Gombin: The Life and Destruction
of a Jewish Town in Poland
(Gąbin, Poland)

Translation of
Gombin: Dos Lebn un Umkum fun a Yiddish Shtetl in Poylin

Original Yizkor Book Edited by: A. Shulman

Published in New York, 1969

Published by JewishGen

**An Affiliate of the Museum of Jewish Heritage—A Living Memorial to the Holocaust
New York**

Memorial Book of Gombin
(Gąbin, Poland)
Translation of: *Gombin: Dos Lebn un Umkum fun a Yiddish Shtetl in Poylin*

First Printing: December 2020, Kislev 5781

Editor of the original Yizkor Book: A. Shulman
Published in New York, 1969
English Translation Coordinators: Leon Zamosc and Ada Holtzman z"l
Layout: Jonathan Wind
Cover Design: Jan Fine
Name Indexing: Jonathan Wind

Published by JewishGen, Inc.
An Affiliate of the Museum of Jewish Heritage
A Living Memorial to the Holocaust
36 Battery Place, New York, NY 10280

JewishGen, Inc. is not responsible for inaccuracies or omissions in the original work and makes no representations regarding the accuracy of this translation. Digital images of the original book's contents can be seen online at the New York Public Library website.

The mission of the JewishGen organization is to produce a translation of the original work, and we cannot verify the accuracy of statements or alter facts cited.

Printed in the United States of America by Lightning Source, Inc.

Library of Congress Control Number (LCCN): 2020949931

ISBN: 978-1-939561-98-5 (hard cover: 452 pages, alk. paper)

Cover Credits:

Front Cover:

The front cover image is a an original drawing "**Gombin - Wooden Synagogue**" by Grzegorz Worobjew from 1893, that was purchased in Poland by Ada Holtzman. She was the coordinator of the English translation who passed away in 2016. For more details of this drawing, please see: http://www.zchor.org/synagogue/synagogue2.htm

Back Cover:

Photograph taken by Leon Zamosc, the translation coordinator

JewishGen and the Yizkor Books in Print Project

This book has been published by the **Yizkor Books in Print Project**, as part of the **Yizkor Book Project** of JewishGen, Inc.

JewishGen, Inc. is a non-profit organization founded in 1987 as a resource for Jewish genealogy. Its website [www.jewishgen.org] serves as an international clearinghouse and resource center to assist individuals who are researching the history of their Jewish families and the places where they lived. JewishGen provides databases, facilitates discussion groups, and coordinates projects relating to Jewish genealogy and the history of the Jewish people. In 2003, JewishGen became an affiliate of the **Museum of Jewish Heritage—A Living Memorial to the Holocaust** in New York.

The **JewishGen Yizkor Book Project** was organized to make more widely known the existence of Yizkor (Memorial) Books written by survivors and former residents of various Jewish communities throughout the world. Later, volunteers connected to the different destroyed communities began cooperating to have these books translated from the original language—usually Hebrew or Yiddish—into English, thus enabling a wider audience to have access to the valuable information contained within them. As each chapter of these books was translated, it was posted on the JewishGen website and made available to the general public.

The **Yizkor Books in Print Project** began in 2011 as an initiative to print and publish Yizkor Books that had been fully translated, so that hard copies would be available for purchase by the descendants of these communities and also by scholars, universities, synagogues, libraries, and museums.

These Yizkor books have been produced almost entirely through the volunteer effort of researchers from around the world, assisted by donations from private individuals. The books are printed and sold at near cost, so as to make them as affordable as possible. Our goal is to make this important genre of Jewish literature and history available in English in book form, so that people can have the personal histories of their ancestral towns on their bookshelves for themselves and for their children and grandchildren.

A list of all published translated Yizkor Books in the project with prices and ordering information can be found at:
http://www.jewishgen.org/Yizkor/ybip.html

Lance Ackerfeld, Yizkor Book Project Manager
Joel Alpert, Yizkor-Book-in-Print Project Coordinator
Susan Rosin, Yizkor-Book-in-Print Project Associate Coordinator

JewishGen
Yizkor Book Project

This book is presented by the
Yizkor-Books-In-Print Project
Project Coordinator: Joel Alpert

Part of the Yizkor Books Project of JewishGen. Inc.
Project Manager: Lance Ackerfeld

These books have been produced solely through efforts of volunteers
from around the world. The books are printed using the Print-on-Demand technology and sold at
near cost, to make them as affordable as possible.

Our goal is to make this intimate history of the destroyed Jewish shtetls
of Eastern Europe available in book form in English, so that people can
experience the near-personal histories of their ancestral town on their
bookshelves and those of their children and grandchildren.

All donations to the Yizkor Books Project, which translated the books,
are sincerely appreciated.

Please send donations to:

Yizkor Book Project
JewishGen, Inc.
36 Battery Place
New York, NY, 10280

JewishGen, Inc. is an affiliate of the
Museum of Jewish Heritage
A Living Memorial to the Holocaust

Notes to the Reader:

We apologize ahead of time for the poor quality of images in the book. Often these images had been scanned from the original Yizkor books which were of poor quality to begin with, being copies of old photographs. Each transfer results in loss of quality. We have done the best we could, given the original material and the resources and technology at hand. Even though images often appear of higher quality on computer screens, that does not transfer to high quality images in print. A reader can view the original scans on the web sites listed below.

Within the text the reader will note "{34}" standing ahead of a paragraph. This indicates that the material translated below was on page 34 of the original book. However, when a paragraph was split between two pages in the original book, the marker is placed in this book after the end of the paragraph for ease of reading.

Also please note that all references within the text of the book to page numbers, refer to the page numbers of the original Yizkor Book.

The original book can be seen online at the New York Public Library site:

https://digitalcollections.nypl.org/search/index?utf8=%E2%9C%93&keywords=gombin

or at the Yiddish Book Center web site:

https://www.yiddishbookcenter.org/collections/yizkor-books/yzk-nybc313762/zicklin-jack-gombin-dos-lebn-un-umkum-fun-a-yidish-shtetl-in-poyln

In order to obtain a list of all Shoah victims from Gombin, the reader should access the Yad Vashem web site listed below; one can also search for specific family names using family name option. These lists are continually updated by Yad Vashem, so it is worthwhile to periodically search these lists.

There is much valuable information available on this web site, including the Pages of Testimony, etc.
http://yvng.yadvashem.org

A list of this book and all books available in the Yizkor-Book-In-Print Project along with prices is available at:
http://www.jewishgen.org/Yizkor/ybip.html

Geopolitical Information:

Gąbin, Poland

The town is located at 52°24' N 19°44' E and 55 miles W of Warszawa

Period	Town	District	Province	Country
Before WWI (c. 1900):	Gąbin	Gostynin	Warszawa	Russian Empire
Between the wars (c. 1930):	Gąbin	Gostynin	Warszawa	Poland
After WWII (c. 1950):	Gąbin			Poland
Today (c. 2000):	Gąbin			Poland

Alternate names for the town:
Gąbin [Polish], Gombin [Yiddish, German, Russian], Gambin

Nearby Jewish Communities:

- Sanniki 7 miles SE
- Płock 10 miles N
- Gostynin 11 miles WNW
- Kiernozia 11 miles SSE
- Żychlin 11 miles SSW
- Bodzanów 14 miles ENE
- Bielsk 19 miles N
- Kutno 19 miles SW
- Sobota 20 miles S
- Wyszogród 20 miles E
- Łowicz 21 miles SSE
- Lubień Kujawski 23 miles W

- Bielawy 23 miles S
- Czerwińsk nad Wisłą 24 miles E
- Dobrzyń nad Wisłą 24 miles NW
- Sochaczew 25 miles ESE
- Piątek 25 miles SSW
- Krośniewice 25 miles WSW
- Kowal 26 miles WNW
- Drobin 26 miles NNE
- Dąbrowice 27 miles WSW
- Bolimów 29 miles SE
- Chodecz 30 miles W
- Łyszkowice 30 miles SSE
- Głowno 30 miles S

Jewish Population in 1900: 2,539

LITHUANIA

BALTIC SEA

RUSSIA

Vilnius

POLAND

BELARUS

GERMANY

Gombin
(Gąbin)

Berlin

Poznan

Warsaw

Lodz

Prague

Krakow

UKRAINE

CZECH REPUBLIC

SLOVAKIA

ınich

AUSTRIA

250 miles

250 Km   500 Km

POLAND – CURRENT BORDERS

Map of Poland with Gombin (Gąbin)

Yiddish Title Page of Original Hebrew/Yiddish Book

גאָמבין

דאָס לעבן און אומקום פון אַ ייִדיש
שטעטל אין פוילן

אַרויסגעגעבן פון דער גאָמבינער לאַנדסמאַנשאַפט אין אַמעריקע
ניו־יאָרק — 1969

Translation of the Title Page of the Original Hebrew/Yiddish Book

Gombin

The Life and Destruction
of a Jewish Town in Poland

Published by the Gombiner Landsmanschaft in America,

New York, 1969

רעדאַקציע פון בוך:

דזשעק זיקלין

מרס. יעטאַ רעיפל

ד"ר הענרי גרינבאום

דעיוו בערנס

אברהם זיידעמאַן

פּאַל טייבער

יעקב צעלעמענסקי

רעדאַקציע־־סעקרעטאַר: אַ ב. שולמאַן

דער אינהאַלט־פאַרצייכעניש געפינט זיך אויף די זייטן 227 און 228 פון דער
ייִדישער אָפּטיילונג פון יזכור־בוך.

Printed in the U. S. A. by
KNIGHT PRINTING CORPORATION
382 Lafayette Street, New York, N. Y. 10003

The Editorial Board:

Published in New York, 1969

TABLE OF CONTENTS

Gombin
The Life and Destruction of a Jewish Town in Poland

The Editorial Board:

Jack Zicklin
Yetta Rafel
Henry Grunbaum
Jacob Cyrmelinski (Celemenski)
Abram Zeideman
David Burns (Brzezinski)
Paul Tiber

Secretary Editor:

A. Shulman

Published in New York, 1969

Translation Project Coordinators

Leon Zamosc
Ada Holtzman

This is a translation of *Gombin: Dos Lebn un Umkum fun a Yidish Shtetl in Poyln* (Gombin: The Life and Destruction of a Jewish Town in Poland), Editors: Jack Ziklin, et al., New York, Gombiner Landsmanschaft in America, 1969 (English and Yiddish, 390 pages).

Preface to the English edition

by Leon Zamosc
Coordinator of the JewishGen translation of the Gombin Yizkor book

Back in 1995, the launching of its website transformed JewishGen into the most important international resource for Jewish genealogy. At that time, one of its key initiatives was the Yizkor Book Special Interest Group (predecessor of today's JewishGen's Yizkor Books Project), which was fostering the creation of lists of same-shtetl people who could be potentially interested in researching, indexing or translating their town's Yizkor book. In September of that same year 1995, I circulated a call inviting people to join in the effort to create such list for the Gombin Yizkor book. That turned out to be the beginning of a process that eventually transcended the initial focus on the Yizkor book and led to the establishment of the Gombin Jewish Historical and Genealogical Society in 1997. As the process unfolded and the Gombin Society embarked on its ambitious (and demanding) projects to restore the Jewish cemetery of Gombin and build a Gombin memorial monument at Chelmno, the translation of the Gombin Yizkor book was put on hold

Ada Holtzman z"l (1951-2016)

Fortunately, it was a case of "postponed, but not forgotten". A few years after the 1999 dedication of the Gombin memorial projects in Poland, Ada Holtzman initiated the Yiddish-English translation of the Gombin memorial book within the framework of the JewishGen Yizkor Book Project. As coordinator of the Gombin project, Ada supervised the translation of several chapters of the book, but her premature passing prevented her from seeing the project through to the end. Ada Holtzman was an awesome Gombin genealogist, a tenacious fighter for the memory of the Polish shtetls and the Shoah, and a tireless contributor to many JewishGen projects. As the person who stepped into her shoes to coordinate the continuation of the work, I am sure that the completion of the Gombin book translation represents a most fitting homage to her memory.

Like all Yizkor books, the Gombin memorial book is a unique source of information about the town's vanished Jewish community. Its narratives, testimonies and photographs offer a vivid overview of the history, religious and secular institutions, leading personalities, social and cultural activities, and daily life of the Gombin Jews before the Second World War. They also convey the horrors of their persecution, suffering and annihilation following the occupation of Poland by Nazi Germany. As an important addition to the original version, this English edition of the book includes a new appendix with individual information about 2,249 Gombiners who are known to have perished during the Shoah. For me, it is a privilege to have been able to fulfill the duty of remembering their names and transmitting the historical legacy of the Jews of Gombin to new generations of scholars and Gombiner descendants all over the world.

On behalf of Ada Holtzman and myself, I would like to express gratitude and appreciation to the volunteer and professional translators who contributed to the success of this project: Janie Respitz, Dorothy and David Rothbart, Clarice Gostinsky-Horelick, Ida Selavan-Schwarcz, Melvyn Wrobel, and Ada's father Meir Holtzman. I would also like to thank the members of the JewishGen's Yizkor Books Project team who diligently supported the production of the book: Binny Lewis and Lance Ackerfeld (Yizkor Book Managers), Joel Alpert (Coordinator of Yizkor Books in Print), and Jan Fine (Yizkor Books Project Graphic Designer).

Finally, the speedy conclusion of this translation of the Gombin memorial book would not have been possible without the support of a grant from the Gombin Society and the individual donations of the following persons: Harold Boll, Bernard Guyer, Robert Kucinski, Sarah Liron, Richard Lozins, Richard Narva, Marlene Rifkin, Carol Rissman, Edee Simon-Israel, Gayle Frenkel-Sokoloff, Arthur Stupay, Dennis Teifeld, Anna Zamosc-Stone, Leon Zamosc, and Shlomo Zytman. Thank you all for your JewishGen-erosity.

San Diego, November 2020

A Poem – Memorials...

by Mikolai Gibs

Translated by Meir Holtzman and Ada Holtzman
Edited by Leon Zamosc

[Original book: Pages 5-6 Yiddish]

Memorials...

Not everyone can lay
flowers and wreaths
on the tombs of their fathers
and mothers...
brothers and sisters...
Not everyone knows
what fate befell them
in the years of that war.
In vain they search
through the sands of Treblinka
the ashes of Auschwitz,
the extinguished crematorium of Brzezinka...
They lay flowers and wreaths
on all the monuments
for the Anonymous Soldier,
the Godess of Victory,
the National Heroes,
the resistance fighters.
They lay the flowers there because,
so far, no memorial has been built
for the anonymous victims,

who fell with their eyes filled of hatred
against the Germans...
who fell with a last thought
for their lost children...
longing for revenge
because anonymous are their tombs
and the tombs of their fathers and mothers
their brothers and sisters...
You look at the monuments
and sometimes it seems to you
that you see your loved ones there...
But you painfully realize
that no sculptor will ever cast
an image that captures
the torments of humanity.

Warsaw, November 1966

Words of Introduction

by Jack Zicklin
President of the New York Organization

[Original book: Pages 7-8 Yiddish and 5-6 English]

Jack Zicklin
President of the New York Organization

With deep respect and piety we present to our Landsleit and the Yiddish reader this "Pincus".

This memorial volume is published as a sacred obligation to the memory of our beloved city, which together with hundreds and hundreds of Jewish cities and towns throughout Poland shared the horrible fate of the Nazi holocaust.

The idea of issuing this Gombiner "Pincus" was born several years ago at a meeting of our society in New York. Since then our committee has gathered the material that would be representative of the historic past of Gombin from the very earliest days, through the Second World War and the ultimate end. The surviving Jews of Gombin are spread far and wide throughout the world, which increased the time required to assemble the great number of relevant documents concerning our city's past.

We hope that within the framework of our resources we have honored in a dignified manner our tragically vanished city. Our goal was to erect a monument through which the coming generations - the children and grandchildren of the Gombiner Jews - would be able to acquaint themselves with the ancient past of Gombin and the roots of their own origin. In their behalf we have published part of the material in English rather than Yiddish, which was the living tongue of their parents and grandparents.

The work of preparing the publishing of the book was done by many of our landsleit, but it is impossible not to give special mention to our dear Sam our former President. Sam was most active and enthusiastic about this project. He was devoted heart and soul to the idea of the Gombiner Memorial Book as he was previously devoted to helping our needy brethren in a Gombin alive with the vitality of a living Jewish community.

Unfortunately, he did not live to see the appearance of this book, but we want it to be known that it contains much of his effort, loyalty and warm devotion. With the publication of this Memorial Book we pay a debt to his shining memory.

I conclude with the hope that this "Pincus" will be found in the home of every Gombiner. We shall also see to it that the book is placed with historical societies, research institutes and in Jewish Libraries throughout the world. In this manner the memory of our beloved birthplace will forever survive in the hearts and minds of our people.

Sam Rafel - Deserved Recognition

by Louis Philips (Pochekha)
President, Gombiner Society Detroit

[Original book: Pages 9-10 Yiddish and 9-10 English]

Sam Rafel is a well-known name and is synonymous with the activities of the Gombiner Societies in New York and Newark. His devoted spirit for various undertakings have influenced the work of these organizations as far back as forty years ago.

He encouraged our activists even in Detroit whenever measures needed to be taken to ascertain a successful monetary campaign.

He brought his dynamic and loyal energy to fruition during the building of the Gombiner House in Israel, to assure a fund for aid to the needy; and to immortalize the names of our martyrs in our own home in Israel.

I recall the year 1941, when we, residents of Detroit recommended a project to raise the sum of 25,000 dollars - we called it the "post war fund" - and we called all Gombiner Societies to take action immediately, without delay.

Then, during the dark night, during the fearful period, under the shadow of war, we thought the war would soon end (we did not think otherwise) and with the war's termination, the world would live in peace and freedom once more including our town Gombin. Our help must be ready in advance, waiting for the oncoming liberation. Who else, if not us, landsleit, will accommodate and meet the great need that we anticipated for the rebuilding of war-torn Gombin? Who would have imagined at that time that the devastation would be so total, so colossal, and so brutal, that not one living soul would remain alive? At that time, during the projection of our plans for raising this huge fund, we did not have to hold forth with Sam Rafel, with the delegate from Newark and the Newark Societies, about our important task. I have before me a letter dated November 1941, from which I quote: "You have a grand project and I am with you wholeheartedly. I shall do everything possible to bring this undertaking to its successful conclusion. We are calling a meeting immediately!"

Since then, even more than previously, the personality of Sam Rafel has revealed itself to me. I quote from the letter which followed the first: "I am happy to inform you that I have a great deal of support and backing for the fund -and I opine that the sum to be raised should be increased to $35,000. It is a grandiose project and must not remain in the stage of a dream."

Sam Rafel - Founder and President
for many years of the New Jersey
and the New York Societies

The personality of Sam Rafel has revealed itself to me not exclusively in money matters, not only in the realm of material aid and activities in the realm of fund-raising - but, mainly for his individual idealism and heartily warm attitude and devotion to "Gombiner activities" - that were near and dear to him for many, many years. His profound dedication was equal to *Hassidic* rapture and ecstasy. He did not seem to know the meaning of defeat. His deep conviction and belief, his urge to help all undertakings, to help other Gombiner activities, were part and parcel of his daily life.

His life's purpose became the rendering of help to our "brother's house" in Israel through the benevolence fund. Afterward he added to his life-long dream the realization of the Memorial Book in Honor of the Gombin Community. This is a monumental work depicting and reflecting the rise, the growth, the spiritual up swerve, the struggles, the conflicts, the pain and woe, the devastation, the destruction and catastrophe that later befell our home town. He was, until his last breath the leader and symbol of efficiency for this idea.

I had the rare honor and privilege of working with my best friend for over a quarter of a century in behalf of Gombiner activities and never failed to derive inspiration from his optimism and his exaltation and ardor.

I also want to state that he and also his sympathetic, dynamic and charming wife, Yetta, have throughout their lives shown a devoted attitude to everything, pertaining to Gombiner undertaking.

They were both fortunate in having the opportunity to visit Israel several times and to breathe the air of salvation and deliverance. He was destined to reap the joy of seeing his great dream become a reality, to see the turbulent Israel with its intensive life as the creator of energy. There, in Israel, he met with his 'townsfolk of the Gombiner house within the clear white radiant walls that symbolize all that is new and bright and illustrious.

All these impressions he brought with him upon his return home and when he made his reports at meetings he spoke of them as if they were a rare wine to be sipped and enjoyed slowly.

He was always in a jubilant and festive mood; he was a man of the people, our unforgettable Sam Rafel.

History and Memories

The History of Gombin

by A. Sh.

Translated by Janie Respitz
Edited by Leon Zamosc

[Original book: Pages 13-20 Yiddish]

Gombin is a beautiful town that sits on the shores of the Nida river and is surrounded by fragrant pine forests and fruit filled fields. Its distant past is shrouded in various legends. How old was the Jewish community of Gombin? Who were the first Jews to arrive and pitch their tents? We do not have definite answers to these questions. All we have are legends.

If there is a grain of truth to these legends, it would be that the first Jews arrived in Gombin at the time when the Christian Crusaders rode through Europe on the way to Jerusalem to free the grave of Jesus Christ their redeemer. Along their route, the Crusaders robbed, murdered, and plundered the Jewish residents of towns and cities in Western Europe, prompting the migration of groups of Jews who sought safety in the east. One such group arrived in the town of Gombin and were kindly welcomed by the local Polish inhabitants.

However, this is only one version of the story. There is another legend that tells the exact opposite: that it was not the Poles, but the Jews who established the town of Gombin and welcomed the Poles who arrived later. According to this legend, a group of Jewish families wandered from the German lands and camped in a beautiful pine forest. They were so enamoured by the fragrant air, majestic trees, and magical singing of the birds that they decided to stay on the edge of the forest. They settled by a stream that was not far from the Vistula, the grand river that would eventually connect them to farther and larger cities.

While we do not know which story of origin is most truthful, one thing is clear: over many hundreds of years Gombin was a town in which Jews and Poles lived together in relative harmony until the outbreak of the Second World War.

The first historical record of Gombin dates back to 1437 when Siemowit V of Masovia gave residence privileges to the local inhabitants according to Germanic laws. Later, these privileges were confirmed by the Polish Kings Kazimierz IV Jagiellończyk and Zygmunt I Stary. Gombin was completely burned down twice; once in 1540 and the second time in 1545. The town was again destroyed during the Swedish War that is remembered in Polish history as the "Deluge". The wooden homes went up in smoke, and it took a long time for Gombin to recover from those fires and wars.

The existence of a Jewish community in Gombin is first mentioned in documents from 1596. On that year, there was a Blood Libel accusation that resulted in the tragic deaths of two Jewish brothers, Moishe and Yehuda, sons of Rabbi Yekutiel of Gombin. The two young men were accused of committing a ritual murder, arrested, and brought to Warsaw where they were put on trial. The details of the case are unknown except for the fact that the Jewish brothers were tortured. They were taken to the Warsaw dungeon known as "Little Hell", where they were nailed to wheels. Their limbs were attached to pulling horses and their mangled bodies were hanged. One of the brothers, Moishe, was tortured and murdered on May 15th 1596 and the other one, Yehuda, on the following day. The Jews asked King Zygmunt III Waza to hand over the bodies and, on May 19th 1596, their remains received a Jewish burial in the town of Blonie, three miles from Warsaw.

The deaths of the two young Jews from Gombin brought great sorrow to the Jews, who recited special prayers for them. Among those who mourned the blood libel victims was the revered Rabbi Moshe Mordechai Margaliot, a great scholar of Krakow who lived from 1560 to 1636. The tragedy was a shock for all the Jewish communities, great and small, throughout Poland and Germany. The names of the brothers were inscribed in the chronicles and special prayers were recited on the anniversary of their deaths to remember their martyrdom. Every year on Yom Kippur the Jews of Krakow would recite the special prayer written by their Rabbi. The Jews of many other towns in the area emulated the practice.

On the following century, the Jews of Gombin are mentioned again in the chronicles of another tragic event, when Gombin was one of the many Jewish communities that were destroyed during the Swedish War that erupted a few years after the Chmielnicki Uprising, when tens of thousands of Jews had been massacred by Cossack and peasants in Ukraine and throughout central and western Poland. In the course of that war, the Swedes penetrated deep into Poland, making it almost to Krakow under the leadership of Arvid Wittenberg. In many places, the Polish soldiers surrendered to the Swedish occupiers. In the regions of Poznan and Kalish, the Polish nobility took the side of the Swedes. At the time, the country was ruled by King Jan II Kazimierz Waza, one of the weakest kings in Polish history. After many defeats, the Poles began to drive out the Swedes from the occupied regions. With the so-called "miracle of Jasna Gora" in Częstochowa, the Polish army began a counter offensive against the Swedish intruders. It was then that the tragedy began for the Jews who lived in the liberated cities and towns.

The Poles blamed the Jews for being too friendly to the Swedish occupiers. That the accusations were baseless is proven by many documented cases of Jewish communities resisting the Swedes, including a record about the Jews who stood in defense of the city of Przemysl. But the Polish hordes perpetrated horrifying slaughters of Jews as they took back their cities and towns from the Swedes. Entire Jewish communities were annihilated. Jewish men, women, and children were murdered, many of them tortmented before being killed. Some had their intestines and tongues cut out and thrown alive to the dogs and pigs. Jewish women were raped, tortured, and faced barbaric deaths. In some towns, the Jews were brought to the river and drowned. In the few places where the murderers offered conversion, many Jews chose a martyr's death. Some managed to save themselves by escaping to Germany. A few were ransomed by the Jewish communities of Vienna, Venice, Frankfurt, and Amsterdam. Among those murdered were many esteemed people including rabbis and scholars. 1,800 synagogues and Yeshivas were burned, and Gombin was not spared during this wave of bloody pogroms.

In those dark days, the parents of the acclaimed scholar Abraham Abele Gombiner, author of *The Shield of Abraham*, were tortured and murdered in front of his eyes. After their murder, the young 20-year-old Abraham Abele managed to escape from Gombin to Kalish. Here I should pause to talk about his life because he became an important historical figure associated with Gombin.

Abraham Abele, son of Rabbi Chayim Halevi, was born in Gombin. He become a renowned rabbi and scholar in the town of Kalish, where he headed a famous Yeshiva. But, on account of his birthplace, he was always referred to as Abraham Abele the "Gombiner". He was still young in his thirties when he earned widespread reputation for his commentary on the Jewish code of law. The book, originally entitled *Way of Life*, was later known as *The Shield of Abraham*. He would go on to write many other books, including *Bread of Life*, *Rules of the Way*, and a collection of sermons. He also wrote poetry, including a lamentation for the destruction of the Holy Temple and a poem glorifying the Torah. His books were published by his son Chaim in the town of Dyhernfurth in 1692. Reb Abraham Abele was well known in his day throughout the entire Jewish world and was often called upon for his expertise.

Some Jewish historians disputed the fact that the author of *The Shield of Abraham* actually came from Gombin, pointing instead to a small town called Gombinen near Poznan. But the *Encyclopedia Judaica* mentions that the hypothesis of Gombinen as birthplace of Abraham Abele Gombiner is false. This is reaffirmed by historian Yehuda Leib Zlotnik, who was Rabbi of Gombin for several years and has great expertise on the history and folklore of the town. In his work *Remnants of the Jewish Community of Gombin*, Rabbi Zlotnik confirms that Abraham Abele Gombiner actually came from Gombin, arguing that, if he had come from Gombinen, people would have called him "Gombinener", rather than "Gombiner". He adds that, in the tradition of the Gombin Jews, the fact that Abraham Abele Gombiner was born in the town was a source of pride that had never been doubted. Illustrating the point, Rabbi Zlotnik writes that many elderly Jews from Gombin showed him a well where Abraham Abele Gombiner's mother would go to purify herself. According to the elders, every morning she would go to the women's section of the synagogue and say to God: "Good day to you, God. I can't stay long because I must go home to prepare food for my little Abraham so he can have the strength to learn your holy Torah." Rabbi Zlotnik concludes that the author of *The Shield of Abraham* is so present in the folklore of Gombin and the surrounding towns that there can be no doubt about the fact that he was born in the town.

The years that followed the tragedies of the Chmielnicki Uprising and the Swedish Wars are wrapped in the fog of history. How was the community rebuilt? We do not know because there are no remaining historical documents. The next confirmed date in Gombin's Jewish history is 1710, the year in which the town's famous synagogue was built. The synagogue, which came to be considered one of the greatest wonders of wooden architecture in Poland, was renovated in 1893. Both dates were engraved on metal pendants that were attached to the tips of the onion-shaped domes that crowned the two towers.

The Gombin synagogue was known throughout Poland for its unique architecture and the wonderful wood carvings that graced the inner walls, the Holy Ark, and the desk where the Torah was read. The interior was enriched with old Jewish ornaments, valuable fabrics covering the Torah scrolls, and beautiful hanging chandeliers. The synagogue was listed by the Polish Ministry of Culture in the national register of historic buildings. People would come from near and far, even from abroad, just to see it. The Polish government forbade any alteration to the synagogue. At one point, the Polish Ministry of Culture suggested that the Jews build another synagogue to preserve the first one as an historical-artistic monument.

The Synagogue of Gombin

The entrance hall to the synagogue was shaped as a long corridor. A pillory, consisting of two iron half rings attached to the wall, was prominently displayed. In the olden days, Jews who had sinned or committed a crime were taken to the wall and the half rings were locked around their necks, so that those who came in could look at them with contempt. The story goes that the writer Yizhak Leibush Peretz used these neck shackles as inspiration for his drama "Chains in the Corridor".

The covers of the synagogue's Torah scrolls were famous for their incredible beauty. When the writer Sholem Asch, a lover of antiques, visited the synagogue, he said that he had only seen such beautiful fabrics in the famous synagogue of Toledo, Spain. The synagogue in Gombin was seeped in legends. According to one of them, a Polish nobleman had donated the huge amounts of wood required to built the synagogue on condition that the Jews would give a certain amount of money every year to help the construction and repair of Christian churches. When Poland was part of the Russian Empire, the annual budget of the Gombin Jewish community included payments for the two churches of the town.

Bimah, Synagogue of Gombin

Another legend related that Gombin rabbis from previous generations had blessed the synagogue so it would never burn down. For a long time, the town's fires did spare the synagogue. In the end, however, the blessings of the rabbis could not save it from the vandalism of the Nazis who, immediately after the capture of Gombin, torched the magnificent synagogue leaving in their wake a pile of ash.

Besides the synagogue, Gombin was popular among the Jews of the surrounding towns for another reason. According to Jewish law, divorce rulings can only be issued in a town that sits on a river that has a name. Not every Jewish town had a river with a name, but Gombin did have the river Nida. And this brought Jewish couples from towns without rivers with names to Gombin for their divorce. A "divorce industry" developed in the town, providing a source of income for local rabbis, scribes, beadles, and witnesses.

The Jews of Gombin were proud that they had been historically blessed with great rabbis. In the first half of the 19th century, the head Rabbi was Fayvl Gritzer, whose son Rabbi Yechiel Dancyger became the founder of the Aleksander Hasidic dynasty. Later in 1841, Rabbi Gritzer place's was taken by the renowned Rabbi Yehoshualeh Kutner. When Rabbi Kutner arrived in Gombin he was still very young at the age of 26. He was not happy because he felt that it was difficult to please the Jews of Gombin after Rabbi Fayvl. They hardly payed attention to the young rabbi until, one Friday afternoon, he gathered his belongings, loaded them onto a wagon, and left the town. Years later, the Jews of Gombin would take pride in the fact that Rabbi Yehoshualeh Kutner, who turned out to be a prodigy of his generation, had been one of Gombin's rabbis.

In those years Gombin was a fortress of Hasidim. The Hasidim had their own prayer houses, that rang with the melodies of their rebbes. The simple folk were satisfied with psalms, and Gombin was renowned for its psalm reciters. Psalms were recited with great feeling and devotion, with fiery passion. The Jews of Gombin were in intimate conversation with god when they recited the psalms. They had learned this from the illustrious Rabbi Yechiel Meir Lifschitz of Gostynin, who believed that reciting psalms helped as a remedy for everything - health, prosperity, long life, prevention of evil, and protection from all kinds of misfortunes. Among the people in Gombin, the authority of the saintly man from neighboring Gostynin remained strong for a long time after his death in 1888.

We have many details about the Jewish history of Gombin in the 19th century thanks to the fact that two chronicles of the community have survived; one from the Society of Mishnah and another one from the Society of Psalms. Rabbi Yehuda Leib Zlotnik included excerpts from these chronicles in his already mentioned work *Remnants of the Jewish Community of Gombin*. Both societies had been founded at the beginning of the 19th century and their chronicles give a sense of some of the preoccupations of the rabbis and the officials of the Jewish community.

The Mishna Society had special privileges that differentiated its members from the rest of the Gombin Jews. Only those who knew the commentaries of the Talmud were eligible to join, and nobody else was allowed to create a similar society of their own. They were responsible for selling seats in the synagogue and used the proceeds to buy books for the study house and maintain the ritual bath. The Mishna Society also supplied the synagogue with wine for the ritual blessings and the Havdala services to close the Sabbath. The honour of sponsoring the wine went to the person that offered the highest bid. In 1820, there was a debate on who would be the custodians of the Torah scrolls and books for the new house of study that was then under construction. Some were in favor of the elected members of the community council. Others favored the appointed officials of the community. The Rabbi decided that the books would be under the custody and supervision of the Mishna Society.

The members of the Society of Psalms had other concerns. During the summer, the Rabbi had the special task of giving a lecture to the congregation every Sabbath in the synagogue. The members of the Society of Psalms had to pay a fixed amount of money which went to the Rabbi as a donation for his extra work. Another regulation of the society was that, when one of its members passed away and his soul exited his body, all the other members had to come and recite psalms by his side. They also held a special ceremony on the second day of Shavuot (considered the anniversary of the death of King David), when they would gather in the synagogue and recite the entire Book of Psalms, all 150 chapters, from beginning to end. If the second day of Shavuot fell on a Sabbath, they would light 150 wax candles for the holiday on the day before.

As in most of the small towns of those times, Jewish life flowed separately from the lives of the surrounding Polish population. The only contacts with the Polish neighbors and the ethnic German residents of the region were related to business. The Jews protected their lifestyle and religious life, their traditions, and their deep-rooted Jewish distinctiveness. Nevertheless, there were historical moments in which the Jews participated in key political events such as the January Uprising of 1863, when most sectors of society rebelled against the Russian Empire demanding the restoration of Polish independence.

Until the end of the 19th century, Jewish life in Gombin followed the old traditional religious lifestyle. The Jews spoke almost exclusively in Yiddish, learning enough Polish and German from their neighbors to be able to work and engage in business transactions. There were no secular movements and very few individuals were involved in socio-political or Jewish national issues. In his work *The History of the Jews of Gombin*, author Israel Chay (Chayek) offers many details about the years leading to the crisis that affected the Jews of Poland at the turn of the 20th century.

The only places for learning in Gombin were the Heders, religious elementary schools that, in the old tradition, were open for boys and excluded girls. The boys were taught the alphabet, the Pentateuch, and the commentaries of Rashi. Children from Hasidic families or wealthier homes would study the Talmud further in higher level Heders. When they reached the age of 12, the vast majority of the boys left the Heders and began to work, helping their parents earn a living. Only a few would continue studying on their own in the House of Study until the time came for military service or marriage. Pupils were not taught how to write, not even in Yiddish. Those who wanted to learn how to write had to find a private tutor with "nice handwriting" or go to a private school. Girls went to these private schools where they learned to write letters in Yiddish and addresses in Russian or Polish.

At one point, the Russian authorities demanded that the Heders had to teach Russian. To adjust to the demand, the children were sent for a few hours a week to the school for Polish children, where they were taught some Russian.

For the Jewish children who wanted to learn secular subjects but did not want to go to the Polish schools, a private Jewish school was eventually established in Gombin. In that school, professional teachers taught Hebrew grammar and general studies such as history, geography, and mathematics.

Still, going to the private Jewish school was the exception, not the rule. In general, Jewish life in Gombin and in all the other small towns of Poland and Russia was rich in tradition, but it was also marked by profound isolation. It was a separate life, barely influenced by the outside world.

By the end of the 19th century, new times came knocking at the doors of Gombin and the other Jewish communities of Poland. The Jewish Enlightenment, together with other momentous historical processes and events like the rise of the workers' movement, the birth of Zionism, and the 1905 Russian Revolution, were bound to shake the foundations of Jewish life to the core.

Gombin and the Events of 1905

by Jacob M. Rothbart

Translated by Janie Respitz
Edited by Leon Zamosc

[Original book: Pages 21-27 Yiddish]

Jacob M. Rothbart

It was late spring in 1905, in the middle of the month. The wheat in the fields had already grown high and was half ripe, almost ready to cut. The moon was out and threw a bright light over the corn stalks, wheat, barley, and oat fields. The stars sparkled and helped create one of the most magical nights of the Polish spring.

On that night there was a meeting of the leaders of the Jewish self-defence group of Gombin. They had arranged to meet on the outskirts of town near the windmill on the Tzerb pathway that began across the Polish Church and stretched behind the butcher shops to Chanan Reszke's long orchard. A serious issue had to be discussed. There were rumors in town about an imminent pogrom against the Jews. The Polish peasants, known to be very brutal and anti-Semitic, were planning to come to town and carry out the attack on a certain date.

For some time there had been talk about the fact that the Poles in the area were agitated and wanted to unleash their wrath on the Jews. Following the horrifying pogroms that had taken place in Kishinev and Gomel, there have been attempts to orchestrate similar attacks in towns and cities all over Poland. However, most of these pogroms were unsuccessful. For example, there was an attempted pogrom near the iron gates in Warsaw but the Jews managed to defend themselves and escape alive. After the failed Warsaw pogrom, things quieted down but the terror was not forgotten. This was the reason for the organization of self-defence groups in most Jewish towns. Gombin was no exception, particularly when Poles who worked for wealthier Jews began to say that, on the day of their pogrom, they would steal the silver candlesticks and the other valuables of their employers. Some Gombin Poles had no qualms about openly declaring their intention to plunder the homes of their Jewish neighbors.

In the Gombin self-defence group, we were a devoted bunch of close friends. When we met that night, we wanted to make sure that our defence plan was kept secret. We had made preparations against the pogromists and any leaked information would ruin the plan.

I remember the boys and girls, friends of mine who took part in the meeting: Elie Layzer Tiber, Melech Tadelis, Laibl Fishl Beckers, Malka Wolfowicz, Chayaleh Stolzman, and Mindl Wolman. There were a few others whose names I cannot recall after all these years.

The Day the Pogrom Was to Break Out

For days people had been openly talking about the pogrom that was about to take place. The Jews of Gombin were living in fear. Some of them dismissed the talk with a wave of their hands, saying "You will see, nothing is going to happen!" But our gang, the Bundist self-defence group, refused to rely on the opinion of the optimists.

We knew that the simple ignorant people who worked for Jews had been blabbing about the coming pogrom. We also knew from trustworthy sources which day the pogrom was supposed to take place. Our source was the new Polish doctor who had settled in Gombin a few years earlier: he and his wife were among our best friends. They were both devoted activists of the Polish Socialist Party, but their party did not have a branch in Gombin. Most likely, that was why they had joined us and our Bund defense-group. They were very sympathetic to our cause and we learned from them what was going on in the

Town Hall and among the functionaries of the Czarist regime. We also knew that the mayor of the town, a great Polish patriot, also sympathized with us, but we did not have direct access to him. Sometimes we learned things from other sources, but we were in regular contact with the doctor's wife, who brought us the news that the Town Hall officials thought that the pogrom was being planned for a specific date.

A few days before that date, our Bund members got together to re-evaluate the situation and prepare for the outbreak of the pogrom. We went over our strengths and who we could count on for help. We were sure that there was a group that would support us if we requested their help. They were part of the "Rascals" who hung out at the market. Since some of them were really tough guys, we had tried to avoid associating with them. However, we knew that, if something happened, they would certainly take our side. We also laid our hopes on the Jewish butchers, carriers, fishermen, and all the other Gombin Jews who would stand and take our side. But we were not relying on miracles: on the night before the planned pogrom we sent two of our guys in a paid horsewagon to Plock, where there was a well-organized Jewish self-defence group. Their job was to ask the Plock group to urgently come to help us.

We quickly worked out an improvised "strategy". We knew that the peasants who were plotting the pogrom had to enter town from behind the butchers' street. We had to place a strong garrison there to stop the peasants advance into the Jewish side of the town. The fight would occur upon the arrival of the pogromists and, since there were many barns nearby, our people could shoot from hiding places and give them a real "welcome". We also agreed to send patrols to cover the other approaches to the Jewish part of the town.

At dawn we were already on our feet and everyone took position at their designated spots. A small group would patrol the roads and communicate with the other groups, making it easier for one group to help another. To do this, however, they needed horses to move quickly from one patrol group to another. We had to figure out how to get the horses.

A smaller group went through the streets and, whenever they saw a horsewagon, they would ask the owner to let us use the horse to patrol the streets and watch out for the pogromists. It may seem strange, but even though the horses and wagons were very valuable, nobody turned us down. On that day, everyone wanted to help.

We patrolled the streets and roads until midnight. Suddenly, we heard a loud rumble. What happened? Two wagons full of men from the Plock self-defence group had noisily arrived, armed to the teeth. There was no limit to our joy; we felt like great heroes receiving backup in a time of danger. Our morale was sky high, and we felt like we were the bosses in town. We wondered where the three or four policemen of Gombin were (it remains a mystery to this day).

The Jews of Gombin were amazed by what happened that day. The Polish hooligans were afraid! They knew that we were prepared for the pogrom and that we were armed. They and all the other Poles in town had often heard sounds of shooting in the forests where the Gombin Jewish self-defence group learned how to shoot. The pogromists did not have weapons, and the fact that we were armed scared them. They decided to postpone the pogrom for a better time...

I only remember a few names of the group of men who came to our help from Plock. One of them was Moishe Varsheh, who later became well-known in the literary circles. He was an educated young man who possessed clarity of mind and a brilliant memory. He was among the best public speakers in the entire region. There was also Leibush Makover, a healthy, well-built young man who eventually emigrated to the United States. Years later, in 1919, I met him in San Francisco, where he worked for the government. We spent three days together and did not tire of reminiscing about the olden days in Poland. Another one I remember was called Guzhik, a fine educated guy with a logical head on his shoulders. I do not know where he ended up. Unfortunately, I cannot recall the names of the others who came from Plock to help the Jews of Gombin on that day.

After the threat of the pogrom passed, we decided to call a mass meeting. Hundreds of people gathered that night in the home of Yosele Borenshtein, a wealthy member of the Gombin community. It was totally crowded: everyone pushed their way in to hear Moishe Varsheh speak. Even the community outsiders and people who had never attended meetings showed up.

Moishe Varsheh gave a magnificent speech that left a lasting impression on everybody and resulted in many new supporters joining our movement. In general, everything that happened that day changed the people's perception of our self-defence group. From then on, our movement grew and expanded like yeast. This would continue until the mid-1906 crackdown of the Czarist government, which changed conditions throughout the land.

The Celebration of the Constitution in 1905

The year 1905 was without a doubt the stormiest year in the struggle against the Russian Czarist regime. Revolutionary outbreaks took the form of mass demonstrations, strikes, sabotage, and other struggles. The uprisings took place in large cities including Warsaw, Lodz, Odessa, St. Petersburg, Moscow, and in other cities and towns throughout the Russian Empire. The Russian autocracy responded with repression, shootings, arrests, exile to forced labor in Siberia, and organized pogroms against Jews in many places.

After the success in preventing the pogrom passed, our Bund organization grew and grew. It would not be an exaggeration to say that most Jewish youths in Gombin joined our movement. We had active and passive members, and many who were sympathetic to our cause but were unable to join our illegal organization because of their personal circumstances. In general, there was a change in attitude towards our movement even among the more traditional Jews. Older people who used to poke fun at the Bund self-defence group, were now saying that "These are dear children with golden hearts. If only they were a little more religious...." Comments like these could be heard everywhere in the town.

News arrived in Gombin that the Czarist government would hand down a "constitution" to the citizens of the Russian Empire. There were immediate calls from all revolutionary parties to come out and celebrate. The calls were not ignored in Gombin; we began to prepare a big celebration for this great historic event.

The members of our Bund movement were particularly excited. We called a meeting to decide how to prepare: there will be speeches in Yiddish and Polish; should there be boxes or benches to allow the speakers to be higher than the audience? We need flags! Red oncs for sure. Where would we get the flags? If we cannot find them, we must make them.

The female members immediately responded: "Flags? Leave that to us. We will take care of it." On the spot they decided who would make the flags and stitch in white letters "Long live the Jewish Workers' Bund of Poland, Lithuania, and Russia". The text would be in both Yiddish and Polish. The girls needed to decide where they would meet to make the flags.

Saltche Wolfowicz went to her mother's sewing shop and found a nice piece of red fabric, long and wide enough to be used for a flag. She also took the white fabric that would be used to cut out the letters. The girls worked through the night and the flag was ready in the morning, a true beauty to be seen. They did a better job than any expert flag maker, for the girls of Gombin were very talented seamstresses from a young age. Many themed tapestries depicting the Western Wall, the Tomb of the Patriarchs, or Moses Montefiore decorated the walls of Jewish homes in Gombin, and those works of art had been made by these same girls when they were younger.

I do not remember how we decided on the place for the celebration. With lightning speed, it was known that it would take place at the German Market, across the street from the Evangelical Church. It was a huge open space surrounded by homes inhabited by Poles. The roads from Plock and Gostynin converged on the place, with a network of other streets branching out. One of them led to the entrance of the old pine forest. From that large open space, one could see the tall forest trees marking a semi-circular border and casting a blue shadow. It was there that the celebration of the new constitution would take place on an evening in the middle of the week.

It was a sunny day and the people of Gombin were happy and filled with joy for this great occasion. Everyone prepared for the celebrations planned for the evening. By midday people began to gather and by sunset the place was completely packed. Jews and Poles, men and women, children and elders, were celebrating, laughing, shouting, and filling the air with song and joy. It was not fashionable to kiss in public, but here and there you could see people kissing... that's how happy they were. Evening fell and the street lights were dim. Our Bund members dragged out boxes and raised the large red flag. There was an applause, and the first speaker was pushed to climb on a box. The speeches were in Yiddish and Polish. People clapped and cheered. When one speaker finished another began. New people who had never been heard or seen before climbed on the boxes and spoke loudly, giving us hope that from that day on better times would come and people would feel like free citizens. There was a sense that there could be peace and unity in the world, that the many nations in the huge Russian Empire could all live together and in peace.

Books could be written about what went on that evening. The greatest surprise was the sheer amount of people who participated. It seemed that there were more people there than residents in Gombin. How did they know to come to this celebration? There were no radios or even newspapers to announce the event. And where did all of these people come from? Why had we not heard or known about them until now? There were many questions like these, but they were left unanswered. The celebration continued until late in the night. It was hard to say goodbye and go home.

Once again, a question that puzzled many was where the Gombin policemen were hiding on that day and evening. They always showed up when they were not needed, but on that day they did not came out to bother us.

Following the celebrations that took place all over the country to welcome the new constitution, it did not take long for the Czarist government to regret the granting of new freedoms. The repression and arrests came back and the pressures were often worse than before. The clashes between the revolutionary movements and the regime turned sharper and bitterer. Demonstrations and strikes were met with merciless shootings, imprisonments, and exile to labor camps in the most remote Siberian locations. People were no longer taken to courts; they were just arrested left and right and punished without due process.

The new conditions changed life in our region. Before, the police would come at night to find evidence for an arrest. Now, they just arrested anyone they wanted and threw them in jail.

A group of Bundists from Gombin in New York, 1907.
Seated from right: Abraham Solomon, Morris Bernstein, Max Wolfowicz
Standing: Morris Stavy, Dvora Bal, Jacob M. Rothbart

Some of my good friends told me, "Comrade Jacob, you should escape while you can because you will be at the top of the list of those to be arrested. Later, when things calm down, you can come back." At first, I refused to leave my hometown. Then, I began to feel tired and worn out. I thought more about the situation and realized that my friends were right.

Early in the year 1906, I left Gombin with the hope that I would soon be able to return...

A Monograph of the Shtetl Gombin

by Jacob M. Rothbart

Translated by Jacob M. Rothbart and son David Rothbart

[Original book: Pages 13-23 English]

Gombin is a small town in Poland located about sixty kilometers west of the capital city of Warsaw, seven kilometers south of Poland's largest river, the Vistula, and fifteen kilometers southeast of the old city of Płock. It is half-encircled by an ancient pine forest that provides the town with a constant fragrance of fresh pine scent. North of the town stretches the broad valley paralleling the Vistula. It was settled by Germans who had emigrated from Germany hundreds of years ago, although small in numbers that they were amidst a host of Poles with their dominant Polish language they yet adhered to their native German tongue, a dialect long un-used in Germany known as Hoch Deutch.

Seven kilometers to the south there was another settlement of Germans, but these had wandered in long ago from Saxony and they spoke Schwabish, the language of the Saxons, steeped in its own culture and entirely different from Hoch Deutch.

Both of these German colonies were agricultural and they were among the most productive farmers in Poland.

The population of Gombin was mixed in proportions of roughly two-thirds Jews, one-third Poles, with a small number of Germans, and also a few Chenovnikes, Russian officers of the Czar who reigned in Poland until 1917.

The language of the Jews was almost one hundred percent Yiddish, but they also knew Polish, Hoch Deutch, and some were even fluent in Schwabish, in Russian, and in "Loshen Kodosh," the Holy Language (Hebrew). There were hardly any Jews who did not know enough Hebrew to *daven* (pray), to say a *broche* (blessing), or to chant the Sabbath Torah portion of the week. Most were able to comprehend the Aramaic of Targum Unkeles, an original translator who spent day and night studying at the Beit Midrash both individually and in groups. There was no Yeshiva in Gombin, but a good number of young men came from adjacent communities to study "Torah" at the Beit Midrash with local scholars of renown.

Gombin: the center of the town

How many inhabitants were there in Gombin at the beginning of the 20th century? It is hard to be accurate on this question. The Czarist regime evinced little interest in a census, being indifferent to the local population except to preserve order during periodic uprising. Consequently there were only informal appraisals. A fair estimate was that the Jewish population comprised between 500 and 700 families. Other estimates ranged from 650 to 800; at any rate there were between 2500 and 3500 Jewish souls. Together with the non-Jews there were a total of 4,000 to 5,000 inhabitants in Gombin.

How did these nationalities coexist with each other until the year 1906? Tolerably. There were undeniably some anti-Semites. Prominent among them were the Polish shoemakers who made ready-made shoes and had to compete at the marketplace with the Jewish shoemakers whose workmanship was superior. Some could speak Yiddish as well as the Jews, yet were the bitterest of anti-Semites. Another antisemitic group were the slaughterers. A little antisemitism was in evidence among a class of poor farmers who had formerly been well-to-do landowners, and among civil servants such as teachers and government officials. The Polish Catholic clergy headed by the priests helped to spread antisemitic venom. But in general all lived together in a state of passable harmony. Often, indeed, relations between Jews and Poles were quite friendly. Many peasants from surrounding villages preferred to deal with the Jews in both buying and selling. Almost the entire commerce of the German settlements was with the Jews, even though Jew-haters among them were not scarce. Such were the conditions that existed until Polish antisemitism really went rampant in later years when they were stirred up by the reactionary National Democratic Party, which reached its highest intensity when Poland gained its independence during the Kerensky Revolution against the Czar in Russia in 1917.

How did the panorama of Gombin lay itself out in the eyes of the Jews? At the center of town was the market square. This was a large rectangular expanse converged on from all sides by principal thoroughfares and side streets. Across from the eastern corner was the Polish Catholic church. To the left on the other corner was the city administration building, presided over by the Magistrate, and attached to it was the jail house. After that came the market square annex, also rectangular, fronting on the main square and lined by a row of *yatkes*, Jewish butcher shops. There were regular market days twice a week and frequent *yaridim* (market fairs) at irregular intervals. On these events the entire large market square and annex were spread with Polish and German peasants who came by horse drawn carts from the country-side to vend their farm-products. The Langer Gass (Long Street) started between the church and the administration building, extended to the edge of town where it became the highway to Sanniki (where there was a large sugar mill) and continued on to Warsaw, also branching off to the textile center city of Łódź, winding all the way through dozens of villages and estates.

To the west of the square, from the right corner, began the Plotsker Gass (street to Płock) and from the left corner, the Kutner Gass (street to Kutno).

On the days of *yaridim* (fairs), the full length and breadth of the square, from the Płocker Gass to the Langer Gass, was filled to capacity with canvas vending booths covered by over-hanging canopies, each with its own special wares displayed on hooks and tables. There were booths operated by Jewish women selling bread and rolls, fruits and vegetables; then a section of Polish butchers offering *kolbassi*, *vursht* (sausages), and *shinka* (ham); then shoe booths with *shtivel* and other peasant bootery. There were *peltz* booths of readymade sheepskin coats; tailors with ready-made *sarmages*, cheap cloth coats styled both short and long with cotton-quilted liners, *kutkes*, knicker pants, and double-breasted jackets. The cap-makers squeezed in wherever they could with their stiff-vizored *dashkes* and winter *kashkets*.

.On the main square there was also to be found glazed pottery, dishes and tinware; *potcherkes,* cheap costume jewelry; crosses and other religious items; balls and toys for children; *tashmes* women's headscarves; *stenges,* decorating material ; and everything else that could he sold at the fair.

Gombin market square
Source: Gabin Land Lovers Association [not in original book]

On all sides facing the square were elegant buildings of wood and brick, residences of two stories and sometimes three above the standard ground-floor stores. One *kaminitze* (mansion) was five stories high. It was the most beautiful building in town, owned by a Jewish family named Posnanski who was reputed to have interests in sugar mills all over Poland. Grocers and merchants of all kinds occupied the stores. A family called Stolcman and a German family named Shtaily had the busiest taverns in town. In the days of the *torgen* on Mondays and Thursdays, and on the large *yaridim,* all stores and taverns were so crowded that it was difficult to push your way through the mass of people wearing all manner of garments: short European jackets, sheepskin, *peltz, kutzkes* (three-quarter length coats), long *sermeges* (peasant overcoats), and *djubetses*, worn by a Polish peasant sect, resembling the Hassidic *kapote* with the split rear hanging to the ground. There were men with short, colored, pleated pants and red vests, accompanied by women in similar skirts and vests who were members of a sect called *Mazures*. In this potpourri of Christians, the Jews mingled with their own distinctive garb; also in short three-quarter length coats and Hassidic men in their ground-length robes with the split rear. And there were the Jewish women: matronly housewives with wigs, others with gay-colored scarves on their heads who came to buy a live chicken, a sack of potatoes, fresh eggs, beets, carrots, *petroushke* (parsley), onions, cucumbers, radishes, and other products that the *poirim* brought in to sell.

As aforementioned, the square was in the middle of the town and from it on all sides there protruded many streets, both long and short, and alleyways that divided the back yards. There were also other market places in the town, like the Hog Market Square at the side of Plocker Gass, the horse Market at the Kutner Gass, and the Old Horse Market near the German Evangelical Church, which was filled on Sundays with the horse-carriages of the parishioners. Most of the carriages were drawn by two horses; some had four and even six that belonged to wealthy Germans who wanted to display their affluence. Later, about 1904, the city administration decreed that this square should be converted into a park, and it was truly a fine setting for a park.

All these secondary market squares were immense and surrounded by houses where the majority of the Christian community resided, mainly homesteaders enrooted there for generations. These areas too were busy during the market fairs, packed with peasants, who had come to peddle their herds of hogs, calves, sheep, horses, and chickens. Some Jewish traders in livestock also milled about, so there was a mixture of Jewish butchers and Polish butchers, gypsies to trade horses, and plain peasants seeking to barter in livestock. Gombin was a major agricultural trading center where the Jewish population could thrive and prosper to a much higher degree than in many other towns in Poland.

Through the center of town there snaked a stream that the Jews called "The Buch," a German word for "river." The widest part of the Buch was at the base of a hill and atop the hill was the Shul (synagogue). Across the way to the left, going down the hill, was the Beit Midrash (House of Learning) and below that the Mikva (ritual bath), which was part of the *merchetz* (bathhouse), located close to the stream. Behind the Mikva was the main city latrine. Going down the hill to the right behind the Shul were private Jewish homes, and below them the city poorhouse. At the bottom was the old slaughterhouse raised on stilts astride the edge of the stream, into which drained the blood when they were slaughtering. At that place the stream was 25 to 30 feet wide. Later they moved the slaughterhouse outside the town limits.

Group of young Bundists who organized
the first illegal library in 1908

Rats larger than cats and more courageous proliferated at that spot. Nevertheless, intrepid Jewish girls came down in summer months with baskets of laundry and did their washing upstream from the slaughterhouse in the clear cold water of the stream that never ran dry. They brought with them soap and a *prolnik,* a small straight board with a flat handle. They soaped the clothes, laid them on the board, beat them with mighty strokes and rinsed them in the flowing water.

The Buch was a paradise for the Jewish boys. They devised a raft out of a wide board or two, propelled themselves with long poles, and felt like "Gott in Odessa" (akin to the bliss that one reputedly experiences in the resort city of Odessa) until a mother or an assistant teacher from the Heder came to tear them away from their rafts, which then became common property. In the frost of winter they had as fine a skating rink on the frozen stream as a boy could want, no matter how often he felt the sting of the Rebbe's lash. It is noteworthy to mention that the Jewish children referred to the stream as "the Jordan," oriented as they were to thoughts of The Holy Land.

On the opposite side of the stream there lived a German named Schneider who operated a tannery. He employed several Jewish workers who produced many varieties of leather-work. The tannery was located across from the city latrine and drew clear water from the stream through pipes into the large yard of the tannery; there it was treated with chemicals and used to soak the leather in vats. The Buch was deeper at this point than anywhere else for the reason that several houses above was a dyeing establishment which required a lot of clear water so the dyer dammed his part of the stream, slowing the flow and also enabling the development of a deep water basin to provide for the needs of the tannery. It also served as "The Jordan" to accommodate the Jewish boys in their summer and winter sporting pleasures.

The *Buch* showed no other prominent features except that after a heavy rainstorm, and in the spring when the snow melted, the stream overflowed its banks, washing away accumulated debris and flooding the lower pastures outside of town. When the flood waters receded, the fertile pastures were lush with new greenery and it was delightful to observe the rejuvenated trees and sprouting vegetation, which contributed in extra measure to the prosperity of the dairymen who pastured their cows in these areas.

Bridges and roads were ravaged by such floods wherever the meandering stream intersected, like at the Plotsker Gass and at the Kutner Gass, but no really great damage resulted because the stream ran mostly through the lower sections of town bordering on fields, orchards and yards.

I previously described the locales where the Jews and the Poles were concentrated, and I recall some other aspect of the neighborhoods where each nationality lived.

Again, the main square was at the center of town and major streets and small byways fanned out from all sides of the square. All of these were settled exclusively by Jews and by Jewish secular and religious institutions. In this section was located the synagogue which was old and styled in the architecture of the 18th century, with two lookout towers facing west toward the German border. It was built that way to comply with a Polish requirement that all public buildings have watchtowers to forewarn if the Germans, with whom the Poles used to have many battles, could be seen approaching from a distance. Catty-corner from the Shul was the Beit Midrash at the head of a different street. One was called the Shul Gass, the other the Beit Midrash Gass. Between the Shul and the Beit Midrash was the roadway sloping down to the stream. The street that ran parallel east of the synagogue was called the Maissim Gass (street of the dead) because it led to the cemetery outside of town to the north, but it was called the Maissim Gass for only as far out as the Jews lived, and then it become the Shoemaker Gass where the Polish *shusters* lived, though not as far out as the cemetery. Further out on this road lived the *vatelles*, homesteaders who had fields and farm plots away from their homes where' they cultivated gardens and grain and raised livestock.

The Polish Catholic church was situated at the beginning of the Langer Gass east of the main square. It was an enormous structure surrounded by a large park with paved driveways that winded in a circular design that was fashioned for religious processions. Adjoining the churchyard further out on the Langer Gass was the large brick residence of the head priest and his assistants. There also was located the housekeeper of the hierarchy with her dozen children. It was well-known that she had never been legally married, nevertheless she gave birth almost yearly, and her children were raised in luxuriant conditions befitting the housekeeper of such a grand establishment... and nobody in the town asked any questions. All around this complex of church buildings and park was a high solid wall that insulated the lay community.

The cross-corner opposite the Church marked the boundary of a tract of land belonging to a wealthy Jew named Chonnan Resky. The houses that he rented out were known as the "Resky's houses," part of them located on the Langer Gass, part on the street behind the town hall, and behind the *yatkes* (butcher shops) further down began the "Resky's orchards." The houses on this property were laid out in the form of a right angle, one section occupied by Jews, and the whole compound was surrounded by a wooden fence. Next to the Resky building along the Langer Gass were a few additional houses occupied by Jews, and a little further out it became entirely Polish as the Gass continued on to become the highway to Sanniki. The countryside around Gombin was peopled with Poles and more Poles, and perhaps a very few astray Jews.

Now to the spiritual and social life of the Jews and Poles on Gombin.

Having lived for a long time in free America and observed how the new generations of diverse ethnic origin relate to one another, I find it hard to understand how two nationalities can mingle, live door to door, and still be almost completely strangers to each other. That is how it was in Gombin. There were a few exceptional families who lived under one roof and were friendly with each other, but their social and spiritual experience was entirely alien.

I want to describe two such families. When my sister and I were still very young my parents moved us into the large house of a Polish chimney cleaner. Both he and his wife were very friendly. He cleaned the chimneys mainly of

Jewish homes and she was the housekeeper. The house was about where the Maissim Gass ended and the Polish Shuster Gass began. Neither our landlord nor his wife could read or write. They did not even go to church on Sunday let alone participate in any other kind of social activity that was non-existent anyway. Their whole life consisted of working, eating and sleeping. Behind the house was a large yard, and as soon as the man came home from cleaning chimneys he got to work in the garden. They also had two children, a boy and a girl, and though very young they already helped with the household. These mundane considerations apparently summed up the entire inspirational outlook of this family for an entire lifetime.

My parents could not brag of riches either, and had to work hard, yet they had an interesting life. Each weekday when my father was not traveling he awoke at daybreak and hurried to the first *Shachres Minyan* at the Beit Midrash. He returned, ate breakfast, *Opgebenched* (gave thanks to the Almighty) and ran out to earn a livelihood. My mother, *Oleho-hasholom* (May she rest in Peace), besides cooking and cleaning, seeing to it that the children were neat and her husband's appetite appeased, busied herself with all kinds of commercial dealings to help my father get along financially and never be in a position of having to seek assistance from others. Yet she never neglected to invite a poor seminary *bocher* from the Beit Midrash to come and eat his meals for at least one day a week, and if she were otherwise occupied on the day that he was scheduled to come she gave him cash so he would not go hungry that day.

All of the Jewish holidays were strictly observed by my parents in either solemnity or rejoicing as befitted the occasion, but none exceeded the exultation with which they greeted the Holy *Sabbath* each week. Even now the memory of this event evokes in me a nostalgic glow. My father (*Olev-hasholom*) was a man of modest means, nor was he a dedicated scholar, but on Friday evening he became a *Melech,* a King of the *Sabbath.* Before he returned from services my mother blessed and lit the candles at sundown and set the table. He usually brought home with him a poor "*oriech*" (guest) from Shul. They came in; my father said "*Gut Shabbes!*" to his family, and greeted the Sabbath as it were a revelation of heavenly emissaries: "*Sholom Aleichem, Malache Hashoretes, Malache Elyon*" -- "Angels of service, Angels from above". He bestowed a tribute to womanhood by reciting, "*Aishis chail Mi-Imtsu,*" "Who can find a woman of valor! " (Book of Proverbs Ch. 31-10), then poured sacramental wine and made *Kiddush.* He washed his hands, blessed the *chollahs,* and the festive meal began. Between each course he sang *zmires* (songs) and my father's songs of the Sabbath were a real treat to hear! The meal lasted through most of the evening and my father did not leave out even the smallest detail, yet he sustained the mood of grandeur and exhilaration during the entire ceremony.

This was the way the *Sabbath* was celebrated in nearly every Jewish home in Gombin, and by the Jews throughout every country in Eastern Europe.

Living so near his Polish neighbors did not disturb my father in his routine. He was serenely indifferent to how he sounded to them or how his mode of living looked to them. He had nothing to hide and nothing to learn from them, and they were equally uninterested in learning from him. This situation between Jews and Christians was typical. Their values and viewpoints set them apart and they lived as in two different worlds.

Dramatic Circle of the I. L. Yeretz Library in Sholom Aleichem's
Comedy "It's Hard to be a Jew"

It would be too large an undertaking to enumerate in full all of the rich interests and activities of the Jews in Gombin some sixty years ago. Life "roiled and boiled" as it used to be said. There were societies of all kinds. Some were involved with serious matters, such as: the *Chevreh Tehillim*, a group which chanted Psalms; *Chevreh Kaddishe*, a burial society; *Chevreh Mishnayos*, those devoted to the Book of Ethics; *Hachnosses Kalleh*, those who helped in the marriage of a poor bride; and various *Hasidim Shtieblach*, followers of a favorite rabbi. There were Heders where children were taught. On any Saturday afternoon and on many evenings one could hear an itinerant *Maggid* preach on special topics, usually concerning *mitzvas* (good deeds), and regarding "The Other World."

Both rich and poor could find their favorite niche among the many fraternities and associations that existed.

Members of Hashomer Hatzair

For young people whose interests were less sober, there were gatherings for general social intercourse as well as for special occasions. There were occupational groups, such as apprentice dressmakers, wigmakers, servant girls, tailors, shoemakers, and other youngsters, who usually assembled in private homes. In summer they had access to nearby orchards, where they bought and treated each other to gooseberries, currants, strawberries, apples, peaches, pears and plums as they came into season. They strolled in the woods and vented their spirits in song. They danced at home socials and at weddings, and they were patrons of semi-private confectionaries. Such a one was operated by Yochvi Goldberg, an old maid who lived with her father in an upstairs apartment. The apartment was arranged with shelves where she displayed the finest assortment of sweets to be found, and she welcomed them to use it as a meeting-place. She was blind from birth and the object of wonder and admiration for the dexterity with which she handled money and conducted her business. These Jewish young people were exuberant and wholesome. They had fiery romances, but they were decorous at all times and scandal of any kind was unknown.

The Bund's Sport Organization Morgenstern

By contrast, the Polish life looked grey and monotonous. Outside of religious services at the church there was no social life in the town. There is no doubt that there did exist a rich Polish literature and culture that had developed in the large cities but it had not spread to the small-town populations except for an occasional Polish doctor, notary or other professional. The only people who spoke knowledgeably about this culture were some rich Jews who fancied themselves to have been assimilated into the Polish gentry. They were loud patriots of Poland who read Polish books, hired live-in Polish tutors for their children, and spoke Polish even among themselves. Neither they nor the few Polish intellectuals had any influence on the Polish masses and certainly not on the Jews. It must be noted that there were here and there a few Poles who had friendly relations with the Jews, and peasants who were not affected by anti-Semitic agitation.

Everything that I have depicted here about Gombin is the way I knew it up to the year 1906 when I departed from Poland. I am familiar with the fact that many changes occurred after that. Several years before I left, the Bund revolutionary movement had already started among the Jews. We campaigned for support of the Polish youth and we won a small number of friends among them. When some of our Jewish comrades were arrested by the Czarist regime for revolutionary activities and sent to Siberia in 1906, there was one Pole with them whom we had drawn in the movement.

Group of Zionists in Gombin

Later developments and impressions will have to be recorded by those who remained after I left; those who lived through the events leading to the first World War, then the second World War in 1939 with its devilish Nazism and Hitlerism, "*Y'Machshemom Zichrom*" "May their names and memory be forgotten" (a curse that evolved during the Egyptian exodus when the Jews were attacked by the Amelaikim).

I hope that a few of the Gombiners who remained longer in Gombin will be able to continue this narrative beyond the period that I have described.

Jewish Craftsmen and Occupations in Gombin

by Jacob M. Rothbart

Translated by Ida C. Selavan Schwarcz
Edited by Dorothy Rothbart, David Rothbart and Ada Holtzman

[Original book: Pages 28-45 Yiddish]

Market Day in Gombin, 1914
Source: YIVO Digital Archive [not in original book]

Tailors (*shneiders)*

There were all kinds of artisans in Gombin who lived from their labor. The tailors occupied the most important position, consisting of many families who had tailoring establishments: fathers and sons and often sons-in-law worked together. There were also apprentices of various kinds.

There were all kinds of tailors: second-rate tailors who made complete garments from cheap materials, as well as those who made finer garments of better quality. There were tailors who specialized in children's clothing, for children of all ages. The second-rate tailors used to carry around their ready-to-wear garments with them to the frequent fairs where they sold them.

There were also second-rate tailors who made garments for the various Polish sects who lived in the area. There were sects who wore long coats with vents in the back (like those worn by hasidim), and the garments worn by the Mazumim, knee-length coats with loose pants, which were draped over their boots. Over these they wore vests. They also wore long-sleeved blouses whose cuffs covered their knuckles. The women wore short full skirts and short blouses with loose sleeves. Both men and women's garments were made from a rosy yellow material decorated with shiny gold buttons and ribbons. Polish patriots considered these garments their national costume, and even shlakhtshitses would dress up in these costumes for their revels, in order to demonstrate their Polish patriotism.

There were also custom tailors whose clientele were mostly German colonists of the FolksDeutsche as well as the Swabian Germans. Among the best tailors in town were Avremele Melekhs, Yitshak Mayleks and others. They got the best prices for sewing garments to order. Their customers were the Polish nobility and wealthy shlakhtshitses who lived in the area.

There were tailors who specialized in women's clothing. They were called 'damske shnayders" (i.e. dames' tailors). Among them there were seamstresses who had workshops. These tailors sewed for the general public, Christians and Jews, old and young women, as well as brides.

Another class of tailors were those who sewed exclusively for Jews. They made long coats and long pants and knickers and even silk kapotes (overcoats) for Hasidim, and short-jacketed suits for the general male population.

One should also mention another kind of tailor, the village tailors. They worked almost exclusively for the residents of the "Niderung." They did their sewing in the homes of the Germans, making cheap clothing for the workers and maids, for children, and sometimes recycled used clothing.

These tailors were of the lowest class. They worked very hard all week long, slept in the barns or in attics on a pile of hay, cooked a pot of "kloytskes" in milk for their meals. Some who were very pious would take along a kosher pot from home. There were also others who allowed themselves some leniency and used glazed pots in the German homes.

On Monday morning at sunrise, they had already packed their talis and tefilin, shears and iron, thread and needles and other necessities, and set out on foot for the villages. Sometimes they would take a son along, to help out. All week long they worked very hard in strange homes, often in anti-Semitic atmospheres; often they would hear mocking remarks from ignorant, coarse Germans but would not respond. This is how they lived, week in week out, and thanked God when there was enough work and they could earn enough to bring home a few rubles for household expenses and to pay off debts and to prepare for the Sabbath.

With the coming of Friday noon they would become restless, hurrying to get home so they would not profane the Sabbath. If God had given them a good week, and the weather was good, they could come home in time. Meanwhile the wives prepared clean underclothes and stockings. Off they would go to the bathhouse, to wash off the uncleanness of the week and they would feel elated. Coming home they would dress in their Sabbath garments and go to the synagogue to receive the Sabbath Queen.

The khazn chanted the evening prayers, sang the "Lekha Dodi", the congregation responded and they received the Sabbath Queen.

At home they would find their wives and children dressed up for the Sabbath; they greeted the angels with the chanting of "Shalom Aleykhem Malachey Ha-Shalom. Malakhey Elyon" (Peace to you angels of peace, angels of the Exalted One) then they would chant "Eyshet Hayil" (Woman of Valor), make kiddush, wash their hands for hamotsi [blessing over bread] and sit down at the table to celebrate at the Sabbath feast. The downtrodden Jews of the weekly toil were completely transformed, possessors of an additional soul.

After the delicious fish which their wives had cooked, they would sing the Sabbath hymns: Menuhah ve-simhah, or la-Yehudim, Yom Shabaton, Yom Mahmadim, Rest and joy illuminate the Jews, a day of rest, a day of pleasure. That was how the Jewish tailors started their Sabbath.

Cobblers (*shusters*)

There were quite a few Jewish cobblers in Gombin. Most of them made cheap ready-to-wear boots and shoes, They would go to fairs and the frequent "targn" which were held in town and there set out their merchandise in booths and on stands.

There were all kinds of cobblers among them: those who did cheap work and others who were more expensive. In this area there was competition from the Polish cobblers. There were a number of Polish cobblers in town. Their products were of a very cheap quality, and the peasants who came to buy shoes preferred to buy from Jews, whose shoes were pleased them more because they were better made than the once sold by the Poles. This aroused jealousy among the Polish cobblers and some of them showed their anti-Semitic poison. Some of them were close neighbors of the Jews on the street of the cobblers, for example Khoynotski, Vroblevski, and Kovalski. Some of them could read and write Yias well as the Jews but did not diminish their hatred of Jews, even of Jews who were not cobblers

There were also custom shoemakers in Gombin. They measured their customers' feet, the customers chose the leather uppers and the soles, and agreed on a price. Here we can mention something, which is looked at as laughable at present. A new style came out which required men's shoes to squeak. God forbid that a shoemaker should forget to include the squeaky material. The young dandies would never have forgiven him.

There were shoemakers in Gombin who were artists of their craft. I should like to mention one of them. When he made a pair of boots they practically danced off the shelf. His customers used to say that his boots made their feet enjoy themselves. Finally he left and came to Chicago. What he did there I do not know.

Hat Makers (*kirzshners un hitel machers*)

There were a number of hat-makers in Gombin. It was a completely Jewish trade. They made ready-to-wear hats of all kinds: for Poles, with shiny visors, cloth visors, hats with warm line, which the peasants wore in winter time, as well as hats for Jewish customers, and custom-made hats for those with their own particular tastes.

Most of the ready-to-wear hats were sold on "targn" (stands) at the fairs, just as other artisans sold their wares.

Tanners *(gorbers)*

Some Jews in Gombin worked as tanners. To mention only a few who were well known: Barukh Garber and his brothers had a yard filled with large vats sunken in the ground, where the skins lay soaking. From these they made all kinds of leather. Every vat had different kinds of chemicals. They said in town that they (i.e. Barukh and his brothers) were experts in their field.

A group of tanners in Gombin

Another tanner was Mordekhai Garber. There were others as well. There was a German family named Schneider, a father and his sons, who had a big tannery on Plotsker Street. They had a large enterprise and employed many workers, among them also Jews, who worked there for many years. They related sympathetically to the Jewish workers; there were never any signs of anti-Semitism on the part of the owners toward their Jewish workers.

There were gentile workers there as well who worked together with the Jews without any conflicts, as far as we know. Harmony reigned among them, a rare occurrence in Gombin.

Furriers (peltzen machers)

The craft of furriers was completely in Jewish hands. Entire families were occupied in this field. To mention a few: Zishe Peltsmakher and his sons, Neta Peltsmakher and his children, Pinhas Shakher and others, who worked at this trade. Most furriers made a complete garment to sell on stands and at fairs. Others did custom work. This was a group of goodhearted and fine people. They were always ready to do a favor whenever asked.

It is worth telling about Neta Peltsmakher that he was very hospitable. So too were his wife and children. It is difficult to transmit what this family went through with the many guests who always crowded their home. They did not do this for money, but only for a mitsva. They never refused a poor man who came to beg for a night's lodging. All kinds of poor people used to come to Neta. They would often come on an annual basis, and go right to Netsa's house, as if to their own homes.

Every summer a Jew came called by the Gombiner, "The Recluse." He was always dressed the same way: a very long caftan, reaching to his feet, over this a shorter one and another shorter one until he was wearing five or six. The final kaftan was the shortest of all. Older people used to look at him with a gentle smile on their faces in order not to embarrass him, but younger fellows would make fun of how he dressed. The man seemed indifferent to their mockery. He came every year, each time to the home of Neta Peltsmakher.

Bakers *(bekers)*

There were very many bakeries in Gombin, much too many to serve the Jewish population alone, but they also served many Christian customers.

There were frequent "targn" (market days) when the Polish peasants and the German householders would come to town and bring all kinds of agricultural products, some a few sacks of potatoes, chickens, eggs, ducks, geese, sometimes a cow tied with a rope to the back of a wagon, or a calf bedded down with straw in the wagon, as well as other products. As soon as they sold their merchandise, they would go shopping for their necessities. Many were also customers of Jewish bakeries.

The Jewish bakers of Gombin also had a side occupation. In Gombin at the beginning of this century there were no proper ovens for baking bread. When a Jewish housewife wanted to bake bread or hallah she had to go to a bakery. After she kneaded her dough she would bring it to the baker, who would bake it for her.

Some Gombiner still remember the hullabaloo at the bakeries on Thursday nights. Women would crowd into the bakeries and it was lively on Thursday nights or before the holidays. Some women even prepared a "roshtshine" and waited until it was baked. They spent almost all night in the bakery. At dawn they would bring home the freshly baked goods.

Most women who had grown daughters would give over the baking chores of baking hallah, honey cake, "stunikes" and other baked goods for the Sabbath to their daughters. This leads me to tell of something that happened when the Bundist movement began in Gombin. It was not easy in such a small shtetl as Gombin to meet Jewish girls and carry on propaganda to influence them to join a new movement. Jewish girls were guarded by their parents and siblings and relatives. It was not customary for a Jewish girl to just meet young men. It was not considered proper. There might be gossip about her that she was a loose woman and that could harm her chances for a match. The shutters to the new times were already half open and the young people were drawn to them as if by a magnet. They wanted to know, what do the "ahdusnikes" Bundists want? What do they have that makes people want to join them? They longed for something unexpected and looked for opportunities to meet with a Bundist and hear what he had to say. The Thursday night baking was the easiest and best time and place to meet. During these evenings the Bundist movement got many new members. A few of them became active members and were even in the executive committee.

Another side income for the bakers was putting the cholent pots in the oven on Fridays and Saturday after prayers the women came to take them out.

There were some exceptional bakers in Gombin: Mendl Baker and afterwards his son Adam. Avraham Baker and Fishele Baker's breads had the taste of Paradise. Many people said it was better than honey cake. Yitshak Baker used to specialize in baking rye bread, which was finger-licking good. Each baker had his own specialty and his steady customers. The Jewish baker families lived not worse than other artisan families. They brought up fine families and were respected in town, and took and occupied an important place in Gombin's economy.

Butchers (katzavim)

There was a considerable number of butchers in Gombin who served the Jewish public, as well as some of the Gentiles. Which Gombiner does not remember the butcher shops with their wooden stands, which stood in front of the butcher shops most of the year? The shops were long, sturdy buildings, on the extreme Eastern side of the market place, left of the council building.

There were thirteen or more businesses in this long building, all of them Jewish butchers. Most of them were assisted by their sons and even by their wives before the Sabbath or holidays when there were many customers.

Most of the butchers were well-built, tall, and healthy men. Their sons and daughters took after them. Most of them were pious Jews. It was rare that one heard them insult or embarrass their customers. But if a Polish anti-Semite ever felt like starting up with one of them, he put himself in an unenviable position. He soon swore off startinup with Jewibutchers.

The merchandise, the cattle, calves and sheep were purchased from the peasants who brought themto town twice a week, Mondays and Thursdays, the famous Polish 'targn' (market days) as well as during the occasional fairs.

Some of the butchers used to travel out to the villages to buy a cow or a calf, bring it to town, to the town slaughterhouse, and let the shohet [ritual slaughterer] slaughter it. The shohet was usually there in the mornings.

If a lesion was found on an animal's lungs, and it was certified trefa (not kosher) and its owner was a poor butcher who had borrowed money to buy it, it was a pity to look at the poor man. He had to sell it as trefa meat and take a big loss. It took him a long time to cover his losses and pay back the money he had borrowed.

However, in general, Jews were able to make a living as butchers. They raised their families and after the fathers' departure the sons continued as butchers in Gombin.

Fruit Traders *(sadovnikes)*

Quite a large number of the Jews of Gombin worked in the marketing of fruit and with orchard keeping in the summer months. As far as I know, there has been no research into the major role of the Jews of that region in the development and spread of fruit commerce (this is a separate profession, which is not part of my experiences). I only wish to mention briefly how Gombin Jews occupied themselves in this.

With the beginning of spring, and the blossoming of the fruit trees, a large number of Gombin Jews set out for the nearby villages, especially those in the "niderung" (lowlands) almost completely settled by Germans. They would negotiate with the owners of the orchards and make agreements to buy the fruit when it ripened and was picked from the trees. It was understood that the owner of the orchard would build a straw hut into which the sadovnik and his family would move as soon as the fruit began to appear on the branches. They would live there until all the fruit had been picked from the trees. A portion of the fruit would be dried and packed in sacks to be sold in the winter months when no fresh fruit was available.

Around the end of the month of May there began the exodus to the villages. The families which leased the rights to the fruit had to watch to see that no fruit was stolen, and make sure that as soon as the summer apples or pears were ripe they would be picked and sent to be sold. They also had to prepare special trays for the drying of the fruit. In short, there was no lack of work. They had to work very hard, often to exhaustion. Everything had to be done at the right time. The fruit could not be too ripe. It had to be picked, properly packed in cartons or vats, so that it was not crushed or spoiled before it was taken to the big city, mainly to Warsaw and Lodz. It took almost 24 hours before the fruit arrived there. They had to know how to pack the cartons of fruit onto the big wagons, which took them to the big city. Afterwards the sadovnik and the waggoner would set out on their way.

If there were not much fruit in the market of the big city, the sadovnik would sell his merchandise at a good price and would be pleased. Sometimes he would even bring home presents for his children. However, if there was a glut of fruit on the market, he had to sell his fruit for almost nothing. One must also keep in mind that most of the sadovnikes leased the orchards with money borrowed from their families or from others. Even if the price of fruit was low, they still had to sell it, because if held too long the fruit would spoil and anyway there was no place to store it. In such cases, after the hard work of the whole family and the difficult two days and two nights of travel on the wagons, which shook up their bodies, the sadovnikes would come home to their wives and children bitter and disappointed. It could happen that the money earned did not even cover their expenses and they had to cover the losses from their pockets.

Drying fruits (dos trukenen di fruchten)

Gombin Jews were great experts in drying fruit. For those who do not know how it was done, I shall give a brief explanation and overview. A lasye, as it was called, was in the form of a wide bed, like the one used for sleeping. All around it was nailed a border of two-foot smooth boards. Over this was attached a thick wire net. Then a hole was dug in the earth, five or six foot deep, over which this lasye was set, so that it would not fall into the hole. Near it another hole was dug, with steps going down. Between these two excavations another hole was dug to connect the two large holes. This hole also served as an oven which was heated with wood. The heat went into the hole under the lasye. The oven had to be heated so that it gave off an exact amount of heat. The lasye was filled with plums or apples, covered with smooth boards of the same size, and the crevices covered with cloths, so that the heat should not escape. And in this way the produce was dried. The sadovnikes knew when it was time to uncover the lasye and take out the fruit that was ready and then to leave it in the baskets until it had cooled off. Afterwards they would put the fruit in sacks and it would be ready to store for winter. All the Gombin Jews who ever ate the dried plums or pears prepared by the sadovnikes will testify that it had a heavenly taste, which they cannot forget until this day.

It is difficult to categorize this occupation--were they merchants or artisans. However they are classified, their work was very important. They provided a necessary addition to nutrition and they also stimulated the owners of the orchards and provided an important part of their income. And our "good-hearted" neighbors looked down their noses on these hard-working and useful Jews and called them "shakher-makher." As I have mentioned earlier, I am not doing a scientific research on Jewish sadovnikes. I am only reporting what I saw with my own eyes in my youth. Before I conclude, I wish to add one fact: the night fears from which these sadovniks often suffered.

The "dear" FolksDeutsche in the lowland, who leased their orchards to the Jews for good sums of money, also wanted to have some fun on the Jews' account. In the middle of the night they would cover themselves with sheets, take along their big dogs and go into the orchards where the Jewish sadovinks were spending the night. They would incite their dogs to howl, run past the straw huts, making terrible noises. The Jewish children would wake up and see the white "jokers" with their dogs dancing around in front of them. The children would be terribly frightened and cry to the high heavens. After they had thoroughly frightened the Jews and had worn themselves out, the Germans would leave with much laughter and satisfaction. They called this adventure a "wachnacht".

This "experience" was in addition to the hard work of the sadovnikes to support their families. If they would have a good season, and make a profit, they would forget all the difficulties and the fears and would wait for the next year, God willing, when they would again lease a "sod" (orchard) perhaps even from the same German owner. But if they had a bad season and were left with a loss and had to find a way to pay off their debts, it was pitiful to see. The next spring they might not even have the possibility of trying their luck (because they could not afford it). So went the life of the Gombin sadovnikes.

Makers of boot uppers *(volkers)*

Quite a few Jews in Gombin worked as makers of boot uppers. Most of them were young children of middle-class families. At that time (between 1900 and 1906) there was a movement to free oneself from the old concepts that an artisan was not as important as someone who studied Torah. The young men did not desire to sit on the yeshiva benches and study until someone would find a suitable match with a large dowry with some years of free board from a father-in-law and afterwards one would look for some way to make a living in business. Young men felt that they should look fora way of life, and many dto learn a trade. There were not too many choices in Gombin so some young men began to learn how to make boot uppers which was quite a respectable trade and widespread Gombin.

For those who do not know what this trade is, I will try and explain: A piece of wood was cut into the shape of a human foot. One took a piece of soft leather, used for boot uppers, soaked the leather in a thick oil, and then put the leather on the form of the foot. It was then worked with a blunt knife until the leather took on the form of a human foot. Then it was attached with small nails and put in a suitable place to dry out. Afterwards it was given to a shoemaker who sewed up the bottoms and put on the soles and heels and it became a finished boot. Mostly these boots were bought by the cobblers to be sold to the peasants who came to the fairs to buy boots for themselves and their children. All sizes of boots were available from the cobblers. The peasants would try them on and if they fit, they would come to some arrangement as to price. The peasants were happy to buy ready -to-wear boots like these, because they were as strong as iron.

There were a number of workshops where such boot uppers were made. The largest was Mordekhai Garber's workshop where only Jews were employed. At the time when I left Gombin, my closest friends worked there - Eliyahu Leyzer and his brother Yankele Tiber, Yosele Berishes, Yitshak Moshe Geyer, and it seems to me, also Shmuel Leyb Volman. These young men who worked for Mordekhai Garber were the most important members of the illegal Bund workers' movement. Later others joined them who also studied this trade, among them Henekh Goldshmidt, and Yerahmiel, the son of the teacher of

Talmud, who had become famous as the genius of the town when he studied by himself in the Beit Midrash. Later he was also the elected representative of the Jews of Gombin in the Town Council.

I want to tell an episode about Henekh Goldshmidt. When he still sat in the Beit Midrash and studied, when the Bund organization in Gombin was still new, the Jews gave the leader of the movement the nickname "Czar". They argued with their children and made fun of the "Czar". Look at this young snot nose, the son of such and such, wants to take over the Russian Empire and become the new Czar. In this way they wanted to frighten their children, so they would not be led astray by the Bundists. But their words had exactly the opposite effect. The children were eager to become acquainted with the Czar. One time Henekh decided he would go to the woods where the Bundists used to meet, and since he knew the Czar very well, since he had studied Talmud with his father. He laid out all the proofs from the Torah that the new ways were no good and would lead nowhere. Well, let me make it brief. Henekh met the "Czar" and from that day on they became the closest comrades and friends until Henekh's death in Rio de Janeiro, Brazil. They corresponded with each other throughout their lifetimes.

Henekh Goldshmidt, 1925
Source: YIVO Digital Archive [not in original book]

Not only were the makers of boot uppers excellent craftsmen who lived from the honest toil of their hands, but they were also considered very important people in Gombin.

I want to mention here that there were people in Gombin who worked in other trades. For example there were some stitchers of low laced boots who worked for shoemakers, locksmiths, carpenters, turners and belt makers and saddle makers and tinsmiths (Yitshak Blekher and his father), carriers, makers of Kashe, soda water makers, those who made oil from flax-seeds, soap makers, glaziers, wig makers, egg chandlers, fishermen (quite a few), bagel bakers (quite a few), waggoners, water carriers, feldshers [paramedics], barbers, teachers, and some other trades which I cannot remember just now. They all earned their bread from their toil.

Musicians *(kleizmerim)*

At the entrance of a narrow little street that started from the Maissim street, there were two stores at each intersection. One store belonged to Itsik Zionts. It was a large flour establishment. At the second intersection was the grocery store belonging to the son-in-law of Leybele, Hanan Klezmer [the musician]. As soon as I walked into this little street, I would hear music being played. Sometimes I would hear only a violin, but often I would hear an entire band. Right behind Leybele's store lived Hanan the musician, the leader of the Gombiner klezmorim [musicians].

Honele Klezmer had in his band, in addition to his two sons, Hatzkel and Yosele (all three played the violin) also Volf Dude, who played a big bass violin which was almost as tall as he was. In Gombin such a bass violin was called a bandure. Nu, how far is dure from dude? So all his life he was called Volf Dude. There were others in the band who played other instruments. In short, it was a whole orchestra.

When Honele and his band played at a wedding, especially for well-established householders, it was something to hear. When they played the melody for "Kale basetsen" [seating the bride] especially if the girl was an orphan, it could break your heart. Not only the bride cried with bitter tears, but all the in-laws wept as well. And their "mitsve tentsl" [the dance of the bride with various male members of the family each one holding a kerchief] was something special. The day after the night of the wedding Honele and his band would come to the home of the bride's parents and play a merry "Dzshien dobri" (Good morning), which cheered everyone up and which refreshed them after they had been celebrating almost all night long..

Occasionally Honele's band had a good bit of income. That is, if the hosts were generous and gave a lot of tips for playing extra dance music they liked, the days after the wedding were also joyful ones for the band. Musicians, as most artists, are something of bohemians, even in such a "metropolis" as Gombin there were rumors that after such a wedding the musicians would whoop it up until the early dawn.

Honele's son Yosele was a very fine violinist. His son while still very young showed great talent as a violinist. It was thought in Gombin that he would grow up to be a famous violinist and that he would make his mark in the world. What happened to these hopes I do not know, for I left Gombin and lost contact with most of my landsleit.

It is important to emphasize one thing here, that a number of Gombin Jews made their living from music, and were also talented Jewish musicians.

Village Traders *(dorfsgayers)*

There were many Jews in Gombin who did not have any special occupation. They tried all kinds of ways of earning a living. When they could find nothing to do in town, they would go out to the village to try their luck. Some peddled with household goods, which the farmers needed. Others sold all kinds of odds and ends especially for women and children. If they noticed that the farmers had things to sell, they would buy them, even if they were not sure what to do with them. Perhaps with God's help they could earn something from them.

Other village wanderers were more knowledgeable about what to buy. They did not bring things to sell, only went out to buy. They bought pigs' hair, horsehair, flax, hides of cows or calves, linseed and other articles, whatever they found. They were quite knowledgeable about the things they bought. There was quite a large trade in animal hides and pigs' hair in Gombin. There were set prices for them, and the merchants knew where to make more profit, what the different qualities were, etc.

There were other kinds of village wanderers as well, for example, butchers often went out to the villages to buy a cow, calves, and sometimes a sheep. This walready routine the Gombin butchers. Most of them had sons and sons-in-law working with them, so one of them would go to the villages to make the purchases needed for the week or for a holiday.

There were also dealers who would go to buy their wares in the villages. I remember my uncle, Avraham Pitel, who lived his whole life in the village of Yuleshev, around 7 kilometers from Gombin. He lived there for the sake of the pasture for his herds of cows and horses, always held in reserve for sale in other towns where he could get better prices.

Once, before the decrees of the 1890's which forbade land ownership to Jews, even in those Polish villages where it had been allowed until then, he had owned his own fields where he had pastured his herds.

Some of these village wanderers did other things as well. They might be in the villages until Thursday, and then go out to the lakes and help the fishermen bring in their nets full of live fish, buy them and bring them to sell to Jews for the Sabbath. Thus the village wanderer became a fisherman on Fridays. Or, on a fair day or market day the same village wanderer would take over a corner and spread out his wares of glazed pots and pans to sell to the peasants. Or sometimes he would sell all kinds of tin and porcelain ware.

In the springtime the village wanderers would go out to the villages or to the German colonies and rent an orchard and become a "sadovnik" over the summer.

That is how Jews who did not have a trade in hand tried various ways to support their families. Only not to have to ask for charity, God forbid. There was a proberb that said "A melokhe is a brokhe" (a trade is a blessing).

The same Jews, who worked so hard to make a living, did not feel happy if they did not have a guest for the Sabbath or holidays. These same Jews would also sometimes offer a "day" [food for the day] to a poor boy who sat in the Beit Midrash and studied Torah. They would also not allow a beggar to pass by without giving him a contribution.

One should mention these Jews with a word of praise. In Gombin no one was ashamed of working hard at any kind of work, in order to support one's family and live an honest life.

Market Women *(mark zitzers)*

One of the ways women earned a living in Gombin was sitting at market stalls. These women were among the poorest of the poor.

At the west side of the market place, leading to Plotsker Street and on the right, to Maissim Street, to the middle of the market place to Long Street, was the beginning of the market women's realm. At the beginning of the market place there were a few permanent wooden sheds. There all kinds of baked goods were sold. The sheds had wide roofs, which overhung both sides, to protect the goods from rain and snow. Right next to them were the stalls of the market women, and they reached all the way to Poznanski's house.

On days when there were fairs, there were stalls put up by Polish butchers where they sold all kinds of sausages and hams and other pork products. Further on, till the municipality, where Long Street begins, there were stalls with all kinds of goods for sale, for example, short pants, trousers, and other cheap clothing.

The Polish butchers were the market women's closest neighbors. They sometimes did disgusting things to the poor Jewish market women. When a woman was busy with a number of customers she did not notice one of the Polish youths throwing a piece of pork into her little pot of food, which she had brought from home to sustain her during the day. When she put her pot on her fire-pot, used to warm her on cold days, she smelled a strange odor, She was greatly distressed, but what could she do? She realized that one of the Polish "bastards" had played a trick on her, but how could she identify him? That was a fast day for her, poor thing. The Polish youths enjoyed the joke they had at the "kike's" expense.

Market Day in Gombin
Source: Gabin Land Lovers Association [not in original book]

The market women displayed many different items in large troughs. At the beginning of the summer they sold red and black cherries, the first summer apples and pears, and all kinds of chickpeas and beans, carrots and cucumbers, sorrel. They sold the first ripened fruits and vegetables that were available in town. In the fall their troughs were full of later ripening produce, dried plums, apples, pears, and other good things. Much of the foodstuffs sold in Gombin was sold by the market women. It is difficult to imagine how Gombin would have managed without them.

They worked hard long hours to earn their bread. They sat at their troughs in the heat of summer and the cold of winter. In the wintertime the kheyder boys would run to the market place to buy frozen apples, which they considered more delicious than the fresh ones. But the market women's lives were not so delicious. They had hard and bitter lives.

Shopkeepers *(kremers)*

The groceries were the most important stores in Gombin. First, there were the stores where all kinds of flour were sold. There were three large flour shops on the Maissim Street alone, owned by Taubers, Itsik Zayonts, and Leybele. Besides selling retail to selected customers, they also sold to bakers. They also had unmilled grain: wheat, chickpeas, beans, and other unmilled products. They sold them for the spring sowing to peasants and farmers who had not preserved the grains from the previous year. They also sold rice and other similar products. In addition to the shops on Maissim Street, there were quite a few flour stores scattered throughout the town.

In the market place between Plotsker and Kutner Streets, was Rasha's large store where many items besides flour were sold, such as all kinds of herring, kerosene, oil, and many other things (I seem to remember that they supplied herring to all the food shops in town). Besides her large store, which was at the front of her building, there was also an entrance on the side for wagon vendors. There it was always noisy with the unloading and loading of all kinds of merchandise, such as sacks of flour, vats of herring, tins of kerosene, sacks of sugar, rice, beans, grain, and other products.

There were always Jewish porters around the building, loading and unloading merchandise onto and from the large wagons. There were always more porters than Rasha needed, and when one of the other storekeepers needed someone to load merchandise he would come to Rasha's building and call one or more of the porters.

Rasha had been born in Plock and married a man from Gombin. Right after the wedding it was obvious that she was better suited to business than her husband. Thus the store was called Rasha's.

Rasha was a sister of Rabbi Yehuda Leyb Zlotnik. Rabbi Zlotnik was chosen to be the rabbi of Gombin in 1911 when he was 24 years old. He held this post until 1919. By the way, one should mention that the late Rabbi Zlotnik was one of the best known folklorists in Poland. I mention it here because I am convinced that in Gombin Rabbi Zlotnik was able to learn a great deal of Jewish folklore, and Gombin has a share in his later fame.

Rasha Holcman nee' Zlotnik, 1870-1937
Source: Ada Holtzman's Collection [not in original book]

There were also a number of dry-goods stores in Gombin. The largest were those belonging to Itele Zelig, Abbas Rosental, and Leyzer Vigderovich. In addition there were smaller stores, like the one belonging to the Chassid Zander, on Kutner Street. At Zander's one could buy all kinds of linens. There were also stores, which specialized in fittings used by tailors of men's clothing and seamstresses: linings, buttons, needles, etc. There were also stores, which sold leather for shoes, boots, and soles. In these shops one could find everything necessary for shoemaking.

As for Jewish saloons, I remember only Bibergal and the tavern belonging to the Shtolcman family which was in the middle of the market place, near Long Street. Menashe Shtolcman was in charge of the tavern, which was a large fbusiness, and was comparato the lartaverns in the big cities of Poland. Most of the other taverns in Gombin were run by Poles, except for a German family named Schteile. They owned a large tavern, situated opposite the Shtolcman's tavern.The Schteile family had quite good relations with Jews. Perhaps it was because they disliked Poles as much as they disliked Jews.

From Shtolcman's tavern up to the Polish church, where Long Street began, there were a number of two story "mansions," the most beautiful buildings in town. There resided the wealthier Jews, many of whom had assimilated to Polish culture, and they spoke Polish exclusively.

Karapki's food store was exclusive. There one could buy the best-imported foodstuffs, for example sardines, lox, little herrings from abroad, almonds, dates, oranges, lemons, pressed dates, figs, chocolate, candies, and whatever one could wish for. But these were not for the ordinary Jews of Gombin. Very few of them tasted or even knew about the taste of what was in this shop. Karapki's customers were the Polish aristocracy and office holders as well as the rich German colonists of the environs. I do not know whether Karapke had other businesses as well besides his imported foods. In any case, he was considered one of the richest men in Gombin and his family lived in a fashion so lavish that the Jews of Gombin could not even dream of it.

There were also wheat merchants in town, who sent their goods to other cities. There were also wood dealers and a number of iron stores. One of the iron stores, the largest in town, belonged to the Krasek family. This family, too, lived on a richer level than most of the Jews in Gombin.

There were also lumber merchants in Gombin, but their business was not in town, but far from Gombin, and the Jews of Gombin had only a vague idea of their business. It was rumored in town that they had big sugar factories, but nobody knew for certain.

There were probably less than ten very rich Jews in Gombin. Shmulik and Poznanski were among the wealthiest Jews, it was said. Then came Zelig Abba Volfovitch, Yosele Borenshtein, and after them less and less wealthy men, Nobody actually knew how rich they were, because people had a very vague idea of what real wealth meant. They were compared with the majority of the Jews of Gombin Even if there were a handful of rich Jews, ninety percent of Gombin Jews were poor, hardworking laborers, artisans, and small storekeepers who worked even harder than the artisans. They worked by the sweat of their brows, in order to earn a living.

Mordkhele, the rope maker *(shtrikmacher)*

Tevya Shtrikmakher lived on Maissim Street in the heart of the poorest neighborhood in town. There were always newly arrived paupers in his home, even though he himself had a house full of children. His oldest son Mordekhai was twelve or thirteen years old.

I knew Tevya Ropemaker, or Tevya Ropetwister, as the Gombin jokesters used to call him, because in order to make the ropes he had a kind of "machine" which twisted the linen fibers into all kinds of ropes, from thin strands to thick ropes.

His workshop was in the middle of Maissim Street during the summer months. He used to station his son Mordekhai at one end of the street (according to how long he planned to make the rope), would place a "machine" in his hand, to which he attached the long fibers into which he had twisted his "twister" and gave his son signals: "Ho! Ho-ho!" Then he would approach the boy. The wheel turned and by the time he reached his son the rope would be made.

Children and passers-by would stop and stand around to watch eagerly as ropes were made. If a gentile would come by from the meadow with a wagon of hay, Tevya would move his whole "factory" to the side of the street and when the wagon had passed he would return to the same position as before and continue twisting the rope. Then he would continue sending loud signals to his son: "Ho! Ho-Ho!"

The second reason I knew the Ropemaker was because of his son Mordekhai who could tell wonderful stories. We children could simply not get enough of them when he would begin telling his tales,

In the summer evenings a group of children would gather in the synagogue yard which bordered Maissim Street. We would sit on the boards scattered here and there. They were needed for fixing the wooden walls of the synagogue. Due to age, the walls were bowed and "bellied" and were under constant repair. There was always a supply of boards of various sizes there. That was our meeting place. We would sit there with pieces of bread and khale in our pockets. Sometimes we would also bring other things for our "rebbe," Mordekhai the Ropemaker.

Even though Tevya's family was always hungry, Mordekhai was a stocky, well-built boy. His appetite was without limit. No matter how much we children (younger than he) would bring along, it was still not enough to satisfy him. He would take a large piece of bread in his mouth, curl his tongue, and the bread would disappear. But as soon as he would finish off the bread and sometimes a piece of gefilte fish, then he would wipe his mouth with his sleeve and would begin to spin his tales, and all kinds of legends, and we boys would sit as if in a dream. Occasionally a boy would actually fall into a sweet sleep.

Books could be written of Mordkhele's stories. When he would begin a story he would put in all the details. His princes and princesses traveled in palaces on rubber wheels. They were served all kinds of meats and poultry, even roasted doves. They ate with silver and gold utensils. Their bedding was of the richest embroidered linens. He saw to it that they had all the conveniences. He did not even omit an indoor toilet for the prince and princess.

He told stones of a king and a king's son who had sinned against his father, who exiled him to distant lands. The prince went around there in rags. He decided to become a doctor. And he wandered the world dressed as a vagabond until he came close to his hometown. . There he discovered that his sister, the princess, was terribly sick, and no doctor could help her. Meanwhile the king made known all over the country that whoever would heal his daughter could marry her. And would become the king's heir. The prince quickly went to the palace and announced that he would undertake to heal the princess. The servants drove him out of the courtyard --such a tramp, dressed in rags, wants to heal the princess! So he again came and announced that he undertook to heal the princess, and again the servants threw him out. And so on and so on until the king heard that a vagabond wanted to undertake to heal his daughter. He ordered: Let him in!" The end was that the prince healed the princess, and when it came time for the wedding, he revealed who he really was. You can imagine the joy in the palace.

The younger boys sat enchanted by the story and some of them were already deeply asleep.

Mordkhele was a magnificent storyteller. His voice was clear as running water. He also had stories about Polish "Paritzim" landowners and their wives. He had stories about the Polish revolt and how the Jews hid the rebels. He had stories about "Zadikim" the Jewish Righteous, magic and wonders. He told about Jews who came from far-away places and settled in Gombin. And if ever there was a slanderer or a wicked person, he was always only from those foreigners who came from far away.

As the years passed, and I grew up and new ideas conquered me, I lost the connection with Mordkhele the rope maker, but the tens of his legends and stories remain for ever in my memory and for remembrance I now put them on this paper.

My Shtetl Gombin
Reminiscences of a Lost World

By Henry Greenbaum

[Original book: Pages 25-41 English]

Henry Greenbaum

On April 17, 1942 the Jewish community of Gombin, my birthplace in Poland, was savagely wiped out by an act of Nazi brutality. The small number of survivors chose not to return to their hometown, where their ancestors had lived and worked for some five centuries, in an effort to forget the unbearable catastrophe in which their loved ones perished mercilessly. They preferred exile, and so the Shtetl Gombin that I knew is no more.

The Polish Magazine Nasza Ojczyzna (our Fatherland) reported in its September 1964 issue: "Gombin is smaller than before the war when it counted six thousand inhabitants. Now there are less than three and a half thousand. The Jews who made up almost half of the population of Gombin were murdered by the Hitlerites. Gone from the streets are the *Hassidic* Jews with their *yarmelkehs* (skull caps) and from the fronts of the small stores the bearded tailors and shoemakers. In the small Gombin now there is almost no industry nor commerce."

It is with deep sadness that I write of my life in Jewish Gombin where I grew up and lived, except for some interruptions for studies from 1907 to 1937. My painful awareness of its extinction may best be described by my paraphrasing the words of the Polish Poet Adam Mickiewicz as follows: Gombin, my dear shtetele, you were like health. How much I miss you only he knows who lost you.

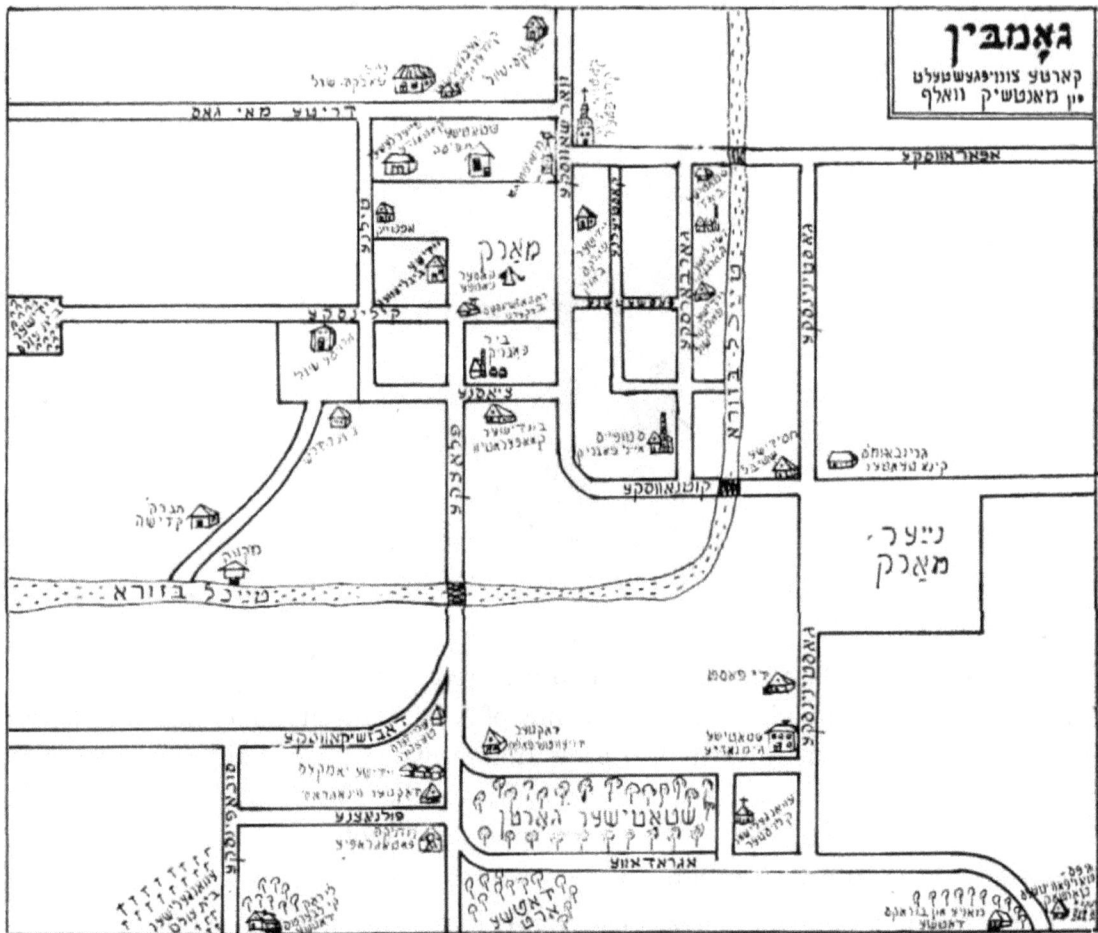

Map of Gombin, by Wolf Mantzyk (Israel)

The memory of Gombin, of its people and its religious, cultural and social institutions, lives in the minds of the few survivors who are scattered over the face of the earth. When we are gone, Gombin will cease to exist even in memory and this would be its second extinction.

To prevent this tragedy, this book is being published as a memorial to our town in hopes that in years to come it will be read from time to time by people who will tell their children that once upon a time there was a Shtetl Gombin and so keep the memory of this town alive after all, like an eternal flame.

And what kind of a Shtetl was Gombin?

To some it would probably seem to be a Shtetl like many others dispersed throughout Poland. But to me it was something very special. I grew up there and it was there that I had my roots and tasted life in all its variety for the first time. And it was also there that I derived my chief values, aspirations, and drives which have become my guidelines in life and have contributed to my achievements.

Regardless of how far away I was from Gombin and from the family I left behind and no matter what I was doing, I always had a feeling of nostalgia and a desire to visit home. So whether I was attending high school in Warsaw or Medical School in Paris, I always liked to return home for vacations. Now that my Shtetl is no more, my old longing to return there has left me.

The Wish to Leave the Shtetl

Looking back to the early days, I can say it was fun to grow up there. Yet paradoxically, as far back as I can remember, there was also the wish to grow up and leave Gombin and make my way to faraway cities or lands. Everybody in the Shtetl at one time or another dreamed of getting away from it, and those who could not hoped that at least their children would have a chance. It was therefore no coincidence that at the age of twelve I wrote a school composition to the effect that I would like to be an explorer of unknown lands like Christopher Columbus.

Nor was it accidental that shortly after World War I, two young boys of about fifteen, David Meilekh Brzezinski (now Burns, living in New York) and Haim Luzer Ciuk, ran away from Gombin and got as far as Holland before they were apprehended and returned home. How I envied them their courage. The aspiration for traveling was in the very atmosphere of the Shtetl. Few were able to get away, but almost all of those who did emigrate thrived in other lands for it was at home that they acquired their stamina and courage.

Gombin Was Isolated From the World

When I was growing up as a child, Gombin was pretty much walled off from the rest of the world. The nearest railroad station, Żychlyn, about fifteen miles away, could only be reached by horse and buggy, and the nearest boat to the outside world was in Dobrzyków on the River Vistula, about five miles away over a stretch of sandy road easier to traverse on foot than by horse and buggy, which often got stuck in the deep sand, causing impatient passengers to miss their boat.

The *Maggid*

The influx of people from the outside up to the beginning of World War I only amounted to a trickle. From time to time a *maggid* (preacher) would arrive in Gombin and spend a Sabbath in town, giving a sermon to the men foregathered in *besmedresh* (house of learning) on Saturday afternoon. On such occasions, the place was filled to overflowing. My father liked to take me along. Although I did not understand the *maggid's* teaching, I remember how I enjoyed the melody of his words, but above all the atmosphere he created by his sermon. When he finished, the people clustered inside and outside in small groups and commented on his wisdom and learning.

Since my father was considered to be a *Lamdan* (Talmudic scholar) people would turn to him on such occasions to ask his opinion on many fine points of interpretation of the Torah. I was always surprised to hear him quoting from memory extensive Hebrew passages from Talmud in support of his reasoning, and of course that feat made me one of the proudest boys in all Gombin.

The effects of the *maggid's* teaching did not stop there. After my father came home, he would take down from the shelves of his large library heavy Sforim (Hebrew religious books) and study them, sometime far into the night. I imagine many other learned Jews acted in a like manner.

Fierce was the devotion to learning of the Torah among a number of *balebatim* (burghers) in the Shtetl.

The *Oyrekh*

Among the people who came from the outside world to pay a visit to Gombin were the beggars. The shtetl had its own poor who on Fridays and holiday eve used to go from house to house to beg alms. But not infrequently transient beggars came to town and did the same thing. It was the custom for the *balebatim* to invite a beggar in as an *oyrekh* (guest) to the Sabbath and Holiday meals.

More often than not the *oyrekhs* turned \out to be interesting characters and I liked very much when my father, after Friday evening prayers in Shul (synagogue) chose one of the beggars standing in the door as an *oyrekh*. That was when the meal-times were gayer and livelier than ever. Once the initial bashfulness was past, the oyrekh often grew quite talkative and told exciting tales about his travels to various towns and cities, and frequently discussed religious, political and business matters with sophistication and wisdom one would hardly expect to find in an *oyrekh*.

My Family

I remember after one of them left the house how my father and mother expressed astonishment, how amazed they were that a beggar should be so smart yet unable to achieve for himself a life of dignity. My parents' wonder stuck in my mind for a long time, and it was not until many years later when I became a psychiatrist that I understood the paradox of being intelligent and capable and yet unsuccessful.

Gombin was an isolated shtetl. But in its isolation it was a microcosm where the people experienced, as they do anywhere, a wide spectrum of emotions ranging from joy to intense sorrow.

It is fair to say that the Jewish emotional life in Gombin was fashioned by two forces - Jewish religious fervor and the ever-present hostility of the non-Jews.

Yom Kippur

The religious fervor manifested itself especially during the Sabbath and all holidays. Of all the holidays, *Yom Kippur* (Day of Atonement and Pardon) has left on me an unforgettable impression. Although *Yom Kippur* is the culmination of a period of the Days of Awe, which begin with *Rosh Hashanah* (New Year) when each person's fate for the year is inscribed in Heaven, and ends ten days later when the fate is signed, I do not recall this period as being grim and gloomy. Rather it was a time of magic like prayers, of warmth and love in the family, of brotherhood among people outside the family, and of delicious meals which bore all the earmarks of feasts. I recollect that as a small boy I never worried about the fate of my parents, my sister, my brother or myself during Yom Kippur. For I believed strongly in the magic protective power of the ritual whirling about my head of a cockerel which was supposed to take over all my sins.

During Yom Kippur Eve all the members of the family went through this ritual, father using a rooster, mother a hen and the children cockerels or pullets. Then I felt immensely reassured as to the fate of my whole family.

But most reassuring of all was my parents' love around this time. They loved their children all year long, but when the high holidays came, they showed more warm tenderness and affection than ever, as if they were trying with their love to wash away our sins.

After the sundown feast of *Erev Yom Kippur* (Yom Kippur Eve) came a most solemn moment which always moved me very deeply. Father dressed in a *Kittl* (white garment) over his holiday silk Kaftan, and mother dressed in a long black silk gown and a black shawl on her head. They kissed each other and shook hands, wishing each other, "*Beyt sich oys a good johr*"! (Pray yourself out a good year!). Then father would bless us children and kiss us. After that mother remained at home with the younger children and a thick Hebrew prayer book with Yiddish translation and legends and parables that she loved to read, while tears poured out of her eyes. By the time the evening was over, the pages were quite damp.

While the women prayed at home on Yom Kippur Eve, the men and older boys set out for the Shul, *besmedresh* or the *Hassidic shtiblekh* (little shul). A blanket of quiet covered the town. The stores and shutters were closed and the people (with a sense of gravity and solemnity) went to the houses of worship to face their Creator. On the way when they met they shook hands and wished each other, "May you pray yourself out a good year." Besides expressing good wishes, some people asked forgiveness of others for any offenses committed in the past year.

The Shul was filled as at no other holiday. The crowd of worshippers overflowed into the large vestibule. It felt as if the whole town were in the Shul. Every year a few non-Jews, usually members of the town's Polish intelligentsia, came to the vestibule to listen to *Kol Nidre*, a very sad and moving prayer, sung by the cantor and his choir in front of the Arc of Torah at the *Mizrakh* (Eastern wall).

This ancient and poignant musical prayer set the tone and opened the Yom Kippur services of unremitting and intense prayers which were interrupted only for the night and then lasted until sundown the next day. The following morning the women and girls came and joined the prayers in the balcony of the Shul.

The chanting, the weeping, the swaying, the fasting, the blessing by the *Kohanim* (members of the tribe of priests) and the fumes from the hundreds of candles on brass chandeliers suspended from the high ceiling, created a climate of intense religious devotion which culminated with the blowing of the *Shofar* (ram's horn).

I have no words to describe the effect of the Shofar on me. The sound filled me with a hypnotic sense of awe and a conviction that God Almighty had descended into the Shul to bless us personally and protect each of us from evil. After the services, I felt elated and purified. Outside the Shul, mother and father met and wished each other a good year, and then exchanged this wish with everybody they met on the way home to a delicious dinner.

To me Yom Kippur meant being in communion with God and with people. It also meant loving and being loved. It inspired an exalted sense of the sublime which comes from the feeling of being purged of sin and evil. But above all, the religious intensity of Yom Kippur imparted spiritual strength and elevated the mood which was so indispensable for Jewish survival in the hostile environment of non-Jews.

The Hostile Environment

As far back as I can remember, I felt the hostility of non-Jews which ranged from condescending attitudes, through subtle as well as overt unfriendliness, to various degrees of violence. This unremitting hostility was depressing to the spirit and highly exasperating. For instance, how can I describe my desolation when at the tender age of eight or nine I happened to meet in school a gentile boy with whom I had played the day before, done homework together in my house, and whom I had invited to dinner. There he stood with a group of other gentile boys, acting as if he had never laid eyes on me before, and together with the others hissed at me and called me dirty Jew.

My brother Stan (1910 -1942) and his wife,
my sister-in-law Helen (Zayontz) (1917-1942)

Or how can I express my shame and humiliation when a Polish teacher, in order to illustrate the concept of race, called up in front of the class - a short, fat, homely Jewish boy - and compared him side by side with a tall, slender, good-looking gentile boy as two specimens of different races.

These and other painful experiences in Gombin were numerous, but of a relatively minor nature. However, from time to time, there were experiences which were overwhelming in character. One such episode shook me up so deeply that I have never forgotten it and even now when I think about it I am moved to tears.

My Father is Nearly Killed by a Cossack

It happened during World War I, at the end of 1914 or the beginning of the following year. Russian soldiers, coming or going to the front, were milling about in the streets of the Shtetl. A big tall Cossack with a mop of hair sticking out from under his hat to one side of his forehead came into my parents' grocery store and ordered a large amount of groceries. After his order was packed in a burlap bag, he took it and walked out without paying. When my father called him back, he made an insulting remark and spat on the ground.

My father, in a rage, ran out into the street after him and grabbed his arm. They grappled with each other and when my father did not let go, the Cossack pulled out his sword and threatened to thrust it into my father's chest. Meanwhile, soldiers with ugly, cruel and laughing faces gathered around as if it were a circus, urging the Cossack to go ahead and kill the Yevrey (Jew).

My mother, the tears streaming from her eyes, begged the Cossack not to harm my father, and pleaded with my father to let the Cossack go. I watched this ghastly scene from the doorway of our store, dreadfully scared and horrified and crying "Totteh! Totteh!" (Father! Father!) For a moment the world stood still on the edge of disaster, the image frozen into my mind of the soldiers' fierce, pitiless faces, and my father deathly pale, his life in danger, and my mother in extreme agony before me.

Suddenly and miraculously, a Russian chaplain, tall with flowing hair and dressed in a long Kaftan, appeared on the scene and angrily ordered the Cossack to put away his sword and return the groceries to my father, and then he dispersed the crowd. My joy and gratitude to that chaplain knew no bounds.

Mother and father returned to the store badly shaken. Of course she scolded him for risking his life and he defended himself, insisting that the Cossack had no right to act as he did. As for me, I agreed with mother that life is sacred, but I was also immensely proud of my father and the courage he showed in making his stand.

Since then I have always believed in the sacredness of both life and human dignity and have longed for a world where no human being would have to risk his life to defend his dignity. Although scientific, technological and economic progress is necessary for the achievement of man's goals, the real barometer of progress toward a humane society is the preservation of human dignity.

The Location of Gombin

To pinpoint Gombin geographically, it was a small town situated in the plains of central Poland, some sixty miles northwest of Warsaw, the capital, fifteen miles south of the ancient city of Płock, sixty miles northeast of Łódź, eighteen miles northeast of the railroad junction, Kutno, and fifteen miles southeast of the county seat, Gostynin. By the time I reached adolescence, the shtetl was connected with all these places by relatively good highways of compressed pebbles.

When a traveler came into town from Kutno or Łódź, the highway ran through pastures, wheat, rye and potato fields. On the outskirts of town there were four huge windmills which manufactured flour from local farmer' grain. A similar landscape presented itself when you arrived from Warsaw, only instead of windmills there was at the entrance of town a flour mill, a tall red brick building with modern machinery. The road from Płock and Gostynin crossed miles of beautiful pine forest, and as you approached the town you could see from afar the tall steeple of the Protestant Church. At this entrance there was a mechanized lumber mill.

When I was a little boy I used to love to play in the fields, watching horses pull the plows and beautiful colts running along beside them, and cows grazing on the grass. But more than anything else, in the summertime I liked to walk through the tall rye and wheat with the stalks high above my head. It was thrilling to see the waves created by the breezes along the surface of the rye and wheat fields. The shimmering golden color of the ripe rye and wheat gave me the impression of a sea of gold.

Then as an adolescent I took great pleasure in strolling for hours at a time in the forest of tall thick pine trees, daydreaming about the wide world and my

place in it. One of the people I frequently met in the woods was our poetess Reisele Zychlinski who like myself was fascinated and absorbed by the unusual loveliness of nature and the whispering orchestration of the trees..

In the center of this beautiful countryside nestled the shtetl, with its two markets and two dozen cobblestoned streets. On its periphery were dispersed farms with small houses, large stables, and huge barns with thatched roofs. In the middle of the farmyard there was usually an open well.

The Old Market, the center of town, was a rectangular place with two manually operated water pumps, one in the center, the other about two hundred feet to the east. On the southeast corner stood the Catholic Church, a beautiful red brick edifice with two towers. Across the street was the Town Hall, a plain stucco building which housed the administrative offices, the police and the town jail. Adjoining was the firehouse. All around stood two-story brick or stucco houses with store fronts. They replaced the wooden houses which had been burned down by a big fire at the turn of the century. The few wooden houses that survived the fire stood at two opposite corners of the market.

Gombin Market Square
Source: Ada Holtzman's Collection [not in original book]

About four blocks to the west was the New Market lived my parents and grandparents. It was a huge, rectangular place, paved with cobblestones, a water pump in the center. At its west end was a huge wooden cross and all around were small farmhouses. In the summer at sunset, it was quite a picture to see the farmers with their horses and cattle returning from the nearby fields. Many Jewish mothers liked to bring her children to the farm to have them drink the fresh warm milk, supposed to have health-giving qualities.

The streets were narrow and lined on both sides with low one-story wooden houses, devoid of beauty or ornament or any modern comfort. There was no running water and until the end of World War I no electricity. Water was brought into the houses from the nearby wells and pumps, and light was furnished by kerosene lamps.

Poor working-class people lived in one room with a brick or tile stove for both cooking and heating in winter. The more affluent could afford a kitchen, a combination dining and living room and one or more bed rooms. In each room there was a high tile oven for heating.

About one block from the Old Market was the Jewish religious complex of the *shul*, *besmedresh*, and the *mikve* (public bath for ritual). The shul was a charming old wooden structure about three or four stories high with tall windows, a copper roof and two copper onion-shaped cupolas. The outside walls were quite weatherbeaten. Inside the walls were covered with natural wood boards with no ornamentation except around the Arc where the Torah Books were kept. There at the Eastern Wall were beautifully carved wood decorations of an ancient design. In the center were carved tablets with the Ten Commandments inscribed in Hebrew. The pulpit, the elevated platform with its Arc and decorations, gave the Eastern Wall a most impressive quality.

In the middle of the shul was the *bimah*, an elevated platform where the Torah was read, the *shofar* blown, and speeches made. From the high ceiling dozens of brass chandeliers were hung. In the rear was a balcony where the women prayed. In front of the *bimah* were benches with pulpits for the *balebatim* (burghers), in the rear the reserved place for the artisans and workers.

At the northern end of town there was a large park and the near-by Protestant Church with its beautiful high steeple. A narrow creek divided the town in half, and two wooden bridges connected both parts. In the spring the water of the creek often came up to the top of the bridges. In winter the water froze and boys and girls skated on the ice in their homemade wooden skates. In the summer the creek usually dried up.

Gombin could not be called a beautiful town. But the synagogue and the two churches towering over the narrow cobblestoned streets, and the two markets with their low small houses, all surrounded by magnificent natural beauty, imparted an aura of charm, the sort of thing that was captured so well by Chagall in his many paintings of small Russian towns.

The People of Gombin

The Jews lived in the center of town, and by their industry and commerce served the other inhabitants who lived on the periphery. Most of the non-Jews were farmers. Some were carpenters, shoemakers, construction workers, blacksmiths, town employees and unskilled workers. Although the Jews constituted about half the population, no Jews were employed by the town hall or the post office.

Gombin was also the commercial and religious center for a peasant population of several thousand people, living within a radius of five to ten miles in an outer belt of villages. A few Jews lived in these villages, but the great majority was non-Jews. I guess about ninety percent of all the non-Jews of Gombin and the surroundings were Catholics and they were referred to as Polish, the rest being Protestants of German origin who were called Germans.

On Sundays and other Christian holidays, the non-Jews came to town in large numbers on foot or in country horsedrawn wagans to attend religious services in the two churches. They were dressed up in their holiday clothes. The men were usually attired in dark, poorly tailored suits with high shiny boots and round caps with gleaming leather visors. The women wore colorful pleated skirts and blouses, homespun kerchiefs on their hair. They would arrive in town to the tolling of the great church bells that could be heard for miles around. After the services they would mill about in the streets. I remember as a child feeling apprehensive on such occasions, because from time to time the Catholics would emerge from church displaying hostile feelings towards the Jews.

Other times when the farmers and the peasants used to come to town were the marketing days on Thursday of every week, and during the two semi-annual fairs held in the spring and fall. They came with wagons laden with grain, potatoes, fruits, vegetables, eggs, butter and fowl for sale. Horses, cattle and pigs were also on sale. The merchants, usually Jews (except when it came to purchasing pigs), met the peasants and bargained with them before a deal was consummated. With money in their pockets, the peasants then went to the stores to purchase food, cloth-shoes and assorted articles for houses and farms.

The stores were well stocked by Jewish merchants. Almost all the grocers, except two or three, were Jewish. Of seven bakeries, five were Jewish. The Jews were shoemakers, tailors, hatters, rope makers, blacksmith, barbers, roofers, metal stove and kettle makers. Haberdashery, dry goods, hardware, leather, book and stationery stores were owned by Jews. The seltzer and oil factories and one of two tanneries were run by Jews. The bicycle repair shop and watch repair shops were Jewish-owned. One out of two physicians and the *Felttsher* (medical practioner without university training) and the dentists were Jews.

The Jews organized passenger and truck transportation to nearby and distant towns and cities to which they exported grain, butter, eggs, and other farm produce, and imported goods needed by the local population. In a word, the Jews in Gombin were an intelligent, industrious and enterprising people in all avenues of endeavor.

A few Jews also lived in the country as farmers. My paternal grandparents, Abe and Hinda, lived in a village a few miles away when I was a child. But then two of my uncles emigrated to Great Britain shortly before the outbreak of World War I and one uncle was taken into the Russian army, so they moved to Gombin. I especially remember the fun of visiting them in the country, running around in the field, riding on wagons stocked high with hay, and going horseback riding.

Relations Between Jews and Non-Jews

Social relations between Jews and non-Jews were almost nil. The only contact between them took place in the course of business and service transactions, and at such times human warmth sometimes did seep through. I remember my parents inviting customers from the countryside to come into the house and warm up with some hot tea and sandwiches during the bitter cold winter. Occasionally they came to my parents for advice on matters of family troubles. On such visits, deep family secrets were frequently bared, with tears in the eyes of the confider.

During my excursions in the countryside I used to meet peasants who knew me and my parents, and they were quite hospitable, inviting me into their huts and treating me to good peasant homemade dark bread, fresh milk, cheese and fruit.

As for intermarriages, they were most infrequent. In thirty years I recall only two such instances. Two Jewish women converted to Catholicism and their families suffered unbearable anguish equal to the pain caused by the death of a child. Indeed the members of the two families said *Kaddish* (the prayer of mourning for the death of a close relative) and all relations with the converts were severed.

Individually, some Poles were able to show friendliness toward Jews. But in a group they were often unrecognizably changed because of the tendency to display, overtly or covertly, anti-Semitic attitudes. From the earliest years of my life I often suffered from humiliation and even physical mistreatment brought about by anti-Semitism.

As in all other shtetlekh, anti-Semitism was endemic in Gombin, a constant threat to the physical and spiritual survival of the Jews. To keep afloat in the treacherous sea of hostility, the Jews needed a cultural compass. During the long dark years of political reaction and hopelessness in Eastern Europe in the nineteenth and at the beginning of the twentieth century, such a compass was supplied by the conviction that the Jews were God's chosen people, that the Messiah would come and free them from oppression.

Religious Fervor in Gombin

Until the end of World War I, life in Gombin had a twofold rhythm of *yomtov* (holiday) and the struggle for *parnosseh* (livelihood). The latter took place during the week and was referred to as *vokhendik* (weekly) life, in contrast to the religious life on the Sabbath and Holidays. For the religious Jews, the *vokhendik* activities were subordinated to the Sabbath and holidays which seemed to serve the very purpose of their lives.

For it was during these days that they were in communion with God. Activities in Gombin were spoken of as taking place before or after Sabbath, since Sabbath was a day of complete rest, of praying, learning, and good eating.

From my earliest childhood on I preferred the spirit of the Sabbath to the spirit of the week. During the week, Jew competed with Jew for *parnosseh*, and this competition frequently led to quarrels and animosity which always filled my heart with sadness. But the spirit of Sabbath and holidays personified friendliness and serenity among Jews.

The devotion to studying the Torah was intense, and the respect for the *lamdn Talmud Khochem* (wise student) was great. When I was a child, my father spent perhaps more time in *besmedresh*, along with other students of the Talmud than in his business. According to custom, young married men, students of the Torah, continued to study, while their wives attended to the matter of *parnosseh*.

The shtetl had a well-organized system of *kheyders* (religious schools) extending from the elementary level of learning the Hebrew alphabet and reading the prayers and understanding the Bible in Yiddish, to the level of *Gomorrah kheyder* devoted to the study of the Talmud. I began *kheyder* at the age of three and spent my whole day until dusk studying. By the time I reached the age of eight, the first public school had been opened in Gombin. The young men and women teachers and the modern classes attracted me and I made up my mind not to go to the *kheyder*. I shall never forget my father's reaction. One evening, thinking I was asleep, he complained bitterly to my mother that I would grow up to be an *amorets* (boor v'am haaretz - ignorant boor) and bring shame on the family. My mother tried to assure him that I would grow up to be a good Jew.

I remember how I brooded over my father's prediction, for I certainly did not want to become an "amorets" and how grateful I was to my mother for having faith in me. Finally, my parents resolved the conflict by allowing me to attend public school in the morning and then having me attend *kheyder* in the afternoon.

Gombin synagogue, front view
Source: Ada Holtzman's Collection [not in original book]

The most religious Jews of all were the *Hassidim* (members of a religious movement founded by Israel Baal Shem Tov in the seventeenth century). There were two sects in Gombin, followers of the Gerer Rabbi and Alexander Rabbi. Each sect had its own shul where besides the usual praying they danced and sang in great ecstasy. Most of the Jews in the shtetl wore long kaftans and beards. Besides wearing long beards, the *Hassidim* distinguished themselves by their earlocks and their silk Sabbath kaftans.

My maternal grandfather, Yoyne Ryster, a tall, slender man with a long beard and earlocks, was a Hassid, and he inspired in me an intense desire to emulate him. As I watched him during his silent prayers, eyes closed, swaying to and fro and twisting his body rhythmically to right and left, while exclaiming ecstatically from time to time the Hebrew word, *Adenoy Elohim Echad*! (God of the Universe) *Shmay Isroel*! (Harken onto Israel), I was convinced that my grandfather was in direct communication with God and it filled my childish heart with a sense of deep admiration and reverence for him.

The other person who inspired great reverence in me was Rov (Rabbi) Zlotnik, head of the congregation. He was a distinguished-looking man with a beautiful pale face and a long beard, tall and thin in stature. By his appearance and comportment he conveyed a sense of holiness and dignity. I remember him as a fascinating orator, and during his *droshes* (sermons) from the pulpit I had the distinct impression of Moses talking from the mountain to his people. A few years after World War I he left Gombin to become a national leader of the Mizrachi (religious Zionist party).

My sister-in-law, Helen with her and my brother's son,
Izia (November 1941 - April 1942)

During this period of profound religiosity, the Jewish community was united, and such occasions as a marriage or funeral brought almost all the people together for celebration and dancing in the streets, or for the expression of sadness and grief. I remember always being moved to tears during a funeral, as I watched the men sighing deeply and the women weeping and lamenting loudly.

This was also a period of medieval superstition. It was alleged that at the turn of the century an epidemic had broken out in Gombin and many people died. To stem the scourge, so the story went, two town idiots were married off on the cemetery, and many people believed in the efficacy of this act, the epidemic having supposedly abated after that.

Secularization of Jewish Life

The period of religiosity in Gombin and all other shtetlekh coincided with a time of general political apathy. The Jews could only turn to their historical past and their religious traditions for hope, identity and spiritual survival. *Leshana Habaa B'Yerushalaim* (the coming year in Jerusalem) often repeated in Jewish prayers, expressed the hope of returning to past Jewish glory. But in the midst of this political apathy two political movements were born in the year 1897 - Zionism and Bund, which at the end of World War I contributed greatly to the secularization of Jewish life and the awakening of the Jews to political action and modern Jewish culture.

At the First Zionist Congress in Basel, Switzerland, in 1897, under the leadership of Theodor Herzl, it was decided that "the aim of Zionism is to create for the Jewish people a publicly secured and legally assured home in "Palestine". Soon afterward, the *Keren Kayemet* (Jewish National Fund) was organized to purchase land in Palestine and further the mass colonization of Jews. At about the same time, Ahad-Ha-Am, the philosopher of cultural Zionism, maintained that Palestine had to be restored as a Hebrew spiritual center for the harassed Jewish people.

The Bund, a Jewish Socialist Party, founded in Russia also in 1897, opposed Zionism and Hebrew culture from its inception. It considered Zionism a dangerous utopian philosophy because it diverted the Jewish masses in the countries where they lived from struggling together with the non-Jewish people for Socialism which alone could create genuine conditions for Jewish emancipation and a Jewish cultural autonomy. The Bund exerted great influence in promoting cultural works in the Yiddish language among the Jewish workers and lower middle class.

These two ideologies had the effect of completely revolutionizing Jewish life in Gombin. Many young people broke away from the religious restrictions and traditions of education, dress and daily habits. *Yeshiva bocherim* (Talmud students) left the *besmedresh*, shaved off their beards and earlocks, gave up their traditional clothing for western type dress and took to reading secular books. Many joined the Bund or Zionist movement and became intensely involved in questions of social, political and national purpose. There were other smaller groups, such as *Poale Zion* (Labor Zionism) and Jewish communists. But the two main parties were the Bund and the Zionist party. They opened libraries with thousands of books in Yiddish, Hebrew and Polish. People read avidly and debated with vigor and deep feeling, especially around the time of elections.

The Bundists and Zionists opened up kindergartens in Yiddish and Hebrew respectively. Each party offered youth organizations, sports clubs, theater groups and glee clubs. Speakers came from Warsaw and discussed political, social and literary themes. Many Jewish women became emancipated from the subjugated role assigned them by religious tradition. A new four-year gymnasium (corresponding to the American junior high school) was opened, and many Jewish boys and girls enrolled in it. Among them was our present president of the N. Y. Gombin organization, Jack Zicklin. Some of them continued their secondary education in other cities, such as Gostynin, Płock, and Warsaw.

Joseph Tadelis, fighter in the Warsaw Ghetto uprising,
murdered by the Gestapo in 1942

For the first time in the history of Gombin, a number of young people studied at universities. The late Abram Finkelstein studied at the University Of Frankfurt School Of Medicine in Germany, Natan Gyps, the late Lea Frenkel, the late Israel Wolfowicz and I studied at the University of Paris Medical School in France. Joseph Tadelis finished Medical School in Warsaw. My late brother Stan studied at the University Of Warsaw Law School. The studies abroad were mainly due to the practice of *Numerus clausus*, a restriction of the number of Jews to be admitted to universities and professions.

The religious Jews felt threatened by the extreme changes and innovations in the traditional life, and made every effort to oppose and combat the new wave. However, the process of change made deep inroads into many families. My own family underwent a radical change, starting with my father. He became an *apicoyres* (freethinker), changed to western clothes and trimmed his beard. My mother took off her wig and let her beautiful black hair grow, and dressed modishly.

It was about this time that my parents built the first movie and legitimate theater in the shtetl. When movies were shown for the first time on Friday evening, Hassidic Jews threw picket lines around it to protest the profanation of the Sabbath and threatened my parents with *kheyrem*(excommunication). My father replaced his studies of the Talmud with reading secular books. Now, during his long walks with me, he talked to me not about the Bible and the prophets but about Darwinism and Spinoza. I was pleased with the changes at home.

Maccabi sports organization in Gombin

I myself joined the Maccabi sports organization where I played soccer, and the Has*homer Hatzair* (Young Watchman) in hopes of getting to Palestine to a Kibbutz (an agricultural settlement). But then in my mid-adolescence, Socialism caught my fancy and I joined the Bundist Youth Organization, remaining a member until I left Poland in 1927 to study in France.

During this period I was a militant Yiddishist, Yiddish being the everyday language of the Jewish people, the Bund was fighting for a Jewish cultural autonomy and for the official Polish government's recognition and support of

Yiddish schools, theaters, libraries and other cultural institutions. I remember when I applied for a passport, I had to answer a question about my maternal language. Although all my education had been in the Polish language, I answered Yiddish to register my solidarity with the Yiddish speaking people. The passport was refused to me and I had to go to great lengths and insist on my constitutional rights to obtain it.

Now, in retrospect, I ask myself how I stand in relation to those ideals of my youth. I believed then that Zionism was Utopian in nature. However, the tragic aftermath of Nazism and the vicissitudes of postwar international developments have contributed to the fruition of the Zionist half-century struggle for the establishment of the Jewish National State of Israel. About two and a half million battered Jews have founded a home there and a purpose in life. My sympathy is with them.

As for my Bundist dream of a social order of equality and social justice for all, without oppression and discrimination, it is rather an incentive to pursue this ideal without respite: "He only earns his freedom and existence," wrote Goethe "who daily conquers them anew".

My Cousin, Reisele (1933 - 1942), daughter of Shyiyah
and Sarah Greenbaum, who perished in 1942

The last time I visited Gombin was in the summer of 1937. There for the first time I met the late Sam Rafel who had not only come to Gombin to see his family but also to make a financial contribution from the New York Gombiner Society to the mutual savings and loan association. The shtetl was pulsating with life. The cultural, political and religious activities were carried on with vigor, as if there was no end in sight. Everywhere I was greeted with warmth and affection as if I were a son and a brother to all. The young men, women and children looked healthy and beautiful with a zest for life.

As a young physician, I was invited to give a lecture on "Planned Parenthood" which attracted a throng of people. They filled the theater to capacity, with many having to stand outside and listen through the open doors. I remember the intelligent faces and the knowledge-thirsty eyes looking at me as I was speaking. Little did my audience and I knew then that four and a half years later, on April 17, 1942, all my compatriots who came to listen to "Planned Parenthood" would be faced with planned destruction by Nazis.

As these reminiscences come to a close, I must add that they called forth in me the most poignant emotions. But the constant feeling that I experienced throughout my writing was one of ardent love and affection for the memory of all my landsmen who lost their lives. Especially do I cherish the memory of my beloved father Yankev Leib, 59, my beloved mother, Hena (Ryster) 57, my beloved brother Stan, 32, his wife, my beloved sister-in-law Helen (Zayontz) 25, their son, my beloved nephew Izia, seven months old, and all my lost beloved uncles, aunts and cousins.

Between the Two World Wars

Social and Cultural Life

by M. Guyer

Translated by Clarice Gostinsky Horelick
Edited by Ada Holtzman and Leon Zamosc

[Original book: Pages 49-52 Yiddish]

M. Guyer

In Gombin, as in the other towns and cities of Czarist Russia, a mood of resignation and apathy had settled down after the failure of the 1905 revolution. In those times of general passivity, only the small Zionist and Bundist groups were engaged in some cultural and political work.

The outbreak of the First World War brought months and years of need and hunger. In the first days of the war, it seemed that everything we had built would go up in smoke. The Germans arrived in Gombin on August 2 1914 and, with very little interruption, stayed in place until the end of the war. On November 11 they put in place a civilian government appointing Schneider, a local ethnic German who owned a clothing store, as mayor of the town.

Among the Jews, and despite the difficulties and the shortages of food and basic goods, the passion for social and cultural work continued. Before the outbreak of the war, we had asked our Maskilim contacts in St. Petersburg to obtain permission from the Czarist authorities for the opening of a legal library in Gombin. When the war erupted, however, we lost all contact with St. Petersburg. Then, near the end of the war, the establishment of the library was authorized by Schneider, the mayor of Gombin.

Now that we had the permission we discovered that we did not have a place or money for the library. In the past, we had had a small, half-legal library that circulated books once a week. Later, during the war, we had packed these books into crates and had hidden them.

Finally, we found a space in Poznanski's house, a three-storied building facing the town's main square. We rented the second floor, removed the internal walls, and replaced the separate rooms with a large new hall that could accommodate two hundred people. Inside we installed a backdrop with a curtain that had been painted by the German soldiers. Abba Wolman arranged the lighting with gas lamps because, back then, there was no electricity in Gombin...

Now we had a place where we could organize lectures and performances. The difficulty was that Gombin's local intelligentsia was rather small. The wealthier young men and women who could afford a higher education went away to the bigger cities. However, we managed to recruit some of them to come back from their gymnasiums or universities, to give lectures for organized audiences in Gombin. The Bundists had also established cultural circles that offered various scientific and educational courses.

The Gombiner youngsters' thirst for knowledge facilitated the effort to raise money, and we were able to buy almost 2000 books. We numbered and catalogued them and, pretty soon, they were ready to be borrowed by readers. We formed a multi-party committee of five members, including three Bundists and two Zionists. They recruited a group of young people to help check out the books.

The opening of the library brought a fresh breath of life to the town. Adults and children flocked to the library. When the set up was completed and the lending of books was routine, we began to think about more uses for the large hall. We organized a "drama society" and we had a number of capable talented directors like Weislicz, Domb, and others. With great success we produced Uriel Acosta's *Chashe the Orphan*, and other dramas by Sholem Asch, Stanis&322;aw Przybyszewski , Anton Tshechov, and Leonid Andreyev. From time to time we also organized concerts.

The Bund's Jewish Kindergarten
Teachers: Sonia Cemelinski-Nowogrodska (right)
and Channa Celemensky (left)

Jewish public school, with teachers
Abram Kalmus and Ignacy Sztokhammer, 1924

A big attraction were the open readings, to which we brought famous speakers- like Israel Lichtenstein, Wiktor Szulman, N. Szafran, M. Kasher, and many others. The young people received the lectures with great enthusiasm. The culture work was done collectivelly, but each separate organization also arranged its own political and educational activities. By the end of 1919, the Zionists and the Bundists had separate libraries in Gombin.

By the end of the First World War we organized a concert garden, and it was about that time that the Bundist teacher Sonia Cemelinski-Nowogrodska came to teach in Gombin (she would be later killed by the Nazis.) The political groups grew stronger and involved larger and larger numbers of Gombiner Jews. The end of the war brought the restoration of Poland's independence. There were local elections to choose the new municipal authorities. In Gombin, twelve Christians and six Jews were elected as members of the municipal council. Four of the six elected Jewish councilmen were activists of the Bund.

One of the consequences of the war was a shortage of food. A special appropriations committee was appointed to bring flour, potatoes, fat, and other foodstuffs from neighboring larger towns. When the war with the Soviet Union broke out in 1919, the Polish government arrested the four Bundist councilmen: Melech Tadelis, Ignacy Sztokhammer, Abraham Tiber, and Yizhak Mosze Chaja (Guyer). Other political activists were forced to escape, and I was one of them. I ran away to America with my family. On October 17 1920 we joined my brother in Detroit.

The teacher Sonia Cemelinski (center) when she was freed from prison. Near her sits comrade Emanuel Nowogrodzki

Despite the setbacks, the groundwork for Jewish cultural and social work in Gombin had been laid out and would continue to bear fruit. Until the outbreak of the Second World War, we maintained permanent contact with our colleagues and friends in Gombin. The political and cultural activities prospered and flourished. Gombin became a place to which prominent Jewish political leaders and speakers were drawn. Lectures and discussions, concerts, and artistic presentations were organized. The young people had a deep lust for learning, and the Jewish organizations from all political stripes actively responded to their desire to learn and their hunger for social activity. Like hundreds of other Jewish cities and towns all over Poland, Gombin was immersed in a powerful cultural movement that enriched anyone who wanted intellectual freedom. Many referred to Gombin as "Little-Warsaw", so intense was the town's Jewish social life.

And it went on like this until the outbreak of the Second World War, when the Nazi demon of death descended over the Jews of Poland.

The Social Assistance Work

by Chaim Rafel (Szacher)

Translated by Clarice Gostinski Horelick
Edited by Ada Holtzman and Leon Zamosc

[Original book: Pages 7-8 Yiddish and 5-6 English]

Chaim Rafel (Szacher)

This chapter of Chaim Rafel's memoirs (his name in Gombin was Chaim Szacher) describes the broad, multi-faceted activities of the town's Jewish social support institutions between the two world wars.

My father Pinchas Szacher spent his entire life working for the welfare of Gombin's Jewish community. When I was still a child, I would accompany him to the Jewish schools, the *Cheders* and *Talmud Torahs*. He was always busy raising funds to pay for the poor students' tuition fees and provide clothing for the needy. We also distributed bread and herring and, when any of those poor children showed special ability to learn, my father would try to provide them opportunities to benefit from a higher education. Neta Pelzenmacher and Jecheskel Blacharz worked side by side with my father, also assisting the poorer students.

I mention this as an introduction to the kind of social assistance work that was done in our town. The Jews of Gombin had always distinguished themselves by their open eyes - and open hearts - to the needs of the poorer members of the community, and there was not a single case of a poor Jewish child or a destitute Jewish family that did not receive some warm support from their more affluent brothers.

The social assistance work developed in stages. It began in a spontaneous way, when a group of wealthy residents of Gombin, on their own initiative, took simple steps to help individual children in need. In time, the social assistance became more and more organized. There was a reception area for the needy, Hachnasat Orchim, in a room above the Mikvah (bathhouse). Later, a Bikur Cholim organization to help the sick was established in a much larger hall located behind the Beit Midrash (Study House). The work of Bikur Cholim, which was supported by 40 to 50 Jewish families, consisted in visiting sick people in their homes, bringing them food, and paying the pharmacist for the medicines they needed.

Jewish Kindergarten group with the teacher Rajzel Zychlinski

The money for these activities was raised in the old and traditional Jewish way. Every Friday, we simply "went to the houses" and the Jews of Gombin did not refuse. The doors were wide open for those who went around collecting funds and the Jewish families contributed their charities. A second source of donations were the *Nedarim*, pledges of money that the Jews made in the synagogue when they were called up to the *Torah*. A portion of those donations were designated for *Bikur Cholim*.

Every year, *Bikur Cholim* organized a big *Kiddush* on *Shmini Etzeret*, the eighth and last day of *Succoth*. They would invite the "*pnay*" of the shtetl (the "VIP" of town) and also the rabbi with the *Klay Kodesh*.

However, the social assistance work was still affected by chance. Since the income from "going to the houses" and the *Nedarim* pledges varied a lot, the distributed aid was not constant but random. It took many years until these goodhearted but amateurish activities took on the form of true, planned social work. The turning point for the establishment of a more stable, organized effort was 1915, the first year of the First World War.

Gombin's economic life was shattered by the war. Yesterday's rich men became paupers and yesterday's poor became even poorer. Since Gombin was located on the front lines between Germans and Russians, the local traders and artisans were cut from the neighboring areas connected with their businesses. The crisis was so deep that it was no longer enough to go around "to the houses" and collect funds for the neediest. It was now necessary to run a larger operation that would allow the provision of help to all the needy. The conditions were right for the emergence of the first Gombiner assistance institution, which was called *Yugent Hilf Verein* (the Youth Assistance League). The founders were Melech Tadelis, Abba Wolman, Yossel Yarlicht, and myself among others. At first, we raised funds through assessments to the wealthiest members of the community, but as soon as the war ended and the links with the rest of the world opened up, we began to receive help from America.

It is necessary to mention that, by this time, the town's emigres in America had created their own Society of Gombiners. In their evaluations, they had accurately predicted that the war would cause an economic upheaval and that the Jews of Gombin would be in urgent need of material help. One of the leaders of the Gombiner organization in the United States was my brother Sam Rafel, who came to Gombin immediately after the war bringing with him a considerable amount of money.

By then, a group of Jews whose children had emigrated to America before the war, had also created their own committee in Gombin. The committee included Jecheskel Holtzman, Jakob Leib Zychlinski, Hersh Nussan Zolna, Abraham Tiber and my father Pinchas Szacher. The task of this committee was to distribute the money received from the Gombiner emigres in America. A big part of the money went for clothing and food for the most needy.

Feeding the children in Gombin's Jewish public school No.2

The year 1922 was particularly important for the assistance efforts in Gombin. On that year, the much-travelled landsman, Abraham Max (Manczyk) came to Gombin from America bringing a large sum of money that included the funds sent by the Society of Gombiner emigres and a substantial donation from his own pocket. That was the basis for the People's Bank, which was established with the active participation of Abraham Zamosc, Abraham Leib Gibs, Melech Tedelis, Abraham Tiber, my father Pinchas Szacher, Jecheskel Holtzman, and others whose names unfortunately I cannot remember. In time, the support that the People's Bank received from the Gombiner Jews in America was boosted by additional grants from the American Joint Distribution Committee, which was active in Poland and was popularly known as simply "the Joint".

The People's Bank became an important institution that played a big role in the life of the Gombin Jews during the interwar period. Its main purpose was the provision of loans, which were given out to those who could offer substantial guarantees of repayment (collateral) or were deemed capable of repaying a certain percent of the loan on a monthly basis. This, however, implied that only a relatively small part of the population could benefit from the support of the People's Bank, the most important group being the merchants.

Board of the Gombin Savings and Loans Kasse, 1913
From right to left, top row: Abraham Zamosc, Melech Tadelis,
Louis Philips (Pochekha). Middle row: Fajwel Borenstein, Hirsz
Jakob Wrobel, Shmuel Kraut, Mosze Glikzeliger, Abraham Shlomo
Plonski, Abraham Fried, Yankel Hodes. Bottom row: Henech
Zorkawski, Mordechai Szwartzberg, Noah Teifeld, Abraham
Wolfowicz, Israel Rozen, Josef Gibs. Bottom left: Leibel Drachman

The limitation of the People's Bank, then, was that it did could not help the poorer Jews, which included the many craftsmen who were not capable of fulfilling the bank's conditions. In this respect, I should mention another important institution: the Handicrafts Union, which had been established in 1913 to look after the professional interests and needs of the artisans: tailors, shoemakers, bakers, hat-makers and poor Jews. Those who were active in the Handicrafts Union included Chaim Luria, Meir Laski, Wolf Laski, Zalman Bol, Hershel Finkel, Jonah Bibergal, and myself.

The Handicrafts Union was very useful in resolving disagreements and helping improve conditions for the working people, but it could not meet all the needs of its members. Its main drawback was that it could not offer financial help. The fact that the People's Bank's was also unable to assist the poorest sectors of the community gave rise to the idea of forming a second, separate bank for the artisans and the poorer Jews.

Meeting of the Gmilot Chasadim Bank in Gombin in the year 1921
Seated from the right: Meir Zeideman, H.N. Zolna, Pinchas
Szacher, Abraham Tiber, Yitzhak Szikarka, Sam Rafel, delegate
from America, S. Borenstein, M. Celemenski, H. Holtzman.
Standing: S. Holtrzman, F. Finkelstein, Bauman, Abraham
Wrobel, Meir Laski.

The idea became a reality in 1927 – another important moment for the Gombin Jews during the interwar period. On that year we received another visitor from America, the landsman Szoiman, who came with his wife bringing funds from the Society of Gombiner emigres. At a meeting in the house of Jecheskel Holtzman it was decided to use the funds for the establishment of *Gmilot Chasadim*, a new bank for the poorer Gombiners.

The founders of the *Gmilot Chasadim* were Abraham Tiber, Chaim Leib Borenstein, Yitzhak Szikarka, Abraham Wrobel, and Pinchas Szacher. The goal of the *Gmilot Chasadim* Bank was to lend money without interest, allowing borrowers to repay the loan over longer periods of time. At the beginning the loans were small, but they did get bigger in the following years. Right before the

Second World War, the bank was giving loans of 300 zlotys, which was a nice sum at the time.

Like the People's Bank, *Gmilot Chasadim* was supported by funds from the American Gombiner Society and the Joint. In the year 1930, when my father passed away, I replaced him in the committee. By then, In addition to the already mentioned founders, the committee also included Chaim Luria, Meir Laski, Hersz Madera and Meir Zeideman, an honorable, dedicated and loyal Jew, who did not want any reward or pay for his work. Our meetings took place on a weekly basis. We were in constant contact with the American Gombiner Society, sending reports to New York every two months. The Secretaries were Abraham Tiber and Meir Zeideman.

A group of social work activists with Abraham Max (Manczyk),
delegate of the Society of Gombiner emigres in America

The social assistance work in Gombin was very developed. Considering that our town was small and was relatively isolated from the surrounding towns and cities, it could serve as an example, and a standard, for every scholar interested in the history of the shtetls – those small Jewish communities in which everybody was closely related to everyone else. The most important point was that individuals did not live for themselves, but they also lived for the others and every Jew was a part of the total. My account of the social and philanthropic work in Jewish Gombin only reflects a small portion of all that was done over many years of work. The great tragedy of the Second World War marked the end of Gombin and its living Jews. The books, documents, ledgers and notes from all the institutions that took care of their welfare were also destroyed.

These few lines should remind us of the historical accomplishments of the activists involved in the social work in Jewish Gombin. They should also uphold the memory of the fact that mutual assistance and concern about everybody's welfare were central values for the Jews of Gombin.

Gombin and its Rabbis

by Michael Rozenblum

Translated by Clarice Gostinsky Horelick
Edited by Ada Holtzman and Leon Zamosc

[Original book: Pages 60-63 Yiddish]

Many cities and shtetls in Poland became famous all over the Jewish world because of the greatness of their rabbis, scholars, writers, spiritual people, and political activists. Our Gombin achieved that kind of fame thanks to its native son, the renowned scholar and interpreter of Torah laws Rabbi Abraham Abele Gombiner.

Rabbi Abraham Abele Gombiner
author of "Magen Abraham"

Abraham Abele Gombiner was the author of the influential book *Magen Abraham* (Shield of Abraham), an interpretation of Rabbi Joseph Caro's

Shulchan Aruch, in which he sought to meaningfully relate the everyday customs of the Polish Jews to the Jewish code of law. In recognition of his contribution, Abraham Abele Gombiner would become known as "Magen Abraham". His first scholarly nickname had been "Ner Israel" (Candle of Israel), but his son, Rabbi Chaim Segal, with the agreement of the Council of Four Lands in Lublin, changed it to "Magen Abraham".

The "Magen Abraham" always wrote his name as follows: Abraham Abele son of the holy man, Rabbi Chaim Halevi from Gombin. About his father Rabbi Chaim we know very little, except that he died in *Kiddush Hashem*, for the Sanctification of the Holy Name, at the hands of Chmielnicki's Cossacks. His son Abraham Abele, who had been born in 1635, was nine years old at the time. Following his parents death, he moved from Gombin to Kalish, where his accomplishments would transform him into a leading Talmudist and religious authority of his times. Abraham Abele Gombiner, the "Magen Abraham", died in Kalish in 1683.

A hundred years after the "Magen Abraham", the rabbi of Gombin was Rabbi Aleksander Yehuda Leib ben Naftali Margaliyot, author of the book "*Midrash Ketubah*" on a tractate of the Mishnah and the Talmud that deals with marital responsibilities, especially those related to "*Ketubot*" (marital contracts). After him, but not for very long, the rabbi in Gombin was Rabbi Israel Jehoszua Trunk, who was wooed from Gombin by the Jewish community in Kutno and would become a famous Gaon, known by the name Rabbi Jehoszele Kutner. He authored rabbinical works including *Yeshuot Israel*, (Salvation of Israel), *Hoshen* (about the fourth part of *Shulchan Aruch* by Joseph Caro), *Yeshuat Malko* (Salvation of the King), *Yavin Shmua* (the Rumor of Yavin) and other books.

After Rabbi Jehoszele Kutner came Rabbi Simchale Gombiner, who served as rabbi of Gombin for a long time. He was the author of the book *Ramzei Ash* (Hints of Fire) and a commentary on *Tanna Eliyahu* (an authority quoted in the *Mishna*). He was a Kocker and Gerer *Hassid*. Rabbi Simcha Gombiner was followed by Rabbi Nathan Natanovich, who was known as a highly learned man and was also a Gerer *Hassid*. His grandchildren, the brothers Mazur (children of his son Rabbi Meir Mazur, rabbi of Nieszawa), became known as the Brothers Mazur who were wealthy and famous in Warsaw. One of the brothers, Elijahu Mazur, was head of the Warsaw Jewish community before the war. Now he is in Israel, one of the biggest merchants in the diamond industry.

Gombin's next rabbi was Rabbi Yehuda Leib Zlotnik, who was popular in Poland under the name "the Gombiner Rabbi Zlotnik." An important public leader and speaker, he was among the founders of the *Mizrachi* religious Zionist party and later of the *"Histadrut Hazionit Haklalit"*, the General Zionist Organization in Poland. Rabbi Zlotnik became famous under the pen name "Yehudah Elzet", publishing important books like "The Wonderful Treasure of the Yiddish Language", "Jewish Traditions", "Reshumot" (edited by A. Droianov), and "The Beginning of the Hebrew Rhetorical Language" (printed in Israel). Rabbi Yehuda Leib Zlotnik was rabbi of Gombin for about ten years until 1921, when he left Poland for Canada, where he served as Secretary General of the Zionist Organization. Later he was invited by the Jewish community of South Africa to take responsibility as Director of Jewish and Hebrew education. From South Africa he immigrated to Israel, where he was active in literary circles and published notable essays in the periodical *"Yeda Haam"* (Popular Knowledge) and the daily newspaper "Hatzofe" (Spectator).

Rabbi Yehuda Laib Zlotnik.

I was a little boy when Rabbi Yehuda Leib Zlotnik came to Gombin. I remember well that the *Hassidim* were not pleased. They worked very hard to prevent his election, and when Rabbi Zlotnik was finally elected with a large majority of votes, the *Hassidim* appealed to the magistrate of Gostynin (the jurisdiction to which Gombin belonged) with the complaint that the vote had not been "kosher". The magistrate, whose name was Naczalnik, ordered new elections under stricter supervision from the Polish government. In the second election, Rabbi Zlotnik won by an even larger majority. After a while, the Rabbi received recognition also from the Hassidim. They appreciated his dedication to Jewish affairs in general, and particularly to the Jewish community of Gombin.

Rabbi Natan Neta Nutkewicz

When Rabbi Zlotnik left Poland, Rabbi Natan (Nussen) Neta Nutkewicz came from Rypin to serve as the Rabbi of Gombin. He was followed by Rabbi Zalman Unger, the son of the famous teacher, Uriah Unger of Wloclawek. He was the last rabbi up to the Second World War and the Holocaust. It has been told that the Nazis tied Rabbi Unger to the tail of a galloping horse and that his how he died. God will avenge his blood, together with that of all the Jewish victims.

Scholars and Hassidim in Gombin

Hassidism in Gombin was not as strong as in neighboring towns like Zychlin and Gostynin. In Gostynin lived the virtuous Rabbi and *Tsadik* Yechiel Meir Lipszyc of blessed memory, known as the *Gostyniner Tsadik*, who was very influencial in the entire region and in Poland at large. To him came not only Hassidim to hear about the *Torah* and *Hassidism*, but also ordinary people, even *Mitnagdim* who were generally opposed to the Hassidim. The *Gostyniner*

Tsadik attended to all who had requests. To those who were ill, he advised to recite *Tehilim* (Psalms) and prayers in public and in private. The *Gostyniner Tsadik* Yechiel Meir was very popular in Gombin and was described by Sholem Asch in his great work "Jews of Tehilim", the praying Jews.

Sholem Asch himself was from the neighboring shtetl of Kutno. In his famous book "Dos Shtetl", he described Gombiner personalities like Rabbi Jecheskel Gombiner, Rabbi Shlomo Nagid, and others.

Though there were few Hassidim in Gombin, there were renowned scholars and *Bnei Torah*, learners of Torah, in the shtetl. About a hundred years ago a resident of Gombin was known as "little Rabbi Abraham" by the Hassidim of Kock (Kockers) and Gora Kalwaria. (Gerers).

Gombin's Beit Midrash
Source: Sam Rafel's 1937 Gombin Film [not in original book]

The well known *Nagid* of that time, Rabbi Fajwel Orbach, was the father-in-law of Rabbi Menachem Landau, a brother of whom, Rabbi Mendel, lived in Gombin. Rabbi Mendel was the son of Rabbi Wolf Strikower, who was the son of the Gaon and Tsadik Rabbi Abraham Landau from Ciechanow. Rabbi Fajwel Orbach was in his time the wealthy philanthropist of the Hassidim in Kock and in Gora Kalwaria.

Forty or fifty years ago, the Hassidim of Gombin did not have their own *shtibel*, (small hassidic house of prayer). On *shabbes*, they prayed in the town's *Beit Midrash*, after the prayers of the rich people. But the Hassidim came to the *Beit Midrash* very early and they studied while the rich people prayed. Frequently, this was a source of disagreements. The rich people said that the Hassidim's vocal studies disturbed their praying. When the arguments became stronger, the Hassidim rented a shtibel for themselves alone.

From the various Hassidim, the Gerer Hassidim from Gora Kalwaria were the brightest scholars. After the Gerer were other groups of Hassidim like the Cocker, Alexan, Radzyminer, and others. The scholars and accredited teachers in Gombin included the town's Rabbi Natan Neta Nutkewicz, Rabbi Benjamin the teacher of religious subjects, the great *Gemarah* scholar Rabbi Jerachmiel Goldszmid and his son Rabbi Zalmen, Rabbi Bunim Menasze Lubinski, Rabbi Henich Rozenblum, Rabbi Gedalia Noach, Rabbi Lajbl Sztolcman, and Rabbi Herszl the son-in-law of Rabbi Yossel Chaiek.

Back view of the Gombin Synagogue
Source: The Gombin Society [not in original book]

There were also respected Hassidim who distinguished themselves in Gombin as important merchants and learners of *Torah*. Among them, I should mention Chaim Luksenberg, I. Sikorka, Yossel Luksenberg, Lajzer Wigdorowicz and his son Jakob Wigdorowicz, Yossel Chaiek and his brother Mosze Mendel Chaiek, Lejzer Mosze Tiber, Jecheskel Rozenblum, Yossef Menche and his son Mosze Menche, Mendel Temerson and his son Abba, Abraham Elia Sochaczewski, Haim Josef Ejli, Mordchai Jarlicht, Jakob Grinboim, Mendil Szczewinski, Israel *Shochet* (ritual slaughterer), Lajbisz *Chazan* (cantor), and Josef Dawid Klapman, a *shochet* who left Gombin to became *shochet* in Switzerland.

Finally, I should also mention Ezriel Yehudah Etinger, the son of the old teacher of religious subjects M. Etinger. He was a *Mitnaged*, an opponent of the Hassidim. But he was considered a *Ben Torah*, a respected scholar of *Torah* He was a *maskil*, an educated person who practiced his religion.

I was born in Gombin and grew up in the town until the age of fourteen, when I moved to Lodz with my family. For me, it is a great honor to remember and write about all the dignified, prominent Gombiner Jews mentioned in these notes.

Religious Life

by E. Finkenstein

Translated by Janie Respitz
Edited by Leon Zamosc

[Original book: Page 64 Yiddish]

I would like to comment on some aspects of the Jewish religious life in Gombin.

My father Fishl Jonah Finkenstein donated a house for the establishment of an orthodox school. A large number of children studied there. I am sure that some of the Gombin youngsters who survived the catastrophe and are now themselves fathers of grown children certainly remember Fishl Jonah's heder (religious school).

The Jewish religious party "Agudah" also used the house for meetings and lectures. The work of "Agudah" was broad, covering many topics related to all aspects of religious life. Unfortunately, we do have documents about the activities of "Agudah". They were consumed in the terrible fire of the Shoah.

I will recount from memory some names of religious Jews who were active between the two World Wars.

The chairman of "Agudah" was my father Fishl Jonah. He was elected to the city council as a representative of "Agudah". My father also served as a director of the loan society Gemilat Hesed Kasse and was an active member of the Burial Society, the Psalms Society, and the Society to Visit the Sick.

Yitzhak Shekerke was also very involved in the work of all the societies. He was one of the most important Jews in Gombin and a great philanthropist.

Hersh Lajb Shekerke was one of the most active members of "Agudah". He served as representative in the Gombin municipal council for a time.

Gedaliah Noach Shlang was another active religious volunteer. He was a learned Jew who devoted his life to community issues and the promotion of Jewish education for the younger generations.

Gombin synagogue tower
Source: Ada Holtzman's Collection [not in original book]

Moishe Celemensky was a Jew with a caring heart who sacrificed everything for the community. He was an active and influential member of all the religious Jewish institutions.

I would also like to pay tribute to Chaim Lajb Borenstein, a pilar of Gombin's religious institutions. He was the heart and soul of "The Bread House", which assisted the poor Jewish people of Gombin with life's basic necessities every Saturday and on the holidays. More than once, he covered the expenses out of his own pocket when there was not enough money.

As in all the other Jewish cities and towns, the religious institutions of Gombin played an important role in sustaining everyday life and preserving its Jewish character.

My Bundist Years in Gombin

by Jacob Celemenski

Translated by Janie Respitz
Edited by Leon Zamosc

[Original book: Pages 65-71 Yiddish]

I arrived in Gombin at the age of thirteen. It was there that I spent my most beautiful, romantic years. My life took shape in the town, as I enhanced my learning and embraced socialist ideals. I still get strength from those sources, which allowed me to persevere and keep faith during the most tragic years of the Holocaust.

As I prepare to share a few memories of my years in Gombin, my eyes fill with tears. I see this beloved Jewish town through the distant fog of the tragedy, the cruel extermination that swept away almost everyone, including those who were dearest and closest to me. My father, sisters, brothers, together with their husbands, wives and children, along with the entire family, uncles, aunts, cousins, all died as martyrs.

During the First World War, when Poland was occupied by the Germans and the Jews of Warsaw suffered from hunger, disease and death, our home was also hit. Two of my youngest brothers died. My parents decided to leave Warsaw and move to Gombin, my mother's hometown. We were then a family of ten, my parents and eight children. For me, arriving in Gombin was an emotional experience. For the first time after the crowded, shabby streets of Warsaw, I breathed the fresh air of Gombin, full of the scent of wonderful pine forests. In the stream that meandered through the town, women would wash their laundry and dishes.

Jewish houses and shops were situated around the market place and on sandy roads, hunched wooden houses with moss on the roofs. Gombin was like an isolated island, far from the railroads. To get to the closest train station in Zychlin, you had to take a horse and wagon. To go to nearby towns like Plock,

Wyszogrod, and Wloclawek, we used the Vistula river. Later on, there would be buses connecting Gombin with Warsaw.

Under the occupation, the agricultural production of Poland was exported to Germany, leaving the local population without grains and other essentials. In Gombin, as in most rural towns, people went hungry, particularly among the poor. Jewish workers had great difficulty to earn a living and, very often, children as young as ten had to help with daily work. It was at that time that the Polish Jews began to receive assistance from the American Jewish Joint Distribution Committee, popularly known as the "Joint". The food and clothing distributed by the "Joint" helped ease the situation of the people.

Jacob Celemenski with his son Bronek, who fell as
a pilot in the Sinai Campaign, 1956

Despite the crushing poverty, a diversified Jewish spiritual life flourished in Gombin. There were many social and cultural activities, and one could see the steady growth of political groups and parties reflecting different ideologies. Among all those movements, the "Bund" played a central role. Boys and girls enthusiastically embraced the appealing ideals of freedom and humanity. All kinds of topics were debated in our long walks through the fields and forests. We talked about justice and fairness, about the differences between rich and poor, and about Zionism, Bundism, and issues of war and peace. The Peretz

Library, which had been illegal under the Czarist regime, came out to the open and was moved to the home of the Holtzmans, a beautiful location with a large reading room in the center of town. In time, the Peretz Library became one the most popular cultural institutions in Gombin. The members and activists came from all levels of society, from the poor houses of the artisans, market merchants and workers to the most established and wealthiest families. The library grew to five thousand books in Yiddish, Hebrew and Polish. It was the largest and richest library in Gombin and the surrounding towns. Among those who dedicated their time and energy to the library I recall Sarah Golda Frenkel (today in America); Liber Lizerstein (today in Brazil); Shloime Wolman, Moishe Orbach and Yechezkel Hodes (all three were murdered). The library offered evening lectures on social and literary themes, bringing distinguished speakers. Among them I remember Victor Shulman, Melech Ravitch, Yisroel Lichtenstein, Natan Shafran and Luria (who was from Gombin and would be later killed in Russia). There were also courses where people learned a variety of things, from Yiddish reading and writing to a course on Esperanto taught by Chaim Kerber, who lives today in Paris.

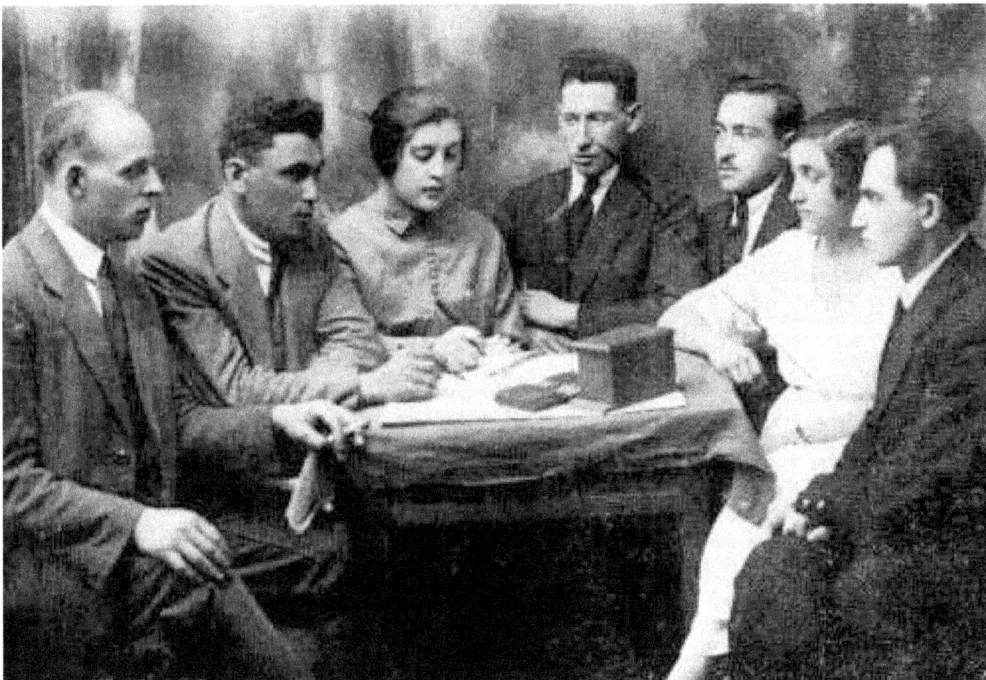

The Bund Committee
From right to left: Yechezkel Hodes, Blume Lizerstein,
Shmuel Borenstein, Hanoch Goldshmidt, Sarah Golda Frenkel,
Yitzhak Moishe Chaja, Shloime Adler.

Like many other Jewish cities and towns, Gombin had an amateur theatre. One of the most active cultural leaders was comrade Chaim Luria. In addition to his extensive knowledge of Yiddish and general literature, he was an accomplished actor with a talent for directing. He organized a group that performed important plays such as Peretz Hirshbein's "Infamy", August Strindberg's "Father", Jacob Gordin's "God, Man and Devil", Sholem Aleichem's The Lottery", Abraham Goldfaden's "Shulamis", as well as dramas by Mikhail Artsybashev, Stanislav Pshibishevsky, and many others. Every production of the Gombin amateur theatre was celebrated as a great event and was performed many times. In later years the director was Chaim Sender Zandman from Gostynin (today living in Israel). The proceeds from the performances were used to support cultural activities and buy food for the orphanage.

The choir, which was also an activity of the library, had a special place in the cultural life of Gombin. The choir master was Leizer Finkelstein, who already at eleven apprenticed with the town's cantor and displayed his great talent as a musician. He later learned to write music. The choir was one of the most successful cultural institutions in Gombin. Its repertoire included classical songs and Yiddish folk songs. When the choir performed, the hall was always full. Their popularity went well beyond Gombin. They were invited to perform in all the surrounding towns. Before the outbreak of the Second World War, the choir master Leizer Finkelstein was hired as a cantor by the large "German" synagogue of Częstochowa. He was murdered there during the Holocaust.

When Poland became independent a tailors' union was founded in Gombin, a branch of the Warsaw Textile Workers' Trade Union Central. Also belonging to this union were shoemakers, boot stitchers, bakers and servant girls. This was a period of actions and strikes for better working conditions, regular working hours, and more humane treatment by the bosses. In some cases, even the bosses' sons and daughters joined the union and the workers in the strikes against their parents. The union, which also organized reading and writing evening courses, had its own office with a paid secretary, comrade Moishe Orbach. The members of the fist board of directors were: Yechezkel Hodes, Simcha Chaja (today in America, Sidney Gayer), Meir Zelig Kerber, Litzek Maydat. Abraham Zhychlinski, Dvorah Lizerstein, Sh. Winter and Miriam Lichtenstein as representative of the youth.

On May 1st 1920, the Bund and the Polish Socialist Party organized a joint demonstration that marched from the marketplace through the streets of

Gombin with red flags. This made a great impression in town. Later that year, when Bundists were being rounded up throughout Poland and sent to a camp near Krakow, Gombin's Bundist city councillor Melech Tadelis was arrested together with Simcha Chaja and the chairman of the union Yechezkel Hodes and his brother.

A Bund circle named after Engels, the lecturer is Hanoch Goldshmidt

My father was a devout orthodox Jew and so was my entire Gombin family, my aunts, uncles and their children. However, my older brother Yosl was already a Bundist in Warsaw and an active member in the textile workers' union. He was the first one in our family to change religion for socialist ideals, while still wearing his long black coat, Jewish cap and boots. In Gombin he was active in the library and was a prompter in the theatre.

He began to bring books to the house and for the first time wore a "kurtz" – a suit with a short jacket. When my father saw this he angrily threw the suit out the window: "You will never wear this in my house!" But my brother knew that he would have to suffer for his convictions. He paved the way for all his sisters and brothers, all of whom eventually joined the Bund. I felt the need to read the Yiddish books and newspapers that he brought home. Even though I was still studying with my grandfather, I yearned for the library. I went there one evening when it was already dark. I stood confused. I saw people sitting around tables reading and discussing books. Here is where I first heard the names of Marx, Engels, Hirsh Lekert, Vladimir Medem. For the first time I heard that on the Sabbath people went to the forest for a "picnic". I did not sleep that night. I knew that I had to discuss this with my brother, that he had to take me with him to the forest. The gathering in the forest intoxicated me. There were boys and girls from Gombin, from poor families, but they all beamed. I barely understood what they spoke about, but I was completely charmed by the atmosphere.

After that, I did not rest until I became a member of a Bund circle. That was the most beautiful day of my life. The best day of my youth. The year was 1919. I joined the circle named for Hirsh Lekert. The circles were like seminar classes, with groups at different levels.

Board of the Tailors' Union

In those years I worked as an apprentice with the master tailor Kukuridza, whose workshop was in his small home. He lived with a daughter, Bayle Ruchl, who had a child. Like all the other apprentices I had to help her with the housework. Summertime, I went with the whole family to an orchard, which master Kukuridza rented for the summer. I helped picking apples, pears and plums and then went with them to the market to sell the fruit picked. There was a goat in their house. My work included feeding the goat and holding the child. This was my start in learning how to be a tailor. In time, I joined the union.

The youth branch of the Bund was called "Tsukunft" (Future). For the members, it was more than a political organization. It encompassed every aspect of personal life, world outlook, personal honesty and morality. Often, the youth were so excited and uplifted by the socialist ideals that they drew in their parents to join the Bund. Many of those youngsters would come to play important roles in Gombin's communal life. The first members of the youth committee of the Bund were: Chane Tatarka, Rude Gostinsky, Yechezkel Hodes, Blume Lizerstein (today in Brazil) and Hindele Zajonc. All four died in the gassings at Chelmno.

Childhood friends who left Gombin in 1922: Abraham Finkelstein, Yankele Zhychlinski, Jacob Celemenski and Abraham Zhychlinski

My weekdays were very ordinary: filled with work and worries. But my holidays were the hours, evenings, and days when I went to the library for the meetings of the youth circle, when we went on our many walks in the forest, when we had a great time. Those days were filled with joy. We felt uplifted when the leaders of "Tsukunft" came from Warsaw to talk to us: Yoshke Lifshitz, Leon Oler, Pinhas Shwartz, Sholem Hertz and others.

It was delightful to have close and intimate friends. One of them was Abrumeleh Finkelstein, who later went to Germany and became a doctor. He was later killed in Treblinka. My second closest friend was Yankele Zhychlinski.

He left for America. Today he is the chairman of the Gombin Society in New York. A third, David Melech Brzezinski, who is also in America. A fourth, Abraham Zhychlinski, now in Paris. I dedicated all my free time to the movement.

I will never forget the day I was chosen to bid farewell to our comrade Yitzhak Moishe Chaja who was leaving for America with his wife Bracha. It was my first public speech, and I said goodbye on behalf of the whole youth branch "Tsukunft". Yitzhak Moishe Chaja was my first Bundist teacher in the "Hirsh Lekert" circle. He is still a devoted Bundist today in Chicago (where he is known as Morris Guyer). He was the first Bundist councilman in Gombin, loved by his friends and respected by his opponents. He was involved in all aspects of Gombin's communal life. He devoted special energy to the orphanage. His wife Bracha was very active in the cultural area and played a special role in organizing the drama circle. She took part in many performances.

I left my home in Gombin and returned to Warsaw in 1924. However, throughout my entire life I have carried with me the inspiration of the exciting days of my youth. These feelings gave me strength to endure the darkness of the Nazi occupation, which I described in my book "Mitn Farshnitenem Folk" (Elegy for my People).

I dedicate these recollections to the idealistic youth of Gombin, who passionately served socialist ideals and were so tragically exterminated. Also, to my father Moishe, my mother Shaine Bineh, my brothers, sisters and their children. And to my beloved Bronke, who fell as a pilot in the 1956 Sinai campaign in Israel.

The Children's Association "SKIF"

by L. Wolman

Translated by Janie Respitz
Edited by Leon Zamosc

[Original book: Pages 72-73 Yiddish]

Meeting in Warsaw in 1926, the central committee of the Polish Bund launched an effort to promote the education of Jewish children in the values of the movement. That was the origin of the Socialist Children's Association (Sotsyalistishe Kinder Farband) or, for short, "SKIF". A year later, the Gombin Bund, together with the local branch of the Bund's youth group "Tsukunft" (Future), founded the "SKIF" organization in Gombin. The members of the founding committee were Yosl Kohn, Moishe Frenkel, and Leybish Wolman. Their first task was to recruit Jewish children from the Povshechner school (the Polish public school) and among the boys and girls who for material reasons had to leave school and learn a trade.

A group from the Socialist Children's Association "SKIF",
in the middle, the instructor Leybish Wolman

I remember well the first meeting with the children. We explained the goals of the "SKIF" organization and our desire to offer a place where they would be able to grow, become more aware of what was happening in the world, and learn to face the important questions of life. The "SKIF" wanted to promote a sense of autonomy among the children and its activities included entertainment, singing and sports.

The first meeting was very successful. The children were excited about the plans and almost all those who attended became members of the new organization.

The children spread the news about the Bund's new organization around Gombin. In a short time the membership grew. Very soon, the "SKIF" became the largest children's association in town.

The Bund's "Tsukunft" youth circle "Marx",
in the middle, the instructor Abrumeleh Finkelstein

We divided into groups and began cultural programs for the children. With the help of Freydl Finkelstein we started a mandolin orchestra. The director of the Gombin sports organization Abraham Frenkel began a physical education program. The children also enjoyed excursions to the forests and surrounding villages. The goal was to familiarize them with the beauty of nature and help them develop strong friendship bonds and a sense of family. For the children, every outing was a holiday. They waited impatiently all week for Saturday, when the field trips took place.

In those expeditions, we would play a variety of games. There was singing, dancing, and conversations on different topics. At the end of the day, we would sit around a fire and sing until late at night. We would then march back to town, still singing loudly.

In 1928, if my memory is correct, we organized the first "SKIF" summer camp under the leadership of comrade Bromberg from the Bund's Warsaw central committee. It was a great success, an immensely happy experience that made a big impression on everyone.

The summer camps were run like a children's republic. The boys and girls planned their own activities. As part of the program, we went to visit other children's groups in neighbouring towns like Gostinin and Plock. In 1937, the summer camp received important guests: Victor Alter, Sarah Shweber and Abraham Stoler.

It should be mentioned that one of the important components of the educational activity of the "SKIF" in Gombin was the "members' court", where the children were encouraged to solve their own conflicts among themselves.

There were other children's groups and institutions in Gombin but, for us, "SKIF" will always shine in our memory with a special light.

The Zionist Movement

by Rivka Frenkel Halpern

Translated by Janie Respitz
Edited by Leon Zamosc

[Original book: Pages 74-76 Yiddish]

Rivka Frenkel Halpern, Israel

Before the First World War, the Zionist movement and all other political organizations were illegal in Russia and Poland. The Zionist groups had to operate under the pretense that they were conducting social or philanthropic activities. After the occupation of Poland, however, Germany and Austria relaxed the restrictions on political activities. That created favorable conditions for a rapid expansion of the Zionist movement.

The 1917 "Balfour Declaration", which announced the British Empire's disposition to allow the construction of a Jewish national homeland in Palestine, fired up the enthusiasm for the Zionist cause throughout Poland. In Gombin the activists of the movement significantly expanded their work. They distributed Shekels, collected donations for the National Fund, and launched a whole slew of new activities, including a Hebrew language kindergarten, Hebrew classes for adults, and a variety of lectures and cultural events focused on national and Zionist themes.

In 1920, news arrived from Palestine that Yosef Trumpeldor and his comrades had fallen in the defense of the settlement of Tel Chai. In Gombin and many other places in Poland, the news stirred a great deal of interest, particularly among youth groups that began preparations to move to the Land of Israel

I remember being at the Palestine office in Warsaw just before I left for the Land of Israel. When I told the officials that I was from Gombin, they honored me, saying that my town was known for its meritorious Zionist work. That reputation was certainly deserved. Gombin had a small group of devoted Zionist activists who fulfilled the movement's tasks with a great sense of responsibility. Thanks to their efforts, a large portion of the previously apathetic Jewish youth of Gombin were now committed to the fulfillment of Jewish national values.

Committee of "Keren Hayesod" (National Fund)

I have fond memories of many of these Zionist activists. Most important among them was Rabbi Yehuda Leib Zlotnik, a blessed man whose spiritual personality influenced an entire generation of Gombin Jews. His arrival marked the beginning of a true national Jewish renaissance. The establishment of the kindergarten and the "House of Judah" school made possible the education of a generation of Zionist pioneers, many of whom are now living in kibbutzim and towns in Israel. Rabbi Zlotnik's sermons in the synagogue influenced all social classes, bringing them closer to Zionist belief and activities.

One of the most the most important persons at the helm of Zionist activity in Gombin was Abraham Zamosc, a man of blessed memory who was murdered in Treblinka. For many years he carried the entire burden of Zionist work in Gombin, neglecting his private interests. He was a bachelor without a personal family life. People jokingly said that Abraham Zamosc had married the Zionist cause.

Abraham Zamosc, activist of the Zionist movement
and director of the People's Bank

It is also necessary to remember the valuable help of Rabbi Natan Nutkewicz, the brothers Melech and Avremele Tadelis, Abraham Prawda, Abraham Chaim Zychlinski, Moishe Glickzeliger, and my closest friends Rivka Leah Opatowski and Shaindl Zychlinski. There were many others whose names I do not remember. Many perished in the Konin forced labor camp. They had dedicated so much of their lives to the Zionist movement...

I would now like to mention my friends (may they live long lives) Yechiel Chajek, who lives in Israel, and Yitzchak Eiley who devotes a lot of time to communal and social work in Montreal and is active in all the Canadian campaigns for Israel. They contributed a lot of time and energy to the Zionist activities in Gombin. I would also like to fufill a personal obligation and mention the devoted and well-loved teacher Yakov Gazalka, who taught in the Hebrew school and gave courses for adults. Many of his students remember and greatly admire him. Gazalka, who moved to Israel in the 1930s, is known as Yakov Gurali and worked for many years at the Hebrew University in Jerusalem. He wrote three important novels, a trilogy about Jewish life in Poland, and made a huge contribution to the Jewish national renaissance in Gombin.

Tarbut School kindergarten
From the right: M. Glickzeliger, Rabbi N. Nutkcvicz, A.L. Gips, M. Todelis

Last but not least, I want to mention our dear friend Louis Philips (Pochekha) who currently lives in Detroit. He was active in the Zionist movement until the day he left Gombin. Today, Louis is active in all things related to Gombin and in the work to support Israel.

To conclude, I would like to emphasize that, thanks to the blessed work of all those who have been mentioned here, there are hundreds of Gombiners who survived and are now living in Israel.

Givataim, Israel, January 1968.

The Beginning of the Zionist Movement

by Louis Philips (Pochekha), Detroit

Translated by Janie Respitz
Edited by Leon Zamosc

[Original book: Pages 77-81 Yiddish]

Louis Philips (Pochekha)

One cannot look back at the history of Zionism in Gombin without a certain amount of nostalgia. Those were times of faith, hope, and joy.

The Zionist movement developed spontaneously, out of a group of dreamers. In 1909, my brother-in-law Mordechai Schwartzberg moved to Gombin from Plock. The Zionist organization began with his arrival.

My brother-in-law's neighbor was Moishe Glickzeliger. They struck a close friendship from the first day they met. Their group of friends included Abraham Zamosc, Melech Todelis, Melech's younger brother Avremele, Yitzchak Wolfowicz, and many others.

I remember that Yitzchak Wolfowicz made a big impression on me. He was proficient in Hebrew, read a variety of publications and journals, and was also well versed in Polish literature. He was a man with a vast knowledge of literature and culture.

When Mordechai Schwartzberg arrived in Gombin, his place became a centre for scholarship. He was a gentle man, educated in the Torah, who knew how to inspire his listeners with humor and logic. He came from a family of "Eastern Rabbis" (religious Zionists), "Lovers of Zion" (early Zionists), and secular enlightened Jews. His grandfather was the famous Lipno Rabbi Yehuda Leib Schwartzberg, who had been active in the religious Zionist party "Mizrachi". And his uncle, Sh. B. Schwartzberg, would become the editor of "Ner Hamerkaz" in New York. Mordechai Schwartzberg brought those kinds of spiritual influences to Gombin.

Schwartzberg's perpetually happy neighbor, Moishe Glickzeliger, was a hardworking Jew with polite manners who was always eager to learn about Zionism, Hasidism, and socialism. In his house, Schwartzberg met people with whom he could spiritually identify.

The youngest was Abraham Zamosc, who was a frequent visitor to Schwartzberg's shop. He was an expert in Hebrew literature who interpreted for others the Book of Prophets, the novels of Abraham Mapu, the poetry of Hayim Nahman Bialik, and of course the works of Ahad Ha'am and the founder of Zionism, Theodor Herzl.

Schwartzberg subscribed to "Ha-Tsfira" (The Epoch) and other newspapers that served as a source of information and education for his listeners. At times, when he was busy dealing with some customer, Zamosc would take over the reading, explaining the brainy materials that filled the pages of "Ha-Tsfira", such as the essays by Nahum Sokolow and the "Blossoming Letters" of David Frishman, which flowed in impeccable Hebrew prose. Zamosc was clearly in his element, translating the articles in his own fluid style.

Another member of that first Zionist group in Gombin was Melech Tadelis or, as he was called, Yankele's Melech to make sure he was not confused with Melech Tadelis from the Bund defense group.

Melech was very handsome and looked indeed as a prince (the word "melech" means "king"). Everybody loved him and he was always smiling and in a good mood. He never antagonized anyone. When people talked about going to the Land of Israel, he would immediately produce a map that he always carried with him in order to find the perfect spot.

His brother Abraham Tadelis also joined the movement, helping out wherever he could. Both brothers were tall and handsome with black hair, like true children of kings.

Another person in the group of friends was the Talmudist Tamel Menche, a brilliant man who was the son of the hasid Yosef Menche. He felt comfortable in the group but he had his own path towards the Zionist ideal. He liked to quote from the Gemara and always had an appropriate passage concerning the topics that were being discussed. He was a sympathizer of the Zionist movement but he was not active in the organizational work. His response to any suggestion was: "We'll see..."

The group held a meeting in Mordechai Schwartzberg's place to organize a Zionist circle in Gombin. It was decided that every Sabbath they would pray at Moishe Glickzeliger's. They did not want to attract too much attention. That was how the Zionist political organization began in Gombin.

With the growth of the movement and new members, we set out to find a location for our Zionist activities. We illegally bought Shekels, distributed collection boxes, organized celebrations, and distributed Hebrew journals.

Since we could not find a stable place to meet, we used the homes of Schwartzberg and Glickzeliger. Like all the other tenement houses on the market square, they had shops facing the street and the living quarters were in the back. To this day I cannot figure out how we all managed to squeeze in. Glickzeliger's kind wife made sure there were enough places to sit.

Our small Zionist synagogue did not have a Torah reader. Everyone could stand at the pulpit, but there were a few who truly deserved the honor. It was usually Elie Baron or my father Reuven Pochekha who would stand at the pulpit.

The Zionist movement in Gombin gained momentum. A special episode was the 1911 election of the new Gombin rabbi. The group, led by Mordechai Schwartzberg, actively campaigned to rally as many votes as possible for Rabbi Yehuda Leib Zlotnik, a founder of the Zionist religious party "Mizrahi" who was strongly opposed by the town's Hasidim.

Schwartzberg's home became the general headquarters of the campaign. There were feverish preparations for the debates of the upcoming elections. Rabbi Zlotnik's father-in-law, M. Kalisher from Plock, stayed at the

Schwartzberg's place during the elections. It was his dream to see his son-in-law become the rabbi of a progressive town like Gombin.

The election battle was won and Yehuda Leib Zlotnik became the rabbi of Gombin. It was a warm, beautiful summer day when the leading citizens, led by the Zionists, went out to the Plock highway to welcome Rabbi Zlotnik. The group included my father Reuven Pochekha, Mordechai Schwartzberg, Yitzchak Wolfowicz, Isroel Rozen, Henech Zurkowski, Abraham Plonski, Abraham Fried, Shmuel Leib Wolman, and Noach Tajfler. Leibl Drachman and me, who were barely of Bar Mitzvah age, were also there, along with other youngsters who identified with the Zionist ideal.

Until 1911 it was not possible for the Zionists to organize large-scale events and celebrations. Since the activists were not wealthy, we could not afford a house with a large hall. On the other hand, it was not advisable to call the attention of the Czarist regime to our activities.

I suggested to my parents that Hanukkah should be celebrated at our home. My father quickly replied, "By all means, it would be a great honor!"

When I shared the news with the Zionist committee they worried: "How can we ask Pochekha to do this for us? He has business with the Russians. We cannot cause problems for him..." But my father responded: "Prepare for Hanukkah evening and let the first Zionist celebration take place in our house!"

The celebratory evening began with the singing of "Hatikva". Schwartzberg gave a lecture and there was more singing: "Jerusalem", "Zion Zion My Holy Land", Sabbath and holiday songs. Wolf and Chana Green sang a duet and the audience praised them with applause.

Among the youth in the hall, I remember many who already belonged to the Zionist movement or sympathized with the cause: Aron Wajfe, Tzvia the daughter of Leibush the ritual slaughterer, Abba Wolman, Zygmunt Stoltzman, Idel Tiber, Yitzchak Fleishman. Shmuel Leib Wolman, who arrived late, was received with clapping and shouts of "bravo!" He did not belong to the group, but he had great respect for progress and culture.

After the holiday the regular weekdays returned. I went back to my studies and was unable to do much for the organization, but I tried to help out whenever I could.

Activists of the Zionist Organization
Top row, from right to left: Yakob Gazalka (teacher), Abraham Zamosc,
Sarah Yesenovicz, Melech Tadelis, Landinski (teacher), Rivka Leah
Opatowski. Second row: Abraham Prawda, Motka Chajek, Chaia Libe
Karasek, Rivka Frenkel, Yechiel Chajek

The Zionist organization participated in activities for the benefit of the community. Among other things, they helped develop a Savings and Loans operation that became a public institution. Shvartzberg was the bookkeeper and I helped as his assistant. The Savings and Loans bank played an important role in the Jewish life of Gombin. It was a democratic institution that belonged to all social classes including artisans, merchants, and other groups.

The meetings of the board of directors remain fresh in my memory. Every member reacted in his own way when there were decisions to make about loans. For example, I recall the polite tailor Faivel Borenstein, whose eyes would lit up with joy every time that his suggestion to increase a loan was accepted, particularly when the applicant was a fruit seller.

Through my work at the Savings and Loans bank, I learned a great deal about the difficulties of people and their feeling of relief when they were able to collect or borrow some money. With the exception of about fifty families, everyone in Gombin benefited from our support.

The Poles had already founded their own Savings and Loans bank in Gombin. People referred to it as the "first" bank; ours was the "second". A member of our board of directors, Abraham Wolfowicz, had many acquaintances and social influence. He managed to convince some wealthy ethnic Germans from around the region to invest money in our Savings and Loans bank. It was a big success that helped us develop the operation. We were proud that people had more trust in the Jewish bank.

The Zionist Savings and Loan bank had directors, administrators, and auditors. They were all devoted to the institution with heart and soul. And they made an important contribution to Jewish communal life in Gombin.

Pioneers

by Zelig Etinger (Kibbutz Evron, Israel)

Translated by Janie Respitz
Edited by Leon Zamosc

[Original book: Pages 82-83 Yiddish]

A small Jewish town, there were thousands of them. The place where I spent my childhood and youth. My town Gombin... I see you now like through a painting by Marc Chagall. Crooked blue-grey houses, the old cemetery... Green and brown Jews floating in the air.

Poverty, an existence without purpose, without a future. We felt that our lives were becoming more difficult and restricted day by day. We went on walks to the beautiful forests of Gombin. Some of us believed in humanity and a collectivist form of life. Under our arms we carried the book "Flames" by Stanislav Bzshozovski. We saw people joining the nation, unafraid of suffering or sacrifices. We studied the teachings of Ber Borochov, Marx and Herzl about the reality of the Jews. We went out to the people and summoned them: "come, let's go to Zion".

We organized the youth movements "Hashomer Hatzair" (The Young Guardian) and "Hechalutz" (The Pioneer). We searched for inspiration to escape towards something new, a different way of life. We worked and studied by an oil lamp until late in the night, trying to obtain a better understanding of the world.

While many others followed the revolutionary slogans of the communists or the rousing calls of the Bund, we nourished from the renaissance of Yiddish culture, reading the books of Peretz, Bialik, and Mendele Mocher Sforim. Through them, we found our path to Zionist activism, and later to the Land of Israel.

In the evenings we strolled along the sidewalks of the market square. We gathered around the pump. On one side of the square stood the town hall. We saw the big clock at Spiewak's and the vaulted windows of the stores and tenement houses. A little further down, the beautiful wooden synagogue, pride and joy of our town. The study house, the washhouse, the synagogue street.

Holidays in our town. Yom Kippur, the mystical Kol Nidre, the conscience of the world is trembling. Passover, the beautiful holiday, filled with tradition and alluring melodies mixed with revolutionary tunes, the songs of the pioneers. Exodus from Egypt, liberation, and the most important blessing: "Next Year in Jerusalem".

A wedding in town. Celebration with jubilant music. People dancing and crying from joy. We should live to be proud of our children... A funeral. Crying and wailing. The long black procession to the cemetery.

The Rebbe comes to town! People are dancing in the street with the Torah. Summer visitors, happiness and misery, old and young, lights and shadows. Merchants, artisans, workshops, libraries, organizations, sports, soccer, dramatic circles.... Who can remember all the details?

Hechalutz organization in Gombin

Far away in the forest, the campsites where our big evenings took place, filled with the content of our youthful dreams. Festive meals and songs to bid farewell to those who departed, those who are today in Israel living the life they strove for, a life that is free and proud.

I lay these words, like flowers soaked in tears, on the grave of my town, for those who were closest and dearest to me...

Hashomer Hatzair

by Abraham Etinger (Kibbutz Kfar Menahem, Israel)

Translated by Janie Respitz
Edited by Leon Zamosc

[Original book: Pages 84-86 Yiddish]

The first groups of "Hashomer Hatzair" (The Young Guardian) began to form in 1923. The majority of the participants were boys from the "Tarbut" school and girls from the Jewish pubic school.

We were Zionist youngsters who organized social and cultural and activities, but we were never completely satisfied. We were always looking for new forms of organization and action.

While we were not fully aware of it at the time, the ideology of "Hashomer Hatzair" and the scouting character of the movement helped us to become self-sufficient.

The Plock branch of "Hashomer Hatzair" had a big initial influence on us. Later on, we were in close contact with the branch in Zychlin. In those times, there were many joint activities for groups of neighboring towns, which frequently visited each other.

In the groups, we read the "Memorial Book" to remember those who had fallen in the Land of Israel. We learned and discussed Jewish history, organized a variety of scouting exercises and games, and there was a lot of singing and dancing. Everybody loved the plays. I remember our first performance as a new organization: we presented "To the far-away land" by Jacob Pat.

In 1925 we formally joined the central organization of "Hashomer Hatzair" in Poland and we absorbed "Guard Trumpeldor", another group that had been recently created in Gombin. Our core initial group grew and we began to organize new younger groups following the model of the organization.

One of the difficulties we had to face was finding an appropriate place for our activities. That was not an issue during the summer, since Gombin was blessed with forests and our activities could take place in the open, close to nature. The problem was during the winter, when everything had to be done indoors. We did not have the money and government permit that were required to rent a place. Somehow, however, we eventually managed. Our first place was a house near the forest, close to the German cement factory.

Seminar-group of Hashomer Hatzair
Standing from right: P. Sochaczewski, Y. Lisak, Ch. Zolna. Kneeling: B. Ber,
A. Etinger. Seated: M. Glickzeliger, Ch. Zaideman, M. Stupaj, Ch. Kerber

I recall with nostalgia our passionate discussions about redeeming the Jewish nation, about the problems of the world, about justice and injustice.... The debates invariably ended with cheery dancing and heartfelt singing by the boys and girls.

Most of our members were children from working families and everybody wanted to learn. "Hashomer Hatzair" was much more than scouting and games. There was a lot of self-teaching, individually and in groups, and we spent a lot of time reading and studying until the late summer hours by an oil lamp during the winter nights. We were interested in social relationships, in the individual and group aspects of the Jewish question, and in the plight of Jewish workers and all the workers in the world. Most of all, we dreamed about our future collective life as kibbutz members in the Land of Israel.

A group of Hashomer Hatzair
First row from right: M. Zaideman, F. Bibergal, Woideslawski
Second row: Makower, G. Gelbart (Zaideman), F. Bol, D. Tiber
Standing: E. Zaideman, G. Rusak (from Plock), M. Gelbart

The ambitions of our founding group grew as we started to prepare for "aliyah" (emigration to the Land of Israel). The first stage was "hachshara" (preparatory agricultural training). The first group left for Dombrovitze. When they returned they brought with them new words, ideas, and practical experiences, which served as a model for the younger members.

In the summer we organized camping colonies. We left our small, cramped homes and spent a couple of weeks in the forest or by the Vistula river. Days and nights were filled with scouting activities and games, group talks, singing and dancing. Everything was planned and organized by the groups of youngsters themselves. They spent the entire year preparing for the summer camping colony, organizing gatherings and fundraising events. When summer arrived, everyone was there, despite the fact that many parents worried about their children going away on their own, without adult care or supervision.

A big day in town was when we returned from the camping colony. Younger and older scouts marched through the streets, refreshed and bronzed by the summer sun.

A group of Hashomer Hatzair

The conditions in Gombin were not good. The situation of Polish Jewry was difficult and hopeless. Still, in our clubhouse the youngsters were joyful, always playing and singing. We organized literary evenings, ideological discussions, recreational activities, summer strolls in the countryside and winter walks through the snow covered pine trees.

The growth of the "Hashomer Hatzair" energized Zionist activism in Gombin. We raised funds for the Jewish National Fund and worked together with "Hechalutz" (The Pioneer) and other young Zionist groups.

In 1929 the older group left for agricultural training. Brimming with pride and devotion, the younger members replaced them at the helm of the organization. They were able to continue the work of the older instructors because they had received preparation on how to educate children and run the activities of the movement.

The first cohort of "Hashomer Hatzair" pioneers left to the Land of Israel in 1930. The group was small because of the lack of visa permits.

Our organization continued to grow. The small lions became older. At our ceremonial gatherings we lined up by groups and divisions, wearing our scout uniforms, flying our colourful pennants, and singing the anthem of the movement "Tehezaknah". We were convinced that we would achieve the ideal of our dreams - "aliyah" to the Land of Israel.

Many of us were able to emigrate before the war. But many more stayed behind. They went the way of martyrs, in pain and suffering, unable to fulfill their life's ideal.

Today one can find "Hashomer Hatzair" pioneers from Gombin in various kibbutzim, cities and villages in Israel. Some of the comrades that survived the Shoah ended up in various other countries. They all carry with them the memories from our beautiful youthful years in Gombin.

Kfar Menachem, Erev Rosh Hashanah, September 1946

Leaving to the Land of Israel

by Bella Tiber-Tzifris

Translated by Janie Respitz
Edited by Leon Zamosc

[Original book: Pages 87-88 Yiddish]

After three periods of training in agricultural camps, the time has finally come for me to fulfill my dream. Today is July 26 1939. I leave my parents' home and my small town.

I go out on our home's balcony to look around for the last time, to see the town and everything that is close and dear to me.

It is a bright summer morning. The sun is already high and its golden rays shine on the beautiful synagogue of Gombin. The synagogue, surrounded by colorful summer flowers, has stood for hundreds of years. At that holy spot, many generations of our family have prayed. As kids, we had heard the cantor chant Kol Nidre, the blowing of the shofar, and the Hakafot of Simchat Torah. The old synagogue is the pride of the Jews of Gombin.

My father and sister call out to me: "It's getting late, hurry up or we'll be late!" I take in the surroundings with all my senses. The house where I grew up, and the town that was so friendly and known for its hospitality.

I'm leaving home...

Surrounded by my family, friends and neighbors, we approach the market square. Today we are leaving Gombin. We are a group of pioneers on our way to the Land of Israel. A large crowd has gathered in the square. We see our families, friends, childhood buddies, and old Jews in long black coats wrapped in prayer shawls after morning prayers. "Where are you children going?" they ask. "To the Land of Israel," we reply. "Travel in good health and be successful! Send our regards to the holy land and the holy city of Jerusalem..."

We say our goodbyes. We cannot tear ourselves away from one another... Everybody has tears in their eyes... The truck is already moving, we are leaving Gombin.

The last kisses and hugs from my dear ones, who knows if we will ever see each other again...

The last words: "Travel in good health! Write! Stay healthy!"

I take my last look at our house, at the streets, at and the pump in the middle of the market square, at everything... We are off.

Through the window, with tearful eyes I see our town of Gombin for the last time. Jews in black hats, the Jewish children, the streets where every stone is familiar to me. We pass city hall, the Jewish school where I received my education. It seems to me that I can hear the school bell, the shouting and laughing of the Jewish children, the voices of their caring teachers...

My father Abraham Tiber, community worker
and secretary of the Gemilat Hesed Kasse

The truck moves on. We are crossing the Christian neighborhood. Jewish women with jugs of milk keep waving at us: "God is with you, travel in good health!" I see the top of the church. Slowly, slowly we leave our town Gombin. The last contours disappear... My heart is grieving, the tears are streaming down my cheeks, I cannot utter a word.

On that day, I saw my unforgettable family and all those dear to me for the last time.

The Jewish Library

by Sidney Guyer (Simcha Chaja)

Translated by Janie Respitz
Edited by Leon Zamosc

[Original book: Pages 89-90 Yiddish]

Sidney Guyer

At the beginning of the 20th century a group of boys and girls who were active in the revolutionary movement laid the foundation for a Jewish library in Gombin. They knew well that, in those times, opening a library was a very important deed. They also knew that they would have to face material and political difficulties, but they deeply believed in their dream and made it happen.

They began to collect books, but they soon realized that this would not be enough. There were problems to solve. The biggest problem was: where do we keep the books? And how do we get money to buy new ones? Luckily, the sons and daughters of some well-to-do families liked the idea. They worked hard raising money at various events. Some went to collect bones from the butchers, then sold the bones and saved the money to buy books.

This continued for a few years. Another issue came up: where should we hide the books? Some parents did not allow their children to bring books to their homes because, in those days, many books were forbidden by the authorities or considered "non-Kosher" by the Jews. Therefore, it was necessary to permanently move the books from one place to another. This would change as a result of the First World War, when the Germans chased out the Russians. What had been previously forbidden was now permitted, and we eventually received permission to open a Jewish library in Gombin.

Now the question was: where would the library be located?

A shoemaker by the name of Hersh Mantchik lived on Kutno Street. He was called the "Kutner shoemaker". There was also the tailors' workshop of Chaim Lurie, where Yosef Laski was a partner. They gave permission to open the library at their place. At that time, I was working as a tailor apprentice at Chaim Lurie's workshop.

Moishe Orbach, "The Rabbi's grandson",
library and workers' union secretary

I helped carrying boxes of books and building the shelves. Other helpers included Hanoch Goldshmidt, Yitzchak Moishe Chaya, Sh. Adler, Tadelis, Bracha Wolman, Sh. Sochazevski, and many others whose names I no longer remember.

The Jewish library was a great success. The number of readers quickly increased and very soon the space in the two workshops became too small for the library's activities. A larger, more appropriate place was needed. This dream was also realized when the library was moved to a large brick building on the main Market Square.

The new location was bright and nice. It was no longer just a lending library - there was also a reading room where everyone felt at home. There were pictures of Yiddish writers hanging on the walls, and the tables were always full of readers. The book collection continued to grow.

The board of directors of the choir at the library
Standing at right: Choir master Leyzer Finkelstein

In time, the library became the most important cultural institution of Gombin. It hosted a variety of community activities, lectures, meetings, and fundraising events. It was also the home of the drama circle and other cultural groups of the town.

I continued to help as an active member of the library until my departure for America.

The Drama Circle

by Sidney Guyer (Simcha Chaja)

Translated by Janie Respitz
Edited by Leon Zamosc

[Original book: Pages 91-93 Yiddish]

At the turn of the 20th century, Yiddish theatre was very popular in Polish cities and towns. In Gombin, a drama circle was founded by a group of talented people who were active at the library. Eventually, the Jewish drama circle of Gombin became the most popular amateur theatrical group in the region.

The board of directors of the Drama Circle, 1910
Seated from right: Yosl Szklower, Hershl Luschinski, director
Chaim Lurie, Yitzchak Moishe Chaya-Guyer, Leybl Drachman.
Standing: Hanoch Goldshmidt

At first, the group faced difficulties. The library hall, for example, was not large and comfortable enough for the growing audience. However, the dedication of the founders and participants allowed them to overcome the difficulties and, in time, the drama circle achieved important accomplishments.

The group's theatrical director was Chaim Lurie. He was very talented, always brilliant in the many roles that he played. He taught evening classes in Gombin, and he was always helping others to develop their acting skills.

The drama circle: director Chaim Lurie playing King Lear

Hershl Tajfeld gave a lot of his time to the drama circle, together with Yitzkhak Moishe Chaya and his wife Bracha, who left for America in the 1920s. For many years, Hanoch Goldshmidt was responsible for the technical aspects of stage and sound. I learned a lot from him. Hershl Luschinski, a well-to-do Gombiner, provided financial help.

Naturally, not everything went smoothly. There were parents who did not like the idea of their children becoming actors. Chana Zychlinska had that problem with her father. She was very talented but her father was opposed from the beginning. He would storm in from behind the scenes and make a scandal. At first he succeeded, but in the end she came back and for many years brightened the amateur group with her talents. She later married Yosl Celemensky who was a prompter as well as a good performer in the drama circle.

Now our town had a group of youngsters who were attracted to the theatre and did not want to wait for the holidays to perform. They wanted to have a stable theatre that performed regularly.

Teatr—POLONJA—Gąbin.
KOŁO DRAMATYCZNE przy BIBLIOTECE
Powsz. Społdz. Robotn. w Gąbinie.

PROGRAM

Sobota dnia 5-XI-27 roku.

„Trudno być żydem"

Sztuka ludowa w 3-ch aktach z prologiem.

— OSOBY: —

Dawid Szpiro	p. Ch. Zandman
Sara , jego żona	R. Gostyńska
Beti] ich dzieci	Z. Tajfeldówna
Sjomke]	Ch. Łęcki
Sznajurson — student	M. Zając
Iwanow ,	M. Wolman
Grynsberg ,	D. Blawat
Fratkin ,	A. Szczawiński
Hurwic — nauczyciel	M. Chaja
Kecele	S. Mocny
Starszy żandarm	M. Chaja

Studenci, koleżanki Beti i żandarmy.

Reżyser—Ch. Zandman ——— Sufler—Ch. Hodys.

Druk. Kliper i Taub Płock 816-27

טעאטער **פאלאניא** נאמבין.
דראמאטישער קרייז ביי דער ביבליאטעק
פון אלג. ארב. קאאפעראטיוו אין נאמבין.

פּראגראם.

שבת ד. 5-XI. 1927

שווער צו זיין א ייד

א פאלקס-שטיק אין 3 אקטן מיט א פראלאג.

===== **פערזאנען:** =====

דוד שפירא
שרה , זין ווייב
בעטי
סיאמקע
שניאורסאן א סטודענט
איוואנאוו
גרינסבערג
פראטקין
הורוויטש א רערער
קעצעלע

דער עלטסטער פון זשאנדאריסטען — ח. מ. הייא
סטודענטן, בעטיס חברטעס, זשאנדארן.

רעזשיסער: ח. זאנדמאן ——— סופלאר: ח. האדיס.

Theatre Polonia, Gombin
Program in Yiddish and Polish, May 1927: It's Hard to be a Jew

The move from the library to a larger new location energized the drama circle. Our group was in contact with theater groups from other towns. We would visit them and they would come visit us. One of our most talented actors was Sh. Laski, a great character performer. Other very talented members were: Hershl Karo, Mendl Frenkel, and Lazar Finkelstein who had a beautiful voice. He later organized a choir within the drama circle. By occupation, he was a tailor, but his singing vocation prevailed and he eventually became a famous cantor in Poland and Germany.

The Drama Circle Youth at the Library

First from right: Director P. Zandman. Standing: Hanoch Goldshmidt

Other active members of the drama circle were: Yakov Celemensky, Lipek Maydat, Moishe Wolman, Hinda Schwartz, Rude Gostynska, Chaya Wrubel, Chatzkel Hodys, Moishe Orbach, Zelda Tajfeld, Moishe Chaya... It is impossible for me to pay tribute to all those who helped with the plays, with the technical work, and with their support and encouragement. But one thing can be said: the Gombin drama circle was one of the most prized cultural gems of our town and it continued to be very active until the war. Eventually, however, the storm that hovered over Poland would not spare anything. The star of the drama circle, like every other light of Jewish existence in Gombin, would be ruthlessly extinguished by the Nazi murderers.

The Sport Associations in Gombin

By Wolf Maintczik

Translated by Meir Holtzman and Ada Holtzman
Edited by Leon Zamosc

[Original book: Pages 94-96 Yiddish]

The most important sports association in Gombin was no doubt Maccabi. But there were other associations. One of them was the Bund's sports club Morgenstern (Morning Star), popularly known by its Polish name Jutrznia. Later on, the Zionist workers' movement also opened a branch of their club Hapoel in Gombin.

The beginning belongs to Maccabi which, if I remember right, was founded in 1921. Among the founders of Maccabi were Abram Zychlinski and the sons of the Glass, Stolcman, Teyfeld, Holcman, Baum and other families.

The early activities of Maccabi centered on two sports groups: football (soccer) and gymnastics. The football team was very strong and popular in the surrounding shtetls. They had many fans who attended the matches, applauded with enthusiasm, and cheered the players with all their hearts. In the flourishing period, the team included the following players: Zeidman Benyamin, Szlomo Maintczik, Herszek Stolczman, Ignesz Stolczman, Motel Pelka, Dawid Toyber, Abrahamele Stolcman, Israel Moshe Zolna, Icze Szreks, Dawid Hodys, Zelig Rochberger and Szmulik Luszinski.

In the reserve played: Szimon Toyber, Gerszon Klinger, Mendel Kilbert, Dan Tayfeld and Reuven Tayfeld. Over time, of course, the players changed. The seniors left and youngsters appeared on the field, including very talented players like Arcze Tiber, Dawid Zychlinsky, Moshe Hodys, Moniek Lask, and Benyamin Chaja, who was a superb goalkeeper.

Maccabi played against amateur teams, and I can remember several memorable games. On one occasion, Maccabi beat the Christian football team Sokol 3:0. It was an exceptional victory because Sokol had some professional players such as the brothers Stille, Frank Kopiczki and Bulek Mrozek. Since Sokol was by far the stronger team, Maccabi's win brought tremendous joy to the fans and all the Jews of Gombin. In another unforgettable match, Maccabi Gombin beat Maccabi Plock 3:0. The referee of that game was Wolfewicz.

The committee of the sports association Maccabi

In 1923 Maccabi played two games against Szczelec, a Polish team from Plock. In the first round, Maccabi won 3:1. In the second match, which took place on the Christian Holiday "Bostwo Cialo" (Body of God) there were anti-semitic assaults. Maccabi led 1:0 after a goal scored by Aron Hodys. But Aron was hit and badly wounded. He could not play again for a while. For a long time after that incident, Maccabi abstained from playing in the Gombin football field. Instead, they played in other towns. One consequence was that the team got weaker. The good players retired and Maccabi was no longer considered the best in the neighborhood.

Maccabi's gymnastics team did not excel. It could not be compared to the brilliant gymnastics team of Jutrznia. So when there was a gymnastics competition in Gombin, they invited the teams of Maccabi Plock and Wloclawek to represent Maccabi in the competition.

It is worth mentioning that Maccabi had an independent wind instruments orchestra. The conductor was Moshe Hodys. The orchestra offered public concerts in the town and the nearby woods. The concerts in the woods usually took place on Lag Ba'omer. Among the participants in the Maccabi orchestra were: Azriel Tatarka (played the Clarinet), Meir Zelig Kerber (played the lyric tenor), Tiber, Zychlinsky and Wruble.

Maccabi in Gombin
Source: album of Meir Holtzman [not in original book].

In 1938, the football team regained strength and once again played a visible role. It attracted very good players like Benyamin Chaja, Moshe Grziwacz, Yosel Blawat, Szimon Spodek, Fajwisz Boll, Moniek Laski, Yankel'e Zolna, Mechle Ber and many others. Until the break of the Second World War, the team had many successes in matches with Jewish teams from Gombin and the surrounding area.

When the Nazis occupied Gombin, only a few people were able to flee to the Soviet Union. Most of the Maccabi members shared the same terrible fate of most of the Jews of Gombin and Poland at large.

Parallel to Maccabi, the Bund's Sport organization Morgenstern, known as Jutrznia, was very active in the sporting life of the shtetl. It had two teams as well: football and gymnastics.

As stated above, Jutrznia's gymnastics team was excellent. They had very good coaches: Kroy in the beginning, and later: Abram Frenkel. Jutrznia organized public shows under the slogan *"A healthy spirit in a health body"*. Their welcoming message was *"Frish-frei, stark-trei"* (New-free, strong-faithful).

Board of the Bund's sports organization Morgernstern,
popularly known by its Polish name Jutrznia

The football team of Jutrznia only played amateur games. It was not a strong team, but they were very enthusiastic. I remember the names of many of their players: Somel Szczerb, Hersz Natan Zeidman, Fajwisz Gurker, Szlomo Blawat, Chaim Gurker, Zalman Klinger, Moshe Schwarcz, Moshe Tipiel, Israel Stupai and Lazer Kuczinski.

I remember a game between the two Gombiner groups: Maccabi and "Jutrznia". Maccabi won 3:1, while it appeared with its strongest team. Most of the members of Juczinia shared the destiny of their brothers in Poland and perished in the Holocaust, except very few who survived. All the others were killed by the hands of the Nazi murderers.

The Years of Destruction

The Devastation

Translated by Janie Respitz
Edited by Leon Zamosc

[Original book: Page 99 Yiddish]

After existing for hundreds of years, the Jewish community of Gombin was destroyed by the German Nazis. As everywhere else in Poland and Europe, the murderers were methodical in the consummation of their crime: anti-Jewish decrees, spreading of terror, vicious beatings, people forced to work as slaves, plundered, individually murdered, and finally confined in a ghetto as a prelude for their deportation to death camps and total annihilation.

Very few survived. Only individual crumbs of entire Gombin families were spared the destruction. This section of the memorial book includes the testimonies of Jews from Gombin who outlasted the catastrophe.

The memories of Ben Guyer, Jack Frenkel, Abraham Zeideman, and the Greenbaum brother and sister exemplify the ways in which some Jews managed to stay alive in dreadful conditions.

Ben Guyer and the Frenkel brothers were dragged by the Nazis to forced labor camps and eventually to Auschwitz. Very few outlived that death factory. Four million people were killed, most of them Jews.

Abraham Zeideman illustrates another path to survival, followed by thousands of Jews from Nazi-occupied Poland who escaped to the Soviet Union, where they endured appalling conditions and investigations.

The Greenbaum brother and sister tell the dramatic story of their survival in the so-called "Aryan side". Albert was hidden by a farmer. His sister Rose succeeded in "passing" as an Aryan woman. They separately describe the emotional moment in which they were finally able to get together again.

Concentration camps, "Aryan side", Soviet exile... That was how a small remnant of the Polish Jews got through the Holocaust. But the descriptive accounts of Guyer, Frenkel, Zeideman, and the Greenbaums have another value. In addition to illustrating the cases of Jewish survival, they give us some details about the war days in Gombin and the terrible fate of the town's Jews in the hands of the Nazis.

Poems

by Rajzel Zychlinsky

Translated by Janie Respitz
Edited by Leon Zamosc

[Original book: Pages 100-101 Yiddish]

God Hid His Face

All the roads led to death,
all the roads.
All the winds breathed betrayal,
all the winds.
At all the doorways angry dogs barked,
at all the doorways.
All the waters laughed at us,
all the waters.
All the nights fed on our dread,
all the nights.
And the heavens were bare and empty,
all the heavens.
God hid his face.

I Want To Walk Here Once More

Dedicated to the 3030 martyrs from my town Gombin who were murdered in the gas chambers at Chelmno, Poland, April 1942.

A.

I want to walk here once more
on the grass
and weep
to the sky

and to the wind
that howls in my face.
I want once again to measure the calamity
that befell this piece of ground
where once was my home.
The door is gone
and my mother---
she will not come home any more
covered with snow,
with a blue pitcher of milk in her hand--
and with the blue light of dawn in her eyes.
The windows are gone,
the sun will no longer wander
from wall to wall,
from corner to corner,
and conjure up for me
a green cat on a chair.
Only the willows at the river are here--
my tear falls into the waters
and for a while disturbs their calm.

B.

Yellow leaves fall, fall.
A tale wanders around on the roads,
a tale about people herded together on a field--
a spring rain was falling.
Three thousand Jews without water, without bread,
four long spring days.
Little children were crying under the stars--
they wanted to eat.
The surrounding forest did not grow darker
from the children's crying.
Here they are, the green forests,
the forests of Gombin.
The deep blue sky
did not send fire down from the heights.
Cows are grazing in the fields,
a shepherd roasts potatoes in the smoke...
For what am I still searching in the village?
I encounter the pock-marked Stasha
she lives, she strolls around with soldiers,
she is drunk and unwashed.

C.

Who calls me here in the meadow?
Who still knows my name?
A thorn bush burns in the field--
a child cries from the flames.
I take off my shoes and approach
the little son of my neighbor;
his little hands are charcoal,
but his eyes are open still.
I am leaving you, shtetl,
your roads are blue as before.
You will celebrate autumns and fairs,
and the river will flow on through the valley.

The Destruction of Gombin

by Jacob Grziwacz

Translated by Meir Holtzman and Ada Holtzman
Edited by Leon Zamosc

[Original book: Pages 102-103 Yiddish]

In 1939, right before the war, Gombin had a Jewish community of about 3,100 people. The shtetl was known for its lively cultural and political life. Writers and other public personalities came frequently to deliver lectures in the town's Jewish libraries and reading halls. There was an acclaimed drama group, which had been founded by Adam Tomb and Sonia Altboim. This theatrical circle performed many plays in Gombin and in surrounding towns.

Many youngsters were active in revolutionary organizations, organizing strikes and demonstrations. Some of them spent time in the prison of the nearby city Plock and a few were sent to Bereza Kartuska, which was the main Polish detention camp for political opponents during the 1930s.

Gombin was mentioned in the Yiddish literature. In his stories, Shalom Ash described the beautiful surrounding landscape and the typical characters of the shtetl. Itzhak Leibush Peretz wrote about the "kaneh" that was still chained to a wall in the entrance hall of the synagogue (a traditional punishment device that was clamped around the neck of sinners).

The synagogue of Gombin was one of the grandest wooden synagogues in Poland. It had been built in the 18th century and was considered a national Polish architectural landmark. Visitors from Poland and abroad would come to the town to admire the engravings of its eastern wall and the building's striking beauty.

The Nazis destroyed the Jewish life in Gombin. Immediately upon the occupation, all the Jews were assembled in the new market square. The Germans beat the rabbi of the community and, while the Jews were being abused and forced to perform humiliating "gymnastic" exercises in the square, they set on fire the synagogue and the Beit Midrash. When the fire extended to the nearby buuidings, the Germans pushed the Jews towards the fire, forcing them to remove doors, windows and other property from the burning houses with their bare hands. All this while the amused Nazis were taking photographs of the horrible scenes.

Nazis humiliating the Gombin Jews

In the early summer of 1942, about 600 Jews were rounded up and sent to the Konin forced labor camp. Upon their departure, commander Haag told them: "You are going to work, you have a chance to live. For the Jews who are left in Gombin the death is inevitable."

Out of those 600 Jews, only 18 would survive the camps.

The Nazis ordered the Jews to remove all the tombstones from the Jewish cemetery, forcing them to dig out corpses and take the remains to the nearby Christian cemetery.

In retaliation for the killing of a German, the Nazis staged a public execution of ten local Poles. They executed another ten Poles in the nearby town of Gostynin.

Some Jews from Zychlin and Gostynin escaped to Gombin. They informed about the crimes of the Germans. They also reported that near the city of Kolo, in Chelmno, the Jews were being gassed to death and burned. When people began to talk about running away and hide in the woods, the head of the

Judenrat "calmed" them, saying that they should offer more bribes and appease the Germans with valuables and money.

The day of the final tragedy arrived in the summer of 1942. The German murderers assembled all the Jews in the field of the fire brigade They were surrounded by armed ethnic German, Ukrainian and Lithuanian fascists who kept them for three days and nights under the open sky, with a barrel of dirty water and without any food. When the wife of Naftali Spiewak begged for more water, an ethnic German from Gombin, Maas, shot her on the spot (after the war he was sentenced to death by the Polish authorities).

On the fourth day the trucks of the Gestapo arrived. With murderous blows, the doomed Jews were pushed onto the trucks and taken to their deaths at Chelmno extermination camp.

A short time later, the Jews of the nearby small towns of Osmolin and Sanniki were liquidated in the same fashion.

The German Occupation

Translated by Melvyn Wrobel
Edited by Leon Zamosc

[Not in original book]

The following report describes conditions in Gombin during and immediately after the German occupation. It was found in the Warsaw Ghetto Archives of the Jewish Historical Institute in Warsaw. The archives were compiled by Emanuel Ringelbaum, a Jewish historian who participated in the Jewish underground Oneg Shabbat. During the Warsaw Ghetto uprising the archives were buried in milk containers and, after the war, a substantial part of the material was recovered and made part of the Jewish Historical Institute's collections. It can be surmised that this particular report was written by one of the Gombin Jewish community leaders who were smuggled to Warsaw in order to elude the Germans' systematic killing of the Jewish and Polish "intelligentsia" of the smaller cities and towns.

Gombin, Gostynin County, Warsaw province

The town of Gombin has 6,000 residents. Fifty percent are Jews. As the fighting developed between Warsaw and Lanzig (Lacko) during the first days of September 1939, German airplanes attacked Gombin with regular bombs and firebombs. About 75% of the buildings in the Jewish center of the town were destroyed in the area of the Pieracki and Narutovich streets. Several hundred people died under the rubble. Many of them were people from neighboring cities and towns like Plock, Sierpc, and Rypin. They had come to Gombin in search of refuge from the German invasion. By mid-September there had been direct and indirect attacks on Gombin and, on Sunday September 17 in the afternoon the Germans entered the town. Difficult days were coming for the Jews.

On Thursday, September 21, they ordered all men aged 16 to 65 to concentrate in Pilsudski square at 10 am. The square was surrounded by German soldiers heavily equipped with machine-guns. For six hours we were there, in two large separate groups of Jews and Poles. We waited, afraid and uncertain, not knowing what the outcome would be. At about 2 pm the Germans set ablaze the synagogue, a wooden building with great historical value, and also the Beit Midrash that was on Boznica street. They also put on fire two neighboring streets of the Jewish quarter and also Kilinskiego street. Some old men tried to put off the fire and the women risked their life trying to save the sefer torahs. At 4 pm the men were released and went to watch the smouldering remains of the synagogue and the Beit Midrash.

This took place on the eve of Yom Kippur 5700. The fire was still going on and they attempted to save some of the houses. For trying to do it the Germans started beating them with the butts of their guns and tried to make some Jews jump into the fire. They also forced them to dance and sing, and burned the peyote (sidelocks) of the elderly Jews. Then they started to loot, taking everything from the Jewish stores. There were Poles, underworld types, and also local ethnic Germans doing that. In the days that followed, they issued a decree forbidding the Jews to run their businesses. They confiscated much of the leather goods, flour, sugar, and other products from the stores. And they raided the houses to take people to work, mistreating the Jews in every possible way.

People in all the Jewish organizations in town started to discuss what to do. On October 15, an order came from Gostynin to Abraham Lajb Gips, born in 1878 and President of the Small Business Association and the FolksBank, telling him that he had to form a Judenrat. He had to organize it with seven people from the different organizations in the Kehila.

The Judenrat started to work under the jurisdiction of the municipal authority. They had to supply workers from ages 16 to 60, one day a week. For a while, it seemed that things would get more or less settled, at least in terms of order.

On November 10 and 11, social activists and organizers were arrested in Gombin. Among them was the President of the Kehila and Director of the FolksBank Abraham Zamosc and the director of the Jewish Public School Yitzhak Rembaum, They put them in the school. By the next day, other people who expected to be arrested had left the town and gone to Warsaw, including Abraham Lajb Gips, the organizer of the Gombin Judenrat.

Thanks to the efforts of the Gombiner delegates in Warsaw, Abraham Gibs and Lajb Siekerka, the office of the "Joint" (American Joint Distribution Committee) agreed to organize and open a soup kitchen in Gombin, and also to distribute clothing and medicines to help the Jews. A Help Committee was organized in Gombin to receive the assistance of the "Joint" and explore possibilities for emigration.

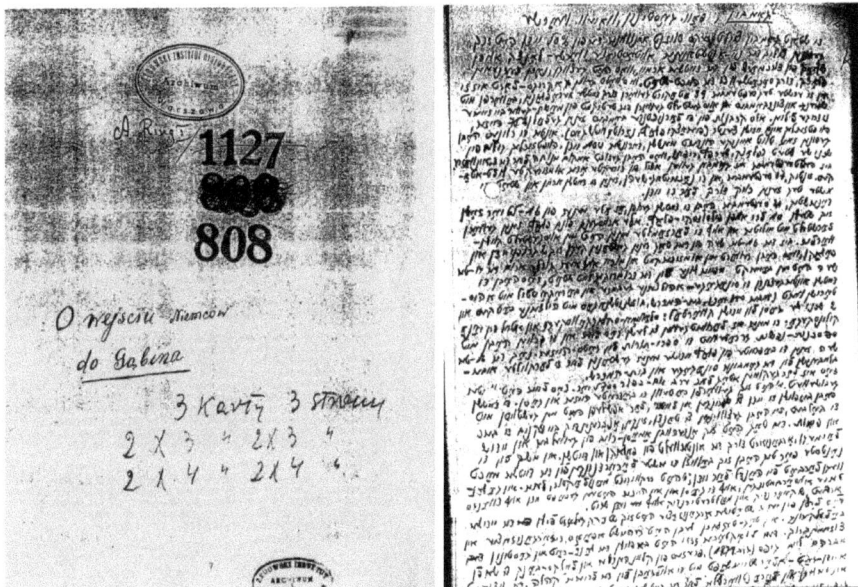

Fascimile of the report on conditions in Gombin
Source: Warsaw Ghetto Archives, Jewish Historical Institute in Warsaw

On November 2/3, the authority issued the order that the Jews had to wear a Star of David on their clothing. They could not walk on the sidewalks, and they had to take off their hats in the presence of any German soldier. They had to wear the yellow markers on their backs and also on the right side of their breast. Then the S.A. (Sturmabteilung) men started to break into the Jewish homes, beating men and women, regardless of age. They poured cold water on naked bodies, beating with sticks until people fainted. One of the houses they raided was that of Gershon Gezeldman. Despite the screaming and desperated pleas of the mother, two S.S. (Schutzstaffel) men took away the 14 year-old daughter. On the next day she was found dead outside the town.

With these events the Jewish population lived in apprehension, feeling insecure, and the parents of the girl who got beaten and raped had to pay for the burial.

An order was given that the Jews could not be seen after 5 pm buying groceries in Pieracki square. Then, in May 1940, they imposed a collective fine of 20 thousand marks on the Jews, making the Judenrat responsible for collecting the money. Some members of the Judenrat tried to appeal, saying that they would not be able to raise that amount. They were beaten unmercifully.

Because of the looting the Jews lost everything they had. Since they could not afford to buy food or medicines, hunger and tifus broke out. The Germans did that to speed up the deaths among the Jews.

The Synagogue is Burning

by Hania Shane Tajfeld

Translated by Janie Respitz
Edited by Leon Zamosc

[Original book: Page 115 Yiddish]

One evening, as we sat at home behind locked doors in fear that the Germans would hear our voices, we heard someone on our stairs. Then, there were knocks on the door.

Some Polish youngsters were looking at us. They said that they needed to install a radio in our balcony.

They were there until late at night. When they left, we heard the heavy footsteps of the German gendarmes on the streets.

Early next morning the German commander ordered all Jewish men to gather at the new market square (the pig market), saying that they would be assigned to various jobs.

Soon, lines of Jews began to form as the Germans gave orders. Machine guns were emplaced in front of the Jews. There was a dead silence.

Suddenly we saw fiery flames coming from the synagogue. We heard frightened screams. The Germans had set fire to the synagogue.

Making fun of the Jews, they sent them to save their holy place.

Then those beasts chased the Jews like a flock of sheep, beating them with sticks, clubs and whips.

The shouts and screams reached the heavens.

The Nazis pushed the Jews into the flames telling them to extinguish the fire with their bare hands. They kept prodding them with whips and bayonets.

It did not take long for the holy synagogue, the pride of Gombin, to collapse into a pile of ash. The beautiful building was quickly consumed by the fire and the towers came down.

The wind carried the sparks and flames to the surrounding houses and an entire portion of the Jewish quarter burned with the synagogue.

A few hours later there were just small smoldering fires amidst the black debris. The place where the jewel of Jewish Gombin had stood for hundreds of years was covered with embers and soot.

This was the beginning of the destruction. After the loss of the synagogue came the loss of the people who once prayed there...

In Gombin Ghetto and the Nazi Camps

by Ben Guyer (Benjamin Chaja)

Translated by Janie Respitz
Edited by Leon Zamosc

[Original book: Pages 104-114 Yiddish and 45-55 English]

Ben Guyer

I was drafted into the Polish Army in March 1939, serving in the 21st Infantry Regiment based in Warsaw. Poland was expecting an imminent attack from the German armies. During that period my family was spread out all over the world. My father, three brothers and one sister were in America. My mother had died in 1934. I lived in Gombin with my older brother, Joseph, who had a wife and a little girl of two.

My Warsaw Regiment was sent on foot in the direction of Mlawa, near the Prussian border. As soon as we reached our destination, war broke out. From that moment we did not have a moment of respite. The Germans poured fire on us - from their planes, tanks, artillery and armored cars. Armed with primitive weapons, we were unable to withstand the pressure of their fiery onslaught. We began retreating from the start, not stopping even once to take positions and engage in battle. Their fire pursued us by day and by night as we retreated, in terror, towards Jab³onna and Warsaw, where we regrouped behind the so-called "Miedszin Line."

There we remained until the day that Warsaw, surrounded by the Nazi armies, blazing from the enemy's serial bombardment, without food or water, surrendered. The Polish regiments defending the capital put down their arms and become prisoners of war.

The Germans packed us into trains and sent us in a westerly direction. But when the train arrived in Kutno, I jumped out and headed to Gombin, my home.

I returned to Gombin during the days of Succoth. The weather had turned cold and the town was unrecognizable. Many homes had been destroyed by the Nazi bombardments and the Jewish population was in the grip of German terror. My brother, who before the war had been a cashier at the People's Bank, was now appointed letter carrier by the Jewish community. Thanks to his job, he was one of the few Jewish men in Gombin whom the Germans did not press into a labor gang.

Jewish forced workers in Gombin
Source: Ada Holtzman's Collection [not in original book]

A half-mad local ethnic German, whose name was Shumacher, was put in charge of the bloody game. It was his task to seize the Jews and press them into labor gangs. Aided by several others, he carried out the task in a barbaric fashion. The Jews were grabbed in the streets and put to clean the debris around the market square and other streets. They were rewarded with insults and murderous beatings. In addition, the Jews were forced to serve the Germans who went hunting in the surrounding forests. There, too, the reward consisted of humiliation and blows. Several times I was seized on the streets, put to work, and felt on my body the blows of the whips and sticks of the Nazis..

One day, four weeks after my return to Gombin, the Germans issued an order directing all former soldiers to report to the magistrate. My brother, fearful of the Nazis' dark designs, said that I should not report. Instead, I should go hide in Warsaw. We hired a Pole who agreed to take me to Warsaw in his horse-and-buggy. Arriving in Warsaw, I went to see the Friedman family on 9 Pavia St. They were a family of weavers from Gombin. Their son had served in the Polish army with me.

In Warsaw, the situation of the Jews was the same as in the other cities and towns throughout Poland. There, too, the Jews were seized, forced to work, and subjected to terror, pain and hunger.

I managed, because of my "Christian" appearance, to avoid being seized to work.

My brother, concerned about my fate, eventually came to Warsaw and took me back with him to Gombin. My intention, in those days, was to follow the example of thousands of Jews who went east, to the part of Poland occupied by the Soviets. We made plans to go with a friend of mine from Zychlin, but I was too attached to my brother and family. In the end, I decided to stay with them and face the dangers together.

In the meantime, the Germans had instituted the Jewish badge, a six-point Star of David that all the Jews of Gombin had to wear on their clothes.

I began working as a tailor and lived with my brother's family untill March 1942. I will not go into the details of the Jewish suffering and pain during those long bloody months. Our life was cheap, worthless. We were in the hands of thugs and murderers dressed in SS and Wehrmacht uniforms. Day after day we were systematically robbed, beaten, humiliated and tortured.

At the beginning, we lived in our old dwelling on 2 Garbarska St. The house belonged to the German owner of the brewery Pivo Okocimskie before the war.

Driven out of there, we lived for a while in another place until they evicted us again. Finally, we found a room in a house owned by a Pole. There were eight of us in that room: my brother, his wife and child, her brother Hershl Santsky with his wife and child, Hershl's father-in-law Shloime Frankel, and myself.

Women and children in the Gombin ghetto

One day of the Rosh Hashanah holiday, when we were voluntarily replacing the religious Jews at work, I committed a "sin". The mayor saw me talking with a Polish acquaintance. He fell upon me with whip and stick and beat me murderously, forcing me to count each lash. In the process, he knocked off several of my teeth.

In the middle of 1941, when the German armies began moving toward the Russian border in the east, we heard that a German soldier had been killed by a Pole. Nobody knew whether this was true or it was a German ruse to frighten the Polish populace. In any case, the Germans seized a large number of Poles and drove them to the market square, locking up the main figures of the local Polish "intelligentsia" in the church. Later, they ordered all Gombin residents, Poles as well as Jews, to assemble at the market square, where they staged an execution. They took ten Poles out of the church and stood them against sandbags. A platoon of soldiers, brought from Kutno for the purpose, shot them. The ten bodies were left on the ground until late at night, when they took them away. After the war, the bodies were found under a road.

Gombin belonged to the part of Poland that was directly annexed to the German Reich. Jewish life was a constant hell, but the Poles were also in anguish. A large number of them were driven from Gombin and "tossed" into the territory of the so called Polish General Government. Their homes were turned over to ethnic Germans from the area or "imported" from further east. However, Polish suffering was nothing compared to ours. Besides, the Poles continued to display hostility and hatred toward their Jewish neighbors, regardless of the difficult conditions of both groups.

Gombin ghetto, main gate

Early in 1942 we received the first disturbing news about Jewish extermination. People who were fleeing from surrounding towns told us that entire Jewish communities were being taken to Chelmno, where they were gassed and burned. We did not believe it. None of us wanted to believe that it could be true. It was not just that we did not want believe it; we did not even want to hear about it. Finally, some Jewish survivors from Zychlin told us that their townspeople had been taken by horse and wagon to Krosniewice and from there by freight train to Chelmno, where they were gassed. Only then did our eyes and minds open to the full extent of the horror that awaited us all.

Around Purim time, the Germans began rounding up Jews in Gombin in order to send them to labor camps. I was among the first to be taken to the firehouse, which was the assembly point. When my brother found out, he came voluntarily with his father-in-law and surrendered to the Germans. Guarding the door of the firehouse, was a local ethnic German, Braun, with whom I had been friendly as a boy. He was now keeping us under surveillance with a cocked revolver.

When the number of Jews who had been rounded up reached about one thousand, a civilian SS man arrived. Armed with a revolver and a club, he did not stop beating us. He made a point of being particularly vicious with those who were well-dressed, whom he called "criminals." But he singled out "Big Moishe" for the worst beating of all. A giant of a man, Moishe aroused the hatred of the SS like no one else in the crowd. He was beaten so long and so mercilessly that he died. Four people who pleaded illness, were taken behind the firehouse and shot to death.

After a night in the firehouse, the Germans released the older men. The rest of us, surrounded by local ethnic German policemen, were loaded on trucks. That was when I got separated from my brother. I found out later that the Judenrat managed to convince the Germans to release him, on the grounds that he was needed as Gombin's Jewish letter carrier.

The trucks took us to the Konin forced labor camp, where we met with Jews from Sanniki, Gostynin and a few who had managed to escape the Zychlin massacre.

The Konin Camp

I spent a year in the Konin camp, until the spring of 1943. More than a work camp, it was a real hell. We slept on wooded boards, without straw. The prisoners died like flies from starvation, unbearable work and constant beatings. The camp was located about twenty kilometers from the extermination center at Chelmno. The sick inmates were shipped to Chelmno, and when anyone caught a contagious disease, all the occupants of his barrack were sent with him to Chelmno and death. We were hungry, surrounded by dirt, and forced to work so hard that many collapsed at work. You knew that, if you suffered any injury, your path led to Chelmno. And yet, the number of Jews did not diminish. New victims were brought from the surrounding towns or other camps to replace the dead.

One day, in the middle of the 1942-43 winter, ten Jews were caught near the railroad tracks trying to steal potatoes from one of the cars. All the Jewish inmates were assembled in an open place to witness their execution. But that was not enough for the murderers. The German commander of the camp summoned a Jewish "elder", Abraham Zeif, who lived in Danzig and had a son-in-law in Gostynin. Zeif was a very refined, educated person, a Talmudist. The commander of the camp had chosen him as his assistant. But now, the commander ordered the Jewish "elder" to select twenty additional Jews to be executed along with the ten. Zeif declined to do it. He stood alongside the ten and declared: "If you are going to kill another twenty, let me be the first of them. You can pick the others yourself." The unexpected response astonished the commander. In the end, he decided to be "reasonable" and "only" execute the ten "criminals."

At that time I was in a tailors' work team. Our situation was a little better than among the people who did physical labor.

In the Konin camp there was a young rabbi from Sanniki, Jehoshua Moshe Aaronson, who was another very refined, cultivated person. We saved his life by "making" a cobbler out of him. The rabbi kept a diary which unfortunately was lost [Editor's note: Most of Rabbi Aaronson's diary was found and eventually published by his family as part of a book in Hebrew: Jehoshua Moshe Aaronson, "Alei Merorot" (Pages of Bitterness), Bnei Brak, Israel, 1996].

We had secretly formed a self-defense group in the camp. We collected knives and were determined to be ready if the Germans decided to close the camp. If that day arrived, we would defend ourselves and try to prevent our extermination.

Among the people in the camp's administration, there was a German socialist who treated us like humans. He would give us information, always in deep secrecy, about what was going on in the outside world. One day he told us that the Jews of Warsaw had risen against the Germans, had fought with guns, and had killed Nazis in that unequal struggle. The news filled us with courage. We were determined to strike at the German murderers before we died.

And that day did in fact arrive. One morning our contact, before leaving for work, informed us that a deportation was imminent. When later in the day the Germans announced that there would be a "delousing," we knew that our contact had told us the truth and the end was coming.

At that time, there were about sixty of us left in the camp. All the others had either been sent to be gassed at Chelmno or had died of starvation, diseases, blows, or the gallows. Soon after the Germans announced the "delousing," two

Jewish camp policemen set fire to the bathhouse and hanged themselves. One of them was Feiwish Kamlazh from Gombin, the other Getzel Kleinot from Sanniki. Philip Kranz, the "Juden-Eltster,", also hanged himself. The already mentioned Abraham Zeif poisoned himself. Two others died of poison: an elderly Gombin Jew by the name of Abraham Najdorf, and Dr. Klappe, a German-Jewish physician who had served as an officer in the German Army in the First World War. My good friend Abraham Aaron Tabacznik from Gostynin committed suicide by letting the flames that were consuming the camp burn him to death.

While all this was taking place in the camp, we were away attending to our various tasks. In the middle of the day, we were suddenly surrounded by German policemen who took us back to the camp. All the buildings were on fire. The ground was strewn with the dead Jews. They assembled the forty-nine survivors in one place and held us there.

We fully expected to be sent to Chelmno on the following morning. But the Germans kept us in the camp for several weeks more. They just left us alone without forcing us to work. One morning, as we came out of the barracks, we were surrounded by SS men who ordered us to leave everything and take along only a slice of bread. They led us towards waiting trucks and forced us to get inside. We were sure that our destination was Chelmno. Inside the truck, we recited kaddish with a rabbi. Several German soldiers sat in the truck, rifles in hand. Knowing that we were going to die, I thought that it would made no difference if I asked one of the soldiers for a cigarette. To my astonishment, he took out a pack of cigarettes from his pocket and gave me one. I took a deep draw and passed it around to the others. Seeing that the soldier was not such a villain, I asked him: "Where are you taking us?" "You are going to a punitive camp - Hohensaltz (Inowroclaw)", he replied. And so it was.

At Hohensaltz, we understood from the start the meaning of a punitive camp. There were "sinners" of many nationalities - Poles, Russians, Germans, but chiefly it was crowded with the remnants of Pomeranian Jewry who were in transit to the death camps. One of the most notorious features of the camp was the "Black Wall" where people were brought to be shot for the smallest transgression. The camp's inmates were not permitted to walk, only to run.

The day we arrived in the camp, they brought a Jewish couple who had been hiding on the "Aryan" side. The young man's name was David Moskowitz. He had been "superintendent" in another camp and the SS themselves had helped him to obtain false "Aryan" identification papers. But now, two SS men began to hit him with heavy clubs as soon as he arrived. They beat him so long and hard that they got tired and had to be replaced by another pair. And yet, the young man withstood all the blows.

It was around Tisha B'Av and the following morning was chilly. They assembled some of us, including the young "Aryan" couple, for "evacuation." We were permitted to take along a slice of bread. Once again we thought that our end had come. They flung us inside a freight train. Every car was guarded by SS men armed with machine-guns. The car was so crowded that there was barely any room to stand. We rode that way for several days. I cannot remember the exact number of days we traveled. Then, in the middle of one night, the train was suddenly brought to a halt. The doors were flung open and we heard a loud barking of dogs and wild shouts: "get out!" We emerged from the cars to be confronted by SS men carrying machine-guns and clubs. We had come to Auschwitz.

Auschwitz

Everything happened with lightning speed. Driven by the SS men, we passed a man who pointed with his finger towards the right or towards the left. Women, children, elderly people, the infirm, were directed to the left. The men, the young, those capable of work, were motioned to the right. I was directed to the right and chased, with the others, toward waiting trucks. I climbed into a truck with two other men from Gombin, Mechl Behr and Mendel Wruble. We did not know whether they were taking us to work or to our deaths. Wruble, who had a slice of bread, said: "Let's eat it, at least we'll die sated." After a half hour's ride, the truck stopped. We got off and saw people wearing striped clothes. I mused: Our chevra kadisha...

But it immediately became apparent that we were not fated for a quick death. They took us into a large hall and told us to undress, leaving on only our belts. The place looked like an ordinary bathhouse, with pipes running across the ceiling. We were certain that it was a gas chamber. The door suddenly opened and two SS camp-leaders entered, wearing black uniforms with red stripes across the back of their shoulders. We held our breaths, but they said that we were there "only" for the purpose of washing ourselves.

After the washing, we were taken to inmates who cut all our hair. Not a word passed between us. Our bodies anointed with salve, each one of us received a striped garment and a pair of wooden shoes. All that took a whole night. In the morning we were driven out early to a square where a band played music. Lining up on the square, we gazed at groups of inmates who were being taken to work. After a while our names were called out alphabetically and we had numbers tattooed on our arms. Mine turned out to be 144-212. It was the fall of 1943 and I was the 144 thousandth, 212th "work-capable" person in Auschwitz.

At noon, one of the SS camp-leaders sent two of us to bring our food. We were then broken up into smaller units that were assigned to tents. I was placed in tent 4.

Slowly we began to take stock of our surroundings. The Auschwitz complex consisted of three parts: Birkenau, Buna, and Auschwitz proper. We were in Buna, which did not have gas chambers and crematoria. That, however, did not spare anyone, since the Buna inmates who were marked to die were taken to Birkenau for gassing and cremation.

Those of us who were from Gombin, tried in every possible way to stay together. In tent 4, I was with Mechl Behr, Yankl Altman, Hersh Zeideman, Hershel Blawat and Shmuel Frenkel. Mendel Wrubel had been sent to another camp to work in the coal mines. In Buna, which was a center of factory-building activity, we were assigned the arduous task of loading coal.

In addition to Jews there were inmates of other nationalities: Poles, Dutchmen, French, Italian, Greeks, Germans and Hungarians. The non-Jews were for the most part criminal types that had been brought from maximum-security prisons. There were also political prisoners who had engaged in anti Nazi activities.

There was not much difference in the types of work assigned and performed by those groups. The only difference was that the Jews wore a six-point star of David made of two triangles: one red and one blue. The others wore one triangle: red for the political prisoners and green for the criminals. Another difference was that, every couple of weeks, the Jews underwent a selection. A "doctor" came to have a look at the inmates. Those who were sick or looked too emaciated, were forced to surrender their cards and dispatched to Birkenau for disposal by gas. Later, the Poles and Germans were sent elsewhere.

After working for six weeks on the coal pile, a kapo sent me away to work in a punitive-commando carrying stones. The work was so dreadfully heavy that the inmates dropped like flies. At the end of every workday, there were scores of dead among the rocks. On the rock pile I saw that Hershel Blawat had broken his leg carrying stones. If the Germans discovered it, they would have immediately sent him to Birkenau. We, the Gombiner group, took Blawat to our tent and succeeded in saving him.

I was fortunate that in the end they put me to work as a tailor. Conditions were better and the food rations larger. I convinced my block leader, a Pole called Vitek, to take in Blawat, whose leg was not healing properly. For this favor I sewed clothes for the Pole Vitek.

A year passed. Nearby, the death factory called Auschwitz, worked ceaselessly. Every day trains bearing Jewish victims arrived to the camp. The infirm, the elderly, the women and children were taken directly to the gas chambers. The ovens were active day and night. During the night, when the wind blew in our direction, the thick smoke from the chimneys filled our nostrils with the stench of burnt human flesh.

Elsewhere in the Auschwitz empire, there was a different kind of hell. Tens of thousands of Jewish inmates performed bone-crushing labor while hooligans were mercilessly beating them. The food we received was calculated to reduce us to cadavers within a period of three months. Every couple of weeks there was a selection and the "unfit" were led away to Birkenau and death. Their places were taken by new victims delivered by the incoming freight trains. Those who ruled over us, from the lowliest kapo to the camp's top commandant, were bloody thugs, cruel barbarians who could do with us as they pleased. Whips, clubs, revolvers, rifle butts and gallows were the symbols of their power. They took pleasure in giving their victims the most gruesome and painful death, inflicting as much suffering as possible.

Many months passed in this fashion. The millstones of Auschwitz did not cease to grind. Each one of us was exposed to the peril of death on a daily basis. In the middle of 1944, young Leizer Bocian arrived in Auschwitz. A native of Gombin, he was only a boy when they took him to the Konin labor camp, where I had taken care of him as if he were a younger brother. Now, he had been told that I was in Auschwitz and he sought me out. Our meeting was a moment of happiness for both of us. I could not have him assigned to our block, but I made arrangements to supply him with some extra food. I also did everything I could to prevent his selection for the Birkenau crematoria.

We suffered and endured until we heard the distant rumble of the heavy guns of the Russian armies. Now and then, a shell would fall inside the camp. Then, on the first of January 1945, we heard that the camp was going to be evacuated. We did not know at the time whether it would be better for us to be evacuated or hide somewhere to wait for the Russians' arrival. But the SS men did not give us much time to think about the matter. They herded us with whips, forced us to line up, and ordered us to start marching. It was a time of numbing frosts and lots of snow. Leaving Auschwitz behind, they made us walk in the middle of the road, flanked on both sides by SS men who killed anyone lagging behind. We spent the night in a brick factory and continued at dawn, walking over frozen ground and wading through deep snows. Our march lasted several days. Hundreds fell by the wayside and were left to die in the snow. Finally, we arrived to Gleiwitz concentration camp, whose inmates had been evacuated earlier.

At Gleiwitz, we were divided into two groups. One group was to continue marching on foot. The other group, including me and the other Gombiners, was loaded into open railroad cars. At that point, our Gombiner group included Abraham Mastboim, Leizer Bocian, Shmuel Frenkel, Mechl Behr and myself. We rode on the open cars for two weeks. Scores died from starvation and cold. Each time the train halted, the dead were flung into the last car. During that entire period we did not receive food even once. We ate snow and sucked ice.

As we were passing through Czechoslovakia, some people tossed bread at us, but this happened seldom. We crossed into Austria and stopped briefly in Vienna. Everywhere people gaped at us, living skeletons, with a shudder.

The train stopped at Camp Dora, situated in a forest. A large detachment of Schutzpolizei, German policemen, greeted our arrival with savage blows. Camp Dora had underground workshops for the manufacture of the V1 and V2 rockets. We spent all our time in the underground tunnels. The number of dead was huge, the corpses were piled up in front of the barracks like planks of wood.

On March 15th, we were given bread and a can of conserves. Then, they took us to open railroad cars with tarpaulin covers. Inside, it was so crowded that we had difficulty breathing. Realizing that we were going to choke to death, I got the idea of hanging a woolen blanket in the manner of a hammock, for Bocian and myself. Others followed my example. In addition, we cut little "windows" in the tarpaulin.

On the way, we were subjected to aerial bombardment. When that happened, the SS men who escorted us jumped out of the train to take cover. Two weeks later we arrived in Bergen-Belsen. Again the Gombin group managed to stay together. We moved into the attic of a house that had been occupied by the camp's officers. Our group included the brothers Shmuel and Mendl Laski, Shmuel Frenkel, Abraham Mastboim, Leizer Bocian and myself. At Bergen-Belsen we were not expected to work. By then, it was just a camp where thousands and thousands of inmates slowly expired from starvation and disease.

On April 15th, the advancing British Army reached Bergen Belsen. Breaking down the gates and entering the camp, the allied soldiers were transfixed by what they saw. There were mounds of corpses, and those who were about to die moved among them like shadows. The British immediately ordered the captured SS men to carry away the cadavers to a proper burial site. When the inmates saw that their former masters obeyed the British with displays of meekness and submission, they were seized by an uncontrollable anger. They pounced on the Nazi assassins and beat them to death. The British tried to stop the inmates, but the criminals who had spilled so much Jewish blood did not escape their proper fate.

Later, Germans living in the vicinity of Bergen-Belsen, were brought to the camp to bury the thousands of dead. When no tools were available, they were made to dig the graves with spoons and bare hands, to make them experience, if only for an instant, the meaning of the hell that Nazi Germany had inflicted on human beings. But for the vast majority of inmates, liberation did not translate into feelings of joy or a desire for vengeance. Weak and reduced to disease-ridden skeletons, we wandered aimlessly around the camp, prisoners of our own nightmares.

Saved By A Peasant Family

by Albert Greenbaum

[Original book: Pages 128-140 Yiddish and 56-66 English]

Albert Greenbaum

The Germans Occupy Gombin

On the twenty-fourth of August, 1939, at seven-thirty in the morning, I received a draft notification to report within two hours to the town hall for induction. From there, they sent me to Warsaw, to join the 21st Infantry regiment. Nobody believed, at the time, that a war was imminent. Our regiment was sent to the Mlawa region, near the East-Prussian border.

When several days later the war did in fact break out, there was not a stable front. The Germans bombarded us day and night, with airplanes, artillery, armored cars and tanks. They did not permit us a moment's respite. We were constantly retreating under the pressure of their fire that inundated us from all sides. When the German steamroller finally came to a stop, our regiment, like the rest of the Polish army, fell apart. I changed into civilian clothes and started on foot for Gombin, walking approximately fifty kilometers a day.

My parents who thought I had perished in the war were naturally overjoyed when they saw me. But soon after my homecoming, in the early hours, in fact, I was struck by the havoc caused by the Germans; half the town was in ruins from the bombardment.

The real hell began when the Germans occupied Gombin. Jewish life became worthless. The Germans kept issuing new orders, but worse than the restrictions was that a German could approach a Jew in the street, beat him savagely and rob him.

Then they began seizing Jews in the streets and pressing them into work gangs, rewarding them with blows and abuse.

On a certain day, I was attacked, near our house, by the son of the Polish stone-cutter. He kicked my head with his boots repeatedly; I thought at the time, I would lose my hearing. He would have killed me had it not been for my mother who, tears in her eyes, pleaded with him to let me go. Another time, when I worked for the town hall, a German peasant who lived on the outskirts of Gombin, Mundt by name, dragged me inside the building. There, three Germans flung themselves at me and beat me until I lost consciousness. Then they poured cold water over me and threw me out in the street.

The civilian Germans, our neighbors for many years, began to cast covetous eyes at our store at the very beginning of the occupation. But the German command let us keep the business until the end of 1940. By a stroke of good fortune, my brother later was taken on as a bookkeeper by a German and when he came home from work, he brought eggs, butter and potatoes. During that period he got married and his wife bore him a son, Izho, a very handsome boy who brought a bit of comfort and joy during those black and hopeless days. But even during the early months of his life, the boy acquired our fears. Each time the door opened, his eyes opened wide, filled with panic. Only when he saw it was one of us did he calm down and smile.

1940: In A Forced Labor Camp

In April or May, 1940, we already wore the yellow Star of David on our clothes. One night when I was fast asleep, the door of my room was smashed by a hand of Germans. They ordered me to dress quickly and dragged me to the marketplace, to a building which once housed the Bund library. Fifty terrified Jews were on the premises, when I was brought in, waiting to find out their fate. On the following morning, my mother and brother came and brought me some clothing and a little food. Soon several German S. S. men descended on us, whips in hand, formed two lines and made us run the gauntlet, beating us mercilessly as we ran, with whips, sticks and cudgels. Under the hail of blows we were chased toward waiting trucks then driven away to Gostynin. There, along with 300 Jews, we were flung inside a church. The doors were locked and we were left inside for twenty-four hours. We were crowded together, barely able to move, without a drop of water, without the most elementary sanitary facilities. It is impossible for me to describe what went on in the steaming, choking place. People simply went wild and many almost lost their minds.

On the following day, we were chased inside the trucks again, guarded by Germans with machine-guns. They drove us to Wloclawek and from there by freight-train to the work-camp Amsee (Janikowo), where we were "greeted" on arrival with fearful blows. Nursing our blows, hungry, thirsty, we were roused at dawn and dragged away to dig slit trenches. It was necessary to dig the trenches two meters in depth, one in width. The work began at six in the morning and not until evening did we receive a black liquid which they called coffee and two slices of bread. After returning from work, we received a plate of soup and a slice of bread. The cook, a Pole, beat over the head any Jew who dared ask for an additional spoonful of soup.

The head of the camp was a German, a former prizefighter. One of his diversions was to select a couple of victims whom he beat until they fell unconscious. To wash ourselves, we had to go outside. The camp was infested with insects and vermin. After several weeks even the healthiest were unrecognizable. On a certain day, three brothers tried to escape. The Germans caught them and hanged them in public, their bodies swinging a whole day.

The Germans continued bringing in new Jewish victims from the small nearby towns who told us horrendous tales which we didn't want to believe. They told us that the Germans drove large members of Jews outside towns and massacred them. Soon S. S. men began visiting our camp on Sundays and when they left, took with them ten men. Later, we heard the men were made to dig graves, then shot.

I found out, during that period, that the Germans had seized my father and flung him in a camp. I was well aware of the fate awaiting elderly Jews and lived in constant fear about what would happen to my father. During the period, too, I was assigned as a helper to a German foreman who walked around with a thick cane and beat all those who did not work rapidly.

My family made repeated efforts to free me, until I succeeded, in escaping and to return home. When I came home, it was the beginning of winter. My brother revealed to me that our father was dead. A German had killed him while he was carrying wood from the forest. My brother told me that our mother and sister did not know of the death and we kept it from them for a long time.

In those days, individuals came on occasion to Gombin and told us how they escaped from their own graves. Led with hundreds of other Jews outside town, they had been made to dig their own graves; then the Germans proceeded to mow them down with machine-guns. The few who escaped, succeeded because they played dead. After the Germans left, they clambered out of the graves and fled.

It can be imagined what impression these tales made upon us. My greatest concern was for my brother's boy, Izho. I was determined, come what may to save him. One day, I mounted my bicycle and rode out to neighboring villages, to find a friendly peasant, an acquaintance, who would take the child. I couldn't find anyone. They all refused.

My brother continued working as a book-keeper for a German firm that was in the construction business. My sister Rozia and I decided to run away from Gombin. Our plan was for my sister to go to the small town of Sierpien and pass as an "Aryan", while I tried crossing the demarcation line that separated our part of Poland from the one the Germans named "Government   General" (Generalgouvernement") where,   I hoped, conditions for the Jews were better.

On The "Aryan" Side

During one of the market-days, I found a peasant woman who agreed to take me in her cart to the border of the "Protectorate". My sister had left, as planned, to go to Sierpien. Prior to leaving, I ran home to say goodbye to my mother. But only my sister-in-law was there. To this day I can't forgive myself that I did not take leave of my mother and brother. I could not keep the peasant woman waiting too long and ran back to the mill where she stood near the cart, impatient.

It was night and bitter cold when we reached the border. She drove on and there I was alone, under the vast sky, in the middle of a winter night, not knowing what to do. I knocked on doors of several peasant huts but nobody let me in.

I spent the whole night in the open. Toward morning, I met a peasant woman who had been at one time a servant in our house. She let me enter her hut, where I remained the whole day until dark.

The woman was to find a smuggler who would take me across the border. She went out to search for one, finally coming back to inform me that the border was well-guarded and nobody wanted to risk taking a Jew across. Staying on in her hut was out of the question, so I left and emerged in the burning frost. I began walking and gazing into the windows of the peasant huts, hoping someone would admit me. I finally came across on old man who let me enter his barn and spend the night. He warned me I must leave with daybreak.

There lived in this village a peasant named Chabar who at one time had been a customer in my parents' store. I asked the old peasant where Chabar lived and he told me. I went to his shack and Chabar let me in. But I perceived that I could not remain there for any length of time as people kept coming all day long and each time someone came, I was forced to run and hide. My situation was unbearable. Chabar, who was eager to help me, suddenly remembered there was a peasant in the village who was friendly to Jews. His name was Grabarek.

Mrs. Grabarek brings me food
to the barn where I was hiding

After darkness descended, he took me to Grabarek's dwelling that consisted of two huts. Both huts were filled with people. In addition to Grabarek and his wife and their four children, there lived two old Poles who had been sent out of their villages. Chabar did not introduce me as a Jew. He said I was a Pole from Poznan who at one time carted stones, when they were building a road to Lonsk. He told me I could remain three days with him and pay him well for it. Grabarek did not suspect I was Jewish and agreed. His wife immediately prepared supper and we sat down at the table. During the meal I became aware of the fact that the two elderly peasants were whispering and darting sharp glances at me. Obviously, I mused, they knew I was a Jew. But they did not say anything about it.

After supper, Grabarek started with me for the barn where I was to spend the night. Walking toward the barn, a very strange thing occurred; I cannot explain it to this day. But it saved my life. As we were nearing the barn, a huge dog suddenly came hurtling out of the dark, barking fearfully. The dog was so wild and mean, his owner kept him leashed day and night. But as it happened, Grabarek had forgotten to tie him up. As the dog sprang towards me, Grabarek feared he would tear me to bits. But here something inexplicable occurred. Instead of attacking me, the dog stopped as though transfixed. The peasant stared at his animal in astonishment and raised his hand to cross himself. This incident evidently convinced him that I was not to be taken for an ordinary mortal. When the three days were over, he let me stay on.

The condition for my staying on, naturally, was bound up with my paying him a large sum of money. Buy this was not the worst of it. My staying at Grabarek's was bound up with other difficulties that were growing more complex every day.

I knew that my sister, Rozia was on the "Aryan" side, in the small town of Sierpien, where she lived as a Christian and I began writing to her. We had made up that she will answer my letters on Chabar's address, the only person in the village who knew I was Jewish. Chabar thus became the intermediary between my sister and me. But soon it became apparent that the enterprise was fraught with danger. The letters, it appeared, instead of going directly to Chabar, arrived at the Town Hall, where the old Grabarek, father of the peasant with whom I was staying, became suspicious. One day he came to the house and pointing at me, said I was a Jew who will someday bring misfortune upon the whole village. He demanded his son send me away immediately, or he would tell the Germans. The younger Grabarek became panicky and was ready to send me away. But I pleaded with his wife, suggesting to her that she tell her father-in-law they had sent me away. Fortunately, she agreed and prevailed upon her husband to do the same. I wrote to my sister, instructing her to stop writing me to Chabar's address and to send the letters directly to me, addressed to one of the elderly Poles. The matter appeared settled but for me there began a period of unrelieved hell.

Until now, I had been able to show my face before people under the guise of a Pole who ran away from the "Reich." But from now on I was forced to hide and not be seen by strange eyes. It meant that outside Grabarek, his wife, their children and the two elderly Poles, nobody in the village must know of my presence. It became necessary to find a hiding place.

The peasant's dwelling consisted of two huts, the second of which had a door leading to the stable, where the Grabareks kept their cow and pigs. During the first few months, I stood for days on end by the window and when someone came near the house, I fled to the stable. This was very tiring and a drain on my emotions, as well. Early in the spring, when Grabarek began to trim his trees, I suggested he place the branches and twigs on a fence and thus make a shelter where I could spend the daylight hours, unnoticed.

The place proved effective as a hiding place, but after a couple of weeks my bones were so stiff, I couldn't stand it any longer. Later, when the wheat in the field grew to its full height, instead of hiding among the branches, I spent my days among the stalks in the field, returning to the stable at night. But lying in the field also had its disadvantages because of the sun that burned pitilessly during the day. Having no alternatives, I lay still, fearing I might bump into some stranger if I rose.

Fortunately, another occurrence took place strengthening my position among the superstitious peasants. One day, while I hid in the field, a gypsy entered the house and told everyone's fortune. Grabarek called me from the field, insisting that I too have my fortune told. I begged him to let me off. Some stranger might enter the house while I was present. But Grabarek was not to be put off. He virtually led me back to the house and nudged me into a chair beside the gypsy.

And again an inexplicable thing happened. No sooner did the gypsy take my hand than she said to the peasants: "This man is a very good friend to you. He suffered much sorrow until now on account of his near ones. But anyway, the person who is very near to him and himself, too, will survive and have a bright future from which all of you will benefit."

The gypsy's words made a deep impression on the peasants. I could discern by their glance that they now held me to be an asset instead of a liability.

The gypsy could not have come at a more propitious time. I had spent all my money and did not have any left with which to pay my host. I had promised Grabarek to reward him a hundredfold, after the war. Now, having heard what the gypsy said, they were inclined to believe what I had promised.

In the meantime, my situation turned for the worse. The wheat having been cut down, I could not lie in the field any longer. I therefore suggested to Grabarek's wife that we dig a pit in the clay beneath the path leading to the stable and the entrance of the pit be covered with straw. After this was done, I would climb down in the morning and remain in the pit until night. But it soon became apparent that the idea was not a very good one. In the first place, the pit was damp and dark and my clothes were soaked through; secondly, the Germans who often came to the peasants in search of pigs, sometimes dug underground for their quarry.

We decided to fill up the pit and find a new hiding place. Stacking the wheat in the stable, we hollowed a little "chamber", with an entrance to the pig-sty. It could not have occurred to anyone that a human being took shelter in this "chamber". There I lay days on end. When I went out, I covered the entrance with straw and dirt. Thus the matter of a hiding place was for the time being solved. During the day I lay hidden in the wheat, at night in the stable. Now, however, new trials arose.

The cause of the new difficulties was the two old Poles whom the Grabareks accused of eating too much. The two old men fought back. "Why", they demanded, "have you sharp eyes for what *we* eat but feed the damn Jew for nothing?" Because of the argument and sudden accusations that the children too ate more than they should, the Grabareks' fourteen year old daughter ran away from the house. I was terrified lest she talk about me to the peasants in the village. But she came back at night, having spent the day in the fields as a protest against her parents' accusations.

To calm the frayed nerves, I reasoned with the peasants that it was not worthwhile to argue over bread and potatoes because after the termination of the war I would reward them for everything. My little talk had its desired effect and the arguments about excessive eating stopped. But for each problem that was solved, a new one emerged.

It suddenly became necessary for me to be doubly careful. In the first place, Grabarek hired a peasant to help him dig potatoes. This hired hand made it a habit of hanging around the stable all night long, intending to steal from the neighboring peasants. So it became necessary for me to be on guard at night, as well as during the day; the tiniest bit of noise might betray my presence. Added to this new peril was even a greater misfortune.

One day Grabarek said to his wife: "Since you took a damn Jew into the house, I'm going to take in three partisans".

Soon they arrived, three young Poles, who remained in the house until the day of liberation. Now my life was in constant peril, making it necessary for me to lie motionless in the wheat "chamber" during the day and at night - in the stable, paralyzing my limbs. My existence became an endless torture.

To my physical difficulties were added moral ones. Returning from the fair one day, the Grabareks told me of a peasant family that was found by the Germans to conceal a Jew. All concerned were shot: husband, wife, their little children, as well as the Jew. I beard Grabarek saying to his wife that day: "If they discover us, I won't wait till they shoot you. On the way to the execution place I will beat you to death".

On another occasion, as I was hiding at the entrance to the hut, I heard him telling his wife: "I can't chase him out. He might inform on us that we hid him. But I got hold of a revolver. I will kill him and bury him someplace and nobody will know".

The Grabarek woman said: "I couldn't endure it if you did such a thing. Yanek's (that is what they called me) sad eyes would always accuse me".

I began to live in constant fear that Grabarek would enter my hiding place at any time and kill me. I wrote a letter to my sister to be prepared for "any eventuality".

The nearer the war's end came, the worse became my situation. My hiding was bound up with new and greater perils. One day Polish policemen, searching for pigs, stumbled on my hiding place. By some miracle they failed to see me but I had no difficulty making out their faces. On another occasion, the Germans came to make a search for someone who thrashed one of their men. Then too they were only a hair removed from my hiding place. A third time, someone came to the stable to steal wheat. Catching sight of me, the thief seized a piece of wood to strike. He would have killed me, had I not jumped aside just in time. Then he fled, believing he'd encountered the owner.

To add to my trouble, Grabareks' daughter married and a new person was added to the household from whom I had to hide. There were now four persons in the house - the three partisans and the son-in-law - who were not to know of my existence.

In the meantime, an uprising broke out in Warsaw and one of those evacuated from that city came to stay with the Grabareks. This added another person from whom I had to hide. But in addition, the new tenant liked to keep busy; he came every night to the stable, where I lay hidden and made brooms and besoms out of twigs. Lying there, hearing his every breath, I was afraid to make a move; if I heard him breathing, he certainly would hear the rustling of the wheat.

To add to my difficulties, there appeared one night in my hiding place a water mouse. I lived in constant fear of being bitten, while asleep, by this mouse that I knew was poisonous. I told my hosts about it and we all started a hunt for the intruder. We blocked all exits and the mouse was forced into my area and I killed it.

No matter bow careful I was, it was inevitable that I be seen on occasion by persons who were not supposed to know of my presence. Several times I saw at close range and from a distance   the partisans who stayed with my host, the son-in-law and even the peasant who made brooms in the stable. But each time I fled and Grabarek made up a story that it was someone passing through the village.

One day I received an alarming letter from my sister, informing me she was in great danger. In order to maintain the fiction that she was a pure "Aryan," and to conceal her Jewish appearance, she periodically washed her hair with hydrogen peroxide to impart to it a blond color. But now she had run short of the peroxide and soon her hair would revert to its natural brown, unless she could get hold of the precious liquid. Could I help her?

I pleaded with the Grabareks to go to the neighboring town and buy at the apothecary's a bottle of peroxide. But they would not hear of it.

As my sister's life was at stake, I warned the Grabareks that I would go myself and risk being caught. But this too proved of no avail. Finally, Grabarek used the incident with the peroxide to try and blackmail me. As my money had run out, he said, and as the war dragged on interminably and he would have to wait a very long time before collecting his reward, he insisted that I start earning money and pay my keep. To begin with, he suggested, I might help him thresh the wheat, although this was bound up with great peril, as someone might come in and see me. Later, be demanded that I go out and steal. His plan was for me to burglarize the neighbors at night and bring him the loot. It goes without saying I would not hear of it; but Grabarek returned to the matter of the peroxide for my sister's hair. If, he suggested, I stole several chicken from the neighbor, he Grabarek, would go to the apothecary's for the peroxide. I had no alternative and acquiesced. But the manner in which I carried out my part of the bargain, was designed to discourage Grabarek from such adventures in the future; instead of taking two or three chickens the night I stole into the neighbors' yard, I took fifteen. Twisting their necks, I brought my haul to Grabarek. Shocked, my host stared at the dead fowl, fearing the neighbor would surely sound the alarm on the following morning. He grabbed the chickens and got rid of them, somehow, instructing me not to go out and steal again on his behalf. Then he went to the apothecary's and bought the peroxide, which I sent to my sister.

The end of 1944 was drawing near. It became daily more apparent that the Germans who were suffering reverses on all fronts, would be compelled to leave our village. But the nearer we drew to the end, the more difficult became my situation.

The Germans, we beard over and over again, although on their last legs, did not cease for an instant their hunt for hidden Jews whom they murdered, when they found them, along with those who had given them shelter. As the retreating Germans neared our village, the fear and terror preceded them. One day several wagons full of Ukrainians dressed in German uniforms arrived in the village. My hosts feared the Ukrainians would invade their stable and take the straw and find me. It was decided to find another hiding place for me, temporarily. There was a recess behind the stable wall with enough room only to stand erect. Here the Grabareks put me and kept me for four days.

What made the ordeal bearable was the knowledge that the front was daily coming nearer. Soon one heard the bombing of Russian artillery. But because of the altered military situation and the ensuing chaos I lost contact with my sister.

Prior to this, in one of our last letters, we pledged to return to Gombin, after it was all over, and there be reunited. And that is what happened.

Liberation And Reunion

In the house the refrain became louder about the Germans fleeing west, often leaving their arms behind. My isolation in the hiding place became daily more unbearable, but the Grabareks would not let me out. There were reports that the Germans, even with their dying gasp, continued searching for Jews. In one of the neighboring villages, it was said, a couple of Jews were discovered and shot with their Polish hosts.

One day, the three partisans who lived in the Grabarek house dug out their guns and left. A day later, we heard one of the partisans had been killed attempting to disarm a German. Despite the fact that German demise was near, the peril was still very great. All the roads and paths were blocked by German wagons, trucks and motorcycles. The sound of Russian artillery drew nearer daily. I lay in my hiding place in a feverish state wondering whether I would survive these final hours. The Grabareks insisted I must be more careful now than in the past and I obeyed. But I longed to go out and behold with my own eyes the humiliation and defeat of history's most bloodthirsty murderers.

Finally a day came and the shooting ceased. The Grabareks informed me there was not any longer a German in sight but it was advisable for me to stay in hiding and avoid unpleasant surprises. That day darkness came early. It was a wintry day, January 1945. In the middle of the night there was a loud knocking on the door. The Grabareks opened and saw Russian soldiers who asked for a place to spend the night. Among the Russians were several women attired in military uniforms. Grabarek ran inside the stable, roused me and said: "Come. You can come out now. Our liberators have come.

I followed Grabarek into the house. I gazed at the Russian uniform, at their insignia: the hammer and sickle. But I was too spent to feel or display any joy. The Russians paid no more attention to me than they did to the others, taking all of us to be Polish peasants. There were a couple of bottles of vodka on the table and Grabarek was soon drunk. He embraced me and said: "Well, what do you say now? I rescued you, eh?"

His son-in-law could not get over the fact that I had been hiding in the house all this time without his discovering it. Mrs. Grabarek and the children appeared genuinely happy that I had survived.

I was to leave for Gombin in the morning but my hosts counseled me not to do it; the roads were still unsafe, infested as they were by retreating Germans and hostile Poles.

Helena and Vladislav Garbarik, who saved my life
during the Nazi occupation. In the middle: their boy Stanislau

I remained with the Grabareks three days longer. I did not even venture into the village, reluctant to test the peasants' reaction to a living Jew. But on the fourth day my patience had run out. I said goodbye to my hosts and asked permission of several Russian soldiers in a truck if I could ride with them.

They let me mount and we started off. My fear and premonition increased with every passing mile. When we were quite near Gombin, I asked the driver to let me off; I would go the rest of the way on foot.

I got off and walked. Nearing my town, tears filled my eyes. I did not encounter one person; it was a cold day and the people remained indoors.

Approaching Nowy Rynek, I met a former neighbor, Tadeusz Jankowski. His face brightened and he flung his arms around me. As his house was directly across the street of ours, I asked him: "Has my sister come back?" It was the first question I put to him.

"No," he replied and led me into his house. There I met his wife and children and they all seemed genuinely happy to see me.

Jankowski informed me that some strangers were occupying our house. At first, the Germans lived there, but several days ago they left and a Polish family moved in. I ate a warm meal and went across the street to our house and knocked on the door. There was no reply. The "owners" were not at home. I waited until they came back and told them the house was mine and demanded they leave. They regarded me without saying a word.

I went inside. Everything seemed familiar and yet strange. The old feeling of cozy intimacy had evaporated. The walls were permeated with the odor of Germans and Poles who lived here for three years. My eyes filled with tears, I started a fire in the oven and lay down to sleep.

I spent a whole week in the empty house. Although I was in constant peril of being murdered by some hostile Pole in my sleep, I remained in the house, clinging to the window from morning till night, hoping for my sister to come.

And it finally came to pass. On the eighth day of my watch, I heard someone at the door. The movements, it seemed to me, were familiar. Bathed in sweat as though I had a fever, I flung myself at the door and opened it. There stood my sister.

Survived as an "Aryan"

by Rose Greenbaum-Dinerman

[Original book: Pages 116-127 Yiddish and 67-78 English]

Rose Greenbaum-Dinerman

There were four of us siblings in the family, three brothers and myself, the youngest. My parents were well-known not only to the Jewish population of Gombin but among the Gentiles, as well. My father purchased wheat from peasants in surrounding villages and sent it to Kutno, Plock and Warsaw. In addition my parents owned a motion picture theater which they built themselves after the first World War. At the beginning, our cinema was called "Polonia", later renamed "Adria". In the building housing the cinema, there occasionally appeared Yiddish theatrical ensembles traveling through the province. My parents also had a food store in our Gombin house. Everything my parents did had one purpose: to achieve security and a better life for their children. But fate willed it otherwise...

The summer of 1939 was a pleasant one. September appeared full of promise. But along with the splendor of nature, the bloody was suddenly burst over our heads.

The Germans fell upon Poland on the first day of September 1939. In spite of the fact that Gombin did not have military installations, they bombarded us for three days in a row, sowing death and destruction among the helpless populace.

When the bombs began to rain upon us, we ran to the fields for shelter. My father stayed behind, refusing to leave the house. He spent most of his time aiding the wounded and the maimed.

Then the Germans entered Gombin and transformed the life of the Jews into a gehenna. Soon after their arrival, the Gemans rounded up all Jewish males between the ages offifteen and sixty-five and took them to the large synagigue, which had the reputation of being one of the finest in Poland. They put the synagogue to the torch and burnt it down. The assembled Jews were pushed and shoved toward the billowing flames, beaten savagely all the time. My brother, Stan, was among those beaten and tortured; he hardly escaped with his life.

Every passing day the Germans beat their drum and announced new disabling decrees aimed at the Jews. The Jews were ordered, from start, to turn in their gold, pay all kinds of fines and wear the yellow Star of David on the chest and shoulder. We were forbidden to walk on the sidewalks - only the middle of the road. We were ordered to clean up the debris caused by the German bombardment and to keep the business establishment closed.

The disabling decrees multiplied daily and life became unbearable.

One day, twenty German soldiers poured into our house, led by a young Gentile, Albert Fatt, the son of a German, who used to deal with my father. The Germans said they came to search for weapons; but this was nothing but a badly-disguised lie.

The Germans turned our house upside down, taking away all objects of value. Many of the things which they seized, Albert brought outside, where a crowd of Poles assembled to enjoy the pogrom. I had been away from home, returning in the middle of this scene. Seeing me approach, Fatt pointed the gun at me, threatening to kill my whole family, myself included, unless I revealed where we hid the weapons.

"You can search wherever you please," I told him. "You know very well we don't have any weapons."

Shortly, the Germans emptied my father's store room of the wheat and went through the legalistic ritual of signing for it.

On the following Christmas it turned colder. On that day there arrived from Lodz a Gestapo man who walked the streets of Gombin and wheneve he saw a Jew, beat him with a rubber truncheon. He broke into Jewish homes, ordered the women to remove all their clothes and beat them witin an inch of their lives.

One day, accompanied by two other Germans, the Gestapo man entered Sala Luszinska's house, where the three of tem got drunk; later they broke into the Rosen's dwelling, where the Tiber family who had a girl of eleven and a boy of six, lived. The besotted Germans ordered the little girl to accompany them. Pleas and tears proved no avail. They took the girl with them. The parents ran to the Jewish Committee, to the police, the mayor, pleading for her release. A day later, she was found in the field, dead naked, violated.

The despondent parents never recovered from the blow. The mother would not let anyone tear her away from the girl's grave; she died several months later.

The kidnapping of Gombin Jews on the streets to be pressed into work gangs, the beatings and the tortures became a daily occurrence. But the news trickling in from surrounding towns was even more gruesome. The Jews of Kutno were all ordered by the Nazis to abandon their dwellings and move into a vacant factory. Early in 1941, the Jews of Kutno, Kolo and other towns were deported to the Chelmno death camp. It was the first time we heard of vans in which Jews were being gassed to death, of mass graves, of Jews being forced t dig graves then being shot and buried in them. At the start, none of us lent any credence to these stories, but daily the evidence increased that what we did not wish to believe was a fact of life.

Early in the fall, the finger of death began to point at Gombin. At first, the Germans deported a hundred young Jews to the Amsee forced labor camp. My brother, Albert, was among the first to be taken. They came for him in the middle of the night. His hands trembled when he got dressed to follow them. My brother, Stan, who was married, ran to the Judenrat, accompanied by our mother and myself, to plead for Albert. But it was to no avail. Depondent, we stood by, gazing at our loved ones being loaded onto open trucks and driven away to the camp.

In the fall of 1941, the Germans issued a decree interring the Jews of Gombin in two Ghettos. One of the ghettos was near the forest, the other was along both sides of Cobbler Street, not far from the cemetery. We were forced to leave our house and moved into dentist Greenbaum 's dwelling. Soon afterwards, the Germans issued another decree: head-tax. From two Jews who escaped from Kolo, we found out that the head-tax was the beginning of the end, that after this decree the deportations began.

One night we heard heavy foot steps nearby, blows and screams. Our door flew open and a German entered. His murderous gaze fell on my father whom he ordered to dress and accompany him. We knew they would send my fater to a camp, but all our pleas and tears and words to the effect that our father was old and unsuited for heavy work proved to no avail. With the arrival o dawn, we made up a package of food and clothing and I took it to the town garage where the Jews were being held, pending deportation. I found my father deep inside the garage, sitting in the company of his friends : Zalman Kerber, Yankl Klinger, Yankl Tiber, the teacher Frenkel and others. When he saw me, my father's face became even more somber, as my coming was a perilous thing and might end tragically for us both.

My father's last words to me were: *"Don't lose courage, daughter, our enemy's end is near..."* We embraced and I left. I never saw my father again.

My father's letters from the camp were comforting and uncomplaining. He seemed determined to cause us no anxiety. But from others we learned that conditions in the camp were unbearable. We sent food parcels, but he received only a couple of them, as they deported him to another place.

The last letter we received from my father was from Libernu, a camp in Poznan.

One day we received a letter, but it was not from my father; it was from the Jewish congregation informing us briefly about my father's death. According to them, he died in the following manner: he had gone to the forest to chop wood for the camp; on the road he was struck by a Gestapo motorcycle and died of a hemorrhage.

My father did not live to receive the last parcel we sent him, nor did he live to witness the enemy's demise, for which he so fervently hoped and prayed. Tragic was his death and sacred his memory.

The numbing frosts came early in the winter of 1941. It was so cold, each morning children were found frozen to death. During that period, my brother Albert, accompanied by two young men, Rosenberg and Zalmen Bressler, ran away from camp and returned to Gombin. We sat in our house and talked about the possibilities of saving our lives. My brother and his friends brought up the notion about seeking shelter on the "Aryan" side, outside the ghetto. But we had heard not long ago about the four Zychlin girls who fled from the ghetto to the "Aryan" side and there, found by the Germans, were shot to death. Our mood was a despondent one. It occurred to us that instead of dying by the Nazi hand, we take our own lives. But we also knew that we must cling to life to the very end, no matter how small our chances of survival, to spite our enemy.

Soon afterward, it was decided that my brother Albert and myself try to break out of the ghetto, as our only chance of remaining alive. My brother left first and my turn came on March 17.

I rose early, said goodbye to my mother. She wept, embraced me and said: "*Remember, no matter what happens to us, you must do all you can to live.*" My brother's son, Izho was asleep. I stood for a long time over his little bed, gazing at his bright, innocent face.

My eyes filled with tears, I left the house, accompanied by my brother and sister-in-law who took me to a waiting cart which was to take me to the peasant village of Szczegowo, in East Prussia. According to rumors, the Germans' murder gangs were less in evidence there than in the "Government General" and chances of survival were better.

Riding on the cart along with me, was a Jewish couple named Glass, who had relatives in Szczegowo. They assured me that on arrival at our destination, their relatives would help me.

The day was cold, the sky seeded with dark clouds. Snow began falling on us who sat in deep silence, wrapped in our own thoughts.

After we'd covered ten kilometers without incident, there suddenly emerged from the blinding snow a man who stopped the cart in which we were riding and asked the driver: "*Who are your passengers?*"

"*'Wealthy Jews,*" the driver replied.

The stranger measured us with a sharp gaze, left and soon returned, accompanied by a German policeman. The policeman ordered our driver to a nearby courtyard. The Glass couple trembled with fear and my heart beat wildly.

We were led into a room full of uniformed Germans: Their first order was for us to give them all we owned: money, gold; diamonds. They searched us but found nothing. After detaining us for hours, they took us back to the cart and said we would now be taken to the Gestapo head-quarters. Hearing the word Gestapo, my blood froze. But most frightened was Glass, who had a bad heart. He seemed crushed by the news, his face pale, his lips trembling. He appeard on the point of a heart attack.

The distance between the courtyard and the Gestapo headquarters was short. A German soldier led us inside. We saw behind a large, shiny desk a German who appeared to be in his fifties. He regarded us with his blue-green eyes, then turning to me inquired whether the Glass couple were my relatives. I replied in the negative and pleaded with him to have pity on my "old mother" and let me go back to her. He grew thoughtful for an instant and it seemed to me I noticed in his eyes a spark of human empathy.

Suddenly two young well-fed Gestapo men came in from another room. They did not come near us, but remained at a distance, gazing at us with disgust, as of our presence in the room made the air unclean. Gazing into the eyes of these men, made me shudder. These were the eyes of sadists and murderers. A moment later, they left the room. The older man who sat behind the desk, followed them. We heard them conversing behind the door, first in even tones, then shrilly and loudly. Soon the older man returned, his breath wheezing. A tall Gestapo man followed him and motioned with his finger to Glass. The sick old man rose and followed the Gestapo man; his wife who stayed behind, turned chalk white. An instant later we heard piercing cries of pain that chilled the heart. Then Glass came stumbling in, white foam at the corners of his mouth, his body trembling. The husky, red-headed Gestapo man turned toward me and roared: "Come here!" I followed him into a large room in the center of which was a large table, its top a forest of large spikes. On the floor were large metal chains. The windows were laced with iron bars. The four Gestapo huskies ordered me to take off my coat. One of them demanded I give them my gold, money, diamonds and other valuables; if I failed to comply and if any found anything on my person, they would beat me to death. I reached for a kerchief in which I had tied a watch and a gold ring and was about to give it to them, when one of the Gestapo men said: Put away that dirty handkerchief you dirty Jewess!"

I was ordered to bend over a chair. An instant later, the red-headed husky stood over me with a rubber truncheon in his ham-like hands. I fell on my knees and bent my body over the chair and the German began to beat me. Suddenly, goaded by the unbearable pain, I turned and grabbed the rubber truncheon and actually wrested it from him as strength surged through my body from some inexplicable source. His anger rising to fever pitch, he pulled the truncheon out of my hands and began striking me with the handle.

Each blow was a knife-thrust. The pain was maddening and I screamed wildly. When he stopped to rest, I rose to my feet, seized my coat and ran to the door. Nobody made an effort to stop me. I ran past the older German who sat behind his desk and the Glass couple who huddled in the corner. I plunged for the door and emerged on the street. Outside, I ran the length of two blocks before stopping exhausted, gasping for breath. A curious calmness possessed me as I turned a grievous glance at the Gestapo building.

Approximately an hour later the Glass couple emerged from the Gestapo building. They walked slowly, barely able to raise their feet from the ground. Their faces were tear- stained as they held on to each other like two children lost in a storm. The old woman was in a bad way; I thought her end was near. The cart in which we had been riding, was waiting for us. We got in and continued our interrupted journey to Szczegowo. The Glass relatives were on hand to greet them. That night, the woman died of a heart attack.

Life in Szczegowo was a little less hectic than in Gombin, but this did not last long. Jewish refugees began arriving from various towns, from Mlawa, Gostynin and Sierpce. Living conditions became progressively worse. The Germans rationed our water for which we stood in long lines. But one was more secure here than at home and I began thinking about bringing the family. After several inquiries, I found a young Jew who undertook to do it for me. Lindenbaum by name, a dental technician by trade, he planned to go to Gombin to buy instruments. On his return, he promised to bring my mother, my brother Stan, his wife and seven-month old boy.

Several days later Lindenbaum did in fact come back, but instead of my family, he brought us the dreadful news that Gombin Jewry was no more.

The end came in the following manner: on the 17th of April, the ghetto was surrounded by the Germans. Then they went in, gun and truncheon in hand. They beat those who were well and shot to death the sick. Among their first victim were Leizer Kot and Helena Zychlinska. My mother was seen heading toward the deportation point, dragging a parcel of clothes. She threw away the clothes, as they were heavy. A German began raining blows on her, ordering her to pick up the package. The cries of the people as they were being driven to the deportation point, rose to heaven.

The Gombin Jews were held for three days near a forest, without food or drink. The men were separated from the women and the women from the children; the young from the old. From Christians I found out later that mother succeeded in escaping from the clutches of the Germans and hiding with a peasant family. But some Poles informed on her and she was dragged out, beaten murderously and brought back to the group held near the forest. On the following day, the people were taken by trucks to their death. The road was soaked with blood. In this manner did the Jewish town of Gombin come to an end.

Conditions in Szczegowo grew daily worse. People were being seized in the streets and put to work; they were arrested and murdered. One of the first victims was Lindenbaum whom the Germans wounded, then buried alive. He was twenty two years old.

The terror increased. One day, the Germans put up fifteen gallows in the middle of the marketplace. They hanged fifteen Jews in the presence of the whole populace which had been forced to witness the gruesome ceremony. One of the victims, an instant before the noose tightened, cried: *"Long live freedom! Death to the murderers!"* The man's defiant cry died in his throat as the noose tightened. Blood-curdling sobs and shrieks filled the marketplace as the Germans rained blows on the people and the families of the fifteen victims who watched them dangling from ropes.

It was then I began seriously thinking about running away to the "Aryan" side. My hair which was black, I dyed blonde and left Szczegowo for a nearby village. The first peasant household where I inquired, had a bed for me. The peasant who knew I was Jewish, entrusted me with the task of teaching his children. I also worked out in the fields and learned how to milk a cow. During my leisure time, I studied by myself, in privacy.

At the time, the Germans issued a decree forbidding Jews from leaving the ghetto under the pain of death. On my part, I made up my mind that my only chance of survival was to go to the "Aryan" side and assume the role of a Christian. I could not go on staying with the peasant, who knew I was Jewish.

I put on several summer dresses, made a parcel of the rest, and started out. I recalled being told by a Jewish inhabitant of Szczegowo that in the vicinity of Koszcebrodi, not far from Sherpts, the Poles were less antagonistic toward the Jews than elsewhere.

I asked one final favor from the peasant: to take me part way to my destination in his cart. He complied, trembling from fear the whole of our journey. Arriving at the road, where I was to proceed on my own, he urged me to get off and quickly disappeared.

I remained alone in the middle of the road. What was one to do? Where does one go? In the distance, across a vast field, I saw a spot which I judged to be a house. I started across the field, in the direction of the house, my spirits buoyed. Nearing the dwelling, I pushed open the door, went in and called out in a loud voice: *"Jesus be praised!"* I paused, waiting for a reaction to my words on the part of the people in the room. Had they recognized my being Jewish? But apparently they did not recognize it because they replied: "Through all eternity, amen!"

I told them I was on way to a funeral in Yunieck, but lacked a German permission; could they tell me how to get there without attracting attention?

They obliged by showing me a path and I left in a good frame of mind, having passed my first "Aryan" test.

Out on the road again, I approached a peasant with a cart and told him I was sick and on the way to a doctor. Would he take me along? I did in fact look sick, my hands trembling. The peasant nodded assent and I got on. We rode until we reached a forest. I thanked the peasant for the ride and got off. I entered the forest. Dark began descending. The thought uppermost in my mind was: where would I spend the night?

I spied a little tumble-down shack among the trees, went towards it and knocked. A voice from the inside asked: " *Who is there?*"

I opened the door and said:

"*Jesus be praised!*"

The people in the room came back with the refrain: "*Through all eternity, amen!*"

I told them I was on my way to a funeral. Would they allow me to spend the night? Their friendliness surprised me. They fed me and put me up for the night. In the morning, they assured me I could stay longer if I wished. But I thanked them and left. Later, I regretted, not having accepted their kind offer to stay.

I spent the day walking across many roads and paths. The shadows of evening began to descend. I picked out one of the sturdier dwellings, knocked on the door and went in, saying: "*Jesus be praised!*" I then asked for permission to spend the night. I was invited to join them at the evening meal. After we ate, I was asked to show my identification paper. I took out a paper, one I wrote myself and signed with my assumed Christian name. Later, I retired for the night, but at two in the morning, my hostess woke me and said I must get up and leave; they could not let me stay as they did not know who I was. She told me to go to the German police and ask for written permission to stay. But before going to the police, she suggested I stop to consult the village head.

A sickening fear gripped me. All now depended on how I would do in my role as a Christian.

My hosts took me to the village head and left. The man was friendly and tried putting me at my ease. My hosts, he said, suspected I was Jewish. I struck a pose of one maligned. But the village head, maintaining his friendly tone, suggested it was best for me to leave the village without delay.

The night was cold and pitch black. I started across meadows and fields, gazing up at the sky thick with clouds. Around me the stillness was that of a tomb. My eyes filled with tears of despondency. All hope was drained out of me. My legs could barely carry me. Suddenly I perceived a small light. Coming closer, I realized it was a little mud hut. I knocked, the door opened. In front of me stood a woman of about thirty, with a Jewish appearance. The hut, I saw, consisted of one room, with a table in the center, a couple of benches and an oven.

I told her half the truth that the rich peasants with whom I was spending the night, had become suspicious of me and the village head ordered me to leave.

The woman heard me out and startled me by saying I could spend the night in her place, in fact, I could stay as long as I wished. She told me she had a son of eight. Her husband, a chimney-sweeper, traveled around in surrounding villages, coming home on Sundays. She worked for others, supplementing their income. She showed me the hut and the little alcove, where she kept a pig.

I will never forget her warm, friendly tone. But I declined her invitation to stay. Her dwelling was too near the village where they suspected me of being Jewish. I rose at dawn and left quietly, without a sound, not wishing to wake the others.

After walking several kilometers, I came to a body of water, spanned by a frail-looking little wooden bridge that groaned and swayed underfoot. I was afraid to cross it. Out of nowhere there appeared a young Pole who offered to help me across. Judging by his tone of voice, he harbored no suspicion of me.

The brief encounter boosted my sagging spirits and gave me the courage to go on. My goal was the village of Yavorovo, where I hoped to get in touch with the Polish family, Soldanski. I had been given the name by a Jew in Szczegowo who told me the Soldanskis were friendly toward Jews. I inquired after these people and was told where to find them. When I arrived there, two families lived in the house.

I knocked on one of the doors. It was opened by a young Pole. I greeted him in a calm tone of voice. I told him a fictitious tale about my family having been deported by the Germans to perform slave labor, while I escaped and was now seeking a place to stay for the time being. He asked me to come in. Inside, I met three of his younger brothers. I gathered from their conversation that they were five brothers, all living under this roof. Their parents were dead. The oldest brother, who came home several hours later, was not averse to helping out a Polish woman who managed to escape the German clutches. On the contrary, he deemed it a patriotic act. He volunteered to provide me with false identification papers; as one who escaped German slave labor, I could not use mine.

The other half of the house was occupied by their uncle, his wife and two daughters, one seventeen-year old, the other - seven.

I concluded it would be a good idea to make myself useful to both families. As soon as I became part of the household, I began thinking about my brother.

This much I knew about my brother's circumstances: he was hiding in a peasant's hut in a village. I had his address and wrote him a letter. This was the first instance when he was provided with evidence that I was still among the living. Subsequently, all our ordeals notwithstanding, we maintained contact with each other through letters. We realized that we were the family's only survivors, that we were fate's play things. The letters we wrote to each others gave us courage and the will to survive.

My first few days in the Soldanski household passed without incident. It occurred to me that my life was entering a period of relative security; I might, in my new guise as a Christian, survive the Nazi deluge. But fate willed it otherwise.

Of the five Soldanski brothers, the oldest displayed the most kindness, while the youngest proved the most hostile. He began arousing his brothers against me, warning them of the terrible consequences owing to the fact that I did not possess the proper papers. The situation became so aggravated, the oldest one took me to a cousin of his who was reputed to be a communist. But it became immediately apparent, during our conversation, that the communist was at the same time a vicious anti-Semite. *"The only positive thing the Germans are doing,"* he said, *"is killing Jews."* I did not remain there very long. The host told me to take my things and leave.

It was the middle of winter. Outside the house, the snow lay thick on the ground. Where was I to go? A young Pole - he was the peasant's son - took pity on me and told me of a family living nearby that needed a servant-girl. He showed me in what direction to go and left. Barely dragging my feet in the snow, I managed to make it to the hut, gasping for breath. I knocked on the door and when a woman opened it, told her I heard she needed help. She led me inside a large kitchen and told me to wait. She left and came back fifteen minutes later to inform me I could stay for the duration of the cold weather. On the following morning, I began doing my chores. I milked the cow, knitted sweaters and helped in the kitchen. Three weeks passed without incident or suspicion. But one Sunday, a friend of the household, a Pole named Tobtshinsky, came to call. This man, whom the Germans appointed manager of the dairy, did not take his eyes off me. After he'd had his fill of staring, he took aside my hosts and talked to them in whispers.

His visit sealed my fate. Several days later, the woman of the house informed me that I could not remain any longer; the neighbors were suspicious of me. However, she did not let me go empty-handed, giving me an address of a family that was seeking a teacher for their children. But in the new place, too, I remained a short time, the woman of the house telling me I must leave as a German search was in the offing.

I went back to the house of the Soldanski brothers and sought the eldest one's advice. What was I to do? During my absence, a Jew from the Szczegowo ghetto had come to the house and asked for me, unwittingly betraying me.

Soldanski led me out on the road and pointed to a house in the distance whose owners were always in need of help. The woman of the house hired me without any preliminaries. I worked very hard. I carted heavy buckets of water from the well, did the laundry and washed the floors. I fed the pigs and during my leisure time, knitted sweaters. The work exhausted me and I slept poorly. But here, too, my employment was brought to a sudden end by circumstances beyond my control. One day, returning from the shed where I milked the cow, I heard unfamiliar voices in the room, I stopped to listen. They were talking about me. My hands, they were saying, were very delicate; how come I never complained of the hard work? I must be Jewish, they concluded, with no other alternative.

I packed my few belongings and left. After covering a sizable stretch of road, I stopped near a house and knocked; they opened the door and shut it in my face. I had no more luck in the next house. I went back to the road. In the distance, a forest cast its vast shadow. I started walking again, letting my feet carry me across the desolated fields and meadows and I began thinking, for the first time, of suicide. I had not the strength to carry on the struggle; I was wrung out, physically and spiritually. I entered the forest and began seeking a stout branch from which to hang myself.

I removed the belt from my nightgown, plunging deeper into the forest. The prickly shrubs and twigs tore at my skin and drew blood, but I did not feel any pain. An inner compulsion drove me on, until I stumbled against a fallen tree and sat down. My feverish brain played tricks on me: I was surrounded by hostile peasants, by Gestapo men, by bloodhounds. I must get up and run. I closed my eyes but could not shut out the images of my pursuers, tormentors; they were gaining on me, coming closer and closer. My pulse beat wildly, my temples hurt. *"You must be going out of your mind -"* I said to myself. Suddenly I perceived my mother's face and heard her gentle but urgent voice: "*No matter what happens to us, you must live... This is my last wish -*"

I sat on the fallen tree for hours, unmoving, as though I'd turned to stone. Night spread a thick mantle over the forest. I possessed neither the strength to live or to die.

I don't know whether I slept or not, but when I opened my eyes, shafts of light stabbed at the damp ground near me. I raised my eyes and saw rays of the sun penetrating the thick foliage. It was morning. The birds were singing. The world was stirring, alive. I took out my little mirror and gazed at my own image. What I saw, shocked me. I did not recognize myself. My eyes were sunken deep in the caverns of my sockets; my face was pale, bloodless.

An urge to live seized hold of me. "*You must live -*" my mother whispered. I rose with great effort. My legs were stiff and I rubbed them furiously to restore the circulation of the blood. I seized hold of a tree to keep from falling. My eyes were filled with tears, but I felt a reawakened desire to live. I combed my hair, put on lipstick, pinched my cheeks to put the flush of life into them and started out of the forest.

Pan Ostrowski, he saved my life!

After walking a short distance, I spied a house and knocked on the door. "*Jesus be praised* !" I said, when the door opened. I was invited inside and treated to a large bowl of food. Eating my fill, I thanked my hosts and left.

I walked a long time until exhaution overwhelmed me. I saw a trim little white house and started toward it. What made me feel salvation was there I don't know. Was it fate? An accident? But there, in that trim little house, I found what I was seeking. The wonderful people who lived there, took me in and gave me shelter.

I will not take up space here to describe my stay with the Polish family Ostrowski.

During my stay with them, I was surrounded by warmth and friendship. Nobody in the family knew that I was Jewish, until the day the Russian patrols first entered the village and I revealed the secret to my hosts.

After the liberation of the village, I decided not to put off returning to Gombin. In our letters, my brother and I vowed to go back to Gombin, soon as the war ended, and wait for each other in my parents' house. Pan Ostrovski tried persuading me not to go; the highways were clogged with military vehicles and unsafe for a young woman. But I was very eager and found it impossible to put off. Old Pan Ostrovski escorted me to the highway and helped me get on a Russian military truck that was heading in the direction of Gombin.

I slept in villages. We passed through Sierpc and Mlawa. When the truck came near Gombin, I asked the driver to stop at the outskirts and let me off.

I was determined to make it the rest of the way on foot. It was a cold January day. All that I saw was familiar, part of my childhood and recent past : the woods, the meadows surrounding the town, the paths. A lump in my throat, I gazed through tear-filled eyes at the dwellings, my town. I walked slowly, hoping to arrive at the house at twilight, one thought alive in my mind to the exclusion of all else: was he alive? Was my brother there, waiting for me?

Entering Gombin proper, I lowered my head to avoid being recognized. It was evening. The streets were empty. My legs, as though possessing a will of their own, carried me nearer our courtyard. Reaching our house, I stopped and raised my eyes. The house looked neglected and empty. A door opened in a nearby house and a woman came out. She gazed at me and smiled in recognition. "*Our Miss is back*," she said, embracing me. "*Quick, go inside the house, your brother is waiting!*"

I plunged for our door and opened it. On the other side stood my brother, waiting for me...

Gombin Children in Nazi Camps

by Jack (Yankl) Frenkel

Translated by Janie Respitz
Edited by Leon Zamosc

[Original book: Pages 141-145 Yiddish and 79-82 English]

My childhood name in Gombin was Yankl Frenkel. I was ten years old when the war broke out in 1939. My brother Chaim was twelve and my brother Shmuel was fifteen. Today, their names in America are Henry and Sam. Our father was a cap maker in Gombin. There were seven children in the family, all boys. Only the three of us survived. This is the story of how we managed to stay alive throughout the war, a period fraught with peril for all Jews, without exception, and children in particular.

I clearly remember the Germans' arrival in Gombin. During the first few days the soldiers drafted some young men for work. After a few days, the Gestapo arrived and everything changed. They chased all the Jews out of their homes and assembled them in the market square under heavy vigilance. Then they poured gasoline on the houses near the synagogue (one of the oldest in Poland, artists came before the war from all over Europe to paint our synagogue), and started the fire. The Jews, surrounded by soldiers, watched as their homes and synagogue burned down, and could not do a thing. By the end of the day they ordered the Jews back to the houses that were still standing.

Soon after that, the Jews were forced to leave their homes and move into a ghetto area from where the Poles had been removed. The Jewish elders assigned rooms to each family according to their needs, as best as they could. Whenever the Germans wanted something they notified the Jewish elders, and there was a Jewish police force that rounded up the young men who were sent to the labor camps. Every now and then they called for 200-300 men to be sent to the camps. On March 9 1942 the Germans took the first step leading to the total annihilation of the Gombin Jews. On that day the Germans rounded up all the adult Jews capable of work, concentrated them in the firemen's building, and sent them away to labor camps. The rest of the Jews were slated for deportation and extermination.

Two weeks earlier an unexpected guest had arrived at the Frenkel home, a cousin of our mother, a Jew from Gostynin. He had escaped from the Nazi camp Anze, and now he was telling us things that filled us with horror and disbelief. In attendance were my parents, six brothers and myself. Vy the light of a flickering candle our cousin told us that he had witnessed with his own eyes the mass burning of Jews. When our youngest brother Michael heard it, he ran over to our mother and asked whether they would burn us too. We all started to cry. There had been rumors of mass murders before, but the Jews of Gombin refused to believe the horrible stories. Now, a live witness confirmed the unbelievable, but the Jewish elders told our cousin to stop spreading rumors and leave town.

From that day on, it was clear that the Jews of Gombin would share the bitter fate of the rest of Poland's Jewry. Thus, on March 9 1942, when the armed Germans surrounded the ghetto and began rounding up men and youngsters for work, the Jews of Gombin knew that death awaited them. The first act of the drama was now being played out. Soon, the second act would lead to the destruction of another small-town Jewish community in Poland.

By then, I was twelve years old. Since I was always out trying to bring customers for my father, I was among the first to notice that something was going on. I saw local ethnic Germans armed and a truck with soldiers at the ghetto entrance, and then I saw another truck on a side street. I ran home with the bad news, which soon spread to the whole neighborhood. In no time at all, the Germans raided one Jewish home after another, seizing all the males between the ages of eighteen and forty five. My oldest brother Beniek, determined not to be taken, hid in the attic. The Germans took my father and my brother Chaim who at fourteen was the third oldest, but looked more mature. I was twelve, but I followed the men as they were assembled in the street. A Jewish policeman pulled me out and tried to send me home, but I ran into a different line, and they led us away to the hall of the firemen's building, which was very large. A German in civilian clothes, a stranger in town who most likely had come to Gombin for the occasion, shouted that we should all sit motionless on the floor folding our hands. He then went around among the rows beating people murderously on the heads with a heavy club. He noticed a Jew who was one of the strongest men in town, and he told him to stand up. He asked him who he was and, when he received the response "A Jew", he hit him on the head and face. Next he ordered a man called Moishe to stand up against the wall. Moishe was a wood chopper, another strong man. When asked, Moishe gave the same answer, "A Jew", and the man kept hitting and hitting him regardless of what Moishe was trying to say. We could all see the blood pouring on Moishe's face, until they took him into another room and we heard a shot. We all knew right then and there what had happened. Next they took a young man named Eighel and also shot him. Later, the civilian was replaced by a local ethnic German named Braun, who warned the Jews that they would be shot for the slightest movement. He did not wait long to fulfill his threat. Hershl Kerber, an elderly man, could not stay still. When he stirred a little, Braun pulled his revolver and shot him on the spot.

A friend of mine, Hershl Schwartz, was sent home because of his age. I walked over to the policeman Braun, who knew us personally because he was a customer of my father and I used to deliver his caps. I asked him if I could also go home, he said "No, you are better off here".

At dawn the trucks arrived with armed German guards. Earlier, the ethnic Germans from Gombin had removed several Jews from the hall saying that their services would be needed in the town. My father, considered "useful" as a cap maker, was one of those who were sent home. My brothers and I were ordered into the trucks with all the others.

Thus began our ordeal. My brother Shmuel was 17 years old. Chaim and I were still virtually children: I was twelve and Chaim fourteen. We were not just sentenced to death as Jews; we were also vulnerable as children, a fact that from then on we would try desperately to conceal by standing on the tips of our toes, performing work meant for adults, and generally trying to behave ourselves as grownups. Jewish children served no useful purpose for the German murderers: they were shot or gassed or clubbed to death with the butt of a rifle.

The five hundred Gombiner Jews seized in the raid were taken to Gostynin, put on freight trains filled with Jews from other communities, and transported to the forced labor camp in Konin. We were assigned to a barrack with triple metal bunks, one on top of the other. It was already evening and they gave us a portion of bread for the next day. Chaim and I ate one portion and saved the other for the following day. That evening we saw our father's partner, who promised that he would look after us. In the morning when they woke us up for work, we discovered that the bread was gone. Our brother Shmuel was in a different barrack. When we told him about the stolen bread he talked with the camp's elder and they transferred us to Shmuel's barrack. Later on, we found out that our bread had been stolen by my father's partner.

Shmuel Frenkel

The Konin camp was a place of work and death. The work consisted of unloading heavy boxes and blocks from freight trains, but some Jews also worked on the railroad, building tracks for a German company called DST Deutsche. The deaths were caused by murderous beatings, overwork and starvation. The only way to avoid death by starvation was leaving the camp stealthily at night, maneuvering past the barbed-wire fences and coming back with some potatoes from neighboring villages. The children were best suited for that task. Chaim and I were not the only children in camp. Every night many of us would disappear in the dark and return with a little food to keep body and soul together. Some of us made it and some did not. In the mornings, those who did not make it were lined up dead on the ground for the rest of the inmates to see.

About two hundred Jews from Konin Camp were taken by train to the Guttenbrunn camp in the Poznan region. My two brothers and I were among them. We had taken a vow that we would be one for all and all for one. Wherever possible the three of us would stay together and share the last morsel of food.

Arriving in camp, we were treated to a spectacle prepared by the Nazis for the new "residents". In the middle of an open area they had built four gallows. Four Jewish boys aged ten or eleven were standing by them. The Nazis lined us up and said that the four "criminals" had been caught smuggling food, a crime for which they were about to pay with their lives. The noose was placed around the little neck of each child and German "justice" was carried out: four helpless Jewish children swinging in the gallows. That was the picture that greeted us when we arrived to the hell known as Guttenbrunn.

Once a day we were fed a watery substance called soup. The work consisted of loading heavy sacks of cement on freight cars. After the cars had been loaded, we were ordered to unload them, then load them again and again. Scores of prisoners fell dead while performing the work. Some died as they rose in the morning, others died in their sleep from starvation. From Guttenbrunn we were sent with other people to the Stadium camp in the Poznan area. Most of the inmates in that camp were Jews from Lodz and Ozorkov. Stadium was another camp where Jews perished from blows, hunger and inhuman labor. At that point, we were well aware that while we were being tortured and starved in the slave labor camps, our father, mother, four brothers and the rest of the Jews of Gombin had been sent to Chelmno, which was the first camp where the Germans applied "scientific" methods for exterminating the Jews — gas chambers. But we stayed together and miraculously survived.

A number of Jews from the Stadium Camp, including the three of us, were assigned to a work detail that was fairly good. They took us to the village of Zbaszyn to perform irrigation work. We slept under Nazi vigilance, but the work in the field was bearable. Most important of all, we were given enough to eat.

Unfortunately that paradise did not last very long. One day in September or October 1943, we were deported to Auschwitz. By then, I was thirteen years old, Chaim was fifteen and Shmuel "fully grown" at eighteen.

In Auschwitz, there were selections when the train transports arrived. Women, children, and the elderly were sent to the ovens. Only strong young men were spared. Since we were coming from a work camp, we did not go through selection. They put us on trucks and sent us directly to the slave workers' section. In the morning they assembled all the new arrivals. A kapo with a striped uniform, accompanied by a SS guard, yelled that all the children and elderly had to assemble on the left, and the rest on the right. Chaim and I were told to go to the left with other children. As we were standing, I talked with an inmate who was sweeping the pavement. He pointed to the chimney, saying that tomorrow there would be smoke going up. Chaim and I realized that "left," where we now stood, meant death. The inmate said that our best chance was getting numbers tattooed on our arms. Our brother Shmuel was already on line to get a number. I said to Chaim: "Let's go to the toilets". Luckily, they were not watching too closely, so we were able to sneak away and hitch on different lines to get a number. I stood on my toes to look taller. We were then "transformed" into inmates. We got the number tattoos, our hair was shorn and we were given a striped garment as clothing.

After being in Auschwitz for a couple of weeks they began to assign men for work detail in neighboring camps, like coal mines. Shmuel was picked, but Chaim and I were left behind. At that point we were separated for the first time in our lives, and we would not see Shmuel again until the end of the war.

Chaim and I were in quarantine for a while. Finally they picked us for brick laying, building stables for horses. Every so often they had selections, where Dr. Mengele stood and looked at you. In one of those selections a young boy who was my same age but skinnier was asked how old he was. Next thing you know Dr. Mengele pointed to the left, and that was his death sentence. That boy had been with me in the other camps.

Staying alive as children in Auschwitz was an endless struggle. For a whole year our children's bodies and faces were death sentences worn like signs. During the selections, we tried to stand next to inmates that were short, we rose on tip toes when walking past the Nazi guards, and during work we tried to outdo the others. We had to deceive the enemy, conceal the fact that we were children. To be a child meant the gas chamber.

The road we travelled was long and arduous. It led from Auschwitz to Glayvitz, to Gross-Rosen, to Dachau, and to the Charnitz river where a desperate band of SS men assembled the skeletal remnant of Jewish inmates to execute us before the Russian armies, whose heavy guns rumbled in the distance, arrived on the scene.

We had arrived in Dachau in early January of 1945, coming from Gross-Rosen. In addition to Jews there were people of various nationalities from all over Europe (Belgians, French, Polish, Germans, Greeks, etc.). Most were assigned to workshops where they made German uniforms. Chaim and I were taught to make button holes.

After being there for a few months, we began to hear bombings in neighboring towns. There were rumors that the war might be over soon. But that did not stop the fulfillment of Hitler's final solution to annihilate the Jews. One day the Jews were ordered to assemble in front of the barracks. We were told that we were being transferred. The trucks came and took us to the train station. They gave us packages from the Red Cross, we thought we were in heaven. The train took us to the Tyrol mountains where we got off and were told to start walking. After a few miles we reached a river. The SS men ordered us to sit down as machine guns were being set up around us. We knew that they were going to shoot us. After a while, however, it got dark. Chaim and I were in a group with four other friends. We put blankets over our heads and waited. But when we saw that nothing was happening, we began to slowly move away from all the others. We decided to hit the road. It was dark and we did not know where we were going, but we kept on walking.

We spent the night in a barn. In the morning a farm woman found us. We told her that we were on our way home after being dismissed from the farm where we worked. She invited us to come in and have breakfast. After all the years in the camp, we felt that we had never had a better breakfast. In Dachau we had been given regular clothing, not striped uniforms. But there was an X on the backs of our jackets. When the woman noticed it, she immediately told us to leave.

Back on the road, we saw a check-point and soldiers. We had no alternative but to proceed. Luckily they did not care what we were doing, so we kept marching. There were loads of soldiers running up and down, also lots of civilians driving. In the next village we found another barn. At dusk I went out to try to get some food. A women gave me something to eat. I saw German soldiers changing into civilian clothing. We stayed in the barn for a few days. Nobody bothered us.

One morning a woman came to the barn yelling in German: "The Americans are here, the Americans are here". We immediately ran to the entrance of the village, saw a soldier on a tank, and then more soldiers coming in. There was still a lot of sniping going on. When we told them who we were, the American soldiers told the farmers that they had to feed and house us in their farms, in groups of two or three. For a couple of weeks we thought we were in paradise. Then the Americans went around the village assembling all the concentration camp inmates. They took us to a displaced persons camp where there were people of all nationalities.

The DP camp was in a former German military compound. Like everybody else, Chaim and I were interviewed. They asked us if we wanted to go back to our country, but we told them that we had no desire to go back to Poland. We knew that nobody from our Gombin family had survived, but we were not sure about Shmuel, our oldest brother, who had been sent to the coal mines in Auschwitz. Then we had a meeting with Jewish soldiers from the Palestinian Brigade stationed in Italy. They explained that they could help us go to Palestine. They would take us by truck to Innsbruck, Austria, were we would be able to get on one of the trains of Italian prisoners of war who were going back to Italy. When the train arrived in Verona we had to get off and go to town were we would see army trucks marked with a Mogen David. Sure enough, that was exactly the way it was. The trucks took us to the Jewish Brigade's base, where we stayed for a few days. They gave us clothing and fed us well. Then they sent us to Bologna, and later to camps in Santa Maria and Santa Cesaria, so that we would be closer to the port of Bari.

Brothers Yankl and Chaim Frankl after liberation

In the Italian camps of the Jewish Brigade, young men of military age were given priority to go to Palestine. Chaim and I were always left behind because we were too young. One day Zalman Tatarka told us that he had heard that Shmuel was alive in Frankfurt, Germany. We rushed to Frankfurt, where we were told that Shmuel was in Hannover, in the British zone. We immediately went to Hannover where we finally met Shmuel and his future wife. We were all overjoyed with happiness. The rest is HISTORY.

I have shared these brief and unadorned notes to account for our survival as three Jewish children from Gombin. Perhaps it is better that the notes are brief and "unadorned." A more explicit account of the ordeal suffered by Jewish children in the German death camps would make the reading too gruesome an experience.

Survived in Soviet Russia

by Abraham Zeideman

[Original book: Pages 146-162 Yiddish and 83-98 English]

We realized, even early in the Occupation, what the Nazis had in store for us. The town was in the grip of terror. Placards began to appear on many walls, informing the Jews what they could and what they could not do. Any violation or infraction of a decree carried with it the death sentence. In town there appeared German landowners, former neighbors, wearing the swastika and taking over power. These same Germans who for many years had lived peaceably with their Jewish neighbors, were transformed overnight into savages. They installed the miller, Albert Fuss, as mayor and as his assistant -Wittenberg who taught German in the Polish school. They took over the town government and following Nazi directives, transformed the lives of the Gombiner Jews into a veritable hell.

From morning to evening started kidnapping to forced labor which was connected to hell of agony and sufferings. The payment was murderous blows. I was caught few times and every time I returned wounded and hurt. After day of misery I had to look for food. The Polish neighbors with whom we lived for generations together watched our sufferings with contempt and mockery. They lost their homeland within matter of days, but comforted themselves that the destiny of the Jews is worse. Every time when the Germans marched a group of Jews to forced labor, the Poles stood by , watching and enjoying "now is your turn zyd to work finally".

I would also like to note that right upon occupation, many Jews lost their livelihood, The Germans immediately confiscated the Jewish business. They took all the warehouses of those who run the trade of eggs commerce (storing in lime pools) and left many without sources for income. They ordered a decree which prohibit the Jews to appear in the market fares which were held once a week. On the other hand, they were forced to open their shops every day, if not they would have been accused of sabotage. In their shops they were the prey of any German passing by. And another common scene in Gombin was, right from the beginning, kidnapping the Jews in the streets and cutting their beards. Some of the Jews did not surrender and they wrapped their faces as if they were sick, to avoid the Nazi abuses.

One morning, it was a Thursday, the Germans issued an order for all Jews to assemble at the pig-market, threatening to shoot all those who failed to appear. That same day, my brother Hersch Nissen and I went out in the street to try and obtain some bread. As we made our way along the street, several Germans pounced on us and dragged us off to the Firemen's Hall, where we were put to work loading boxes of ammunition. There were in our work group about twenty five or thirty Jews. The "procedure" was the customary one, the work accompanied by abuse and blows. We were aware of the order to assemble at the pig-market and wondered whether we were better or worse off. Suddenly, at two in the afternoon, we saw smoke billowing from the center of town. I suspected the Germans set fire to the Large Gombin Synagogue. Taking advantage of a lapse on the part of those who were guarding us, I left the work group and ran toward the market. The sight that greeted my eyes was terrifying. Our shul, our magnificent wooden shul, one of the jewels in all of Poland, was enveloped in flames. Approximately forty Jewish dwellings, surrounding the shul, were also on fire. Standing nearby, but at a safe distance, were a group of Nazis who divided their attention between the burning synagogue which moved them to laughter and raining blows on Jews.

Later in the day, while the embers were still smoking, the Germans dynamited Jewish stores and plundered them.

Those who excelled in the burning and the plundering, were not the lowly privates but the officers. A large number of Jews were assaulted and murderously beaten. Among the seriously wounded, was my wife's uncle, Wolf Laski (who later shared the fate of most Gombin Jews, perishing with his wife and two daughters in Chelmno's gas chambers. Two of his sons, Shmuel and Mendl live in Detroit today). I too was murderously beaten that day. I managed to save my life by escaping into Faivish Prawda' house, the Germans firing at me, as I ran. All week long my body was swollen and I was unable to move. It was on that bloody Thursday that I made up my mind to escape Gombin and go to the eastern part of the country, occupied by the Russians.

There were, during that period, others, mostly young Gombin men, who fled "east." Lying swollen in bed, I discussed the matter with my brother, trying to induce him to go with me. But he would not hear of it. Russia, he argued was a "locked cage," and whoever crossed the border into that land, was lost forever. As for staying behind, one might hope, he said, after the war's end and the departure of the Nazis, Gombin would again be free.

My brother was not the only one to entertain such notions. Nobody could remotely imagine, at the time, what the Germans had in store for us. But I became daily more determined to leave Gombin. I talked over this matter with the girl I intended to marry and she expressed a willingness to go with me. It was decided that we marry before leaving. The wedding took place in my bride's mother's house. Present at the wed-cling which took place in the after-noon, were my two brothers, Hersh Nussen and Mayer, my sister Ruzia, my bride's mother, Malka, Freydl Laski, her daughters Sarah and Chana Laski, her brother-in-law, Itzhak Bauman, Wolf Laski, Mayer Kesele and his wife, Mordechai Findik and Miriam Ettinger. We received the blessing from my bride's cousin, the sexton Itzhak Bauman. Moishe Niederman, was placed outside the house to stand guard, in the event a German came upon us and found a group of Jews assembled in one place.

On the following day, Sunday, November the 20th, we left Gombin, Moishe Shlang who had a "permit" to travel, drove us in his wagon. With us on the journey, was a son-in-law of Shekerka's (whose wife and daughter perished in the bombardment). He was a resident of Eretz-Israel who had come to Gombin on a visit only to be caught in the war.

The road to Warsaw was fraught with peril. We were stopped by the Germans several times and were pressed into work gangs.

Arriving in Warsaw we first perceived the full extent of the destruction. Whole blocks were levelled to the ground. Among the ruins, people moved like shadows. An acrid odor of smoke permeated the air. Two bridges, spanning the Vistula River were smashed and we crossed on the third which was crowded with German schutz-polizei and soldiers.

Approaching the Jewish section, we found the destruction worse than elsewhere. Every second Jewish house was a fire gutted ruin; in many places it was impossible to pass owing to the mounds of rubble. The Jewish faces one saw, were filled with sorrow and grief and - fear.

After only several hours in Warsaw, we learned that here, too - in Europe's largest Jewish community -the Nazis "caught" people on the streets and pressed them into work gangs. Every day fresh placards were pasted on the walls, announcing new disabling decrees. There was also widespread talk about instituting a ghetto. The prevalent mood among the Jews, was despondency.

We went to an address which we received from home, to the son-in-law of Manyale Wolman, Manek. We stayed there a few days and prepared to continue our journey.

In her house we met some Gombiners: Chaja Ajdel Mitzenmacher, Gitl Celemenski, her husband and son Brunek, Wowa Appel from Sanniki. Also during the few days we stayed in Warsaw, we were grabbed to forced labor. Over there we saw for the first time the S.S. with the red skulls on their uniforms.

After three days in Warsaw, we left in a wagon. Among the passengers, besides my wife and myself, were Chaja Aydl Mitzenmacher, Chawa Appel, Gitl Celemenski and her four-year old boy. Our destination was the small town of Slovatich on the Bug River which divided Poland from Russia. The man who drove us was a Pole.

Arriving at the border town, we were surrounded by Germans who beat us mercilessly and locked us in a fortress. Inside, it was so dark, we could not see one another. When, later a German opened the door, we were almost blinded by the light. He let us go free, but we didn't know what path to follow. As if by some miracle, a Polish woman appeared and signaled us, with her eyes, to follow. Arriving in front of her hut, in a nearby village, she volunteered to row us across to the opposite shore of the Bug. She led us inside a large white washed dwelling, left us there and came back later carrying food for us to eat. She was very friendly and did not demand an exorbitant amount of money for rowing us across. She treated us decently. Considering our recent unfortunate experiences with the German barbarians, we were very moved and grateful. In the middle of the night, she led us to the river and we took seats in a little boat -in two's and three's - and she rowed us across. Nor did she abandon us on the other side, till we were shown the road to Brest-Litovsk. In parting, she wished us luck. May you never experience misfortune again, she said. Her wish did not come true.

Several kilometers from Brest-Litovsk, we happened upon a peasant who regarded us with a hostile expression and did not let us out of sight. Wherever we went, he followed. We realized he planned to report us and offered him some money to leave us alone. But to no avail. Spying the first Russian militiaman, the peasant told him about us and the other commanded us to follow him.

We were taken to the militia headquarters, where a heavy-set N.K.V.D. lieutenant sat behind a desk and questioned us in Russian, through a translator. He asked us who we were and where we planned to go. Gitl Celemenski and her husband and child were allowed to go to Brest-Litovsk, as he had been born in Byalistok and was thus a citizen of the "Liberated Territories." But the rest of us made the mistake of telling him the truth - that we were Gombin Jews who suffered untold agonies at the hands of the Germans; but now that we were in the land of the Soviets, we were hopeful of finding protection and freedom. The N.K.V.D. lieutenant heard us out calmly and just as calmly informed us we would have to go back where we came from, in view of the fact we crossed the border illegally.

And that is how it was. After spending the night under arrest, a militiaman put us inside a train (for which we had to pay) and we returned to the Bug. There, a Russian peasant, whom we had to pay, rowed us across to the Polish side. Fortunately when we crossed, there was not a German in sight. We came upon a tiny Jewish village, Swislowicz, and found an inn that was crowded with Jews who had run away from German-occupied towns and villages. Now they were waiting for an opportunity to cross into Russia.

The owner of the inn brought us food and put us up for the night. In the morning, he found a Polish woman who, like the peasant woman before her, rowed us across the river. This time we were lucky and made it to Brest-Litovsk without untoward incident.

Our first impression of Brest-Litovsk was shattering. People walked about in the streets without fear or hindrance. Jewish children, clutching books, were on the way to school; business establishments were open. Soldiers promenaded on the sidewalks, engaging passersby in friendly conversation. It seemed incredible that only a few kilometers separated us from the gehenna, where the

Nazis stalked their prey like animals, where each and every Jew had a death sentence hanging over him.

The Russian soldiers had a popular song about Russia, where one could "breathe free air." Our initial impression was, after the German nightmare, that this was indeed so. Everything we saw that in ordinary times would be considered as a natural state of affairs, we held to be a wondrous revelation. Even the fact that we could appear in the street without fear of being assaulted by a hate-filled German who could torture and kill us at will, we deemed a miracle. We entered an inn and spent the night. As our money soon gave out, we went to the "tolczok" (free market) and sold a few of our personal belongings.

Although we felt good in Brest-Litovsk, it was not our plan to remain there but to go on to the small town of Yanov, near Pinsk, where, we hoped to find my wife's brother, Moishe Gelbert, who at the start of the war, had been a soldier in the Polish army. After the invasion of the Germans and the rout of the Polish forces, he returned to Gombin where he stayed only briefly. He left for Yanov, where a friend of his, a former Gombiner resident, Benyomen Baruch, a locksmith, lived. From Yanov, my brother-in-law sent regards to us through another Gombiner resident. Noah Zielonka who had come back with his wife. We, therefore, decided to go to Yanov and settle there with my brother-in-law.

Before the departure to Yanov we phoned and talked to Baruch who informed us that my brother-in-law, Moishe Gelbert decided once again to return to Gombin, but he offered us to join him in Yanov. Only later it was discovered to us that my brother-in-law, Moishe Gelbert was caught before arrival to Gombin, murderously bitten. He lied a few days afterwards with destroyed lungs and died from the blows.

Travelling to Yanov was not a simple matter. To begin with, it was difficult to get a railroad ticket. But even after standing many hours in line and finally obtaining a ticket, you had to force your way into the train which was frightfully crowded and did not run regularly. But in the end, after much effort, we found ourselves inside the train. There were only my wife and myself, Appel and Aydl Mitznmacher having stayed behind in Brest-Litovsk. On arriving in Yanov, several militiamen were on hand to take charge of the refugees and find quarters for them in private homes. We were put up with a couple, Moishe and Brayne who ran a small bakery. They treated us in a friendly manner. Yanov was not far from the small town of Motele, where Chaim Weitzmann, the eminent Zionist and first President of Israel, was born. The town was very small but colorful. It consisted of a large rectangular market and little streets that led out toward open meadows. The early weeks in Yanov were for us a transition from a nightmare to sunny reality. The little town Yanov was quiet and Jewish and after the ordeal of Gombin everything appeared as though it were a pleasant dream. But the dream did not last long.

In the first days I started to work at a private tailor workshop Zanwel. After a week of work I asked for my salary and he fixes payment which you couldn't live on it. I left him and started to work by my own as a private tailor. I succeeded. Work was not missing. People were afraid to leave material for fear of confiscation. Everybody wanted new clothing. So income was sufficient for both me and my wife in those days.

When we stayed in Yanov, I was in contact with our Gombiner Jewish friends from Gombin, who escaped also and lived in the surrounding towns and villages. Some of them even came themselves to visit us, like Jazik Zaliszynski, Welvek Friedland, Lajzer Cohen, Fawisz Bol, Menasze Ber and others.

In January arrived and settled with us the brother of Benyomen Baruch. He enlisted to the Polish Army afterwards, survived and killed afterwards in the Independence War of the State of Israel.

I traveled a few times to visit Gombiners in Bialystok and Brest-Litovsk. In Bialystok on Kazikowa Street 16, lived 30 Gombiners. I remember Moshe Wolman, Rachel Lajzerszteyn, Natan Schwartz, Lajzer Cohen and his sister Rivka Cohen, Natalia Fuks, Mendel Wruble, Jazik Zaliszynski, the two Rogozynski brothers, Muniek Laski, Itzhak Wirobek and others. They all lived in a small room with a kitchen which looked terrible and frightening from poverty, dirt and hunger. The little bread they found they used to hang on the ceiling so that rats will not eat it. They fought hard and sold some clothes in the market, to gain some money. I met them in most depressing situation and they were all desperate and home sick, longing for the relatives who stayed behind in Gombin. Some of them had thoughts to go back to Gombin, and so it was. Part sent deep into Russia and the others who returned to Gombin were liquidated.

Second time I traveled to Brest-Litovsk to visit group of Gombiners who fled to that town. I found there the former chairman of the Jewish Community of Gombin: Chaim Lurie. Also he told me he is desperate and wish to go back to the home town. And he did return, and shared the bitter fate with all the Jews of Gombin.

Several weeks after our arrival in Yanov, a new decree was issued by the local authorities, evicting the local "rich" from their homes. One such person, a Jew named Pomerantz whose mill and store had been nationalized earlier, was quartered with our landlord. It was therefore necessary for us to find a new place to live. We moved in with an old Jew who had a much smaller and poorer house than the baker. The second change was a 'social" one. The local Jewish communists discovered that I worked privately as a tailor; they came with the intention of forcing me to open a large workshop specializing in ladieswear (there were many Soviet officials in town with their wives). I tried to beg off and made a counter-proposal that my wife shall be employed in the workshop. They agreed. But soon a third change occurred, a radical one, destroying all our previous plans. Some time ago, the authorities had come to us with a choice: either we accepted Soviet citizenship or registered for the purpose of returning to Poland. Owing to the fact that both my wife and I had relatives in Gombin, we decided to register as Polish citizens desiring to go back. Morever, we knew if we accepted Russian citizenship, we would, as my brother once said, get 'caught in a trap." We registered and for a long time heard no more about the matter. But one Friday evening a large number of Russians appeared in the town and we became suspicious something was afoot. But we did not know what it might be; there was not one among us who had an inkling of the misfortune that was in store for us.

In the middle of the night, we were awakened by a knocking on the door. Several N.K.V.D. members entered, guns in hand. They were here on an inspection, we were told. But instead of inspecting they told us to get dressed and accompany them. We had not the slightest notion, at the time, that the scene unfolding in our house was being repeated a thousand-fold throughout the "Liberated Areas" of former Poland. Permitted to take along a few personal belongings, we were led outside, where a horse and wagon was waiting. Only now we saw that we were not alone. Horse and wagons were strung out in front of virtually every dwelling. Refugees, like ourselves, were being led out of the dwellings, carrying their personal belongings. We were ordered to climb in and driven to the railroad station. It was summer, the end of June. We were put inside the cars and spent the whole day here in the unbearable heat. Towards evening, soldiers sealed our doors and put huge locks on them.

We spent ten days in the sealed freight-train that moved slowly across Russia's vast and endless steppes. We did not have the slightest notion where the train would stop and let us out. At each railroad station we saw throngs of people who gazed at us from a distance, tears of pity in their eyes. Toward the end of the tenth day, the train stopped and soldiers removed the locks. Now, for the first time after so many days and nights in the airless, fetid, unsanitary cars, with all of us on the point of being asphyxiated, we emerged to breathe the free air.

The place where we stopped was called Kotlas, on the River Severnaya Dvina, Archangelsk region, Siberia. As evening settled, it did not grow dark. Even later, in the middle of the night, it was so light, one could read a newspaper under the open sky. Towards nightfall, we were divided into small groups and put in small open wagonettes. My wife and I and several other refugees were taken to a place about twenty-five kilometers from Kotlas to a village surrounded by an impenetrable forest, named Basharova, where exiles were held. We arrived at our destination at three in the morning. The insects were unbearable. Clouds of mosquitoes swarmed over us, stinging our faces, hands and all exposed parts of our bodies, It was impossible to drive them off; they appeared determined to eat us up alive. When we reached our destination in the middle of the forest, the insects were even worse. The place consisted of several wooden barracks, subdivided into one room compartments. Two families were crowded into each room. Entering our "dwelling," we were horrified by the sight of red worms covering the walls. These live, squirming objects were soon in our clothes, on the table, in our beds, in our food.

The barracks were furnished with little iron beds and crude tables and benches. Owing to the bright light, the worms and the insects, crawled out of the walls; sleeping was out of the question.

At dawn, we were summoned to a meeting. There were several Russian families in our camp who took charge of us. At their head was an N.K.V.D. official, Bayoff who had an assistant, named Samsonov. Bayoff greeted us with cold harsh words. "You were not sent here for a certain period," he said, "you will remain here forever. You declined to become citizens of the Soviet Union; you declined to accept Russian passports offered you; you are, therefore, traitors to the Fatherland. Those of you who want to live will have to work. All others will be buried here, under the firs. Here, in Russia, we firmly believe in the principle that he who does not work, does not eat."

Many of those present began calling out their skills. One man declared he was a doctor; others called out they were tailors, cobblers, tin-smiths. But the commander dismissed them all with a wave of his hand. "Here," he said, "you will forget what you were in the past. Here, you will chop down trees." As the work was being assigned, I was put in with a group of "Drivers" whose task it was to haul the logs from the forest with horse and sled. The work was much more difficult than cutting wood in the forest, but the commandant promised us we would be better fed than the others. However, the difference between their portions and ours, was two hundred grams of black bread.

Our work-day began at five in the morning; we returned to our barracks twelve hours later, exhausted and hungry. There was only one break during the whole day, during which we received a piece of bread and a liquid they called "soup," for which we had to pay. It became apparent during the very first day that being a "driver" was extremely hard work. In the first place, it was very difficult to put the felled trees on the sleds; but our real trouble started when the horses tried pulling the loaded sleds. The horses were skin and bones, perennially hungry and exhausted. The Russian had told us we could use the horses for work only, not, under any circumstances, for pleasure. The life of a horse, they told us, was to them of greater value than a human being. We heard this refrain many times. It was true, the horses were more important to the Russians than human beings.

The food we received, barely appeased our hunger and we were forced to seek additional sustenance in the forests. In the summertime it was bearable, as the forest provided berries, mushrooms, roots and certain vegetables with which to still our hunger. But the winter was insufferable. In the first place, it was numbing cold and none of us had the proper clothing. We still wore the clothes in which we came in the summer. Now, during the numbing winter nights, when the wind knifed through the barracks, we covered ourselves with all the belongings we'd brought along from Yanov. But even worse than the cold, was the hunger. The berries and mushrooms of the summer months were gone and we were forced to live on the rations we received for "fulfilling the norm." This consisted of a piece of pasty bread and thin, unappetizing soup.

With the arrival of winter, hunger began to exact its toll. Many of us became ill and bloated with swelling. It became a vicious circle: the weaker one became, the less work he was able to perform; the less he worked, the less food he received, the weaker he became. Realizing that some of our people were on the point of dying from hunger, we organized a secret group whose task it was to help the weaker ones in every way possible. But the commandant found out about it and warned us that forming such "secret" organizations could lead to severe punishment. The position of those who received occasional packages from the outside, was less intolerable. But there were only a very few of those in our barracks. Another way of acquiring a little food was to sneak out of camp and go to a kolhoz (collective farm), about ten kilometers away, and barter clothes for something to eat. This could be done only on Sunday, our free day. But not every Sunday was free. The authorities "invited" us meetings and tried to prevail on us to "voluntarily" give up our free Sunday for the "Soviet Union." It goes without saying everybody "volunteered." The medicinal care we received was minimal. They did not provide us with a doctor altogether; we were dependent on a Russian woman who claimed to be a qualified nurse. On her "diagnosis" depended whether a sick person would be allowed to remain at home a day or whether, in his indisposed state, he would have to drag himself to the forest to work. Under such circumstances, a number of people collapsed and died. A number of infants also died.

There wasn't any school available for the children; but there was a prison. People were imprisoned for the slightest infraction of rules, put in a cold cell and received nothing to eat, as 'those who did not work, did not eat." As for the outside world, we had not the slightest idea what was happening. Often we spent nights on our iron cots, thinking about Gombin and what was happening there, how our relatives fared. Only the Russians in our camp received an occasional newspaper, but there was little in them about the events transpiring in the world. The winter, arriving early, increased in severity, bringing with it heavy snows and arctic winds. And just as on our arrival, there had been tweny hours of light and four of darkness, there were now no more than a couple of hours of light, the rest, pitch-black night.

We kept track of Jewish holidays and when Yom Kippur came, we decided to go to the forest but not to perform any work. The leader of our brigade was a Jewish attorney from Warsaw, named Glicksman.

Came Yom Kippur, we rose and went to the forest. But nobody made an effort to work. The commandant flew into a rage, summoned Glicksman and took away part of his pay. In the meantime, the temperature continued dropping. After a period when the thermometer stood at fifteen and twenty degrees below zero, it fell precipitously, reaching forty below. It was hell to get up at five in the morning on such days and wade through the deep snows. The forest was a little more congenial than the open, the trees providing a little protection from the winds. Moreover, we built fires in the forest, enabling us to thaw out.

However, the hunger was unbearable. Everyone of us hoped fervently that with the passing of winter, conditions would improve. But when winter finally bowed out, we were beset by new troubles. With the arrival of the spring thaws, we were forced to stand deep in water for days on end, performing our work. The dampness, the work and the inadequate diet, brought on a rash of illnesses. Many of us lost our teeth; some had swellings; virtually all of us suffered of chicken-blindness, the latter caused by a vitamin deficiency. Often, on the way to work, our sight was so deficient, we held hands and probed our way cautiously, led by those who managed to see a little better than the rest of us. The camp administration, moved by pity or concern for decreased production, one day brought in a wagon of old and rancid liver. After we ate the liver, a miracle occurred - our blindness disappeared.

Thus we worked and slaved in that distant, snow-bound, God-forsaken camp in the Siberian forest, removed from the rest of the world. One day, one of the refugees heard indirectly about a startling bit of news that appeared in the newspaper the Russian received, called "Severnaya Zvezda" ("Northern Star"). The news, according to our informant, was that the Germans invaded Russia, precipitating a war between these two countries.

Our first reaction was delight. Such a war, we were confident, meant an eventual defeat for the Germans and their withdrawal from Poland. We had heard so much about the might of the Red Army, we now firmly believed it would prevail over the Germans. Secondly, we were hopeful the new war would somehow bring about a change in our desperate condition, one we could not much longer survive. One day our prayers were answered and our hopes realized. The commandant summoned us to meeting and informed us that the Soviets signed a pact with General Sikorski. As a result, we would be freed from exile and be permitted to go to designated areas. Understandably, we were overjoyed. After repeated threats that we would be "buried under the fir trees," there was a new hope now of survival, perhaps even of eventual return to our homes, our families and friends.

Our commandant who only recently ruled us with an iron hand, now kept his distance from us as though he wanted nothing more to do with the refugees. We went to our work, as in the past but the administration's control over us was relaxed. Upon receipt of permission to go to south or middle Asia, we packed our few remaining belongings and left the camp. We started, on foot, toward the railroad station and boarded open wagonettes, similar to the ones that had brought us to Siberia. The train started and we were off again across the vast and endless Russian land. It was summer and the heat unbearable. The train was crowded and filthy and we had to provide our own food. And so, at each stop, we were forced to get off and exchange a garment for food.

It was a period when all Russia appeared in motion. All trains and ships were crowded. Millions of people were fleeing from west to east to escape the invading German armies. We saw, along the way, large numbers of Russo-Germans who had been uprooted from their homes near the Volga, where they had their own republic, and driven into exile in Siberia because the Soviet government did not trust them.

Our train moved slowly across the face of Russia. Two weeks later we arrived near the Volga and stopped in a little town called Volsk, in the Saratov region. The whole surrounding area consisted of German villages that bad been emptied of their inhabitants. At Volsk, where we got off the train, we found large quantities of food. The abandoned villages were all amply stocked with food and live-stock and fowl. We decided this was a good place to get off. After many months of starvation in exile, we began the slow process of recovery. For the first time in a long time we ate our fill. We slept in genuine beds and enjoyed long periods of rest. But our paradise was of short duration. The front moved closer and soon we heard the distant rumble of heavy guns. Many of us, the women in particular, became concerned about again falling into the hands of the Nazis. Learning that it was possible to escape to Afghanistan, we boarded a freight-train and got off at a station near the border. The little town's name was Karushi. We were seven couples and our arrival aroused the militiamens' suspicion. In the end they sent us back to Uzbekistan Guzari. The town was crowded with many thousands of refugees, the majority of them Jews. All the little houses and tearooms were thronged. People slept in the streets. Hunger and sickness were rampant. We decided to leave without delay and took a train to Khazakstan, in the direction of Alma Ata. We arrived at a very attractive and well-lighted station, at the town of Djambul. The station being bright and clean, we were certain the town itself must be modern and well-kept.

We left the train with our belongings and started for the town. We soon realized our mistake. What we saw was a dirty, muddy town with muddy huts, many of them windowless. The place was inhabited by Khazaks, a primitive people, who had not heard of such things as beds, spoons or forks. The Revolution changed nothing. The people lived now as they did hundreds of years ago. The town was full of refugees. We succeeded, after expending a great deal of effort, to move in with a poor Khazak family, who let us have a "room," in the middle of which was a place for a cooking and warming fire. Owing to the fact that we had no money, I began immediately to look for work. A tailor workshop hired me but it was twelve kilometers from where I lived, a distance I was forced to walk every day. As a qualified worker, I was paid 300 rubles a month. This sum was barely enough for one day's subsistence. All of us received the same pay. We worked thirty days and were paid for only one. There was no other alternative than to look for other means to earn more money.

The whole of the Russian people were forced to look for other means, to keep from starving to death. This other means was to deal on the black market. This was done by the menial worker as well as high official. Those who did not resort to the black market, died of starvation.

In February, 1943, my wife gave birth to our first child, a girl whom we named Hannah. Pregnant women were treated with a little more consideration than the rest, receiving on their ration cards some butter, fine flour and white bread.

With the creation of Polish committees, there began the registration of citizens of that country for General Anders's army. Soon discrimination against the Jews set in. The Christian Poles, in charge of the registration, refused to accept into the newly constituted army Polish citizens of Jewish extraction. A small group of Jewish refugees went to Kuybishev, headquarters at the time of the Anders army, and prevailed upon the leaders to be taken in. But their number was small. The Poles, by and large, did not long conceal their anti-Semitic bias; they soon began to carry on as though they were home, in Poland. The situation became even worse when the Russians instituted raids, seizing refugees and pressing them into work-battalions.

Six weeks after my wife gave birth to our daughter, two N.K.V.D men entered our room and demanded to see my passport. They well knew I did not have a passport, being a refugee. They arrested me and took me to jail. The cell, where they took me, was large enough for twenty people, but there were two hundred in it now. The conditions were unbearable. As though counting on our being despondent, the authorities again offered us a choice - that of accepting Soviet citizenship, or staying in jail. The majority declined the offer, fully aware that the moment one became a Russian citizen, he severed the last tie with his past. Several days after entering the overcrowded, filthy cell, I came down with a virulent sort of dysentery. The prison doctor doubted I would survive. The prison authorities, convinced I would soon die, called me in the office and said they would release me, temporarily, until such time as I recovered. Then I would have to come back to prison. The distance between the prison and the house in which we lived, was only four kilometers, but it took me eight hours to get there, It was twelve weeks before I could rise from bed. The doctor who came to see me, declared it was a waste of money, my ailment being incurable. But we were able to obtain a woman doctor who used to come to see me at dawn and bring medication she bought on the black market.

In the end, after three months, I recovered, though my body was weak long afterward.

Owing to the fact that the N.K.V.D. raids had not stopped, we decided to go away from the town, to a kolhoz which was about seventy five kilometers away. There we were "made comfortable" in a windowless stable, on a mound of straw alive with insects. Plagued by the filth and the hunger, we decided to return to Djambul, in spite of the raids. Back in town, I succeeded in obtaining a job in a tailoring workshop, connected with the railroad. It was said the workshop was "secure" from raids and work-battalions. But one day, during work, several N.K.V.D. men entered our shop, took away all our identification papers, sent us to the "voyenkomat" (military headquarters), then by freight train to some unfamiliar destination. Only later did we discover that our destination was Karaganda's coal mines.

We rode one hundred and twenty kilometers before I decided to jump off the train. After walking several nights (I did not dare move during the day as I did not possess identification papers) I returned home. I went immediately into hiding and stayed there. I slept in an attic and thus avoided the raids. In due time we made the acquaintance of a woman who was the head of the passport division and through her, with the aid of graft. of course, obtained a Polish passport. This made it possible for us to come out of hiding, to register and receive a bread-card. But this did not make me immune from raids. I was caught in the net several times, but each time I managed to escape. On one occasion they even fired at me, but I was determined not to fall into their hands, come what may.

Time passed and 1944 stood on the threshold. Our condition took a slight turn for the better when wounded soldiers began trickling back from the front, bringing with them all manner of objects, including material which could be used for sewing clothes. Trade increased as soldiers came to the open market to buy, trade, sell. The town revived. One day, a tumult spread through the town. People poured into the streets, shouting and waving. We soon found out: the Germans capitulated, the war was over.

The scenes that were enacted, are indescribable. All of Russia celebrated and wept, at the same time. The outpouring of joy was for the bloody war finally concluded, and the sorrow was for the loss of millions of husbands, sons and brothers. In the hearts of the refugees hope was reborn to come out of the ordeal alive, to go home eventually to our towns and villages and after these many years of suffering untold agonies, be reunited with our families. While in exile, bits of news would reach us about the German outrages, but none of us, even in his wildest nightmarish dreams imagined what had taken place during our absence, the total destruction visited on our people.

Although the war was over, our condition did not improve. The raids continued unabated and it was necessary to hide from the N.K.V.D. Soon we began to hear of Jews who crossed illegally into Poland. Through a friend of ours, a Polish Jew who was the head of a committee, we managed to get on a list of "military families" picked to return to their homeland. We left Djambul in one of the early transports, riding by freight-train again, in the direction of

Poland. Among the passengers were many Poles who appeared friendly enough while we were on Russian soil. But no sooner did we cross the border into Poland than their true anti-Semitic colors surfaced. They accused us of being responsible for the war and all their suffering. According to them, we worked hand in glove with the Russians.

Arriving at the Polish border, we were subjected to an inspection, the last one, after which the train was put in charge of Polish officers. Without losing any time, the officers took charge. They decreed that the Christian passengers on board were free to go where they pleased, but the Jews were ordered to Wroclaw in Lower Silesia.

Arriving at our destination and emerging from the train, we were confronted by a Pole who said derisively: "Moishe, you still alive?!

This derisive question was hurled at us wherever we went. When in the end we found out that our Gombin had been emptied of Jews and that in this land of our birth the lives of those who miraculously escaped the Nazi assassins were not safe, my wife and I said to ourselves: we will not rear our child in Poland which is a mass-grave of our people. We will go elsewhere.

Group of released Gombiners after a gathering in Lodz, 1946

Personalities, Images and Characters

Rabbi Yehuda Leib Zlotnik

by A.I.
Translated by Janie Respitz
Edited by Leon Zamosc

[Original book: Pages 165-166 Yiddish]

Rabbi Yehuda Leib Zlotnik was born in Plock on January 8 1887, but his name is closely connected with Gombin. This is due not only to his 1911-1918 tenure as rabbi of Gombin, but also to the fact that Gombin figured prominently in his scholarly works.

Rabbi Yehuda Leib Zlotnik
Source: Ada Holtzman's Collection [not in original book]

When he was three years old, his father, Abraham Yitzchak Zlotnik, passed away, and he was educated by his mother, Chana-Nekhe, who had to support the ten surviving orphans. He studied until age ten in religious schools, and thereafter with his brother Jonah Mordechai who was the rabbi of the town of Zakroczym. In 1910, when he was 27 years old, he passed the government examinations and left to study at the Volozhin yeshiva. He already had a reputation as a sharp scholar and one year later, in 1911, he was chosen as rabbi of Gombin, where he lived until 1919. During his service in Gombin he did a great deal of work for the community and helped develop the Zionist movement. He became a central figure in the spiritual and cultural life in Gombin.

In 1920, Yehuda Leib Zlotnik was among the founders of the religious Zionist party "Mizrachi" in Poland. His position as general secretary of the party forced him to leave Gombin and settle in Warsaw. In addition to representing "Mizrachi" at the Zionist congresses (1925, 1929, 1931 and 1935), he traveled on assignment to various countries. By the end of 1920 he was chosen as the president of "Mizrachi" in Canada and settled in Montreal. In the service of the international Zionist movement he visited the Land of Israel and South Africa in 1925, Argentina in 1935, and Australia in 1946. From 1938 to 1949, he was director of Jewish education in Johannesburg, South Africa. From June 1949 and until the end of his life he lived in the State of Israel. He passed away in Jerusalem on September 21, 1962.

Yehuda Leib Zlotnik was not only a Zionist leader. He was also a prolific writer and scholar. He began writing at the age of seventeen. He wrote in Hebrew a biography of Jesus of Nazareth, but the work was never published due to censorship. He also wrote poems in Hebrew and Yiddish. Some of them appeared in "Hakol" (The Voice, Warsaw, 1899). In 1915 he published articles about the Zionist program in "Lodzher folksblat" (Lodz People's News) under the pseudonym Yehuda Elzet; and he published tracts in "Moment" against religious Jews who opposed Zionism.

Tombstone of Pinchas Shachar,
Gombin Jewish Cemetery

Some of Yehuda Leib Zlotnik's most significant and interesting works focused on Jewish folklore. He was a contributor to the "Collected Books" of the well-known philologist and folklorist Dr. Noah Prilutsky. He also published a series of booklets on folkloric themes, including "Jewish Food", "Treasures of the Yiddish Language", and many others.

Rabbi Yehuda Leib Zlotnik wrote under the pen names Yehuda Elzet and Yehuda Abidah. The Jewish community of Gombin benefited from his love of folklore. As rabbi of Gombin, he explored the local history and investigated old documents, community chronicles, and the matzevot of the town's old cemetery. His research contributed a great deal to what we know about the past of Gombin

The Poems of Rajzel Zychlinsky

by Abraham Shulman

Translated by Janie Respitz
Edited by Leon Zamosc

[Original book: Pages 167-169 Yiddish]

Rajzel Zychlinsky, our poet born in Gombin, holds an important place in Yiddish poetry. She has recently published a new book of poems called "Silent Doors". The book was enthusiastically reviewed by critics and admirers of her poetry. The following excerpts come from a work on Yiddish writers by the literary critic Abraham Shulman.

It is impossible to read a poem by Rajzel Zychlinsky and not be disturbed by the first two or three lines. Here is an example of the opening words of her poem "Four Corners", which only had eleven verses: "The sea spilled over all boundaries, the night extinguished all the train stations". Or the beginning of another poem of only eight lines: "When I finally reach the bridge, it will no longer exist". Or: "Everything is ready.... For birth or death?" Or: "Do not ask a mute about any street, do not be afraid, do not disturb the continent". Or: "All the trees are waiting for God". All these are examples of a choice of words that suddenly thrusts you into a shocking awareness of a situation.

In Rajzel Zychlinsky's poems the word combinations are unexpected, the scenes are unnatural and weird. Together with the feeling of bizarre injustice, one feels in her lines that the poet is rendering in words our imposing and useless islands of silence.

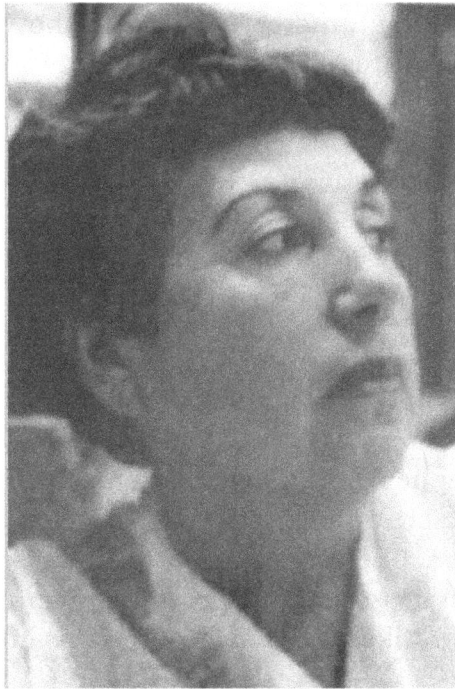

Rajzel Zychlinsky
Source: Ada Holtzman's Collection [not in original book]

Here is a poem where simple words short-circuit into an unexpected experience. The poem, which consists of only ten short lines, is entitled "In front of the Mirror":

How many women have already seen
Their first grey hair
In the cold eyes of the mirror.
The dream has ended,
We step into reality
The world becomes clear and white,
The water freezes.
A blue piece of ice
Becomes our ship.

This poem sums up a personal drama. The drama of passing time, the drama of aging. It is the drama of human fragility, which runs past us and transforms "our ship into a blue piece of ice". This short poem captures the "blindness" of the biological script with nihilistic needles. This poem is a sea where gushing words settle somewhere at the bottom. Only a few shards of the words remain on the surface,

Another poem, a shocking, unforgettable poem that makes us shudder and feeds our depressed and sinister anxieties, has just twenty words:

At night
When I sleep
My skeleton guards my bed.
With white knees
A white fiddle.
From its eye sockets
The moon shines – sonatas
In my dream.

This picture is not simply a momentary hallucination. The "bony skeleton with the white knees" presides over Zychlinsky's poems. Her poems are pervaded by death, the ephemeral, a hovering anxiety... Rajzel Zychlinsky is an absolutely individualistic poet. Her experiences are very personal. She does not try to connect with others. The scenes in her poems are naked, void of people, landscapes or frozen still lives. And if a person appears in one of her poems, it is someone seen from afar, like in a canvas of the misanthropic painter Maurice Utrillo.

The being of her poems is often permeated by madness. Their colors are twilight. Their philosophy is the philosophy of white clinics, scalpels, surgery. But it is interesting that despite this, despite her naked loneliness, Zychlinsky is not an asocial poet. In the backdrop of many of her poems there is a flat improbable reality, characters like "tall, hot black men", "grey women from the shops", "old people, transparent, going from silence to silence", a "chased off drunk from the church. Rajzel Zychlinsky's God? "Every morning I pray at the chimney, to the Godlike fool on my roof". Her desires? "I want to be a black woman with yellow eyes that drinks the moons". Her joy as a poet? "The dialogue of man's candlesticks with green beads is older than me. It will continue after I am gone. I tremble with joy when the sun embraces me". Her accompanying landscape?

The sun set
In its final red.
The birds flew over
From grey to black
And became still.
The blind man
Who looks at eternity
What will he do with our neck?

Yiddish poetry in general is lucky to have good female poets, but Zychlinsky stands alone on an isolated island. It is remarkable that our female poets are generally less lyrical than men. They are more self immersed, and more involved in a traditional, even pious Jewishness. Rajzel Zychlinsky is the Yiddish secular poetess. She is our "window to the world". It has now become fashionable to board up these windows with so–called religious planks. Rajzel Zychlinsky is a child and sister of the poets Rembo, Verlen, Valery and Rilke. She is Jewish, but her Jewishness does not lie in the pre-poetic 613 good deeds, but rather in the deep sense of humanity. A humanity that does not command her to venerate our buried forefathers, but to learn from the misdeed of "Hagar who still wanders in the grey desert and cries". Or the folly of Esau who "ran from the field pleading... for his old father Isaac to bless him as well! Too late, said the buzzing fly licking the last piece of blessing from the bowl of stew... too late. Esau cried".

Rajzel Zychlinsky is a great Yiddish poetess. Saying that someone is "great" may sound like a cliché. For me, it is a real pleasure to be able to use the word and feel that, in this case, it does mean the real thing.

Hanoch Goldshmidt

by M. Guyer

Translated by Janie Respitz
Edited by Leon Zamosc

[Original book: Pages 170-172 Yiddish]

Until my departure to America in 1921, Hanoch Goldshmidt and I were inseparable friends. We were active in the Gombin Bund and we were arrested together. After my release I left for America, but we did not lose contact. The idyllic Polish town surrounded by forests remained deep in the hearts of all those who had left. In America, the Jewish emigres from Gombin followed the news about the idealistic movement that we had helped to build and remained active under Hanoch Goldshmidt's leadership. We continued to help them grow from America, supporting their organization and struggle.

Hanoch Goldshmidt came to the Bund in a peculiar way. He was born in 1889 to a poor but respected family. His father was a religious teacher, and Hanoch was a pious child when the winds of revolution galvanized the towns of Czarist Russia in 1905. In our town there was talk about a clandestine group called "Achdut" (Unity), which included youngsters who did not believe in God, wanted to bring down the Czar, and gathered every Saturday in the forest to secretly smoke cigarettes and sing "subversive" songs.

This pious boy, the son of the religious teacher, decided that he must find the leader of the "Achdut" group and "teach him a lesson". So Hanoch went looking for Jacob Rothbart, the founder and leader of the Bund in Gombin (who today lives in Pittsburgh). The result, however, was completely different from what the pious Hanoch expected. He did not teach a lesson to Rothbart. It was Jacob Rothbart who taught the lesson to him. Hanoch Goldshmidt became a Bundist.

Fundamentally, Hanoch was a man who strove for completeness. Simply embracing the ideal of socialism was not enough. He decided to take a more decisive step: he became a worker, learning the craft of boot-upper making. There were not that many Jewish boot finishers *(yiddishe volkers)* in Gombin, but they were known as a very progressive and revolutionary group. Hanoch Goldshmidt set an example for other religious students: in Gombin, one could take the path from the Heder and the Yeshiva to the workshops of the town's craftsmen.

Hanoch Goldshmidt was a calm person, but he was really passionate about the movement. After 1905, when the founding leaders of the Bund left Poland, he became the soul of the movement in Gombin.

Because of a speech impediment (he stuttered a bit), Hanoch was not a great public speaker. But he had a remarkable knack for persuading people to join the movement. After the 1905 failed revolution, he worked tirelessly with the town's youngsters, instilling in them the sense that it was important to read good books, pay attention to social problems and political issues, and join the struggle for a better life. Hanoch spent his Saturdays in the forest, reading books and explaining things to the groups of kids who sat around him.

Hanoch Goldshmidt and his wife Ruchele

Under the Czarist regime, unions were illegal. In Gombin, however, we managed to establish a union that embraced workers of all the different trades. In 1908, the union organized a strike. We opened a free kitchen for the workers and purchased equipment to start a worker's cooperative. It was a bitter struggle in which Hanoch Goldshmidt distinguished himself as the most effective leader.

In 1909, Hanoch and I were denounced by the bosses. We had to leave town. Later on, we returned home. Throughout the most difficult years of Czarist repression we maintained a group of young men and women and a small illegal library. We kept in touch with Bundists from other towns, especially during the summer months when some Bundist activists came for vacations in the forests of Gombin. One of them was the well-known Bundist leader from Lodz Israel Lichtenstein, who would later serve as Bund representative in America, and died in 1933.

During the First World War, when the country was occupied by the German army, the workers' organizations were allowed to operate legally. In Gombin, proletarian institutions flourished, including a party organization, a library, an orphanage, a consumers' cooperative and, a bit later, the youth organization "Tsukunft" (Future).

Hanoch Goldshmidt was everywhere. In addition to working as an employee at the cooperative, he ran educational activities for the youth and was active in all the other institutions of the movement.

Particularly moving was his relationship with the younger generation. He almost never thought of himself. Day and night he was busy with the activities of the movement. A letter had to be written to headquarters in Warsaw? The youngsters needed help with something? The orphanage was running short of coal? Hanoch Godshmid was always busy. Here I should mention that, back then, the Bundist comrade Sonia Celemenski worked in our orphanage. She later married Emanuel Novogrudski and died a martyr's death in the Warsaw ghetto.

The first free municipal elections of the restored Polish republic were held in 1919. The Bund party saw the fruits of its work in Gombin: the four candidates presented by the Bund were elected to the municipal council. Had we presented more candidates they would also have been elected....

In America we closely followed Hanoch Goldshmidt's indefatigable work in Gombin. The repression of 1920 did not slow him down and the party remained united. He remained in his post as the recognized leader of the worker's movement in Gombin until the end of 1938, when he emigrated to Brazil.

In far away Rio de Janeiro, Hanoch remained the same passionate Bundist he had been his whole life. Every letter he wrote reflected the same heartfelt conviction that had been so characteristic of him when we worked together in Gombin.

Marek Wolfowicz

by Dzunia Wolfowicz, Israel

Translated by Janie Respitz
Edited by Leon Zamosc

[Original book: Pages 173-174 Yiddish]

My father Marek Wolfowicz was born in Gombin in 1883. His parents wanted the best education for their children, which was not easy in a small provincial town like Gombin. Marek received his elementary education at home and later graduated from a technical school in Lodz.

From early on, Marek Wolfowicz showed a disposition to help others. Rather than living for himself, he got involved in activities focused on improving the lives of everybody in the community. As a youngster, he became very active in the socialist movement.

Marek's father Zelig Wolfowicz,
from one of the affluent Jewish families of Gombin

Marek participated in the revolutionary outbreak of 1905. After supressing the uprising, the Czarist regime launched a campaign of repression against the socialist and progressive organizations. Fearing arrest, many activists went to exile. My father Marek went to America, staying there until the end of the First World War.

In the United States Marek Wolfowicz worked for the Edison Company. However, he could not stay there. The pull of Gombin was too strong. When the First World War ended, he returned to Gombin and dedicated all his time to community work. He was elected to the municipal council and opened our home to all the needy, Jews and non-Jews. They came to him for help and advice. Many Jews brought letters in English from their relatives in America. My father would spend time with them, patiently translating and explaining the content of the letters. I remember how happy he was when the government placed a huge order designating the shoemakers of Gombin as suppliers of boots for the Polish army.

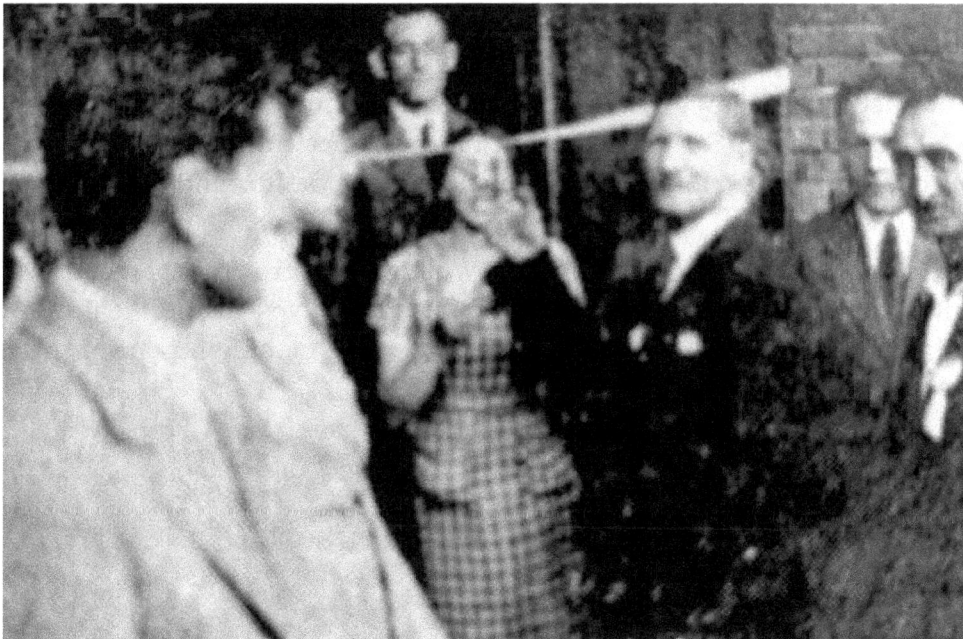

Marek Wolfowicz cuts a ribbon at the opening of the Zionist library

Marek's work as municipal councilman was only one aspect of his activity. He was also a well-known Zionist personality and mentor of Zionist youth organizations. In addition to organizing meetings and artistic performances, he personally assisted many of those who emigrated from Poland to Palestine. He was convinced that a Jewish homeland in Palestine was the only solution for the Jews.

During the day, we the children rarely saw our father. Marek was always busy with his many occupations. Our mother Mania (née Glas) had to look after the house and the business. She never complained and never disturbed our father's community work. She worked from early morning until late in the evening. She was a very good person, a wonderful mother and the best possible wife for a husband who was deeply committed to community activism.

When Marek came home on Friday evening we were a unified family. After the traditional meal we would remain seated at the table and spend time together. Friday nights and Saturdays were the loveliest days of my childhood.

The war put an end to our normal life. In November 1939 the Gestapo came to our house to arrest our father. At the last moment he escaped through a side door and never returned.

Marek went to the Warsaw ghetto where he continued to be active maintaining regular contact with the Zionist organizations. He helped to support orphanages, surrounding himself with the other Jews from Gombin who were in Warsaw.

The last time I saw my father was on September 5, 1942. During one of their selections, the SS included my mother in a transport to Treblinka. My father could have saved himself, but he stood beside her and together they were sent to their death.

Our parents Mania and Marek Wolfowicz were murdered in the gas chambers of Treblinka. They had dedicated their lives to the ideal of a Jewish homeland, but they did not did not live to see the establishment of the State of Israel and the realization of their dream.

Reuven Pochekha

by Louis Philips (Pochekha)

Translated by Janie Respitz
Edited by Leon Zamosc

[Original book: Pages 175-176 Yiddish]

My father, Reuven Pochekha, was born in Plock. He was a tall slender Jew whose demeanor imposed respect. He had bright blue eyes and a Herzl–like beard that framed his gentle face. He was a supplier of boots to the Russian military, a business that offered jobs to many Jewish families of Gombin.

His work required him to go on long trips all over Russia and maintain contact with leading Russian personalities. He spoke perfect Russian and he loved to talk for hours about his travel adventures, keeping his listeners in suspense.

Reuven Pochekha was often asked to intercede for Jewish soldiers who were serving in the regiments to which he supplied boots. I remember incidents in which his intervention helped improve the conditions of the Jewish soldiers, many of whom were far from home in the lonely vastness of Russia.

Despite his prestigious position in the town, he never held any formal office in the community. He saw those offices as a way of exercising power, and he believed that power leads a man to temptation. He was offered important positions numerous times, first in Plock and later in Gombin. He turned all of them down.

When we lived in Plock many inmates from the local prison worked for my father in the manufacture of boots. Most of them had been artisans before their incarceration, and the others had learned the trade while in jail. Of the approximately one hundred prisoner shoemakers, about ten were Jewish. My father sent me to work as a bookkeeper in the penitentiary. I will never forget how the Jewish prisoners opened their hearts and shared with me their tragic stories. They were victimized by the non–Jewish inmates, many of whom were vicious anti–Semites. My father often appealed to the Russian prison director on behalf of the Jews, but there was always the fear that any improvement in their conditions would only inflame the hatred of the anti–Semites. In the end, my father could no longer bear it. He did not renew his contract with the prison, and that was one of the reasons for our move from Plock to Gombin. My father arrived in Gombin with a plan to recruit 100 shoemakers to continue the production of boots for the Russian military.

Reuven Pochekha carried out the plan with his characteristic energy. With the help of his cousin Helerman he called a meeting of Jewish and Polish shoemakers, who at that time were suffering from lack of work. Within a few days, my father succeeded in recruiting enough shoemakers and opened his first large workshop for those who wanted to work in a group. Many others preferred to work independently from home.

The boots for the Russian cavalry had to be of top quality. Gombin was an ideal place to produce them because there were well qualified shoemakers, makes of boot–uppers, and tanneries with first class craftsmanship. My father's business attracted more Jewish families to Gombin, including leather merchants, tanners, and makers of shoes and boots.

I remember well our move to Gombin. Only my mother was sad. It was hard for her to leave our comfortable house and our many neighbours and good friends. My father was filled with enthusiasm and I liked the idea as well, despite the fact that I would have to leave behind the Plock high school and become a "greenhorn" student in Gombin. We packed up all our stuff in large crates - our polished glassware and silver carafes, our silver Menorah, and my father's holy books including the heavy leather–bound Gemara. My father packed his books by himself, he would not let anyone else even approach him. I busied myself with my mother's prayer books and my own Russian books...

Our arrival in Gombin was a big event in our lives. Here, as in Plock, our house became a warm Jewish home. More importantly, we brought new life to the Jewish artisans. Dozens of Jewish families were directly connected to my father's businesses. Throughout the years, Reuven Pochekha's initiatives played a key role in the economic life of the Jews of Gombin.

Meir Zeideman

by Abraham Zeideman

Translated by Janie Respitz
Edited by Leon Zamosc

[Original book: Pages 177-178 Yiddish]

There are many documents in the archive of the Gombin Society that serve as mementos of our destroyed town. They include the letters, reports, and statistics of Gombin's "Gemilat Hesed Kasse" (savings and loans society), all of them written in the clear beautiful calligraphy of Meir Zeideman, secretary of the loans society and of the Jewish community board.

My brother Meir was very popular in Gombin. He was an unusual kind of Jewish intellectual, a self–educated man who put his talents at the service of the community. Everyone in Gombin came to him asking for help with paperwork and official letters, which he would compose in his exquisite handwriting. He was also the chronicler of the town, passing on the local news and information to the Jewish scholar Jacob Leshchinsky, who collected materials from all cities and towns for his economic and demographic research.

Meir Zeideman was born in 1910. At thirteen he ended Polish school and, like many other Jewish boys, he had to stop his studies in order to work and help his family. Fortunately for him, he got a job at the Zionist library, where he avidly read everything he could. Within a short time he was known as the "remarkable guy" who had read all the books available in Gombin. He went on to more ambitious things, taking correspondence courses until he was able to graduate with a high school degree.

When the Union of Manual Workers was founded by Chaim Luria, Meir Zeideman helped as an aide. Displaying his talents, he gradually worked his way up to the important position of secretary.

Later on, he was involved in the establishment of the "Gemilat Hesed Kasse" as assistant of Abraham Tiber, the first secretary of the savings and loans society. Once again, it was only a matter of time for Meir to eventually rise to the post of secretary himself.

Meir Zeideman's main achievement came in the 1930s, when his Union of Manual Workers obtained a majority in the board of the Jewish community.

Meir's popularity lay in the fact that he would do anything to serve the town and its people. He became the official writer for all the Gombin Jews who needed to submit documents and petitions to the authorities. His reputation transcended the boundaries of Gombin. People would come to him from all the neighbouring towns.

When Jacob Leshchinsky announced a contest for the best monograph about a Jewish town there were hundreds of participants, but it was my brother Meir's monograph of Gombin that won the prize.

Meir Zeideman was also a poet. Some of his poetry was published in the magazine "Literary Pages". Proficient in Hebrew, he translated Bialik's famous poem "The Kidnappers". In the town's political circles, he advocated for a combination of socialism, Zionism and religion. His ideal was a movement that would "Keep the Faith" through a mixture of leftist ideology and traditional Jewish piety. At one point, he admitted that it was not easy to find other people who shared that particular kind of vision.

In 1937 Meir married Roize Hodys from Gombin and had a son. The occupation of Gombin by the Nazis sealed the fate of Meir Zeideman, his family, and the rest of the Jewish community. In the Spring of 1942, they were deported to their deaths at Chelmno extermination camp.

Types and characters from Jewish Gombin

by Jacob M. Rothbard

Translated by Janie Respitz
Edited by Leon Zamosc

[Original book: Pages 179-196 Yiddish]

Reb Israel Shochet

Reb Israel Shochet was a Torah scholar. When he was not busy slaughtering animals he was studying the holy texts.

He would mainly slaughter the poultry that the town's pious women brought to him. It was said that when an animal had been ritually slaughtered by Reb Israel, the meat was fit for the consumption of the holiest men. He would slaughter in the yard behind his house on Maissim Street. Sometimes they had to literally drag him away from a book. He was unhappy when someone interrupted his study asking him to slaughter a chicken.

Reb Israel was also masterful when he led people in prayer. One of the best prayer leaders. On the pulpit he was sweet as honey, a pleasure to listen, especially during the Days of Awe and the other holidays. The words would flow from him like a clear stream of water cascading from a mountain. His intonation was extraordinarily harmonious. He would modulate the tones and tastefully bring forth the meaning of the prayer. He prayed in the large House of Study, which was always packed when he stood at the pulpit.

Those who followed him were mainly from the poorer class of Jews in town, including artisans, peddlers, and small merchants. They were fascinated by every word that came out of his lips. They were sure that the Almighty would hear his prayers and show his mercy to the Jews.

Reb Israel Shochet had a lovely family. His daughters were married to important men in Gombin. His children raised beautiful families as well. Some of Reb Israel's grandchildren would later hold distinguished positions in modern Jewish institutions, including the unforgettable Sarah Golda and her husband Shmuel Leib, and Brocha and her husband Yitzchak Moshe Guyer, who are now very active in the Jewish School movement in Chicago.

However, most of Reb Israel Shochet's children and granchildren were among the six million martyrs, our sisters, brothers, and innocent children who were exterminated by the Nazi murderers. Let my words here serve as a memorial to one of the finest Jewish families that ever lived in Gombin.

Yocheved

Her name was Yocheved Goldberg but in Gombin everyone knew her as simply Yocheved.

Yocheved was blind in both eyes. No one really knew how it had happened. Some people thought that she had been born that way. Others said that she became blind when she was a child. In any case, whatever the origin of her blindness, she was doubtlessly one of the most remarkable personalities in town.

Despite her total blindness, Yocheved had an independent business and helped her father bear the burden of earning a living. Neither business was a gold mine, but they managed to make ends meet. Her father Jacob dealt with "non–Kosher merchandise". He sold Turkish tobacco, saccharine and other items that were strictly controlled by the Russian government and required the payment of steep excise taxes. But as the Yiddish saying goes, "a Jewish scholar always finds a solution", and Jacob Goldberg was a bit of a scholar. He had many holy books in his large room. He would always hold a book in his hand and appear to be reading it, pretending to be unaware of what was going on around him. From time to time, he would raise his head and cast an unhappy glance sideways, saying nothing and returning his eyes to the book.

In her store, Yocheved sold sweets to the Jewish children of Gombin. One could buy from her the most expensive sweets and all sorts of candy, shtrudels, and nuts. What sweets could you not buy from her? Her assortment was comparable to anything available in the best shops of the largest Polish cities.

Yocheved's store was on the second floor of a tenement house facing the market square, not far from Poznanski's brick building (which was five stories high and surrounded by a brick wall). Children from all over town came to her place. At Yocheved's, teenagers experienced their first pangs of love in their young hearts. Today it would seem strange and impossible, but in those days young boys and girls hardly ever spoke to one another. They kept up appearances to avoid the risk of a bad reputation. The kids knew that there were people in town who loved gossip and were always ready to speak ill of others. That could hurt your standing and, God forbid, your chance of a good marriage in the future. Everyone tried to behave decently and show respect for each other.

Of course, there were exceptions. A romance would ignite, sometimes even leading to a match and a wedding. But such cases were very unusual. Just the fact of meeting people from the opposite sex made you happy. And if you did fall in love, it was wise to stay quiet, be modest, and wait for a more appropriate opportunity...

Remarkably, despite the fact that she was blind, Yocheved could sense the feelings of the youngsters and made a point of giving them opportunities for conversation. It is easy to understand why everyone loved her. She cared for the young like a good mother, and sometimes more.

Yocheved ran her candy business with great skill and sensibility. Upon receiving payment, she felt the coins in her hand and knew whether they were silver or copper. She calculated how much was owed and returned the exact amount of change, rarely making a mistake. She knew everyone and it would be fair to say that she was a first-rate psychologist. If someone was short a few pennies, she knew exactly who could be trusted. If someone was trustworthy, she would say: come on, take it, you'll pay me later. That was Yocheved, the daughter of Jacob Goldberg. Those who knew her have never forgotten her. She will be always remembered with love and gratitude. She honestly earned it.

Leiser Wigdorowicz

Leiser Wigdorowicz was a distinguished person in Gombin. Just the name Wigdorowicz told people that he was an important man. His stature alone imposed respect. He was tall, with a bright face and a nicely combed beard. His eyes were happy and inviting: "Look at me! See my pious ways, how I sway in all directions when I pray, and the dignified way in which I come down the steps from my favorite spot on the synagogue's eastern wall". Leiser the Hasid admonished the simple Jews to be quiet during prayers. After their Bar-Mitzvah, some boys would wander aimlessly round the House of Study with the tefillin boxes on their heads, trying to show off as "perfect" Jews. Leiser the Hasid would grab such boys by the tefillin box, drag them to the door, and throw them out. Understandably, those boys became his archenemies. But nobody dared stand up to Leiser the Hasid, not even the parents of the boys, who resented the fact that he embarrassed their children.

The respectable Hasid Leiser Wigdorowicz had a dry goods store at the corner of Maissim Street and the market square (where Plock Street began). His residence was on the back of the dry goods store. It was a nice house with good furniture. He had several large trunks where, in addition to his own money, he kept the money "deposited" by humble women who were saving to provide dowries for their daughters. These poor women looked at every saved penny as the parting of the Red Sea. What would not a mother do for her children? Was it not true that they would deny anything to themselves in order to collect enough for their daughters' dowries? Saving for dowries was essential to ensure a good match and, since there was no bank in Gombin, the mothers entrusted their money to wealthy Jews who held it in their secure iron trunks. Depositing money with the rich Jews was considered to be safe, and the house of Leiser the Hasid was one of the places where the poor families kept their savings.

Leiser Wigdorowicz did business on a large scale. He would buy merchandise from large warehouses in Lodz, Zyrardov, and Pabianice and he would sell it in Gombin and nearby towns. His dealings included large transactions based on credit and promissory notes with predetermined conditions.

One nice day, the town awoke to find that Leiser Wigdorowicz' dry goods store was closed and sealed with extra large locks. Leiser the Hasid was bankrupt again. Actually, the people of Gombin knew that he had gone bankrupt before. Some of his detractors would even say that Leiser the Hasid went bankrupt "every Monday and Thursday".

So, what happened to the deposited money that the poor women had worked so hard to save? Leiser's house had also been locked for a few days. But the family eventually returned to town. The poor women came running and, out of breath, knocked at Leiser's door. The respectable Jew and his wife put a sad face, cried, and asked for pity: "We have suffered an unfortunate tragedy, we have lost everything we had, there is nothing left: can't you see good people, that catastrophe befell us?"

To make a long story short, people yelled, screamed and cursed but there was nothing to do. Leiser the Hasid was bankrupt. The poor women lost every penny they had entrusted to him.

After a short time Leiser's dry goods store reopened and was again full of merchandise. The peddlers and the poor women who sat in the market stalls came back, again bringing their saved pennies for safekeeping in Leiser Wigdorowicz' iron trunks.

Gombin types: Abraham and Yosef Pytel,
uncles of Jacob M. Rothbart

The repetition of the bankruptcies of this "righteous man" raises a puzzling question. How was it possible that, after every financial disaster, people would come back and again deposit their savings with the "saintly man in furs" Leiser Wigdorowicz? I highly doubt that even the smartest person in the world would be able to provide a logical explanation...

Hershorn

When Hershorn was born he was named after his two grandfathers, of blessed memory, Hirsh and Aaron. The Jews of Gombin were not always accurate in pronouncing names. When they vocalized the two names quickly together, "Hirsh" and "Aaron" were fused together into "Hershorn", one name.

When he was still very young, not long after his Bar Mitzvah, Hershorn became a tailor's apprentice. Soon, however, an official of Czar Nicholas I came to Gombin to recruit children between the ages of 10 and 15 for military service. In those times, conscripts had to serve the Czar and the "fatherland" for 25 years. Hershorn was one of the draftees. He was torn away from his parents, sisters, brothers, friends and the Jewish life to which he was so attached.

But he turned out to be luckier than others. The Czarist authorities were always looking for free labour and, since he was an apprentice tailor, he was placed in a soldiers' workshop that produced uniforms for the military. Then they sent him to Vilna, where he worked as a tailor in a large military factory for the rest of his 25 years of service.

In Vilna something happened that made him happy and influenced his whole life. He met Esther Malka, a smart, healthy Jewish girl whom he married. When he was released from the military, Hershorn and Esther Malka returned to Gombin with their three full-grown, pretty daughters. In Gombin, Hershorn bought a comfortable home with a large family room on Maissim Street. He installed a big white ceramic-tiled oven in the large room. When he lit the oven in the winter just before the Sabbath, his place remained warm until the Sabbath ended. His large family room and oven became popular in Maissim Street. During the worst frosts of the winter, Esther Malka hosted a lot of guests. In addition to their own family, neighbours and other poor people who lived on the same street filled their large room. She would offer the guests a cookie, sometimes a glass of *kvass* from dried apples, which she would cook before the Sabbath in a large pot. In short, Hershorn and Esther Malka's house on Maissim Street was a very popular place in Gombin.

Their large room was also used to celebrate the weddings of the members of Hershorn's family, which was quite large. Sometimes strangers would ask Esther Malka if they could use the room for their daughters' weddings. Esther Malka did not have the heart to refuse anyone. They always managed to find extra boards for tables and benches to accommodate the crowds.

Funny things occasionally happened during these celebrations. At the wedding of the daughter of one of Hershorn's relatives, the bride's brothers and sisters began to set up the tables and benches for the guests. Realizing that there would not be enough places for everybody, they asked uncle Hershorn to help them find more boards for installing benches. Bringing a board, he asked them to estimate the number of people that would be able to sit on that bench. When they told him, he said that the bench would not be strong enough to support that many. They laughed, ignored his advice, and did what they wanted. Then, when everybody sat at the table with the bride and groom, there was a sudden wham! The bench broke, the guests were on the floor with cutlery, food, and golden broth on their fancy clothes, and everyone was screaming. Some of those on the floor were the same youngsters who had dismissed their uncle's warning. Now it was Hershorn's turn to laugh at them" "Didn't I tell you the bench would not hold?"

Esther Malka had brought with her the Lithuanian Yiddish dialect that she spoke in her hometown Vilna. However, after a few years living with her husband's family and neighbours she began to speak like the other women in Gombin. Very soon her accent disappeared and you would have never known that she once spoke differently. Other traits from her youth did stay with her for the rest of her life, like her sobriety, her strong practical sense, and her calm disposition. She would not get overly excited as the women in Gombin usually did. And she would always take pleasure in Herhorn's comical actions and expressions, despite the fact that it was anybody's guess whether they were deliberate or just a reflection of his naivete. This continued even when they were older with grown children and grandchildren.

Upon his return to Gombin, Hershorn had discovered that his 25 years in the Russian military workshops had made him an exceptionally good tailor. So he did what the Jews had always done when they had something good to sell. He packed his prayer shawl and phylacteries, needle and thread, a lead pot, scissors, and a few other items and set off on foot to visit the villages of the region's ethnic German farmers. Hershorn already spoke the "high" German of the lowlands and, with the help of God and his natural kindness, it did not take him long to acquire a substantial clientele among the affluent German farmers. In fact, the Germans loved him because he had their same mentality. He was outgoing, friendly, and always ready with a joke or a funny expression. The result? Hershorn got a lot of work. In those times, the wealthy Germans took tailors into their homes until their work was completed. Sometimes they would spend weeks in a German house. On Friday afternoon, the tailor (and his assistant, if he had one) would walk home for Sabbath and the weekend. On Monday at dawn he would pack up his sewing accessories, prayer shawl and phylacteries and return to the house of the German farmer until the end of the week.

Hershorn was successful from the start. His first German client received him warmly in his home. On the first Friday, when Hershorn was preparing to go back home for the weekend, the German gave him some flour and a sack of green peas that he had brought from a faraway place... Vilna! Hershorn returned home and surprised Esther Malka and the daughters with the prized gift from their hometown, triggering a memorable scene of overjoy and excitement.

With his natural sense of humor, Hershorn introduced a new style to the German homes. He told all types of jokes, making the entire household happy with his whims. In between, he revamped their clothes and their underwear by hand. Sewing machines were not popular yet, and when they finally arrived Hershorn refused to use those "trinkets", as he called them. "Rather than fooling around with a machine that can ruin the clothes or mutilate my hands, I will sew by hand faster than a speeding bullet and your clothes will be ready before you know it!" He would call everyone in the household including slaves and servants and say: "When my work is done, we must have a party". And he would make all of them, the homeowners and all the servants without exception, sing the following song with him: "The trousers are elegant; tra–la–la, tra–la–la, the trousers are ready, tra–la–la, clothes made by male tailors, clothes made by female seamstresses, tra–la–la, tra–la–la, tra–la–la..." After he taught them the song they would all sing it together several times. The Germans would roll on the floor laughing. No wonder Hershorn got plenty of work from them!

One day an obese German woman asked him to make extra–wide slacks for her. He stood there in shock. What should he do? He would have to measure her big ass for the pants. He placed his right palm on his cheek, as he always did when he had to make a difficult decision. The German woman stared at him with consternation: what he could possibly be thinking about? She did not know that Hershorn would not put his hands around a woman to measure her. Sometimes he allowed himself to use the household's pots to cook himself some pasta, of he would eat a piece of the non–Kosher bread or cheese made by the German women. For these things he could find an excuse. But how could he put his arms around a woman to measure her, and a German woman to boot? Hershorn could not allow himself to do this.

Deep in thought he suddenly had an idea. He fetched his bag, taking out a piece of chalk and one of the large sheets of paper that he always carried with him to make molds. He then returned to the German woman, who was still standing in perplexity. Hershorn spread the paper on the floor and told her to lie down and stretch out her legs. She did as he asked. Like most German women from the lowlands, she was not shy, so she lay there waiting to see what would happen. Chalk in hand, Hershorn began to dance around her, drawing the contours of her hips and legs. When he was finished with his markings he told her that she could now stand up. With great effort, the fat German woman lifted herself from the floor and a smiling Hershorn told her that when the slacks were ready they would organize a special party.

Water carriers in Gombin

Hershele Mulicher

They called him Mulicher , but that was not his last name. A "mulicher" was someone who smuggled people across borders. Since Gombin was far from the border it is hard to understand why they called him Mulicher. But we can leave that for now. Maybe others will want to investigate it. For our description of him, it is not important.

Everyone in Gombin knew Hershele Mulicher. First, because he owned a haberdashery store in the marketplace, right under Poznanski's five story building. Second, because he had a big mouth. He would talk about everybody, always cutting to the quick.

His favourite targets were the religious figures of the town. He would mock the way in which the Rabbi's wife walked to the ritual bath and he would pock fun at the cantor, his wife, and other leaders of the Gombin community.

Hershele Mulicher was surrounded by a group that could not get enough of his jokes. One of his admirers was the writer of official requests, whose beautiful handwriting literally danced on the paperwork. He always took Mulicher's side and often gave him ideas for his jokes.

One would think that Mulicher was an ignoramus or a boor, but the opposite was true. When you walked into his haberdashery he was always reading a holy book annotated by Rashi. He behaved like the other Jews of Gombin. In the synagogue and the House of Study, he would always sit with his gang on the back benches.

In my later years, when I was far from Gombin, I sometimes wondered what sort of person Hershele Mulicher was. Was he an enlightened Jew? If that was the case, why was it that nobody mentioned him when talking about the teachings of the town's Enlighteners? Was he a complete heretic who wanted to avoid hostility in our small traditional town? It is difficult to understand. But one thing is clear: compared to the rest of the Gombin's Jewish population, he was completely different. It is worthwhile, then, to record here the various" types of Jews that one could find in Gombin.

Chayaleh Stolzman

Chayaleh Stolzman did not belong to the old generation of settled Jews of Gombin that I have described in previous chapters of my memoirs.

Chayaleh was the daughter of a wealthy family, the Stolzmans. Her grandmother, who was still alive, reminded me of the matriarch in Jacob Gordin's play "Mirele Efros". She held the whole family together and her sons, daughters, and grandchildren respected every word she said. With the exception of one son who was a Hasid, all her children were assimilationists. They all spoke Polish and when they had to talk with a Jew they spoke German. There were many ethnic Germans around Gombin, and many Jews spoke Yiddish, Polish and German. The Stolzmans owned a large tavern and their children were among the wealthiest German speakers in Gombin.

Now that I have described Chayaleh's family background, I can tell you about the rest of her life.

In her early years Chayaleh received the best education that affluent "half–assimilated" Jewish parents could provide to their children in a small town like Gombin. They hired private teachers who taught them Polish, German and Russian. Chayaleh was taught to play piano and learned everything else that was deemed appropriate for a Polish young lady of Jewish origin. She was a good student, absorbed everything, and became a passionate reader. Her favorite writers were the German poets Goethe, Shiller and Lessing. She also idolized German musicians like Haydn, Beethoven, Schumann, and Schubert. In one word, she was in love with German culture. In addition to being so well educated, Chayaleh was a gentle person who respected people regardless of their nationality and always sympathized with the poor.

Chayaleh's closest childhood friend was Malka Wolfowicz, from a wealthy Jewish family who were not yet as assimilated as the Shtoltzmans. Malka's father, Zelig Wolfowicz was a forestry businessman. On the Sabbath he and his wife Itele would dress up and go to synagogue. He joined the men downstairs while Itele sat upstairs in the women's section. After prayers, they would meet and walk home together. Zelig was a handsome man. Tall, with a broad body and a full blond well–groomed beard, he looked like a giant beside his wife Itele who was short and thin. This did not stop her from giving birth to half a dozen children. With the exception of one (who was not bright) they were all healthy and talented, including their only daughter Malka, Chayaleh's best friend.

When we founded the Jewish workers' organization Bund in Gombin, Chayaleh and Malka were among the first women to join the movement. Despite the fact that they were only teenagers, they were among the most devoted activists. They began recruiting new members and learning Yiddish in order to read the Bund's documents and publications, but they soon proved to be very useful to the movement in other ways.

The Czarist officials in Gombin had detected that we were organizing a revolutionary movement and it was very important to avoid "falling into their hands" before we managed to expand and consolidate. The two girls were good friends with the children of the Polish mayor of Gombin (who, as we learned later, was not a fan of the Czarist regime). Thanks to Chayaleh and Malka, we got detailed information from the town hall about the activities and plans of the police.

When the girls told us that gendarmes would come from Gostynin to carry out searches in the middle of the night, we immediately took steps to hide all the "incriminating" literature we had about the Bund. Many of our members simply did not go home to sleep that night. Later on, Chayaleh and Malka were able to tell us whose homes would be searched. In a nutshell, the help of the two girls allowed us to survive intact the repression of the Czarist regime. I cannot here include all the details of that memorable episode. Hopefully, it will be possible to do it on another occasion.

One more word about Chayaleh and Malka. After almost sixty years, I cannot stop admiring those fine, gentle and moral women. It is true that all Jewish youth at that time were highly idealistic. The activists of the movement thought little about personal matters. The Jewish youth were prepared to sacrifice in order to achieve human dignity and freedom for the Jews and all mankind. As Jews, they felt they had to fight for the general freedom of all. And they wanted to correct all the injustces and humiliations suffered by the Jews throughout their history. That is why they thought little about their personal happiness when they immersed themselves in the struggle.

Until 1909, three years after arriving in America, I would still receive the occasional periodical from Chayaleh. But I did not hear anything from or about her after that. Then, while visiting my sister in Montreal during the winter of 1947–48, I met a recently arrived survivor from Gombin, Abraham Grzywacz (grandson of Boruch Grzywacz). I asked him about various people and, when I mentioned Chayaleh Stolzman, he told me the following story.

When Hitler's armies attacked Poland and occupied Gombin, they immediately began to mistreat the Jews. They made arrests tearing the men away from their women and children. They stole what they wanted and requisitioned many of their houses, killing, beating and throwing out the half–naked Jews after they took everything.

Chayaleh Stolzman could not understand how the Germans, the people of the high culture, the people of her adored Goethe, Shiller and Lessing, could possibly perpetrate such atrocities. She thought that it was a matter of simple soldiers running wild during wartime. She believed that the German officers did not know what these soldiers were doing. So one day, without telling anyone, she went to speak with the commandant of Gombin. She wanted to inform him what his soldiers were doing to the Jews.

The commandant looked at her with contempt and shouted: "You damn swine Jewess! How do you even dare come to me?" He called his soldiers and ordered them to tie her up. For a few days they tormented her with various forms of abuse, and in the end they tied her to a horse and dragged her naked through the streets of Gombin. The Polish neighbours that watched it were laughing with mockery on their piggish faces. That was how Chayaleh Stolzman gave up her clean soul. Let this be written for all generations, and may the nation of murderers that could perpetrate such atrocities never be able to wash away the blood of our martyrs! Honor her holy memory!

Chaimele – Keep it going

There were many Jews in Gombin named Chaimele, and every Chaimele had a nickname, otherwise nobody would know which Chaimele you were talking about. The nickname of the Chaimele I am describing here was "Keep it going". You may wonder: how on earth did he get such a funny nickname? Well, this is the story.

Chaimele was a short, solidly built middle–aged man. He had a wife and a house full of children. His older boys worked with him in his workshop, making peasant coats from coarse fabrics of inferior quality. Chaimele was very good at his craft, and the family lived well compared to other Jewish families in Gombin. He was a good–natured, lighthearted man who sometimes would come across as a bit childish.

On Friday evening Chaimele would sit at the table and lead his sons in lively Sabbath songs. Most of his melodies came from the mechanical music of pianolas, music boxes and carousels or from the songs of the Russian soldiers that often marched through Gombin. His tune for the grace after the meal was playful. It sounded exactly like a Russian military march. Later in my life I was reminded of Chaimele – Keep it going when I read the Yiddish writer I.M. Visenberg's story called "A Father With Sons".

The carousels used to come to Gombin for the summer fairs. They were set up at the German market square and would amuse the town for a week or two. The place was full of children and youngsters, Poles and Jews, who never missed an evening. The carousel was the main attraction for the kids, who loved to climb on the horses and carriages and go round and round with the tunes coming from the music box. They brought every possible penny they could get at home in order to pay for the rides. Some engaged in daring acrobatics, jumping from one horse to another or from a carriage to a horse in the middle of the ride. It was noisy and everyone was thrilled. Chaimele was always there. A man with a beard among all the kids. The Jewish boys would tease him: "Chaimele, I bet you won't be able to withstand one turn on the carousel. You will either faint or fall off the horse. You are a chicken guy who is afraid of everything". Chaimele held back for a long time. He knew that he was the only grown–up man among all these "rascals". He felt embarrassed, but he really wanted to get on one of the horses and enjoy the exhilaration of turning round and round.

One evening the young clowns teased him so much that he could not restrain himself any longer. He paid the few cents for the ride and jumped on a horse.

The kids celebrated a great victory. They stood around the carousel and every time Chaimele passed by on his horse they shouted: "Chaimele, Keep it going!"

In short, when the ride ended, Chaimele came down from the horse looking pale and wobbling from dizziness. Well, I am sure that you are already guessing what happened next. Everybody rolled with laughter when they heard the story. Whenever they met him, they would greet him with the words: "Chaimele, Keep it going!" And that's how he earned his nickname for the rest of his life.

Crazy Ruchele

It was generally accepted as a fact of life that every Jewish community had a crazy person. Gombin had two, a man and a woman. I will first tell you about crazy Ruchele.

She was a tall woman with a pale face, wacky eyes, long hands and feet, and a lunatic's appearance. She spent her days wandering through the Jewish streets in the rags that she received from pious women. She begged for food and very few turned her down.

Where did Ruchele live? No one knew. There were homes that offered her a place to sleep on cold winter nights, but she always refused.

Hardly anyone knew where she came from. Did she have relatives, sisters, brothers, family? It was simply a mystery, and few were interested in those questions. There was a house for the poor in Gombin, but she did not want to go there. She just wandered through the cracks and ruins of the Jewish streets of the town. Christian women would tell us that they sometimes saw her in a barn with the animals. The summer months were not as bad, but people wondered how she managed through the winter. She did not live long, but during her short life she was a rarity even for a secluded town like Gombin.

One night, a few years after she passed away, I was coming home from the Heder of Mordechai the teacher with a lantern in my hand. It was dark and raining. As I turned into Maissim Street I heard someone plodding behind me. I turned my head and saw crazy Ruchele. I began to take faster steps. The faster I walked, the faster she ran after me. I "knew" that dead people assembled after midnight at the nearby synagogue and stayed there until the first crow of the rooster... But it was still early in the night and I was overcome with fear that she would take me who knows where, maybe to the demons. When I finally reached my house, totally pale, my good mother Sarah of blessed memory was alarmed. "What happened my child?" I told her crazy Ruchele had tried to snatch me. "What are you talking about my child? Ruchele has been dead for a long time and dead people don't snatch children."

A funeral in Gombin

Crazy Yosele

Crazy Yosele was the opposite of crazy Ruchele. His madness was of the melancholic type. He would wander around town in silence. He hardly ever spoke to anyone but he would do bizarre things. For example, in the summer he would sleep on the stretcher that was used to carry the corpses to the cemetery. The stretcher had a top cover made of a ripped black cloth that looked like a carriage awning. The bottom was like a bed mounted on posts, with front and back handles to carry the corpse. Since it was quite a distance to the cemetery, they would lift the stretcher and carry it on the shoulders of six or eight men. When the carriers got tired, others would take over. In those days, they did not use wagons to bring the dead to their final resting place.

The stretcher was kept in the anteroom of the synagogue, standing on legs that opened and closed. The burial society was unhappy about the fact that Yosele liked to sleep on the stretcher. Some members would scold him but, when they did it, the other members silenced them. They said that he should be left alone. Why bother about a mad guy?

What Yosele probably did not know was that, in Gombin, some people believed that every night the dead came to the synagogue to read the Torah and celebrate. There was a story that, one night, a Jew was walking by the synagogue and heard their prayers. They called out his name to bestow him the honour of reading the Torah. The man knew that when the dead call you, you have to go. If not, you could drop dead in the middle of the street. And when you enter the synagogue, you must go straight to the pulpit and bless the Torah without looking around. You have to keep your eyes closed and, when you are done, leave the synagogue without looking back until you are safely out on the street.

This legend and others did not make a difference for crazy Yosele. He slept on that stretcher for years and the dead never disturbed his sleep. They left him alone...

In the cold nights of winter crazy Yosele would lie on a hard bench near the warm oven in the House of Study. He slept there through the entire winter.

Yosele did other crazy things. Every day he would go from house to house begging. The women would give him some grits or a piece of bread to eat. Sometimes he got more bread than he could eat. What should he do with the leftover bread? Throw it away? No! Perhaps the next day he will not get anything and go hungry... Where to hide it? He looked for cracks and holes and stuffed them with bread. One of his favorite hiding places was the Holy Ark in the House of Study. There were many small niches... a perfect place to stuff the bread. The result? Lots of mice running around the House of Study!

Shloime Jacob the house's custodian, investigated where all the mice were coming from. He knew that it was not allowed to bring food to the House of Study. He questioned the boys who sat there all day studying the Torah. Maybe they knew something? Maybe it was them that were bringing food to the place? Shloime Jacob was desperate to solve the mystery.

One night, as some boys were deep into their studies, Shloime Jacob heard some rustling near the Holy Ark. He ran to see what was happening and saw crazy Yosele with his head inside the ark. "Yosele, what are you doing? Did you put something in there?"

When Shloime Jacob finally saw what was going on inside the ark he was shocked. Oy! There were pieces of bread stuffed into every corner... It took him a lot of work to clean the Holy Ark and get rid of the mice.

Yosele did this and other crazy things. It was hard to bear. No one could figure out how to stop him and his antics.

The synagogue chandelier

This story goes back to when I was very young. I was a pupil at the Heder of Mordechai the teacher. One day, when we finished studying the portion of the week and were ready to go home, Reb Mordechai told us "Children! Tomorrow, God willing, will be a great day. You do not need to come to school." The rumblings about the new chandelier had been going on in Gombin for quite some time. The people in town had been talking about the need to beautify and decorate the synagogue, which was very old and everyone loved. They decided to hang a big light fixture to brighten and enliven the building.

They collected money and everyone gave what they could. The enterprise took a long time and, at one point, people began to lose hope that enough funds would be raised to buy the fixture.

But the day finally arrived. A young man from Gombin went to Warsaw in order to look around for an appropriate light fixture. If I remember right, it was at Elstein's chandelier factory that he found an antique fixture that was exquisite and the price was right.

He returned from Warsaw and told everyone about the chandelier and its cost. A committee was formed to handle the matter. Everyone was talking about this rare antique even before it arrived from Warsaw.

When the chandelier arrived in Gombin, the committee decided to turn the day into a holiday and organize a parade to take it to the synagogue. I cannot recall who was in charge, but the best director could not have put together a more beautiful mass scene. At the front was a large wagon with the fixture. Following the wagon were the rabbi, the cantor, the rabbinic judge, and other scholars from town. After them came the synagogue administrators and the wealthy Jews, the members of the burial society, elderly Jews with grey beards, middle–aged men with black beards, younger men with incipient beards, and excited children of all ages. On the side of the street were the women, young and old. Everyone was happy, imbued with the feeling of a divine presence, but trying not to display too much joy (Jews are not allowed to be too happy).

In my later years I saw paintings of Jewish artists that illustrated mass gatherings of Jews. I remember one that was called "Diaspora". It showed a large group of Jews walking in the desert. Tired and distressed, they dragged themselves through the wasteland, with disheveled twisted beards, chased by the storm winds.

But I never saw a painting depicting the mass of Jews with happy faces that I saw that day in Gombin when they brought the chandelier to the synagogue.

When they hanged it on the chain that had been prepared in advance, and lit the lights which hung with polished glass on all sides, the synagogue looked majestic. The wooden carved Holy Ark, covered by a blue satin curtain trimmed in gold, stood out more radiant than ever. The coloured glass on the windows took on a new regal appearance as the whole synagogue came alive.

Arieh Zilberstein, the candlemaker

by Julius (Jonah) Green

Translated by Janie Respitz
Edited by Leon Zamosc

[Original book: Pages 197-200 Yiddish]

I will never forget that Jew from Gombin. I remember him from when I was a small boy. Every time he looked at me I felt a throb in my heart. He would often pull me towards him, place his hands on my small shoulders and stare at me from under his thick white eyebrows. His fingers grasped my shoulders tightly and when our eyes met I saw sadness in his eyes. I felt he looked at me through and through. All that lasted barely a second. He would then loosen his fingers and let go my shoulders. I left in silence. I was seven or eight years old at the time. This man would come into our house every day, sit in the same place and observe my father's tailor work.

My father and Arieh Zilberstein spoke rarely, and when they did speak, it was always about the same things. My father spoke about his two sons who had left Gombin and were living in America, and Arieh spoke about his son Shloime and his children whom he missed very much. Shloime and his family were by then also in America, living in Detroit.

I knew this conversation between Arieh and my father by heart. Arieh's beard was white as snow. My father's beard was also white. It was difficult in Gombin to guess someone's age by their face. Every young man already had a beard. The majority looked undernourished, they dressed in rags, and they hardly ever smiled. Most people's eyes were sad, families were large, the children numerous. It was common for a couple to have half a dozen children or more. The parents lived with their married children and hungered together.

There were cases in which the sons and daughters who went to America would not send support to the families they left behind. In such cases the situation of the parents was bitter. Only a few received help from their children in America. Arieh Zilberstein belonged to the lucky few.

By the time of my Bar Mitzvah I began to understand what it meant when they said that Arieh's son was successful in America. His name now was Solomon Zilberstein, he lived in Detroit and regularly, every month, sent money to his father. Arieh did not suffer hunger. He felt secure, protected and proud that his son provided for him. Yet, he continued to live as modestly as before, when he barely earned a living. I heard him tell my father that he does not allow his wife to peel potatoes because she peels off to much flesh. "I peel them, and then sell the peel to the farmers to feed their pigs".

On another occasion I heard him say: "My wife eats too much. A person should not eat in excess, they should always leave something for the next day".

The last couple of years before I left for America, Arieh and his wife would come to our Passover seders. When I said to him "Next Year in Jerusalem" he looked at me and said: "No, next year you will be in America". I will never forget that. The year was 1913. A silence fell over our table. Arieh shook his head and looked at my father. A few minutes later he said to my father: "Don't sin, it is God's will". My father turned his head to me, then to Arieh and said in a trembling voice: "Yes Arieh, it is God's will. We must accept it".

Arieh sat in silence. He looked at his veiny hands, lifted his head and looked far away. A few weeks later a bunch of legal papers arrived from America. We could not read them, but the accompanying letter said that I had to begin to prepare for my voyage.

We read the letter many times at the table. Arieh was sitting there with a gloomy face as white as his beard. His hands, which were resting on his cane, were shaking. By the time that we finished reading the letter he looked very pale. I saw how he lifted his head to the sky and his lips mumbled a soft prayer. I looked in his eyes. There were two crystal tears in the corners of his eyes, and they fell over his beard like a strand of pearls.

That day Arieh remained with us longer than usual. He whispered something to my father, then called me over and said: "Yoinele, this evening you will come with me to the synagogue to pray the evening prayers". I looked at my father. He nodded his head and said: "Yes".

When Arieh and I left the synagogue after prayers, the sky was filled with stars and the moon shone bright. After we walked a few steps Arieh turned around and motioned me to follow him. We sat on the steps of the synagogue.

Arieh stood up and looked at the sky. His lips began to move, his beard trembled and he said this to me: "God created a beautiful world. How nice it is to look at the sky, at the stars, at the moon. Even in darkness there is so much beauty. Only man's heart is heavy. It is filled with sadness. You know Yoinele, I don't suffer from hunger. But no one can look into my heart and see the longing I feel for my son Shloime and his children".

He was quiet for a moment and then nervously said: "You Yoinele, will soon see my son and my grandchildren. I am sending with you a piece of myself. My feelings, my longing... I am planting in you a piece of my soul".

He sat down beside me and put his hand on my knee. He looked me in the eye and said: "Tell my son that I pray for him day and night. I pray to the Almighty that he and the children should be successful, that he should find happiness in everything he does, that he should be in awe of God, and that he should remember that God always listens to my prayers. But please don't tell my son and grandchildren that my heart is broken from longing".

Again he was silent. Suddenly I heard him say something, not to me but to himself: "Why must we be separated? Why did the Master of the Universe give us a heart that suffers so much? Why can't I see my son? It is all so bizarre, my child. We are forbidden to question the ways of God".

It was very sad. I did not understand clearly what Arieh said, but I felt the pain in his heart, his loneliness, his gratitude to his son Shloime and his pride. Of the things he said the words that moved me the most were: "Why do we have to be separated?" I realized that soon I would also be separated, torn away from my family as I left to America.

Arieh removed his hand from my knee, stood up and said: "Good night Yoinele". He walked slowly to the street where he lived.

I remained seated and watched him vanish deeper and deeper into the night's darkness. My head was filled with the words he had said to me. His steps were becoming softer on the cobblestones. My knee, which he had held with his bony hand, kept burning until I no longer heard his steps, until he was swallowed up by the dense night.

Arieh Zilberstein was a candlemaker by profession. He was a strong man. He always looked fresh and healthy. When I left to America he was close to eighty. Many people in Gombin were jealous of his dear son Shloime. People said that he sent so much money that the old man must have a "bundle".

The day of my departure Arieh came to our house. He took me to a corner and whispered in my ear: "Tell my son and his children that when my days on this earth will end, I will pray for them in heaven, and now Yoinele, you shall be under the protection of the Master of the Universe. Never forget Gombin and the Jews of Gombin".

I have never forgotten.

Folk sayings from Gombin

Translated by Janie Respitz
Edited by Leon Zamosc

[Original book: Pages 202-202 Yiddish]

The farmer can't distinguish between a cross and an "A". (Ignorant, illiterate)

Together they sell stolen pigs. (Up to no good)

He is and expert on this matter like a pig is an expert on yeast. (Has no idea what he's talking about)

The farmer and his wife lie for so long on one pillow that they end up having the same thoughts.

The Gentile is not Kosher but his money is Kosher.

It is good to remove hot coals from the stove with someone else's hands.

He did not even say dog… kiss my ass. (A guest that was treated well leaves without saying "thanks")

What a smart man doesn't say, a fool has on his tongue.

A Jewish scholar gives good advice.

I will not sin with talk. (I will not talk badly about people)

I will not be punished for what I say. (What I am saying is true)

My words should not complicate things for him. (When talking about someone who is dead)

Pluck feathers. (Tear the feathers from the stems – do a thorough job)

Don't attempt to do something you can get used to.

Picking peas. (Picking out the lice)

One is to seven as he is to seventy. (He exaggerates)

A punch goes away but words keep hurting.

Naked, bare foot and hungry (Someone who has nothing)

S'Gligen Tuenish. (A nonsense phrase used to begin telling a story)

When the heart is full, the eyes overflow.

Don't overwhelm my teeth with talk. (Don't bother me about other things, don't distract me)

He is already preparing his wallet. (He's waiting for a windfall or an inheritance).

He is an expensive purse. (Likes to keep up appearances)

A mangy horse attracts flies.

A fool must pay twice and a lazy man must run twice.

By day they're ready to divorce, by night they're ready for bed

You study your entire life and you die a fool.

You study until you are seventy and you still die a fool.

If you are lazy, you have nothing to eat.

Nobody has everything.

He lives in a fool's paradise. (Does not worry about the future)

You can always find an excuse for the angel of death.

A taker is not a giver.

Take with a laugh give with a cry. (When you take, you rejoice, but when you give, you weep)

When man thinks, God laughs. (Don't make too many plans)

Jews eat kreplach (dumplings) three times a year – when there are harsh blows. (Jews strike their chests on Yom Kippur, their willow branches on Hoshana Rabba and their feet and hands when they hear Haman's name on Purim – these are three times in a year that tradition prescribes eating kreplach)

When the Angel of Death slays, it always has a justification.

When you are young time crawls, by middle age time runs, by old age time flies.

A guest for a while, sees for a mile.

Someone may be pretty, but I am smart.

May all your teeth fall out, except the one that gives you a toothache. (A curse)

Don't push your hand through a narrow door. (Don't get involved in other people's arguments)

From just a little you can fill a bowl. (A little goes a long way)

When does a poor man rejoice? When he finds something he lost.

For a patient going into the hospital is a big deal, but coming out is much easier.

If you dig a hole for someone else, you may fall into it yourself.

Little goat, little lamb, red oranges. When father beats up mother, the children dance. (A very silly rhyme)

When you can't go over it, go under it.

Go complain on Yom Kippur. (This will get you nowhere)

Go complain to the devil's mother-in-law. (This too will get you nowhere)

Let him be a Cossack, as long as we survive.

Talks about cemeteries, great troubles. (Sarcastic remark in mixed Polish-Yiddish, about someone who brags about his ancestral origins)

He thinks that he is a grandson of Rabbi Tzots. (Someone who pretends to have a pedigree)

If God wants, he sweeps with a broom. (Even a weakling can achieve something big)

Don't examine the mouth of a horse that you received as a gift.

When it boils is bubbles over.

I don't know about any evil feasts, just as I don't know what you want from me.

Purim is no holy day, and fever is no disease.

You don't have to show a stick to a beaten dog.

If someone in your family was hanged, don't mention the word hang. (Don't talk about something you know people are sensitive about)

The apple does not fall far from the tree.

You cannot make a Shtreiml (a fur hat worn by Hasidim) from a pig's tail. (You cannot refine a boor)

Activities of the Gombiner Societies

A Sacred Task

by Sam Rafel

Translated by Janie Respitz
Edited by Leon Zamosc

[Original book: Pages 205-211 Yiddish and 99-104 English]

Sam Rafel

In 1913 I left Gombin and came to America. I was a young man of 17 going to a strange new world. I had an uncle in New York, my mother's brother-in-law, but I knew I could not count on much help from him. Still, I decided to leave home because, at that time, the situation in Gombin had become unbearable.

Gombin had been a quiet, sluggish place until the late 19th century, when the arrival of worldly, secular ideas brought rapid changes and a great deal of excitement. The exhilaration, however, only lasted until the failed 1905 revolution, which led to years of Czarist counter-revolutionary repression. It was a period of terror, police harassment, and general disappointment and resignation. Gombin's youngsters were either sent to Siberia or left for America. There was an unsettling stillness in town. The fresh worldly winds that had briefly blown through Gombin had left everybody with an uneasy feeling. And what was happening in Gombin was also happening in all the towns and cities of Russian empire.

We could feel the anguish and emptiness at home. My only brother Chaim had been arrested during the revolution and was now sitting in a Warsaw jail. At the time I was 17 years old. I lived with my parents and three sisters. My father, Pinhas Schacher, was a tailor. He had a small workshop at home. Feeling suffocated by the depressed mood in the town, I finally convinced him to allow me to travel, promising that I would not go for long and I would return after a short time. My father understood my anxiety. He was an active person who gave a lot of his time to communal work. He was the manager of the society to Help the Sick and the poor Jews of Gombin would always come to our home for assistance. As a child, I had helped my father writing the notes that the sick gave to doctors and pharmacists. I myself had health issues, problems with my lungs, but my father did not stop me from leaving. Eventually, I embarked on a ship to New York.

At the time, there was no visa requirement. All you had to do was show you that had 25 dollars in your possession when you arrived at the port in New York. I went straight from the ship to my uncle's place.

I had learned to work as a tailor at home, but I arrived in America at a difficult time. I walked the New York Jewish neighborhoods stopping at the workshops of the small Jewish tailors, but I could not find work anywhere. Finally I went into a woman's clothing store on Houston Avenue and told the owner that I had just gotten off the ship and needed work. "Alright, you have a job in my store", he said. I worked for a couple of weeks and he kept postponing my wages. Then, one Friday he said: "I'll pay you next Monday". When I came back on Monday there was no sign of the store, clothes, machines or the Jew. He simply liquidated the business and disappeared.

I worked at a small trousers factory, and later at a bigger one. But I did not last very long, the bosses did not like my work. In one factory the only workers were the owners, a couple who were always fighting, and a young man who pressed the clothes. One day, when the owners fired the presser, I left in solidarity. The presser had a wife and child. We tried to develop our own business, but things went poorly and we did not receive any work.

I continued to work in factories but always for short periods of time. I had difficulty adapting to American conditions. In one factory, for example, I messed up sewing sleeves: all the work was returned and had to be done again. The boss immediately fired me. Nevertheless, after a year I had managed to save 180 dollars which I planned to use for a ship ticket to return home. I kept the money in Adolph Mandel's small bank. One day, unfortunately, Mandel's bank and many other small banks declared bankruptcy and I lost all my "capital". That, and the fact that the outbreak of the First World War made sea travel impossible, put an end to my thoughts about returning to Gombin.

Eventually, I left New York for Newark, where some landsmen from Gombin were living, including Hymie Rubin, Abraham Shtiglitz and others. I worked there in various jobs until 1916, when I became secretary of the executive board of the International Garment Workers Union. My material difficulties ended and I finally started to fit in. In Newark I also met my wife, who had came from Gombin to America with her family in 1910. I began to earn more money and, as things improved for me, I began to think about Gombin and its poverty, wondering what could be done to help the needy Jews of the town.

The Executive Committee of the Gombiner Organization in Newark

At the time, the Gombin Jews of New York and Newark were trying to organize a systematic way to send money to Jewish philanthropic institutions in Gombin. In 1920, the Gombin Relief Committee of New York and Newark was founded by the following members: Max Jacklin, the Kraut family (father Simon and sons Teddy, Alex and Philip), Louis Green, Max Green, Ralph Rafel, Louis Koch, Abe Carmel, Abraham Itshe Zichlin, Abraham Max, Nathan

Kleinert, Zishe Zichlinsky, Maitshik, Wolf Kesselman, Jack Sherman, Joseph Stern.

Five years later, after Hersh Karo arrived in America, the "Young Men's Benevolent Association" was founded. Their goal was to give money support to the Gombin landsmen arriving in America. The Relief Committee was also involved in this work: according to its bylaws, help should be given to the Jews from Gombin regardless of their location.

The Executive Committee of the Gombiner Organization of New York

In those days I was the chairman of the Relief Committee. Our job was to collect money for a fund that we had created in Gombin: the Gemilat Hesed Kasse, which offered interest free loans to all the Jews of Gombin. The Joint Distribution Committee helped us with this work. The Joint matched the money we raised with an equivalent amount of its own and sent it to Gombin. Later, in the 1930s, similar Gombin committees were set up in Detroit and Chicago.

I went to visit Gombin in 1930. It is hard to describe the joy I felt after being away from my hometown for 17 years, and finally being able to reunite with my parents, my brother, my sisters, the rest of our family and so many acquaintances and close friends. I did not go empty handed. I brought a large amount of money from the Relief Committee, mainly for the Gemilat Hesed Kasse and also for other Jewish institutions. When I arrived in Gombin, my warm reception at home was followed by a big reception at the the Gemilat Hesed Kasse. The banquet was chaired by Itzkhak Shikorsky, his secretaries were Meir Zaideman and Abraham Tiber. They bestowed honors on me as president of the Relief Committee, but the honors were not only for me, they were for all the landsmen from Gombin who had participated in the American effort to send help to Gombin.

Attending the banquet were representatives from all the Jewish organizations and movements. There was a moving moment in which they gave me a gift, a golden plaque with the inscription: "To our honorary chairman, in recognition of his help".

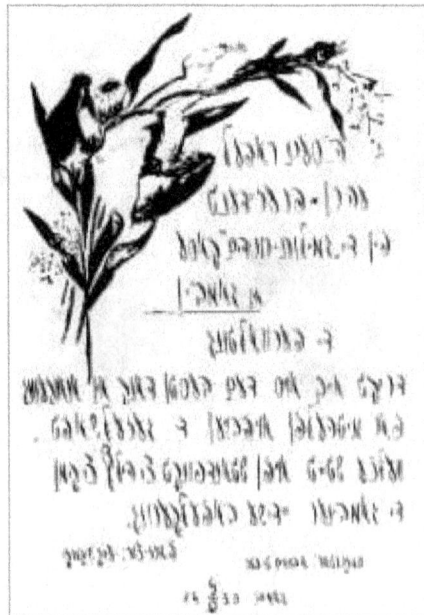

Gift received by Sam Rafel from the Jews of Gombin, 1930.
The text reads: "Mr. Sam Rafel, honorary president of Gemilat Hesed.
We are grateful for your help, which provides assistance to the Jewish community of Gombin. Signed by Itzkhak Shikorsky and Abraham Tiber"

During the two weeks that I spent in Gombin I chaired many meetings, learned about the plight of the needy, and promised that our work in America would continue to grow not only for the Gemilat Hesed Kasse but for all the assistance organizations including the Beit Halehem, Linat Zedeck, and the Children's Home. It was exciting to see how the assistance work was handled in Gombin, and when I returned to America I tried to instill my enthusiasm in the hearts of the other members of the Relief Committee.

Seven years later, in 1937, I visited Gombin again. This time I was accompanied by my wife and, once again, I did not go empty handed. They gave me a reception that was even bigger than the one I got on my first visit. It took place in the large Firemen's Hall and was attended by more than three thousand Jews, virtually everyone in the town. In Gombin, those were years of terrible poverty and anti–semitism, which was incited by the Polish government. This time, I had brought a camera and made a film of what I saw during the visit. Later, I showed that film many times in America and Israel. I believe that it has great historical and cultural importance.

During the visit, once again I spent many hours at meetings in which we discussed the plans to increase the aid from America. Before my departure, I reached an agreement with Gombin's Dr. Dzewciepolski, who agreed to provide free treatment to the Jewish poor and send us the bill at the end of the year.

All this was in 1937, when we did not expect that, two years later, Gombin and all the other Jewish cities and towns in Poland would be swallowed up by the fires of a horrific war. When the war broke out, we lost contact with Gombin. Despite that, I thought that we had to continue our work, collecting money and establishing a fund that would allow us to help the Jews of Gombin as soon as the war ended.

Our organization raised 25 thousand dollars but, unfortunately, the end of the war brought the dreadful news about the Shoah. During those terrible days, we received some letters from Jewish survivors from Gombin. We immediately began to help them with money, packages, clothing and medicines. We then started a movement to bring surviving Jewish Gombiner families to America. In a short time we managed to complete the paperwork to bring fifty families from refugee camps in Poland and Germany.

We also decided to launch a large help initiative for the Gombin Jews in Israel. The first thing we did was to organize a Lending Society in Israel. At our meetings, people began to voice the proposal that we had to build a monument to memorialize Gombin. There was a suggestion to create a Gombin House in Tel Aviv, which would serve as a center for the Gombiner Jews. It would have a memorial hall and would serve as a gathering place for historical materials about Gombin. After much effort, the committee managed to obtain an available lot in Tel Aviv from the Keren Kayemet. We then built the house, with a beautiful Memorial Hall to accommodate 150 people. The names of the martyrs from Gombin were inscribed on one of the walls, illuminated by an eternal flame and covered with a curtain. Every year a memorial takes place in that hall for the murdered Jews of Gombin. In the front room, before the entrance to the main hall, one can see inscriptions with the names of the men's and women's divisions of the American relief organizations, including the names of their officers.

Farewell evening in New York for Abraham Marks,
before his visit to Gombin as representative of the
Gombiners' organization in America, 1927

The Gombin House has a three–room apartment for a family of caretakers. We hired a Gombiner couple, the Segals, with the three children that they found and adopted on their escape road to Russia. As I write these lines, two of those children are already married.

In 1959 I went to Israel with my wife. The members of the Gombin committee met us at the airport. Most of the Gombiners in Israel came from their far off Kibbutzim and Moshavim to the memorial evening in Tel Aviv. That evening I showed the film I had made in Gombin more than twenty years earlier. I will never forget the people's tears when they saw their parents, relatives and close friends. I had also brought money from our American Relief Committee, and we spent quite a bit of time making plans to continue our work.

In 1962 my wife and I returned to Israel again. The Gombiners in Israel were happy to receive us again and expressed their appreciation for our work in America. There was another emotional memorial evening at the Gombin House in Tel Aviv.

Sam Rafel, Max Jacklin and Jack Holtzman

At the present time, our organizations in New York and Newark continue to be very active. We have succeeded in bringing together Gombiner Jews from all over the world. We have also managed to instill in them a feeling of warmth, kinship and intimate friendship. Among the Jews from Gombin, family occasions are not just for relatives. They also invite the entire Gombin "colony", all the other landsmen from Gombin who live in their communities.

Today, our most urgent undertaking is the publication of the Gombin Memorial Book. It is a sacred task that is on the conscience of all of us.

A Visit to the Gombin House in Tel Aviv

by Louis Philips (Pochekha)

Translated by Janie Respitz
Edited by Leon Zamosc

[Original book: Pages 212-214 Yiddish]

I am approaching the house that carries the name of my hometown. I experience a storm of emotions. Feelings of sadness that our former home no longer exists; and a feeling of joy that a clean white building has been built as a symbol of the vanished Jewish life in Gombin.

I am now standing in front of the building that must eternalize the memory of the destruction. A mental image flashes in my memory – a moment, as I lay in the shade of the Gombin forest reading, or perhaps I should say praying over, Herzl's book "The Jewish State". A cloud covers my thoughts: there was a land which was ours – yet not ours... But now, I am standing in front of a Gombin House that was built on our land, in a Jewish country of our own. I happily climb the wide stairs.

Gombin Jews in Israel at the spot where the Gombin House was built

The whole house is filled with dazzling light. The crowd is gathering. The mood is shining and gleaming. Everyone is happy and radiant. The children of Gombin enter in a procession. So many people, close and dear to my heart. I am surrounded by dozens of friends. They gather around me. For them, I am Potchekha's son – their guest who comes from America!

Laying the foundation
From right: Rabbi Shrager, Frenkel and Yakov Finkelstein

Their warm words will keep ringing in my ears. The scene of this day in the Gombin House will always stay in my memory. Among the crowd I see many dear faces, friends from my childhood in Gombin: I see Rivka Frenkel, now Halpern. Thirty five years ago I sent her a twelve–page letter from America. After all these years she still has the letter. Together, we once dreamed about redemption, and now the dream has become a reality...

Inauguration ceremony

I look at the house and the beaming faces and I am overwhelmed by joy. I feel proud that we, Gombin Jews from New York, Newark, Detroit and Chicago, with pious devotion, helped build a bright Gombin House, brick by brick, here in this light–filled Tel Aviv, where thousands and thousands of stars are shining.

Memorial ceremonies at Gombin House, Tel Aviv 1967

I say to my friends Yitzhak and Yakov Finkelstein: "Look, the night is silent and calm, but there is a storm brewing in my heart. The evening has intoxicated me. My mood is feverish, I share your emotions, the air is Jewish, it feels like Sabbath, and now there is even an echo from our old town Gombin... Who can be happier than us?"

The Gombin House in Tel Aviv

The south is covered by shadowy veils. Everything seems to be part of a magical story. The white wall of Gombin peels away from the darkness of the night. Is it real or just a dream?

After we leave the Gombin House there is a deep silence. Someone whispers to me quietly and firmly in Hebrew: "Hope to see you again soon!"

Written during the days of Sukkot, 1967.

The Gombiner Young Men's in New York

by Jack Zicklin
President of the New York Organization

[Original book: Pages 105-109 English]

The purpose of this article is to describe the various members who laid the foundation in forming the society in New York. These men deserve the highest credit for taking upon themselves the responsibility of helping the unfortunate in Gombin. That strong desire forced them together and in 1923, they established a relief fund in that city. The group consisted of: A. Marks; Sam Rafel; M. Jacklin; H. Solomon; Max Green; A. Carmel; Hirshel Caro and others.

Meetings were held often for that purpose at the home of Brother Stern and Kraut. The success of those meetings was overwhelming, because money was raised for the poor in Gombin. At one of those meetings a question was raised as to the formation of a society in New York. This idea spread like wildfire among the few Gombiner landsleit in New York. At that time there were about 40 families from Gombin who immigrated to the United States. Thus, in October, 1923, a meeting was called at the Astoria Hall in New York.

At that meeting, the following were present: Sam Rafel; Max Green; Max Jacklin; Sam Kraut; A. Carmel; Sam Frankel; H. Levy; Jack Holtzman; Jack Stern; Hirshel Caro and a few others. That was the beginning of the Gombiner Young Men's in New York. A charter was formed and we were incorporated in the state of New York. The primary purpose of that organization was to help its people in Gombin. The important object was to get as many members who lived in New York at that time. A committee was sent to all Gombiner in New York in order to become members of that organization. That committee was very successful getting most of the members in.

In 1924, through the leadership of David Frankel and others, a plot at the Beth David Cemetery was bought. At the end of 1925, a stronger society was imminent with many members working hard towards the success of that organization. As the membership grew in numbers, the society became financially stronger, thus money was sent to Gombin in order to help the poor "landsleit" there. It would be impossible to enumerate all the men who contributed towards the success of our organization in New York. I will try to describe just a few of the leaders who did so much for the benefit of our society.

Farewell of Jack Zicklin, on the eve of his departure for the United States in 1923. Surrounded by his friends and two sisters, Anka and Lajka.

The most important member was of course, Brother Sam Rafel. He was the Society. His greatest pleasure was to talk about Gombin, its people and in general about the welfare of our organization. I know that this book is contributing several articles on this great personality, but as President of the Gombiner Young Men's, I would not want to miss this opportunity in expressing my personal opinion and my feeling about our Sam. It was he who, many years ago, was responsible for the relief work in Gombin. Through his effort, money and clothing was sent there to help the unfortunate. He was instrumental in bringing to this country many refugees from Europe who otherwise would have perished with the others under the Hitler regime. He was the one who fought and succeeded in establishing a "Kase" in Israel and laboured vigorously toward the establishment of a permanent house in Israel. Thus, I feel happier that I had the opportunity to work with him since 1960 and see for myself a man who gave his time and energy towards the good and welfare of our organization.

Brother Max Jacklin was another energetic and honest member who contributed a great deal to the growth of our society. Under his leadership, he was instrumental in making our meetings interesting and lively. He was the driving power in making our organization the biggest in New York City.

Brother Max Green, one of the first organizers, was a sincere worker and donated his time towards the success of our organization. I was happy that I had the privilege of working with him for several years and noticed what an asset he was to our society.

Brother Louis Green held various important positions and served them well. As recording secretary and head of various committees, he worked diligently in every capacity.

The success of the Gombiner Society at its beginning was due to the hospitality of Brother and Sister Sam Kraut

Brother Isidore Puro was very active in the Newark branch of the Gombiner Young Men's and was an outstanding worker and head of various important committees.

Brother Harry Solomon was an outstanding member and he will be remembered for his great work and tireless effort to make our organization financially strong and independent. He was the first to answer the call for fund raising activities.

Brother David Plutzer was another member who excelled in fund raising matters. He was a very conscientious worker and also contributed a great deal to the success of our organization.

Brother Joe Stern held many important positions in our society and contributed a lot to the welfare of our organization. He excelled in straightening out matters thus keeping our organization harmoniously together.

Brother Teddy Kraut was our first secretary of the organization and held it for many years. He laid the groundwork for other secretaries who followed him to keep our books in order. Being a personal friend of mine, I know of his ability to fulfil a job with great success. I am sure that he would still be active in our organization if he lived in New York City.

25th Anniversary of the Gombiner Society

Brother Aaron Freisler, one of our first organizers, held many important positions in our society. His outstanding accomplishment was as chairman of the gate committee at Beth David Cemetery and through his tireless effort, the organization became financially stronger.

Brother Abe Carmel served our organization well. A man of small height and big deeds. He worked diligently in every capacity and contributed a great deal to the success of our organization.

Brother Sam Greenzang held important positions in our society. He excelled in being secretary for several years. He was always ready and alert to do his share whenever he was called upon.

A meeting of the New York organization in 1968

Brother Sam Marks was very active in our organization. He held many important positions and served well. Upon his retirement he left for Florida and that's when his activity stopped. I had the pleasure to work with him. His knowledge of the various rules was outstanding. He helped our organization a great deal.

Brother Dave Temple, another outstanding member, excelled in fund raising activities. Through his efforts, our society benefited financially a great deal.

Brother Sam Galvin was instrumental in enriching our treasury. He was always successful in any undertaking.

Brother Ralph Rafel was the orator of our organization. As head of several important committees, he managed to get things done in a quieter way.

Brother Sam Kraut was one of the first organizers of our organization. His house was always open for our members to meet. Hospitality was the key word in Sam Kraut's home.

Dave Burns, Member of the Editorial Staff
and the Executive Committee

Brother David Chitel was very active in many committees. His home was another example of hospitality.

Brother M. Shechter excelled financially. He always succeeded in enriching our treasury.

Brother Wolf Goldman will be remembered in giving a great deal of time for our house in Israel. He was the one who laid the cornerstone of our house in Israel.

Iaul Tyber, Member of the Editorial Staff
and the Executive Committee.

Brother Chaim Opatowsky contributes a great deal to the enjoyment of our members. Refreshments are always taken care of by our well beloved Chaim. I still have the pleasure to work with him and enjoy his work.

Brother Hyman Glickman, our recording secretary for as many years as I can remember, is an outstanding member of our organization. With his humour, he heals the wounds of our organization. He is a soft spoken man with a clear mind and a great desire to keep the organization together. I'm happy to have the pleasure to work with his at present. My God give him strength and long life to carry on the work.

These members were and are to my mind a few of the outstanding men who made our organization a success.

The Activities of the Ladies Auxiliary

by Yetta Rafel, Honorary President, New Jersey

[Original book: Pages 111-112 English]

Yetta Rafel

At the height of the Gombiner Young Men's successful organization, they urged the ladies to form an independent Women's Organization. Its main purpose and function was to raise funds for the Gombiner Relief, to furnish social activities and form a separate chapter. This developed into a very useful group which performed a great number of enterprises.

Who of us can forget the theatre parties which brought in large sums of money and also the exciting get together and the fun we all had from the package parties. Each woman brought a lunch for two and the man who bid the highest bought the package and shared it with the woman who brought it. Thus, we achieved two goals: we raised funds and had fun.

The Chanuka parties were in a class of its own. They were festive with candelabras, "sudah–tablets", etc. They also brought in funds for the relief. The Purim parties were gay and colourful. Who will or can forget the choosing of Queen Esther? The woman who got the highest number of votes was crowned Esther.

There was great competition among the men, everybody wanting his wife to receive the royal title. However, there was no jealousy and no one was hurt as there was great comradeship and sportsmanship and the consciousness of purpose. Thus, money was again raised for relief.

Looking back at the annual meetings in the country which were wonderful occasions for enjoyment, for talk, story– telling and dancing, we shall never forget these beautiful events. Everyone brought back wonderful memories and new plans for further activities.

The same can be said of the women in Newark, Chicago and Detroit. They had the same purpose: funds for relief and a close friendship.

To give due credit to all would require mentioning scores of names. Their thanks lie in the knowledge and satisfaction of having contributed to a human cause.

Let us take the opportunity and mention the names of some past presidents of our Gombiner Ladies Organization: Helen Jacklin; Fanny Temple; Yetta Rafel; Minnie Schacter; A. Offenberg; B. Chitel; B. Lean; L. Green and from Newark: P. Jacklin; B. Kleinert; A. Piuro; R. Levy; S. Winter; M. Tiber and A. Kesselman.

Former presidents of the Gombiner Organization

[Original book: Pages 112-113 English]

Max Green, First President
of the Gombiner Society in New York

Teddy Kraut

Isidor Piuro

Louis Green

Max Jacklin

Philip Kraut

The Organization in Newark

by Nathan Kleinert

[Original book: Pages 115-117 English]

The Newark Gombiners belonged to the New York Organization since it originated. Most of the New Jersey members were very active and due to some outstanding members such as: Sam Fogel; Mr. Bloom; Mr. Jacklin; Mr. Nathan Kleinert; Mr. Kesselman; Mr. Puro and others, the New York Organization grew in membership and prestige.

Around 1939, after being with the New York Organization for about fifteen years, dissatisfaction arose among the New Jersey members; there were various reasons for wanting to form their own organization. Some argued that it was too far to travel from New Jersey to attend meetings in New York. Others claimed that the members of New Jersey had risen to such an extent that they were able to form their own organization. Thus, after lengthy and stormy meetings in New York, the New Jersey members broke ties with the New York organization and, in November 1939, a meeting was called for the sole purpose of forming the New Jersey branch.

Abraham Max, Influential
Member of the Organization in Newark

The first meeting was held at the home of Mr. S. Lasky. Mr. Kesselman, a prominent lawyer, was elected first President and Mr. Nathan Kleinert was elected secretary. After serving 1 year, elections were held and Mr. Jacklin was elected President. It was he who was instrumental in obtaining a charter from the state of New Jersey for their organization. It was a successful and prosperous society. They worked hand–in–hand with the New York, Detroit and Chicago organization. The goal of the New Jersey society was to help financially the Gombiner landsleit wherever they were. New Jersey was active in promoting the building of our Gombiner House in Israel. They also contributed very heavily towards the "Kasa" so that the Gombiner in Israel could borrow money whenever they needed it.

The Gombiner Society, Newark 1968

Several years passed and the ladies auxiliary came into existence. Its purpose was to raise funds for the Gombiner relief, to furnish social activities and to form a separate chapter. Some of the outstanding names were the following: Mrs. Puro; Mrs. Yetta Rafel; Mrs. B. Kleinert; Mrs. Levy; Mrs. Blum; Mrs. Kornfeld; Mrs. Jaclin; Mrs. Vinter and Mrs. Hyber.

When the war in Europe came to an end and it was known that some Gombiner young men were saved from Hitler's destruction, a tremendous task was undertaken in order to bringing them to the United States. Under the leadership of Mr. Sam Rafel, many Gombiner families were brought to America to lead a peaceful life. They, in turn, helped the organization become more successful.

The Gombiner Society in Newark, with representation of the
Society from New York and Mr. Chaim Kerber from Paris

At present, Organization in Newark has a membership of about fifty men
and women. The current leader is Mr. Jack Frenkel and Mr. Janowitz is
financial secretary.

The Gombiner Society in Detroit

by Louis Philips (Pochekha)

[Original book: Pages 115-117 English]

The Gombiner Society in Detroit was founded in 1936 and is one of the outstanding societies in Jewish communal life of that city.

Although Gombiner Landsleit had been living in Detroit for a long time before the society was organized, a small group was active and in touch with various institutions of Gombin in Poland. Among them were the late Shmuel Gayer, his son Sidney Gayer who in the thirties collected funds and kept up a correspondence with the landsleit in Gombin. Also active were Louis Philips Potshecha, Jack Gayer, Julius Green (now living in California), Max Rifman and Mordecai Schwartzberg.

The activities were not planned systematically and because of this situation, it was decided to invite other landsleit to participate. This is how the society came into being.

Louis Philips (Pochekha) succeeded in bringing in the family Silberstein and greatly influenced Mrs. Miriam Silberstein, wife of the famous Solomon Silberstein and proprietor of the department store, to take an active part in the establishment of the society. At the first meeting, 17 members were present: Shmuel Gayer, Sidney Gayer, Mordecai Schwatzberg, Jack Gayer, Mrs. Miriam Silberstein, Mrs. Rose Saf, Louis Philips, Julius Green, Jack Frankel, Mr&Mrs Max Risman, Mr&Mrs Harry Frankel, Yitche Stone, Morris Wispe and Mrs. Morris Wispe. At this meeting it was decided to call the organization; "The Gombiner Society of Detroit" and a committee was elected consisting of the following: Louis Philips, President; Julius Green, Vice–President; Mrs. Miriam Silberstein, treasurer; Jack Gayer, Financial secretary and Sidney Gayer, Secretary.

During the years 1937–38, the sum of $1000 was sent to Gombin from Detroit. Considering the circumstances under which money was raised, it was a great achievement and the following institutions in Gombin received financial support from the Gombiner Society of Detroit: Linas Hatzedek, Beth Lechem, Gmilat Chasodim fund, Talmud Torah, Bikur Holim, the library and others. In addition, $400 was sent in 1938 to the "Building Fund" in New York. Sam Reifel was instrumental in setting up the fund for all monies collected.

Women members were especially active in arranging various affairs such as Purim and Chanukah celebration and others. Just to mention a few of the active women members as follows: Mrs. Anna Philips, Mrs. Pearl Gayer, Mrs. Ray Zatkoff, Mrs. Chana Gayer, Mrs. Shulamith Reich, Mrs. Tillie Mossman, capable financial secretary and her husband Shiye Mossman who was the entertainer at all the affairs. An exceptional member was Sarah Frankel, mother of Tillie Mossman and wife of Harry Frankel. Another very active member was the well–known patron Samuel Frankel of the Frankel family.

We also enjoyed our own entertainer, an accomplished pianist and accordionist, Mrs. Rose Green, wife of Julius Green. Also active was Mrs. Freida Grand, daughter of Jack Gayer and wife of Herman Grand.

A festive banquet was arranged on December 8th, 1940 for the first anniversary of the society. It was a great financial and moral success. Almost all the Gombiner landsleit participated.

Executive Board of the Gombiner Society of Detroit.
Standing, from right to left: Vice President Sidney Guyer, Executive Secretary Sidney Guyer, Vice President Max Rissman, and Barney Zat. Sitting fom right to left: President Louis Philips, Secretary Ethel Philips, and treasurer Herman Grand.

We pursued every avenue of sending help to our brethren in Gombin at the time of the Nazi occupation because we had no means of contacting them. Unfortunately, we were unable to get in touch with our brothers and sisters. As a result, the society became inactive. However, we had our representatives in a number of organizations such as the American Jewish Congress and the Joint Drive.

Before the United States entered World War II, we sent money to a Yeshiva in Poland but the money never reached them. The Yeshiva boys were sent to Shanghai and we lost contact.

At the suggestion of President Louis Philips, we adopted a proposal in November 14, 1943 to raise $25,000 to help rebuilt Gombin at the end of the war. Detroit undertook to raise the sum of $5000.

Sam Reifel was impressed with the proposal. It was then decided to call a conference in Detroit and to invite delegates from New York, Chicago and other cities.

The following participated: Sam Reifel and his brother Hyman Reifel of New York; Mr & Mrs J. Teifeld and Mrs. Kain of Chicago; and the following from Detroit: Julius Green, Sidney Gayer, Jack Gayer, Izzy Ball, Max Risman, Shmuel Gayer and Louis Philips. It was adopted unanimously to raise $25,000.

In 1946, we started a drive to send packages for the Gombiner Jews. At the same time, we carried out a drive to obtain affidavits to bring the survivors from the Nazi Holocaust to the United States.

Social Committee of the Gombiner Society of Detroit.
Standing from right to left: Mr. Barney Zatkoff, Mrs. Louis Philips, and Mr. Herman Grand. Sitting from right to left: Mrs. Henry Rich, Mrs. Herman Grand and Mrs. Barney Zatkoff

With the consent of the New Yorker Farein and the Ladies Auxiliary of Chicago, we decided in 1951 to establish a Gombiner House in Israel to commemorate our martyrs and our Shtetl. We also established a Loan Fund for needy Gombiners in Israel.

The Gombiner committee in Detroit consists of the following: Luis Philips, President: Max Risman, Vice–President; Sidney Gayer, Vice–President; Herman Grand, Treasurer; Freida Grand, Secretary–treasurer; Sidney Gayer, Secretary; Ethel Philips, recording correspondence secretary.

To record, the following people were in various posts during the last 32 years: President Louis Philips Pochekha; Vice–President Sidney Gayer–Chaye; Jack Gayer, Max Risman, Harry Frankel and Sidney Gayer. Financial Secretary: Rose Green, Shmuel Gayer–Chaye, Melvin Wrubel, henry Reich and Freida Grand; Treasurer: Mrs. Miriam Silberstein, Tillie Mossman, Louis Philips, Jack Silberstein and Herman Grand. Various other posts: Ben Silberstein, Morris Bernstein, Barney Zatkoff and Samuel Wrubel.

The Society in Chicago

[Original book: Pages 123-124 English]

Gombiner Society in Chicago, 1935.

Executive Committee of Chicago Society.

The Gombin Society's Initiatives in Poland

by Leon Zamosc

[Not in original book]

The Gombin Jewish Historical and Genealogical Society

The Gombin Society was established in 1997 by people from younger Gombiner generations who were keen on celebrating family roots, remembering the Yiddish civilization that flourished in Poland, and bearing witness to the destruction of the Jewish community of Gombin during the Shoah. In the early years of activity, many participants from several countries joined the society's daily exchanges through electronic mail and the group worked in collaboration with the senior landsmen Gombiner organizations that were still functioning at the time.

The Gombin Society is officially registered in the United States as a nonprofit organization that seeks to educate Gombiner descendants and the public about the history and genealogy of the Gombin Jews. Thanks to the work of its members, it has been able to obtain and publish substantial amounts of information about the Gombin Jewish community. In the process, a variety of pictorial materials and documents have been collected, and the society continues to encourage descendants to investigate their family trees, re-establish contact with relatives and friends, and document the Shoah victims from Gombin.

In 1997, the directors of the Gombin Society decided to undertake special initiatives to restore and protect the Jewish Cemetery in Gombin and to dedicate a memorial to the Gombin Jews at the Chelmno extermination camp. These projects were successfully completed in the course of 1998 and 1999.

Restoration of the Gombin Jewish Cemetery

The Jewish community of Gombin was destroyed in the Spring of 1942, when the Germans liquidated the ghetto and sent the remaining Jews to their deaths at Chelmno extermination camp. After the deportation, the Jewish cemetery was razed: the fences were torn down, the gravestones removed for use in construction, and a trench was dug accross the burial grounds as part of the belt of German fortifications that surrounded the town. With the end of the war, no initiatives were taken to protect the site, and for the next fifty years the Gombin Jewish cemetery was an abandoned wasteland. In the mid-1990s, when the Gombin Society started to explore ways to protect it, the cemetery was being desecrated on a daily basis. Part of the area was used as a soccer playground, most of the ground was littered with garbage and bottles left behind by drunkards, and the cemetery was cited in a study of the Jewish Heritage Council and the World Monuments Fund as endangered by pollution and nearby development.

In August 1997 the Gombin Society approved a project to save the Jewish cemetery in Gombin. The decision came after exploratory visits of members of the society and extensive consultations with the Gabin Land Lovers Association, a group interested in the local history and cultural heritage of Gombin. In October 1997, two representatives of the Gombin Society, Leon Zamosc and Jeremy Freedman, signed a cooperation agreement with Zbigniew Lukascewski, president of the Gabin Land Lovers Association. At the same time, they reached an agreement on a project to restore the cemetery with the Nissenbaum Family Foundation, a Warsaw-based institution that worked to preserve the traces of Jewish history and culture in Poland. The realization of the project was made possible by the contributions of survivors and descendants of Jewish Gombiners from all over the world and matching funds from the Nissenbaum Foundation. In addition to counting with the active support of the Gabin Land Lovers Association, the project was sympathetically endorsed by the civil and religious authorities of the town. Overall, the restoration of the Gombin Jewish cemetery included the following elements:

Demarcation: In the real estate registry, the Gombin Jewish cemetery appeared as part of a larger lot that included a German Military Cemetery from the First World War, a sizeable sand pit, and other adjacent areas. As a first step to protect the cemetery, it was necessary to establish its boundaries. The

Gombin Society hired a surveyor who, on the basis of testimonies and a 1915 chart of the Jewish cemetery, demarcated the cemetery limits. A decree was obtained from the Plock Regional Conservator Office on December 23 1997, officially approving the boundaries of the cemetery with a perimeter of 580 metres and a total area of 3.5 hectares.

Recovery of gravestones: Through a contract with the town's Communal Construction Company, the Gombin Society recovered the gravestones that the Germans had used to line about 80 meters of sidewalk in Browarna Street. The Communal Construction Company, which had already recovered Jewish tombstones and fragments while doing re-pavement work in other streets of Gombin, dug out the Browarna Street matzevot, took them to storage, and replaced the sidewalk's curb. This work was also finished by the end of December 1997.

Enclosure of the cemetery: After designing the project and obtaining approval from the competent authorities, the Nissenbaum Foundation undertook the actual construction work. A quality welded metal fence, set on bases of concrete, was erected around the entire perimeter of the cemetery. Brick pillars and an iron-wrought gate were installed at the entrance, where a marble plaque reads: "Jewish Cemetery of Gombin, destroyed by the Nazis, restored in 1998 by the Gombin Jewish Historical and Genealogical Society and the Nissenbaum Foundation." The enclosure of the cemetery was completed in October 1998.

Lapidarium: In the final stage of the project, the Nissenbaum Foundation brought back the recovered matzevot to the cemetery, where whole stones and large fragments were re- erected and arranged as part of a lapidarium, and smaller fragments were incorporated into the memorial monument's wall. With the construction of the lapidarium, the restoration works at the site of the Gombin Jewish Cemetery were completed.

Gombin Memorial Monument at Chelmno

Gombin was occupied by the German army on September 7, 1939. On arrival, the Germans subjected the Jews to a regime of forced labor and a few weeks later they burned the town's wooden synagogue and Beit Midrash. Early in 1940, the Gombin Jews were evicted from their homes and concentrated in a ghetto. In the following months, about 200 Jews were deported to slave labor camps in Konin, Eindziov, and Hohenzaltz; many of them were later sent to Auschwitz. Then, in the Spring of 1942, the Germans liquidated the Gombin ghetto, dispatching the more than 2,000 remaining Jews to the extermination camp at Chelmno. Only 212 of the Jews who were in Gombin at the time of the German invasion survived the Holocaust.

In the 1990s, the Konin Regional Museum, which was responsible for administering the site of the Chelmno extermination camp, facilitated the installation of monuments memorializing the Shoah victims from individual towns. Some monuments and plaques were erected by survivors and descendants of various Jewish communities, but nothing had been done to perpetuate the memory of the Gombin Jews who were murdered at Chelmno.

In 1997 the Gombin Society approved the realization of a project to dedicate a memorial to the Gombiner Shoah victims. In October of that same year, acting in representation of the society, Leon Zamosc negotiated the details of the monument with Lucja Pawlicka Nowak, director of the Konin Regional Museum, and Jan Rassumowski, the artist recommended by the museum.

In the course of 1998, while the director of Konin Regional Museum obtained all the necessary approvals and permits from the Polish authorities, the Gombin Society raised the funds for the construction of the monument among Gombiner survivors and descendants from Israel, the United States, and other countries. The construction work, which was initiated in 1998, was temporarily suspended as a result of the unfortunate death of the artist, Jan Rassumowski.

Eventually, an agreement was reached with Stanislaw Mystek, colleague and friend of Rassumowski, who took responsibility for the project. The work was successfully completed in the early Spring of 1999.

On the walls of the Gombin Memorial Monument at Chelmno, four plaques bear the following inscription in Hebrew, Yiddish, Polish and English:

> *Gombin In Eternal Memory*
> *In this place of horror*
> *The valley of the shadow of death, Chelmno*
> *in the Spring of 1942*
> *over 2,000 Jews from Gombin*
> *men and women, young and old*
> *were gassed and burned by the German Nazis*
> *If only my head was filled with water*
> *and my eyes were a fountain of tears*
> *Then I would weep by day and night*

Over the destruction of the flower of my people
(Jeremiah Ch.8 v.23)
We are still here
We shall never forget
Survivors and descendants of Gombin
from all over the world

The configuration of the plaques is reminiscent of the classic Jewish Eastern European matzevah, with a semicircular design that features a bass-relief image of the Synagogue of Gombin. The monument is a tall white-concrete structure, in the shape of two integrated triangular obelisks. The plaques, which are made of iron, have been especially treated with chemicals to resist abrasion and weathering. The first column, capped with a Star of David, displays the plaques with the image of the Gombin wooden schul and the Hebrew and Yiddish versions of the text. The Polish and English versions of the text are displayed on the second column, which is topped with the traditional Jewish Menorah.

Dedication ceremonies

On August 15 and 16 of 1999, about fifty people from three generations of Gombiners came from different parts of the world to be present in the memorial services and dedication ceremonies at the restored Jewish Cemetery in Gombin and at the Gombin Memorial Monument in Chelmno. The Israeli ambassador to Poland, delegates of various Jewish institutions, and representatives of the Polish authorities participated in the events. The momentous experience was chronicled in the documentary film "Back to Gombin", produced and directed by Minna Packer.

Dedication, Gombin Jewish Cemetery Restoration Works

Dedication, Gombin Memorial Monument in Chelmno

In Memoriam

[Original book: Pages 215-225 Yiddish and 125-161 English]

Please Note:

The names on the following pages are not included in the Name Index

**We will always hold dear the holy memory of our beloved
who were murdered by Hitler's Nazi beasts**

Mother Zisl Wolman (in the center) brothers Shloime Wolman
with his wife and child, Chava Wolman with her husband Leiser

Morris and Bracha Wolman,
Chicago

Our Grandfather Aaron
Wolman

In memory of my deceased parents in Gombin

Bezalel and Chana Wolman

* * *

With deep sorrow and pain I remember my late
husband

Sylvia Surry, California

We will always mourn those who were closest to us. May their names be sanctified.

Deceased from the Adler family

Rivka Adler's father: **Chaim Yitzhak Rothbart**, of blessed memory, passed away the 22nd of Adar, March 24th 1918 in Gombin Poland. Rivka's mother **Sarah Rothbart**, of blessed memory, passed away the 11th of Shevat, February 6th 1936 in Montreal, Canada. Rivka's son **Jacob Adler**, of blessed memory passed away the 25th of Tammuz, July 20th 1951 in Montreal, Canada. Rivka's husband, **Shloime Leib Adler**, of blessed memory, passed away the 16th of Nissan, April 17th 1965, in Montreal, Canada. Part of this family were murdered by the German Nazi murderers, may their names be blotted out, in the years between 1939 and 1944.

Mrs. Rivka Adler, children and grandchildren

My father **Chaim Yosef**, of blessed memory, passed away February 28th 1934 in Gombin. My mother **Rokhl**, of blessed memory, passed away February 22nd 1931 in Gombin.

Yitzhak Eily and family, Montreal, Canada

We will cherish the memory of our parents, sisters and brothers who were murdered in 1942 together with their families

My sister Chaia with her child

My mother and father Shayna Bine and Moishe Leib Celemensky with the family. My sister Leah and my brother Yosef with his wife Chana and their daughter.

My sister Beila

My brother Abraham

We will always carry them in our memory

Jacob, Pola, and Velvl Celemensky,
Paris

My sister Feige

We will forever carry the sadness in our hearts for our beloved parents and
family who were cruelly exterminated in the death camp Chelmno

Our mother and father Beile and Wolf Zolna of blessed memory, sisters
Dvorah, Rachl, Leah, Sarah and Dena, killed in 1943

Our mother and father Beile and Wolf Zolna of blessed memory, sisters Dvorah, Rachl,
Leah, Sarah and Dena, killed in 1943

Our beloved parents Rochl and Yidel Mokotov,
murdered in Treblinka with our brother Moishe

My unforgettable wife **Sarah** (maiden
name **Schwartz**) with our son **Aaron
Wolf**

Israel Zolna,
Melbourne, Australia

In their memory

**Families Hershl, Reuven, and Tzeshe Mokotov–
Nisenboym**
Melbourne, Australia

The surviving brothers
Kasriel, Israel   **Yitzhak**, Russia   **Israel**, Melbourne

**With pain in our hearts we remember our closest and dearest
who were exterminated by the Nazi beasts**

Our mother and father, **Chaia Ita** and **Baruch Ozer Rusak**.

Our brother **Yankl**, his wife **Ita Miriam** and their children **Chanele**, **Eliezer** and **Aaron David**. Our brother **Yehuda**, his wife **Chaia** and their two children. Our brother **Shmuel**, his wife **Neche** and their child. Our sister **Neche** and brother **Mendel**.

The ones who remained to mourn: **Chana and Chaim Rusak, and their children Baruch and Feigele**

We will hold dear our murdered mother and father, **Leah and Aaron David Yarlicht**.

Our brother **Yacob Yosef**, his wife **Gitele** and their children **Hershl** and **Rivche**. Our sister **Ita Miriam**, her husband **Yankl** and their children **Chanele**, **Eliezer**, **Aaron David**. Our sisters **Neche** and **Mindl**.

Our tragically murdered brother **Yitzhak**, also **Hershl** and **Moishe**.

Mourning survivors: **Yehuda Yarlicht family and the orphaned wife Malka Yarlicht**, Rio de Janeiro, Brazil.

To the eternal memory of our beloved mother and family who were killed in Chelmno.

Yosef and David Blawat, Paris

Our mother Frimet and brothers
Hershl, Lipe and Shloime

My wife Fradel Wrubel
with her mother and child

In memory of our beloved parents Yosef and Miriam Opatowski

Sisters, brothers and their families who were killed by the Nazi murderers

In the centre is our mother Miriam, left, our sister Sarah with her husband Lipe

From this group only two survived

Our brother Rafel with his wife
Kuczynski and their two children

Our sister Libe
and our brothers Moishe, Zishe and Yankl

Chaim and Natan Opatowski, New York
Mordechai Opatowski and family, Mexico
Melech Kuczynski and Mrs. Fradel Opatowski , Mexico

May these lines serve as a tombstone on the unknown graves of my closest and dearest

Sorke Yeshon-Zilberman and her son

The Sochatczewski family

My unforgettable town of Gombin, fate would have it that I would be the only one left to mourn the tragic extermination of the entire **Sochatczewski family** by the Nazi murderers. In my dreams I see my father with his silver-white beard being led to death by the murderers. Who can forget my brother **Jonathan** who stood up to an S.S. officer to protect his daughter and paid it with his life.

Let this Gombin chronicle serve as a monument for the scattered ashes of my parents **Miriam and Abraham Eli Sochatczewski**, my sister Tovah and my seven brothers **Reuven**, **Shloime**, **Jonathan**, **Rabbi Moishe**, **Yankele**, and **Pesach**. I will carry the light of their memory deep in my heart.

Balka Sochatczewski-Yeshin, Chicago

May these lines serve as a tombstone on the unknown graves of my closest and dearest

My unforgettable sister **Esther Manczyk**, born 17th January 1917 in Gombin, daughter of Hersh and Hodes Skurka. Murdered March 1942 in Chelmno by Hitler's barbarians.

Her brother Wolf

We will forever mourn our dearest and closest who were cruelly exterminated

**My father Yosef Wolman, my sister Tovah and her husband Mendel Shapiro,
my brother Moishe his wife Rochl and their four children**

My brother Lozer
who died in the Red Army

My sister Brandl

My brother Wolf

Leiser Wolman, Toronto, Canada

**In sanctified memory of my parents, my brother Leib and my sister Chaia Sarah.
They were among the six million martyrs.**

My father Abraham Moishe

My mother Roize

Yitzkhak Schigel, wife and children,
Winnipeg, Canada

**With pain and sorrow we will carry the sanctified memory of my parents,
sisters, brothers
and my child who were exterminated by the Nazi barbarians**

My father Fishl Jonah Finkelstein
who died a martyr's death

My sister Frida Hinda
with my son Yerachmiel
and my sister-in-law Ruth Lichtenstein

With pain and sorrow we will carry the sanctified memory of my parents, sisters,
brothers and my child who were exterminated by the Nazi barbarians.

My father was the head of the "Agudah" orthodox part and active in various Jewish
institutions. His house was devoted to the study of the Torah, with a school for
children. He was respected by the Jews of Gombin.

With respect and love I remember my mother **Miriam**, daughter of **Moishe** and
Rivka; my father **Fishl Jonah**, son of **Ezriel Zeev Finkelstein**, my sisters **Frida**,
Hinda and **Rachel**; my small son **Yerachmiel**; and my brothers **Shmuel**, **Wolf** and
Israel.

Ezriel Moishe Finkelstein , Israel

My father Wolf Grzywacz,
murdered in Chelmno

Reb Yitzhak Shachar,
distinguished orthodox leader,
died a martyr's death

Abraham Grzywacz, Montreal

SAM KRAUT

FAY KRAUT

We mourn the loss of our parents, who truly were the inspiration
of the beginning of the Gombiner Young Men's.
We shall always cherish their memory,

ALEX, TEDDY, MATILDA, PHIL, BERNARD,
ROSE, MAX (KRAUT)

D A V E

We also mourn the loss of our brother
DAVID who was taken away from us so
early in life.

Brothers and Sisters KRAUT

—————

I mourn the loss of my husband DAVE.

FAY KRAUT

The memories of our beloved parents
ABRAHAM ITCHA ZYCHLINSKY and GERTRUDE ZYCHLINSKY
who died in New York in 1946 and 1942 respectively will always be in our hearts.

We mourn the loss of JACK FRIEDMAN (TEDELIS), husband of GOLDIE FRIEDMAN, our beloved brother-in-law who died in 1948.

BENJAMIN, GOLDIE, JOSEPH DAVE, JACK

Sisters ANKA and LAJKA

JACK FRIEDMAN, Husband of Goldie Tedelis

Sister ANKA and DAUGTHER   Sister LAJKA and SON

We mourn the loss of our sisters ANKA ZYCHLINSKA and daughter, LAJKA ZYCHLINSKA and son who perished in 1943 under the Hitler regime in Warsaw.

RUBIN ROSENTHAL   E V A

In loving memory of our beloved parents

MOLLIE ZICHLIN
IRVING ROSS

In loving memory of my
husband MAX JACKLIN

HELEN, Children and Grandchildren

In loving memory of my beloved husband
HYMAN GOLDSTEIN
who died on February 15, 1955.
He was a charter member and
recording secretary of the Gombiner Society of New York.

Wife E. GOLDSTEIN
Son B. GOLDSTEIN

I mourn the loss of my husband
MAX GREEN
first President of the Gombiner Young
Men's of New York and charter
member, who died in New York in
January 1965.

BESSIE GREEN

We mourn the loss of our father ABRAHAM BRZEZINSKY, Mother CHANA, sister CHAYELE ROTHSTEIN and brother-in-law, who were killed by the Nazis in Gombin in 1942.

They will live forever in our hearts.

We also mourn the loss of our brother CHASKEL MOISHE who died in New York in 1959.

DAVE and GITELE

CHASKEL MOISHE

Sister and Husband
ITSHE LANDAU and wife CHAJELE

All from Warsaw:
YANKEL and HANNAH ORENSTEIN
PHILIP and GOLDA ORENSTEIN
HARRY and BRUNDEL ORENSTEIN
and children
MANYA and ABRAHAM KOTLER
and children
HELEN and LEE SILVERMAN
and children

GITELE BURNS and family

In loving memory of our parents,
LAIBISH and **ESTHER JACOBOWITZ**
BECKY KLEINERT, YETTA RAFEL, BEN JACOWITZ

In loving memory of
BAIREL and **HINDE GITL KURDALUCK**
(Known in America as Mr. & Mrs. **KLEINERT**)
MORRIS, NATHAN, IRVING

Mother MALKE GELBERT   Sister LAJKA   Brother
                                                MOISHE GELBERT

I mourn the loss of my parents ZAJWEL and MALKE GELBERT, brother MOSHE
GELBERT, sister LAJKA and her husband ITZCHOK BAUMAN and their two
daughters, FELA anr SALA.

GOLDIE SEIDEMAN

In memory of my Brother-In-Law

SYMCHA ALONY

of Naviaska Domb.

October 1968

GOLDIE SEIDEMAN

Family of A. SEIDEMAN

In memory of my parents CHASKEL and CHANA GOLDE ZEIDEMAN, and my
brother HERSH NATHAN ZEIDEMAN who was killed in the concentration camp in
1945, my brother MEYER and his wife ROSA ZEIDEMAN and their son CHASKEL,
killed during the liquidation of Gombin, also my sister RAIZEL and stepmother
GITEL ZEIDEMAN killed during the liquidation of Gombin.

ABRAHAM SEIDEMAN

YECHIEL MEYER TYBER
brother

MINDEL TYBER
mother

LAJSER MOISHE TYBER
father

I, PAUL TYBER, devoted son of LEIZER MOSHE and MINDEL TYBER in loving memory to my departed brothers and sisters and their families who were victims of Hitler's massacres.

BELA and YECHIEL MACHL SPEISHENDLER GOLDA and A. BOCIAN

YEHUDA and two daughters ESTER and RACHCIA TYBER and grandchildren

A. and ZELDA BOCIAN
parents of Leonard Bocian

EDZIA and LAJSER
(children of Bella and Yechiel Machel)
from Lowitz

I mourn the loss of my father and mother SCHLOJME LEIB and CYPRA SHPEISHANDLER, my brothers ABRAHAM and MICHAEL and my sister SARAH.

LAJA TYBER

DEBORA
oldest sister of PAUL

MORDECHAI TYBER
brother

RACHCIA
youngest sister of Yehuda Tyber, (drowned in the shore of Tel-Aviv)

BLUMA
youngest sister of Paul

SIMCHA
youngest brother of Paul and his family

In loving memory of our parents

ITZHOK and SACHE FRENKEL

and brothers HERSHELE, MACHEL, MOJSHE and BENEK

Our parents ITZKHOK and SACHE FRENKEL who were so mercilessly killed by the Nazis in Chelmno, came from a large family of Frankels and Puros. Our father was very popular among his tradesmen. As a cap maker he worked very hard to make a living for his family. Like most European fathers his aim was to bring up his children in an understanding and cultural way. The family spent a lot of time together discussing various subjects of great interest to them.

SAM, CHAIM, JACK and Families — Newark

In Loving memory of my parents
CHAJA TOBE and HERSH JOSEL WOJDESLAWSKI,
and brother JANKIEL and sisters FEJGA RUCHEL and PERELE.

Forever in our hearths.   NAHAN WOJDESLAWSKI (WEISS)

I mourn the loss of my dear beloved wife
HELEN GREENZANG.

ABE GREENZANG

In loving memory of my husband
SAM GREENZANG.

Y. GREENZANG

Mother-in-law   Wife ANNA   Sister and husband

BERNARD family

In loving memory of my wife CHANA who was taken away in 1967, so early in life.

I also mourn the loss of my family and my wife's family who perished so tragically by the hands of the Nazis.

ZALMAN   BERUCH

Brother BINAM and
wife EDGA

Brother and wife

In memory of my beloved mother MALKA and father ABRAHAM, brother MORDECAI and sisters RACHEL and LAJA WOJDESLAWSKI, who perished during the Nazi persecution in Gombin.

from their Son and Brother, JOSL WOJDESLAWSKI

In loving memory of my father SHAJA, mother DINA, sister MINIA, brother CHAIM, who perished under the Hitler regime.

family BER, MICHAEL ZELONKA, only survivor

We mourn the loss of our parents ISRAEL and FRIEDA GURKER, our sister RUCHELE and her husband ABRAHAM SCHWARTZ, also our sister CHANA and husband KIBA from Plock.

CHAIM and FAVISH GURKER

We mourn the loss of our parents, SAMUEL HIRSCHBERG and brother ABRAHAM MOSHE and SZYJA and sister ROSE HIRSCHBERG.

E. HIRSCHBERG

In loving memory of my parents CHANA GITEL and MOSHE ARON SOCHACKI my brothers NATHAN, DAVID, SYMCHA, my sister FEIGA and her husband ABRAHAM SHAJA. They will be forever in my heart.

SYLVIA GURKER

Father MOISHE AARON   Mother CHANA

Brother SYMCHA   Brother NATHAN   Sister CHANA GITELE

I mourn the loss of my sister ROSE and JACK SOLOMON and mother ESTHER BASHE.

BESSIE STRESSHEIM

IN LOVING MEMORY OF THE
L U B I N S K Y   FAMILY

Father
Rabbi BINEM M'NASHI

Brother
JACHIEL MAJER

Brother
MENACHEM

Sister DEVORAH

Mother MIRIAM

Rabbi Binem M'NASHI LUBINSKY was one of the seven sons of Rabbi
PINCHAS LUBINSKY of Kownel.

At the death of Rabbi BINEM M'NASHI LUBINSKY all business establishments in his town were closed in tribute to him. He requested his eulogy contain
no praise of him.

HIS daughter, DEVORAH perished at Auschwitz with her entire family. His
son, Rabbi CHIL MEIER, died of starvation at the Lodz Ghetto. His son,
Rabbi MENACHEM, died a violent death in the gas chambers of Chelmno.

PAUL and MORRIS LUBINSKY

In loving memory of my wife
BESSIE KOCH

LOUIS

Children of RAPHAEL

RAPHAEL KUTCHINSKI and family

! mourn the loss of my beloved wife
SALLY LEWIS

M. LEWIS

In loving memory of my husband
SCHLOJME KLEINERT

HELEN and Son

In loving memory of parents, sisters and brothers

Mother MIRIAM   Father ABRAHAM

Sister FRAJDA   Brother ITZKHOK

Brother ISRAEL and wife BALCIA (nee) ZICHLINSKY   Brother MENASHE

MACHEL BER, Montreal

In loving memory of my father and mother SAMUEL and HANAH. I mourn the loss of my brother JOSEPH, and sister SARAH, who were killed by the Nazis in Europe.

Grandma RIFKA and grandpa
LEJBELE BAJGELBECKER

I mourn the loss of my beloved wife ANNA who died in 1968. Our meeting at the concentration camp kept us close to one another. Our marriage bore us 3 children, twins SHELDON and HANNAH and our youngest SAMUEL.

We will always cherish her memory.

BEN GUYER

In Memory of my beloved Parents and Grandparents:

ABRAHAM ZIMALINSKY (my Father)
DAVID GOSTINSKY (my Grandfather)
RIVKA GOSTINSKY (my Grandmother)

Picture of my Mother GITLA ZIMALINSKY not available

The only surviver fom the entire family is **SHLOME** — changed to my present name: **SOL SIMON** and wife **NANCY**, and children: **DAVID** and **EDDY**.

My Father and Grandparents perished in the Hitler Holocaust. My Mother died in Gombin in 1938.

To the holy memorial of our beloved parents
PESE DVORAH and REUVEN YECHEZKEL POYCHEKHA

You dedicated yourselves with love to your children to ensure they grow up to be good Jews. You left us a spiritual inheritance. Today we are alive and breathe by virtue of your ideals. We will continue the holiness of our nation and we will pass it down to the next generations.

Let us also remember forever the names of our beloved sister **Yehudit Schwartzberg**, her husband **Mordechai son of Reb Yosef Pinchas**, and our brother **Chone Yakov**. We will carry their memory forever.

Louis (Leib Eliezer) Philips Potchekha and Gos (Gedalia) Philips Potchekha
Detroit, Michigan   Hightstown, New Jersey

אין היילּיקן אָנדענק...

IN LOVING MEMORY of my DEAR PARENTS

AVROM MOYSHE and LEBA ROCHEL WISPE

Mother died in 1909; Father died 1943 at the age of 92.

We will cherish and honor their memory forever.

HARRY (CHAIM) and HELEN WISPE
and Grandsons RICHARD and ROBERT
Downey, California

In loving memory of my wife PEARL, mother of:
MAE, JOYCE, MELVIN and LARRY

She brought great happiness and joy to her family and friends with her kindness, devotion and love.

As a member of the Gombiner Society (of Detroit) she shared in its organization and worked zealously and with tireless energy to help fulfill its many important projects.

We will cherish and honor her memory forever!

SIDNEY GUYER and Children

IN LOVING MEMORY

of

ABRAM GUYER

by

His Wife EDITH

Children, and

Grandchildren

1 9 0 8 — 1 9 6 4

Died in Detroit, Mich.

In loving memory of our parents JACOB and NETTIE GUYER.

JACOB GUYER was born in Gombin in 1890. He was very active in the revolutionery movement in Gombin.

He was instrumental in organizing the Gombiner society in Detroit.

His love for Gombin made us children believe that his home was there.

STANLEY and IDA GUYER

FREDA and HERMAN GRAND

and all the grandchildren

JACOB and NETTIE GUYER

MY BELOVED FAMILY

Top row, from left to right:

My Mother RAJZEL, Sister RIVKA, Father MEYER, Grandmother BLIMA GUYER,

Sister TOBI.

Bottom row, from left to right:

Brother LEIB and myself (changed to SAUL).

My father was active in Jewish social life.

Son SAUL and HELEN TATARKA, Detroit

ZELDA

ZELDA
and Brother ABRAM

GENIA

In loving memory of my dear wife ZELDA GUYER (TEIFELD), died Sept. 1952.
MAX, DAUGHTERS and GRANDCHILDREN

In memory of ZELDA and her brother ABRAM TEIFELD, who perished by the Nazis.

In loving memory of my dear wife GENIA GUYER (TEIFELD), died 1967.
MAX GUYER

In loving memory of my dearest family
TEIFELD.

Upper row from left to right,

Mother: ITA-MARIEM
Sister: SARA
Brother: ABRAM
Father: NOACH

Bottom row:

Sisters GENIA, ZELDA, and ESTHER
HANIA SHANE (TEIFELD)

Sisters TEIFELD:

From left to right:

ESTHER, HANA, ZELDA, GENIA, and

SARA.

In loving memory of my parents and family . . .

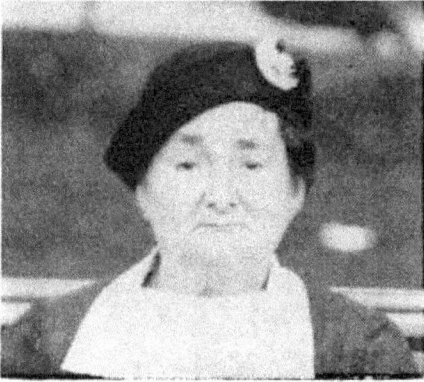

Mother KAJLE

Father BERISH CHAJA

Sister MALKA LAJA

Sister REFKA LIEBE and BAJLE

SIDNEY B. GUYER

I mourn my dearly beloved brother, MOISHE BORUSICK, his wife and children. tante SARAH, her children, my cousins ROSA and HERMAN CERINI who were among the six million Jewish martyrs killed by the Nazis.

Mrs. BETTY LEAN from columbus, Georgia

I mourn the loss of my mother HELENA SZMAJEWICZ (Born SZTOLCMAN), grandma ROSALJA SZTOLCMAN.

HENRYK REICH

My uncle MONIEK ZYGMUND and ALFRED SZTOLCMAN

My greataunts CHANA SZTOLCMAN (wife of MENASHE) and CHANELE SZTOLCMAN (wife of LEJBEL and their families.

HENRIK REICH, Detroit

I mourn the loss of my parents PINCHAS and CHAVE SHACHER who died in Gombin.

HYMAN SHACHER

Our Beloved Brother Dr. JOSEPH WRUBLE

Graduated University of Michigan with a PHI BETA KAPPA.
Had a tremendous practice and a devoted doctor.
He had a AB and MD degree, and interned two years at the
Mount Sinai Hospital in Cleveland, Ohio.

Died February 3, 1966

ROSE AND BEN KASNER

We mourn our beloved parents SAMUEL and SARAH WRUBLE.
Our father worked hard to bring up his family. He was a self educated man.
Father died in 1950. Mother died in 1967.

ROSE and BEN KASNER, and daughter.

**Our beloved father
Dr. MILTON WRUBLE.**

Died 1965.

In memory of our beloved parents

YAHOSHUA and TOBA MOSSMAN
and our beloved brother

DR. JACK MOSSMAN

BEN and TILLIE MOSMAN, Detroit

In memory of our beloved parents

MANELE and SARAH RISSMAN
Sister NACHA and MORDECHAI WOYDESLAWSKI
Brother SIDNEY and Sister ZELDA
Uncle HARRY and Aunt REBECCA LASKI
and beloved friend JOSEPH STUPAJ

MAX and GOLDIE RISSMAN, Detroit

HARRY LASKI

ZELDA

JOSEPH STUPAJ

In memory of our beloved parents —
Father: WOLF LASKI   1887 — April 1942
Mother: FRADEL LASKI
        nee' KILBERT   1891 — April 1942
Sister: CHANNA GOSTINSKI
        nee' LASKI   1916 — April 1942
Sister: SARA LASKI   1820 — April 1942
WOLF LASKI, son of SZMUL ZINDL —
FRADEL LASKI, daughter of JANKOV
                            KILBERT.

        and dear sisters.

Family of SAMUEL and MENDEL LASKI

CHANNA GOSTINSKI nee' LASKI

Survived by their sons and brothers SAMUEL LASKI, MANNY LASKI

I mourn the loss of my parents
VIGDOR and RACHEL WHITHORN

DAVID

In loving memory of my grandparents
MOISHE MENDEL and CHANA CHAJEK
and their children, ITZKHOK BINEM and
RIFKA RACHEL EDELBAUM, JACOB,
AARON, DAVID, MALKA, RACHMIEL,
HERSH LEIB and MENASHE, (killed in
Tel-Aviv), my uncle ZALMAN CHAJEK and
aunt SARAH CHAJEK.

HELEN WHITEHORN

ZALMAN CHAJEK

In loving memory of JACOB and
RACHEL LAJA RUZGA — parents of
MAJLECH, also of my brothers ZYSHA,
SHMUEL, MOISHE, AVRUMELE and sister
ESTHER.

MARK RUZGA

I mourn the loss of SARAH GREEN-
SPAN, born March 23, 1886 in Gombin,
daughter of MOISHE and GOLDIE TYBER.
They lived in Berlin for 19 years. They
perished under the Hitler Regime in 1942.

ROSE GOLDBERG

In memory of Mr. SOL KANE, husband
of ESTHER KANE (ZICHLINSKA) of
Chicago.

In loving memory of my dear wife, KRAUSE, my son SHMULIK and his wife, my son CHASKEL and my daughter LAJELE who were killed by the Nazis in 1942.

HYMAN SHACHER

In memory of my father ABRAHAM ITZCHOK and mother GOLDIE BOCIAN, my brother PINCHAS and sister DEBORAH BOCIAN.

LAJZER BOCIAN

In memory of my beloved grandfather and grandmother RAFEL and ZELDA SHACHER, sons and their wives, BUNIM and SYLVIA, DAVID, ALEXANDER and GUSSIE, ISAAC and BECKIE.
All of blessed memory.

FRANCES and JOSEPH SEID, of Florida.

My brothers and their wives, HERSHEL and FRIEDA, SHOLIM and FEIGA, ISAAC and FEIGA FRANKEL and my sisters and their husbands, MOISHA and CHANA KUTSHINSKY, DEBORAH and JOSEPH PINCHOWSKI.

I mourn the loss of my parents AARON and CYVIA FRANKEL and my wife's parents SHMIEL USHER and DINAH ROSENFELD.

SAM FRANKEL

In loving memory of mother and father HENRY and SUSAN GERTRUDE ZAYAC. HENRY'S family, the wife ETHEL, daughter SUSAN GERTRUDE, daughter RUTH and a son ISRAEL ZAYAC, brother HERSHEL and family, SHAI and family, sister and brother in law, LEAH and MORRIS BORASHACK and family, brother MORRIS ZAYAC and family, sister GOLDIE FELDMAN, born ZAYAC.

CHAIM ZAYAC

I mourn the loss of SARAH GREENSPAN, born Morch 23, 1886, in Gombin, daughter of MOISHE AARON and GOLDIE TYBER. They lived in Berlin for 19 years. They perished under the Hitler regime in 1942.

ROSE GOLDBERG

IN MEMORIAM...

מיר בויגן די קעפ אין טיפן טרויער און אבטונג פאר די מיטגלידער
וואָס זײנען אין פערלויף פון אונדזער עקסיסטענץ ארויסגעריסן געוואָרן פון
אונדזערע רייען. מיר שיקן אונדזער טרייסט צו זייערע קרובים און פריינט.

GOMBINER SOCIETY OF DETROIT

דער גאָמבינער פאַראיין אין דעטראָיט

ISIDORE BALL
CHARLES BALL
HENRY BLOCK
MORRIS BORNSTEIN
MR. and MRS. MAX BRESSLER
JAKE FELDMAN
SARAH FRANKEL
NETTE FRANKEL
REV. SAMUEL and MRS. GUYER
MR. and MRS. JAKE GUYER
PEARL GUYER
ZELDA GUYER
GENIA GUYER
ABRAHAM GUYER
HELEN GREEN
HARRIS GREEN
NATHAN NUDELMAN
MR. and MRS. ABE MOSES
ANNA PHILLIPS
MR. and MRS. HARRY ROSENBERG

MIRIAM SILBERSTEIN
JAKE SILBERSTEIN
JOSEPH SILBERSTEIN
HARRY SILBERSTEIN
Mr. and Mrs. MAX SCHWARTZBERG
Mr. and Mrs. ISIDOR STONE
MORRIS STONE
SAUL SLOAN
SARAH STEIN
ABE SOCHACZEWSKI
LOUIS SILVER
Mr. and Mrs. AARON WISPER
LOUIS WISPER
MAURICE WISPE
MAX WISPE
DAVID WISPE
MR. and MRS. SAMUEL WRUBLE
DR. JOSEPH WRUBLE
JULIUS ZALENKO

HARRY and DORA DRASHINSKY

Mrs. CHAYA TEMERSON and two daughters

MORRIS and LENA GREENFIELD, ISIDOR and ESTHER GOLDSTEIN

In memory of BAJLA ROSENBERG (nee FINKENSTEIN) and her family.

MALKE LEAH and LEIBEL MORDECAI MASTBAUM

In memory of LOUIS FEINGOLD, husband of SARAH FEINGOLD
(ZICHLINSKY)

In loving memory of the STUPAJ family who perished in the Shoah

MOSCHE STUPAJ and his wife
NECHA STUPAJ née **STUPAJ**

their daughter
RUCHLE,
her husband
CHAIM LURIA
and their
children
RACHEL and
**MORDCHAI
LURIA**

their daughter
SURA and her
son
LUZER WYSPA

Also remembering

their son **JOSEPH,**
pre-war emigrant
to the United States

their son **LAZAR** and his wife
MIRLA AKAWIE, survivors

their daughter **MALIA** and
her husband **MOSHE ZOLNA,**
pre-war emigrants to Israel

and **LAZAR** and **MIRLA's** son,
Dr. **MOSHE STAV**

*Remembered by
Jodi, Elie and Meryl Stav
Marsha Rosenberg*

We mourn the loss of the Greenbaum family murdered by the Nazis

Stas Greenbaum 1910 - 1942
Icek Greenbaum 1941 - 1942 son of Stas and
Helene (Zajac Zayontz) Greenbaum 1917 -
1942

Jakob Leib Greenbaum
1882 - 1941
Hena (Ryster) Greenbaum
1884 - 1942

Reiselle Greenbaum
1933 - 1942
Daughter of **Shiyah** and **Sarah**

Including: **Shiyah Greenbaum** 1896 - 1942 and his wife **Sarah Greenbaum** - 1942

We also remember other members of the family from Gombin:

Simon Greenbaum 1886 - 1957
David Greenbaum 1891-
Joseph Greenbaum 1895 - 1955

Henry Greenbaum 1907 - 1992
Albert Greenbaum 1914 - 1985
Rose (Greenbaum) Dinerman 1918 – 2007

Sarah (Rosenberg) Lichtenstein 1852 - 1948
Solomon Silberstein 1861 - 1925
Mary Miriam (Rosenberg) Silberstein 1876 – 1941
Jacob Silberstein 1890 - 1956
Harry Silberstein 1896 - 1955

The Greenbaum, Dinerman, Silberstein, Landau-Chark, and Hamilton families

In loving memory of my grand-parents **Raphael** and **Nacha Bernard** who perished in Auschwitz. Raphael was born in Wloclawek in 1903 and Nacha was born in Gombin in 1907 to Tobjasz and Balka Wolman. They emigrated from Poland to Paris in 1930. Nacha was arrested in Paris on 26th of September 1942 and deported two days later. She died upon her arrival in Auschwitz on Simchat Torah 1942. Raphael was deported on 17th of July 1942 and died in Auschwitz on 24th of October 1942.

Their two children, **Aristide** and **Madeleine**, Paris January 1938.
Madeleine tragically died on 3rd May 1938 at the age of two.

In loving memory of my father, **Aristide Bernard**, 1932-2016. He was a proud and humble Jew. He became an orphan at age of 8 and went through numerous hardships in life. His strength, lovingkindness, simplicity, high moral standards, hard work ethics and constant optimism will be forever a source of inspiration and awe for me.
May his memory be a blessing for all of us.
With love, your daughter who remembers you every day.

Sarah Mayer

In memory of the members of the ZAMOSC family who perished in the Shoah

LEIB ZAMOSC, CHANA PIORO, and their child **CHAIMEK**

ABRAHAM ZAMOSC
Director of the Jewish FolksBank
and President of the Gombin Kehila

HINDA ZAMOSC and her child
LAJZER BURSZTYN

BREINA ZAMOSC, her husband **ZVI HERSZ PROPS**,
and their children **DAVID** and **DVORA**

TZIREL ZAMOSC
and her husband
MOSHE FRIDMAN

We also honor the memory
of our beloved parents,
ISAAC and **NOEMI ZAMOSC**

ANNA ZAMOSC-STONE
LEON ZAMOSC

NAME INDEX

A

A.I., 235

Aaronson, 173

Abele, 16, 17, 102, 103

Abidah, 237

Acosta, 90

Adler, 113, 143

Aleichem, 39, 40, 114

Altboim, 158

Alter, 121

Altman, 176

Anders, 230

Andreyev, 90

Appel, 220, 222

Artsybashev, 114

Asch, 18, 90, 106

B

Baker, 50

Bal, 29

Baron, 128

Baruch, 222, 223

Baum, 149

Bauman, 99, 219

Bayoff, 225

Beckers, 24

Behr, 175, 176, 178

Benyamin, 149, 151

Ber, 132, 136, 151, 223

Berishes, 54

Bernstein, 29, 308

Bialik, 127, 132, 252

Bibergal, 61, 98, 137

Blacharz, 94

Blawat, 151, 152, 176, 177

Blekher, 56

Bloom, 302

Blum, 303

Bocian, 177, 178

Bol, 98, 137, 223

Boll, 151

Borenshtein, 26, 62

Borenstein, 98, 99, 110, 113, 130

Borochov, 132

Braun, 172, 210

Bressler, 197

Bromberg, 121

Brzezinski, 1, 67, 118

Burns, 1, 67, 295

Bzshozovski, 132

C

Carmel, 280, 290, 293

Caro, 102, 103, 290

Celemenski, 1, 99, 111, 112, 117, 220, 221, 244

Celemensky, 91, 110, 147, 148

Cemelinski, 91, 92

Chabar, 184, 185

Chagall, 77, 132

Chaiek, 107, 108

Chaimele, 264, 265, 266

Chaja, 92, 113, 114, 115, 118, 142, 145, 149, 151, 167, 220

Chajek, 124, 130

Chay, 22

Chaya, 143, 145, 146, 148

Chayek, 22

Appendix

Register of **Gombiner** Shoah victims

by Leon Zamosc

This register synthesizes our current knowledge about the Gombiner Jews who were murdered or are known to have perished as a result of the genocidal policies and actions of the German Nazis during the Second World War in Europe. It includes the names of individual Shoah victims who were born in Gombin, were residents of Gombin before the war, or were in the Gombin ghetto during the war.

Sources and methodology

In the register's table, the "Source" column displays the following letters to indicate the origin of the information about each individual person (the sources are ordered by number of references):

Letter	Sources	References
Y	Yad Vashem database of testimonies and historical archival documentation	1086
G	Gombin Ghetto's correspondence with the JOINT (list compiled by Ada Holtzman)	555
W	Rememberance Wall, Gombin House, Tel Aviv	418
B	Gombin Memorial Book	348
M	Survivors and Victims Database, United States Holocaust Memorial Museum	136
K	Rabbi Y. M. Aaronson's lists of Konin camp immates (compiled by Ada Holtzman)	132
L	Lodz Ghetto: Hospital Deaths, deportations to Chelmno, and other records	87
R	Information supplied by victim's relatives	41
F	Serge Klarsfeld's Memorial to the Jews Deported from France	30
H	Meir Holtzman's memories	23
U	Kutno Ghetto List	5

It should be noted that the databases of Yad Vashem and the US Holocaust Memorial Museum incorporate information from vast numbers of different archival sources containing lists of victims' names and various kinds of documents about the fate of individual persons during the Shoah.

The register of Gombiner victims was elaborated on the basis of compiling, cross-referencing and consolidating all the pertinent information from the sources listed above. For verification, the register's entries for individual persons were double-checked against the existing lists of Shoah survivors.

There are 2,249 names in the register. In 156 cases (most of them children) the given name of the victim is not known. In 2 other cases (husbands) it is the surname of the victim that is not known. Such cases are indicated in the table by the following acronyms: (GNU) = Given name unknown, and (SU) = Surname unknown.

Accessibility, corrections and updates

As research continues and new information is found, the documentation of Shoah victims remains an unfinished task. We estimate that a substantial proportion, perhaps up to a third of all the Gombiners who perished, have not been identified yet. We are also aware that, despite all the care taken to avoid them, it is impossible to expect that this register will be completely free of errors or oversights.

For these reasons, we regard the register of Gombiner Shoah victims as a work in progress. Following its publication in this English edition of the Gombin Memorial Book, the original spreadsheet will be posted as part of the online version of the book in the website of the JewishGen Yizkor Books Project. Relatives and researchers will be able to review the information and provide input for the correction of mistakes and omissions. That input, along with any additional data coming from new research, will serve as a basis for future periodic updates.

Finally, it should be pointed out that, due to printing limitations, part of the available information is not visible in the table that is published here. In some cells of the table, the text appears truncated. Also, the black/white format of the printout prevents the use of colors to pinpoint the affiliation of individuals to specific family units. The online publication of the original spreadsheet will not be subject to these limitations.

Family	Person's complete name	Year born	Parents	Other details	Place of birth	Before the war lived in	During the war was in	Source
Adler	Chaim Adler	1889	Jankiel & Lea	Married to Dina	Gombin	Jaslo	Jaslo	W
Adler	Dina Adler nee Frenkel	1870		Married to Chaim	Gombin	Jaslo	Jaslo	Y
Ajtman	Laja Ajtman	1870		Died Lodz hospital 04-Dec-1941	Gombin		Lodz	L
Akawiec	Sara Akawiec	1897		Married to Mosze	Gombin	Plock	Warsaw	Y
Akawiec	Lajzer Akawiec					Gombin		W
Akawiec	Ester Malka Akawiec					Gombin		W
Alterman	Roza Alterman nee Spodek	1913	Moshe & Ita	Married	Lowicz	Gombin	Kiernozia	Y
Alterman	Lea Alterman		Roza nee Spodek	Child		Gombin	Kiernozia	Y
Alterman	Azriel Alterman	1891		Married, buried Konin Catholic	Gombin	Gombin	Konin camp	K
Alterman	Jerachmiel Alterman	1923		Single, "sick" deported 11.5.42		Gombin	Konin camp	K
Altman	Mortcha Altman	1885	Mendel & Khana	Butcher, married to Mindla	Gombin	Gombin	Gombin	Y
Altman	Bella Altman	1919	Mortcha & Mina	Seamstress, single	Gombin	Gombin	Gombin	Y
Altman	Jakob Altman	1917			Gombin		Buchenwald camp	Y M
Altman	Avraham Eliahu Altman	1888			Gombin	Gombin		Y W
Altman	Roza Altman					Gombin		W
Altman	Dorca Altman					Gombin		W
Altman	Lajb Altman			Deported Konin camp to Andrz		Gombin	Konin camp	K
Amzel	Hersz Amzel			Single, deported Konin camp to		Gombin	Konin camp	K
Arbeitsman	Yosef Arbeitsman					Gombin		W
Arbeitsman	Majer Arbeitsman							G
Asz	Masza Dwora Asz nee Grosman	1876		Married to Moshe	Gombin	Plock	Gombin	Y
Asz	Helena Asz	1898			Gombin		Plock	L M
Auerbach	Pola Auerbach nee Stupaj	1890	Solomon & Rebecca nee Wa	Married to Leon	Gombin	Lubraniec	Lodz	Y
Aurbach	Wolf Aurbach	1898		Merchant, married to Bila	Gombin	Piotrkow Kujawski	Wloclawek	Y
Aurbach	Mojsze Aurbach						Piotrkow Kujawski	Y
Baibok	Hersh Khaim Baibok	1875		Shoemaker, married to Hinda	Gombin	Gombin	Gombin	G
Baibok	Felia Baibok	1914	Hersh & Khaia	Sales person	Gombin	Warsaw	Gombin	Y
Baibok	Ester Baibok	1912	Hersh & Khaia	Sales person	Gombin	Warsaw	Warsaw	Y
Baibok	Josef Baibok	1888		Married, "sick" deported 11.5.4		Gombin	Warsaw	Y
Baibok	Hersz Baibok		Josek	Child			Konin camp	G K
Baibok	Rojza Baibok		Josek	Child			Gombin	G
Baibok	Frajdla Baibok		Jde	Child			Gombin	G
Baibok	Fajga Baibok		Jde	Child	Gombin	Gombin	Gombin	G
Baibok	Dubcja Baibok				Gombin	Gombin	Gombin	H
Band	Ester Rivka Band nee Brand	1882	Israel	Married to Lajbl	Gombin	Osmolin	Osmolin	Y
Baran	Khana Baran nee Kam	1892	Yechiel	Married to Shlomo	Gombin	Kutno, Poland	Kutno	Y
Baruch	Israel Baruch					Gombin		W
Baruch	Moshe Baruch					Gombin		W
Baruch	David Baruch					Gombin		W
Baruch	Shamai Baruch					Gombin		W
Baruch	Biniamin Baruch	1908		Locksmith, married to Dvosha	Gombin	Janow	Janow	Y W

1

Family	Person's complete name	Year born	Parents	Other details	Place of birth	Before the war lived in	During the war was in	Source
Baum	Majer Baum						Gombin	G
Baum	(GNU) Baum			Wife of Majer			Gombin	G
Baum	Majlech Nuchem Baum	1892		Died Lodz hospital 15-Jan-1942	Gombin		Lodz	L M
Baum	Ruchla Baum nee Frydland	1895	Szmul & Chana	Married to Szail	Gombin	Lodz	Lodz	Y
Baum	Cypra Idess Baum	1861			Gombin		Lodz	L M
Bauman	Moshe Bauman					Gombin		W
Bauman	Sura Bauman						Gombin	G
Bauman	Hersz Laibusz Bauman	1904	Mordekhai & Rivka	Merchant, married to Golda nee Gombin	Gombin	Gombin	Poland	Y
Bauman	Golda Ita Bauman nee Holtzman	1909	Eliahu & Rasha nee Zlotnik	Married to Hersz	Gombin	Gombin	Gombin	Y
Bauman	Khana Bauman		Hersz & Ita nee Holtzman	Child		Gombin	Poland	Y
Bauman	Ela Bauman		Hersz & Ita nee Holtzman		Gombin	Gombin		Y
Bauman	Mordchaj Bauman			Merchant, married to Ester nee Gombin	Gombin	Gombin	Poland	Y
Bauman	Tzvia Bauman	1908	Mordchaj & Rakhel nee Gold		Gombin	Gombin	Gombin	Y
Bauman	Dvora Bauman	1922	Mordchaj & Rakhel nee Gold		Gombin	Gombin	Poland	Y
Bauman	Yitzkhak Bauman	1907	Mordchaj & Rakhel nee Gold	Clerk, married to Lajka nee Gelb	Gombin	Gombin	Gombin	Y B
Bauman	Lajka Bauman nee Gelbert	1908	Zainvil & Malka	Married to Yitzkhak	Gombin	Gombin	Gombin	Y B
Bauman	Fela Bauman	1932	Yitzkhak & Lajka nee Gelbar	Child	Gombin	Gombin	Gombin	Y B G
Bauman	Sala Bauman	1934	Yitzkhak & Lajka nee Gelbar	Child	Gombin	Gombin	Gombin	Y B
Baumann	Sara Baumann	1901			Gombin	Chemnitz, Germany		Y
Bekas	Mosze Bekas			Married, deported Konin camp		Gombin	Konin camp	K
Bel	Icek Bel	1921		Died Lodz hospital 03-Mar-194	Gombin	Lodz	Lodz	L M
Bel	Cwi Bel	1903		Married, "sick" deported 8.7.42		Gombin	Konin camp	K
Belfer	Moshe Belfer					Gombin		W
Belfer	Sara Belfer					Gombin		W
Belfer	Miriam Belfer					Gombin		W
Belfer	Frajdel Belfer	1921		Died Lodz hospital 22-Aug-194	Gombin		Lodz	L M
Bender	Frimet Bender		Yosef & Khaia	Married to Mor	Gombin	Poland	Lodz	Y
Ber	Awraham Ber	1887	Yitzkhak	Merchant, married to Miriam n	Gombin	Gombin	Gombin	Y W B
Ber	Mirjam Rywka Ber nee Zaiontz	1892	Gitel	Married to Avraham	Kutno	Gombin	Gombin	Y W B
Ber	Jehoschua Chaskiel Ber	1916	Avraham & Rivka	Single	Gombin	Gombin	Auschwitz camp	Y B M
Ber	Menasze Ber	1913	Avraham & Rivka	Married	Gombin	Gombin	Gombin	Y B
Ber	Israel Ber	1916	Avraham & Rivka	Electrician, married to Balcia	Gombin	Gombin	Gombin	Y B
Ber	Bejla Ber nee Zychlinski	1916	Avraham	Married to Israel	Gombin	Gombin	Gombin	Y B
Ber	(GNU) Ber		Israel Ber & Bejla Zychlinski	Child	Gombin	Gombin	Gombin	Y
Ber	Mordechai Ber	1885		Agriculturist, married to Zelda	Gombin	Gombin	Gombin	Y
Ber	Zlate Ber	1905	Mordekhai & Zelda	Married	Gombin	Gostynin	Gostynin	Y
Ber	Male Melania Ber	1907	Mordekhai & Zelda	Married	Gombin	Gombin	Gombin	Y
Ber	Sara Ber	1909	Mordekhai & Zelda	Single	Gombin	Gombin	Gombin	Y
Ber	Bracha Ber	1911	Mordekhai & Zelda	Single	Gombin	Gombin	Gombin	Y
Ber	Yosef Ber	1920	Mordekhai & Zelda	Single	Gombin	Gombin	Kutno	Y
Ber	Mosche Sana Ber	1923	Mordekhai & Zelda	Pupil, single	Gombin	Gombin	Warsaw	Y

2

Family	Person's complete name	Year born	Parents	Other details	Place of birth	Before the war lived in	During the war was in	Source
Ber	Chana Ber	1924	Mordekhai & Zelda	Single	Gombin	Gombin	Gombin	Y
Ber	Jeszayahu Szaja Ber	1889		Married, "sick" deported 8.7.42		Gombin	Konin camp	W K
Ber	Dina Ber					Gombin		W
Ber	Israel Ber	1912		Died 19/01/1943, Auschwitz	Gombin		Auschwitz camp	Y M
Ber	Jakob Ber			Married, deported Konin camp		Gombin	Konin camp	K
Ber	Hersz Lajb Ber			Deported Konin camp to Andrz		Gombin	Konin camp	K
Berenholc	Beniamin Berenholc		Majer	Child			Gombin	G
Berenholc	Cyrla Berenholc		Majer	Child			Gombin	G
Berholc	Maks Berholc						Gombin	G
Berholc	(GNU) Berholc			Wife of Maks			Gombin	G
Berholc	(GNU) Berholc		Maks	Child			Gombin	G
Berholc	(GNU) Berholc		Maks	Child			Gombin	G
Berkowicz	Frania Berkowicz nee Sieradzka	1903	Pinkhas & Dina	Married to Szymon	Gombin	Lodz	Lodz	Y
Bernard	Nacha Bernard nee Wolman	1907	Tobjasz & Balka	Married to Raphael, deported f	Gombin	Paris, France	Auschwitz camp	Y F M
Bernard	Binam Bernard			Married to Edga	Gombin	Gombin		B
Bernard	Edga Bernard			Married to Binam	Gombin	Gombin		B
Berszt	Yosef Berszt	1894	Yona & Khava	Baker, married to Sara nee Pali	Gombin	Warsaw	Uzbekistan	Y
Bibergal	Mordechai Bibergal	1887		Married, "sick" deported 11.5.4		Gombin	Konin camp	K
Bibergal	Jona Bibergal	1892	Zusman & Rivka	Uppers tailor, married to Frida	Gombin	Gombin	Gombin	Y W G
Bibergal	Fraida Bibergal nee Fleishman	1892	Shmuel & Mindl	Married to Yona	Gombin	Gombin	Gombin	Y W
Bibergal	Yaakov Bibergal		...ona & Frida nee Fleishman	Child	Poland	Gombin	Poland	Y W
Bibergal	Mordekhai Bibergal		Jona & Frida nee Fleishman		Poland	Gombin	Poland	Y W
Bibergal	Efraim Bibergal	1916	Jona & Frida nee Fleishman	Uppers tailor, single	Gombin	Gombin	Gombin	Y W
Bibergal	Mindl Bibergal	1920	Jona & Frida nee Fleishman	Pupil, single	Gombin	Gombin	Gombin	Y W
Bibergal	Meir Bibergal					Gombin		W
Bibergal	Mania Bibergal						Gombin	G
Bibergal	Jakub Bibergal		Mordka	Child			Gombin	G
Bicman	Brajndel Bicman nee Spodek	1910	Moshe & Ita	Married to David	Lowicz	Gombin	Sochaczew	Y
Bigeleisen	Yitzhok Bigeleisen	1895	Shmuel & Teltza	Married to Mindle nee Parzenc	Gombin	Gombin	Warsaw	Y W
Bigeleisen	Mindle Bigeleisen nee Parzenczew	1900	Moishe & Baila	Married to Yitzhok	Ozorkow	Gombin	Warsaw	Y W
Bigeleisen	Yosef Bigeleisen	1930	Yitzkhak & Mindl	Child	Gombin	Gombin	Gombin	Y
Bigeleisen	Ester Bigeleisen	1923	Yitzkhak & Mindl		Gombin	Gombin	Gombin	Y
Bigeleisen	Khana Bigeleisen	1927	Yitzkhak & Mindl	Teenager	Gombin	Gombin	Gombin	Y
Bigeleisen	Sara Bigeleisen	1922	Yitzkhak & Mindl		Gombin	Gombin	Gombin	Y
Bigeleisen	Hinda Bigeleisen	1925	Yitzkhak & Mindl	Child	Gombin	Gombin	Gombin	Y
Bigeleisen	Dvora Bigeleisen	1926	Yitzkhak & Mindl	Child	Gombin	Gombin	Gombin	Y
Blamboim	Abraham Blamboim	1879		Married, buried Konin Catholic	Gombin		Konin camp	K
Blank	Perla Blank		Berysz	Child			Gombin	G
Blank	Nacha Blank		Berysz	Child			Gombin	G
Blank	Azriel Blank		Berysz	Child			Gombin	G
Blank	Szyfra Blank		Berysz	Child			Gombin	G

3

Family	Person's complete name	Year born	Parents	Other details	Place of birth	Before the war lived in	During the war was in	Source
Blank	Abram Blank		Berysz	Child	Poland	Gombin	Gombin	G
Blaved	Pinchas Blaved	1890		Horse dealer, married to Roza		Gombin	Gombin	Y
Blaved	Rosa Blaved nee Bzura	1890	Shmuel & Khana	Married to Pinkhas	Gombin	Gombin	Gombin	Y
Blawat	Herzel Blawat		Pinhas & Rosa nee Bzura	Married	Gombin	Gombin	Gombin	Y G B
Blawat	Shlomo Blawat		Pinhas & Rosa nee Bzura	Married	Gombin	Gombin	Gombin	Y B
Blawat	Lipa Blawat		Pinhas & Rosa nee Bzura	Married	Gombin	Gombin	Gombin	Y B
Blawat	Frymet Lea Blawat nee Vrubel	1912	Jakub & Malka	Married to Maier	Gombin	Gombin	Gombin	Y W G B
Blawat	Hanna Blawat	1938	David & Frymet nee Wroble	Child	Gombin	Gombin		Y
Blawat	David Blawat				Gombin			Y
Blawat	Hinda Blawat		Dawid	Child			Gombin	G
Blawat	Chaja Blawat						Gombin	G
Bochka	Salusch Bochka	1925		Died Poznan camp 23-12-1942	Gombin		Poznan camp	Y
Bocian	Avraham Bocian	1903			Lodz	Gombin	Gombin	Y B
Bocian	Genia Bocian nee Tyber	1905	Lajzer & Mindel	Married to Avraham	Gombin	Gombin	Gombin	Y B
Bocian	Pinkhas Bocian		Avraham & Genya nee Tiber	Child		Gombin	Gombin	Y
Bocian	(GNU) Bocian		Avraham & Genya nee Tiber	Child		Gombin	Gombin	Y
Bocian	Laibisz Bocian					Gombin		W
Bocian	Abraham Itzchok Bocian			Married to Abraham Itzchok		Gombin		B
Bocian	Goldie Bocian			Married to Goldie		Gombin		B
Bocian	Chaskel Bocian		Abraham & Goldie			Gombin		B
Bocian	Deborah Bocian		Abraham & Goldie			Gombin		B
Boczko	Zeew Boczko	1922		Single, buried Konin Catholic ce	Gombin	Gombin	Konin camp	K
Boczko	Yekhiel Boczko	1890		Merchant, married to Khana	Lodz	Gombin	Gombin	Y
Boczko	Khana Boczko nee Goldman	1897	Israel & Reizl	Married to Yekhiel	Gombin	Gombin	Gombin	Y
Boczko	Hershel Boczko	1922	Yekhiel & Khana nee Goldm		Gombin	Gombin	Gombin	Y
Boczko	Raizel Boczko	1928	Yekhiel & Khana nee Goldm	Child	Gombin	Gombin	Gombin	Y
Boczko	Zalman Boczko	1926	Yekhiel & Khana nee Goldm	Child	Gombin	Gombin	Gombin	Y
Boczko	Israel Boczko	1934	Yekhiel & Khana nee Goldm	Child	Gombin	Gombin	Gombin	Y G
Boczko	Golda Boczko nee Goldman	1898	Tzvi & Reizl	Married	Gombin	Gombin	Gombin	Y
Boczko	Chilel Meyr Boczko			Merchant, married to Khana ne	Lodz	Gombin	Gombin	Y
Boczko	Szlomo Boczko			Married, deported Konin camp		Gombin	Konin camp	K
Bojl	Zelig Bojl	1897	Elizabeta & Elizabeta	Butcher, married	Gombin	Gombin	Gombin	Y
Bol	Mordka Bol	1909		Died Lodz hospital 26-Jan-1942	Gombin		Lodz	L M
Bol	Symcha Bol						Gombin	G
Bol	(GNU) Bol		Symcha	Daughter of Symcha			Gombin	G
Bol	(GNU) Bol		Symcha	Son of Symcha			Gombin	G
Bol	(GNU) Bol		Symcha	Son of Symcha			Gombin	G
Bol	(GNU) Bol		Symcha	Son of Symcha			Gombin	G
Bol	Abrahm Meir Bol	1870	Menashe & Sara	Butcher, married to Malka nee	Gombin	Gombin	Gombin	Y
Bol	Sheina Bol nee Plonski	1896	Shlomo & Rivka	Married	Gombin	Gombin	Gombin	Y
Bol	Riva Bol nee Kerber	1895	Leibel & Lea	Married to Jacob	Gombin	Zychlin	Lodz	Y

4

Family	Person's complete name	Year born	Parents	Other details	Place of birth	Before the war lived in	During the war was in	Source
Bol	Fela Bol	1922	Jacob & Riva nee Kerber	Student	Gombin	Zychlin	Lodz	Y
Bol	Herszel Bol					Gombin		W
Bol	Mordchaj Bol	1905	Menashe & Malka	Butcher, married	Gombin	Gombin	Gombin	Y W
Bol	Fajge Dvora Bol	1904	Menashe & Malka	Married to Tzipora	Gombin	Gombin	Gombin	Y W
Bol	Chana Bol	1909	Menashe & Malka	Married	Gombin	Gombin	Gombin	Y W
Bol	Benjamin Bol	1901	Menashe & Malka	Butcher, married to Fruma	Gombin	Gombin	Gombin	Y G
Bol	Zalman Bol	1877		Butcher, married	Gombin	Gombin	Gombin	Y W G
Bol	Fryda Bol	1895		Married	Gombin	Gombin	Gombin	Y W G
Bol	Malka Bol	1870		Married to Moshe	Gombin	Gombin	Gombin	Y
Bol	Herszel Bol	1903	Moshe & Malka	Butcher, married	Gombin	Gombin	Gombin	Y G
Bol	(GNU) Bol			Wife of Hersz		Gombin	Gombin	G
Bol	Ester Bol	1942	Benjamin & Fruma	Child		Gombin	Gombin	Y G
Bol	Mordka Bol		Zalme	Child			Gombin	G
Bol	Berek Bol		Zalme	Child			Gombin	G
Bol	Jcek Bol		Zalme	Child			Gombin	G
Bol	Mandel Bol	1922		Died Konin camp	Gombin	Gombin	Konin camp	Y
Bol	Meir Boll					Gombin		W
Bol	Ester Boll					Gombin		W
Bol	Salamon Boll	1881	Jakew & Sara	Married to Rachel nee Ziger	Gombin	Gombin	Gostynin	Y
Bol	Rachel Laja Boll nee Ziger	1886	Mordcha & Ita	Married to Salomon	Gombin	Gostynin		Y
Bol	Jakob Lajb Boll	1913	Salomon & Laja		Gombin	Gombin	Gostynin	Y
Bol	Faiga Boll	1918	Salomon & Laja		Gombin	Gombin	Gostynin	Y
Bol	Etka Boll	1916	Salomon & Laja		Gombin	Gombin	Gombin	Y
Bol	Manes Boll					Gombin		W
Bol	Malka Boll					Gombin		W
Bol	Dawid Boll	1901	Hirsh & Lea	Merchant, married to Khana	Gombin	Juliszew	Juliszew	Y
Bol	Laibl Boll					Gombin		W
Bol	Gitel Boll					Gombin		W
Bol	Sura Boll						Gombin	G
Bol	Fajwysz Boll			Single, deported Konin camp to		Gombin	Konin camp	K
Bol	Zelig Boll			Single, deported Konin camp to		Gombin	Konin camp	K
Borashack	Morris Borashack			Married to Leah		Gombin		B
Borashack	Leah Borashack nee Zayac		Henry & Susan	Married to Morris		Gombin		B
Bornshtein	Avraham Abek Bornshtein	1917	Yitzkhak & Ita		Gombin	Gombin		Y
Bornshtein	Jachet Bornshtein	1870		Died in Lodz Ghetto	Gombin	Lodz	Lodz	L M
Bornstein	Feiwel Bornstein			Merchant, married to Tzivia		Gombin	Gombin	Y
Bornstein	Ciwia Bornstein nee Dziewczepols			Married to Faivel	Gombin	Gombin	Gombin	Y
Borovik	Ester Borovik	1890	Yosef & Frida	Married to Yitzkhak	Gombin	Zychlin	Zychlin	Y
Boruch	Mosze Boruch						Gombin	G
Boruch	(GNU) Boruch		Mosze	Wife of Mojsze			Gombin	G
Boruch	(GNU) Boruch			Child of Mojsze			Gombin	G

5

Family	Person's complete name	Year born	Parents	Other details	Place of birth	Before the war lived in	During the war was in	Source
Borysiak	Mosze Borysiak			Wife of Mosze			Gombin	G B
Borysiak	(GNU) Borysiak						Gombin	B
Brand	Rachel Zelda Brand			Married to Khaim	Gombin	Kiernozia	Kiernozia	Y
Brand	Fajwusz Brand	1891	Yosef & Yeta	Merchant, married to Khana ne	Lodz		Gombin	Y G
Brand	Chana Brand nee Frenkel		Gedalia & Yehudit	Married to Feibush	Gombin	Gombin	Gombin	Y G
Brand	(GNU) Brand		Fajwusz & Chana	Daughter of Fajwusz	Gombin	Gombin	Gombin	G
Brand	(GNU) Brand		Fajwusz & Chana	Daughter of Fajwusz	Gombin	Gombin	Gombin	G
Brand	Berek Brand		Jankiel	Child			Gombin	G
Broder	Icchok Broder						Gombin	G
Bruner	Tauba Bruner	1890		Died Lodz hospital 25-Feb-1943	Gombin	Lodz	Lodz	L
Bryl	Chaim Bryl	1900		Married, "sick" deported 19.5.4		Gombin	Konin camp	G K
Bryl	(GNU) Bryl			Wife of Chaim			Gombin	G
Brysz	Frymeta Brysz	1896		Died Lodz hospital 13-Jun-1943	Gombin		Lodz	L M
Brzezinski	Michael David Brzezinski	1879		Merchant, married to Rakhel	Lowicz	Gombin	Gombin	Y
Brzezinski	Rakhel Brzezinski nee Sloma	1889	Israel & Yokheved	Married to Michael	Gombin	Gombin	Gombin	Y
Brzezinski	Hinde Brzezinski	1917	David & Rakhel nee Sloma	Student	Gombin	Gombin	Gombin	Y
Brzezinski	Genia Brzezinski	1911	David & Rakhel nee Sloma	Child	Gombin	Gombin	Gombin	Y
Brzezinski	Yehoshua Brzezinski	1908	David & Rakhel nee Sloma	Merchant, married to Luchia	Gombin	Gombin	Bielsk	Y
Brzezinsky	Abraham Brzezinsky			Married to Chana	Gombin	Gombin	Gombin	Y W B
Brzezinsky	Chana Brzezinsky			Married to Abraham	Gombin	Gombin	Gombin	Y W B
Burak	Minia Burak nee Fridland	1911	Shlomo & Rakhel	Married to Rafael	Gombin	Gostynin	Gombin	Y
Burak	Gina Burak				Gombin	Gostynin	Gombin	Y
Bursztejn	Maryem Bursztejn nee Frenkel	1914		Physician, deported from Beau	Gombin	Paris, France	Paris, France.	Y F M
Bursztyn	Hinda Bursztyn nee Zamosc	1898	Chaim Yehuda & Deborah	Married to Fishl	Gombin	Gombin	Gombin	Y R
Bursztyn	Lajzer Bursztyn	1930	Fishl & Hinda nee Zamosc	Child	Gombin	Gombin	Gombin	G R
Bursztyn	Israel Bursztyn		Eliahu & Feiga	Merchant, married to Malka	Gombin	Warsaw	Warsaw	Y
Buzin	Yisrael Buzin		Shmuel & Lea	Merchant, married to Menukha	Gombin	Gombin	Gombin	Y
Cadik	Mania Miriam Cadik nee Frenkel	1902	Yaakov	Seamstress, died Lodz hospital	Gombin	Lodz	Lodz	Y L M
Cala (Tzale)	Abram Cala	1881		Merchant, married, Lodz hospi	Gombin	Lodz	Lodz	Y L
Cala (Tzale)	Golda Sara Cala nee Fuks	1887				Lodz	Lodz	Y
Cale (Tzale)	Mosze Aron Cale				Gombin	Lodz	Lodz	Y
Celemenski	Sonia Celemenski			Teacher, Bund activists		Gombin	Warsaw	B
Certner	Mindla Certner	1898		Deported from Drancy 23/09/1	Gombin	Joeuf, France	Auschwitz camp	Y F M
Ciek	Jakob Ciek	1899		Married, "sick" deported 19.5.4		Gombin	Konin camp	K
Chai	Israel Chai					Gombin		W
Chai	Lajzer Chai					Gombin		W
Chai	Dvora Chai					Gombin		W
Chai	Herszel Chai					Gombin		W
Chaim	Huda Chaim					Gombin		W
Chaja	Abraham Chaja			Married to Feiga		Gombin		B
Chaja	Feiga Chaja nee Sochacki		Moishe & Chana	Married to Abraham		Gombin		B

6

Family	Person's complete name	Year born	Parents	Other details	Place of birth	Before the war lived in	During the war was in	Source
Chaja	Sara Chaja			Sister of Ben Guyer (Chaja)		Gombin		W R B
Chaja	Josek Chaja			Brother of Ben Guyer (Chaja), married to	Gombin			Y W H R B
Chaja	Cirel Chaja nee Sanicki			Married to Josek	Gombin	Gombin		Y H R
Chaja	Chana Chaja		Jcsek & Cirel			Gombin		W R
Chaja	Shmuel Chaja					Gombin		W
Chaja	Refka Chaja		David			Gombin		B
Chaja	Liebe Chaja		David			Gombin		B
Chaja	Bajle Chaja		David			Gombin		B
Chajek	Moishe Mendel Chajek			Married to Chana		Gombin		B
Chajek	Chana Chajek			Married to Moishe		Gombin		B
Chajek	Itzkhok Binem Chajek		Moishe & Chana			Gombin		B
Chajek	Rivka Rachel Chajek		Moishe & Chana			Gombin		B
Chajek	Jacob Chajek		Moishe & Chana			Gombin		B
Chajek	Aaron Chajek		Moishe & Chana			Gombin		B
Chajek	David Chajek		Moishe & Chana			Gombin		B
Chajek	Malka Chajek		Moishe & Chana			Gombin		B
Chajek	Rachmiel Chajek		Moishe & Chana			Gombin		B
Chajek	Hersh Leib Chajek		Moishe & Chana			Gombin		B
Chajek	Rachel Chajek	1905	Gotlib & Yehuda		Gombin	Sochaczew		Y
Chajek	Zalman Chajek			Clerk, married to Rakhel nee Fr	Gombin	Sochaczew		Y B
Chajek	Saraj Chajek				Gombin			B
Chencinski	Hinda Chencinski nee Finkelstain	1897			Gombin	Sprendlingen, Germany		Y
Chniel	Raizla Chniel nee Burshtein		Faivel & Tzivia	Married to Moshe	Gombin	Wyszogrod	Wyszogrod	Y
Chodes	Chaim Chodes	1887	Shlomo & Golda	Merchant, married to Pesa	Lowicz	Gombin	Gombin	Y H
Chodes	Pesa Chodes	1887	Yaakov & Sara	Married to Khaim	Gombin	Gombin	Gombin	Y
Chodes	Hinda Chodes	1916	Khaim & Pesa	Married	Gombin	Gombin	Gombin	Y
Chodes	Jakob Chodes				Gombin	Gombin	Gombin	H
Chuczy	Chaim Icchak Chuczy	1878	Zalman & Zelda	Tailor, married to Vital nee Pald	Gombin	Lodz	Lodz	Y
Chudis	Chana Chudis	1927		Pupil, single	Gombin	Gombin	Gombin	Y
Chudis	Chaim Chudis					Gombin	Gombin	G
Chudis	(GNU) Chudis			Wife of Chaim		Gombin	Gombin	G
Cohen	Arie Cohen	1880				Gombin		Y W
Cohen	Chana Cohen					Gombin		W
Cohen	Sara Cohen					Gombin		W
Cohen	Binem Cohen					Gombin		W
Cohen	Yosef Cohen	1904		Married, "sick" deported 19.5.4		Gombin	Konin camp	W K
Cohen	Yochevet Cohen					Gombin		W
Cohen	Chana Cohen					Gombin		W
Cohen	Lajzer Cohen					Gombin		W
Cohen	Moshe Cohen					Gombin		W
Cohen	Khaia Cohen					Gombin		W

7

Family	Person's complete name	Year born	Parents	Other details	Place of birth	Before the war lived in	During the war was in	Source
Cohen	Herszel Cohen					Gombin		W
Cohen	Duba Cohen					Gombin		W
Cohen	Chaim Wolf Cohen					Gombin		W
Cohen	Ester Cohen					Gombin		W
Cohen	Awraham Cohen	1892	Nute & Rivka	Shoemaker, married to Royze	Gombin	Gombin		Y W
Cohen	Royze Cohen	1900	Reuven & Feiga	Married to Avraham	Gombin	Gombin	Gombin	Y W
Cohen	Shmuel Cohen				Gombin	Gombin		W
Cwajchaft	Josek Majer Cwajchaft	1891		Died in Lodz Ghetto	Gombin		Lodz	L M
Cwajghaft	Mordekhai Mendel Cwajghaft	1899	Yona & Ester	Married to Miriam nee Bornsht	Gombin	Lodz	Lodz	Y
Cwajghaft	Bayla Dina Cwajghaft nee Holtzma	1887	Moshe & Riwka nee Frenkel	Married to Jakob	Gombin	Lodz	Lodz	Y
Cymaliński	Szlama Cymalinski	1924			Gombin		Auschwitz camp	Y M
Cywie	Pinkus Cywie	1893		Deported from Drancy 6-03-19	Gombin	Mauriac, France	Majdanek camp	F
Czarka	Lajb Czarka			Married, deported Konin camp	Gombin	Gombin	Konin camp	K
Czarnoczapka	Jechiel Majer Czarnoczapka	1883	Reuven & Lea	Merchant, married to Gitel	Gombin	Rypin	Warsaw	Y
Czarnoczapka	Eljahu Dow Czarnoczapka	1882	Reuven & Lea	Merchant, married to Matilda r	Gombin	Sierpc	Warsaw	Y
Dancyg	Szmaja Dancyg			Died in Konin camp.	Gombin	Gombin	Konin camp	K
Derewiczer	Fanny Derewiczer	1910		Married to Abraham	Gombin	Zuromin		Y
Dobrzynska	Perla Dobrzynska						Gombin	G
Dorembus	Marjem Dorembus	1893		Died in Lodz Ghetto	Gombin		Lodz	L M
Drachman	Abram Chaim Drachman	1860		Died in Lodz Ghetto	Gombin		Lodz	L M
Drachman	Gersz Drachman	1887		Died in Lodz Ghetto	Gombin		Lodz	L M
Drachman	Chaim Drachman	1916			Gombin		Lodz	L M
Drachman	Estera Drachman	1921			Gombin		Lodz	L M
Drachman	Mendel Drachman	1909		Died Flossenbuerg camp	Gombin		Flossenburg camp	Y M
Drachman	Fela Drachman	1917		Died Lodz hospital 11-Dec-194	Gombin		Lodz	L M
Drejwicz	Mendel Drejwicz			Married, deported Konin camp		Gombin	Konin camp	K
Dutman	Mosche Dutman	1879		Died Lobau camp, 1942	Gombin		Lobau camp	Y G
Dutman	Szaja Dutman		Moszek	Child			Gombin	G
Dutman	Sura Rywka Dutman		Moszek	Child			Gombin	G
Dutman	Laja Dutman		Moszek	Child			Gombin	G
Dutman	Pinkus Dutman						Gombin	G
Dutman	Aron Dutman		Pinkus	Child			Gombin	G
Dutman	Majer Dutman		Pinkus	Child			Gombin	G
Dutman	(GNU) Dutman		Majer	Child of Majer			Gombin	G
Dutman	(GNU) Dutman		Majer	Child of Majer			Gombin	G
Dutman	(GNU) Dutman		Majer	Child of Majer			Gombin	G
Dzialka	Shlomo David Dzialka			Merchant, married to Khava	Gombin	Plock	Plock	Y
Dzialka	Khava Dzialka			Married to Shlomo	Gombin	Plock	Plock	Y
Dziedzic	Cerka Dziedzic	1897		Died in Lodz Ghetto	Gombin		Lodz	L M
Dzik	Aron Dzik	1917		Single, "sick" deported 11.5.42		Gombin	Konin camp	K
Dzik	Nathan Dzik	1885		Married, buried Konin Catholic	Gombin		Konin camp	Y K

Family	Person's complete name	Year born	Parents	Other details	Place of birth	Before the war lived in	During the war was in	Source
Dzjedzic	Meir Szmuel Dzjedzic	1878		Married, buried Konin Catholic	Gombin		Konin camp	K G
Dzjedzic	Rafal Dzjedzic						Gombin	G
Edelbaum	Izrael Edelbaum	1910		Died Lodz hospital 16-Jul-1942	Gombin		Lodz	L M
Edelstern	Mosze Edelstern			Deported Konin camp to Andrz		Gombin	Konin camp	K
Elberg	Brane Elberg	1882		Married to Beniamin		Konin		Y
Elsner	Perel Laja Elsner						Gombin	G
Elsner	Chana Elsner nee Lack	1904			Gombin		Krakow	M
Elsner	Zelig Elsner		Rojza	Child			Gombin	G
Elsner	Szlama Elsner		Rojza	Child			Gombin	G
Elsner	(GNU) Elsner		Rojza	Child			Gombin	G
Engel	Hana Engel	1880	Avraham & Yenta	Married to Meir	Gombin		Lodz	Y
Engelke	Frajda Engelke	1897		Died in Lodz Ghetto	Gombin		Lodz	M
Erbst	Frumyt Erbst	1890	Moshe & Dorel	Married to Ozer	Gombin	Sochaczew	Sochaczew	Y
Erdberg	Moshe Erdberg	1919		Single, buried Konin Catholic ce	Gombin		Konin camp	K
Etinger	Szmul Etinger	1927			Gombin		Buchenwald camp	Y M
Etinger	Szewa Etinger nee Zilberman	1890	Etel	Married to Zelig	Gombin	Gostynin	Gostynin	Y
Ettinger	Smuel Mair Ettinger	1888	Zalman & Miriam	Baker, married to Khana nee Ba	Gombin	Gombin	Gombin	Y W G H
Ettingier	Chana Ettingier nee Bauman		Aleksander & Breina	Married to Shmuel	Gombin	Gombin	Gombin	Y W H
Ettingier	Miryam Ettingier	1916	Shmuel & Chana	Single	Gombin	Gombin	Gombin	Y W H
Ettinger	Breina Ettinger	1919	Shmuel & Chana	Single	Gombin	Gombin	Gombin	Y W H
Ettinger	Mindl Ettinger	1926	Shmuel & Chana	Single	Gombin	Gombin	Gombin	Y W
Fajtman	Laja Fajtman	1870		Died in Lodz Ghetto Hospital	Gombin		Lodz	L M
Falc	Aleksander Falc			Single, deported Konin camp to		Gombin	Konin camp	K
Falke	Mindl Falke nee Lipkovitz		Binem & Edel	Baker, married	Wroclawek	Gombin	Gombin	Y
Falke	Rivka Edel Falke		Mindl nee Lefkovitz	Single	Gombin	Gombin	Gombin	Y
Feldchaim	Ester Feldchaim						Gombin	G
Feldchaim	Szyfra Feldchaim						Gombin	G
Feldchaim	Cywa Feldchaim						Gombin	G
Feldman	Goldie Feldman nee Zayac		Henry & Susan			Gombin		B
Ferenbach	Abram Berysz Ferenbach	1878	Mosiek & Itta nee Goldman	Merchant, married to Chana ne	Gombin	Kutno, Poland	Kutno	Y
Fidler	Ita Fidler	1866		Died Lodz hospital 06-Jul-1942	Gombin		Lodz	L
Finkelkraut	Zoner Finkelkraut	1932		Deported 9/23/1942 from Drar	Gombin	Paris, France	Auschwitz camp	Y F M
Finkelstein	Abraham Finkelstein	1871		Tailor, widower	Gombin	Frankfurt am Main	Auschwitz camp	Y
Finkelstein	Ester Miriam Finkelstein nee Laski	1864	Shmuel & Khana	Married to Mordekhai	Gombin	Plock	Zary	Y
Finkelstein	Beila Finkelstein		Yaakov & Gitel	Married	Gombin	Gombin	Gombin	Y
Finkelstein	Yitzkhak Finkelstein		Yaakov & Gitel	Tailor, married to Yenta	Gombin	Gombin	Gombin	Y W
Finkelstein	Yenta Finkelstein			Married to Yitzkhak	Gombin	Gombin	Gombin	Y W
Finkelstein	Avraham Finkelstein		Yitzkhak & Yenta	Physician, single	Gombin	Warsaw	Warsaw	Y W B
Finkelstein	Eliezer Finkelstein		Yitzkhak & Yenta	Cantor, married	Gombin	Riga, Latvia	Riga, Latvia	Y W B
Finkelstein	Bluma Finkelstein			Married to Eliezer	Gombin	Gombin		W
Finkelstein	Hinda Finkelstein		Beila	Married	Gombin	Gombin	Gombin	Y W

9

Family	Person's complete name	Year born	Parents	Other details	Place of birth	Before the war lived in	During the war was in	Source
Finkelstein	Ester Finkelstein		Beila	Seamstress, single	Gombin	Gombin	Gombin	Y W
Finkelstein	Szyfra Finkelstein		Szyme	Child			Gombin	G
Finkelstein	Ester Finkelstein		Szyme	Child			Gombin	G
Finkelstein	Eliezer Finkelstein			Single, deported Konin camp to		Gombin	Konin camp	K
Finkelstein	Fishl Joine Finkelstein		Ezriel Zev	Married to Miriam		Gombin		B
Finkelstein	Miriam Finkelstein		Moishe & Rivka	Married to Fishl		Gombin		B
Finkelstein	Fraide Hinde Finkelstein		Miriam & Fishl			Gombin		B
Finkelstein	Hindl Finkelstein		Miriam & Fishl			Gombin		B
Finkelstein	Rokhl Finkelstein		Miriam & Fishl			Gombin		B
Finkelstein	Shmuel Finkelstein		Miriam & Fishl			Gombin		B
Finkelstein	Volf Finkelstein		Miriam & Fishl			Gombin		B
Finkelstein	Yisroel Finkelstein		Miriam & Fishl			Gombin		B
Finkelstein	Yerakhmiel Finkelstein		Ezriel Moishe	Child		Gombin		B
Finkelstein	Rutke Finkelstein nee Likhtnshteyn			Married		Gombin		B
Finkelstein	Leo Finkelstein	1921			Gombin		Buchenwald camp	M
Fiszbein	Neta Fiszbein	1900		Married, "sick" deported 8.7.42		Gombin	Konin camp	K
Flaiszman	Icchak Flaiszman	1903	Shmuel & Mindl	Merchant, married to Ester nee	Gombin	Gombin	Gombin	Y W G
Flaiszman	Ester Malka Flaiszman nee Vrubel	1905	Avraham & Roiza	Married to Icchak	Gombin	Gombin	Gombin	Y W
Flaiszman	Miriam Flaiszman		Icchak & Malka nee Vrubel	Child	Gombin	Gombin	Gombin	Y W
Flaiszman	Khana Flaiszman		Icchak & Malka nee Vrubel	Child	Gombin	Gombin	Gombin	Y W
Flaiszman	Shlomo Flaiszman		Icchak & Malka nee Vrubel	Child	Gombin	Gombin	Gombin	Y W
Flaiszman	Rivka Flaiszman					Gombin		W
Florkewicz	Chava Florkewicz					Gombin		W
Flaumbaum	Josek Moszek Flaumbaum						Gombin	G
Flaumbaum	Elie Flaumbaum		Jcek	Child			Gombin	G
Flaumbaum	Sala Flaumbaum		Jcek	Child			Gombin	G
Flaumbaum	Jakub Flaumbaum		Jcek	Child			Gombin	G
Frajman	Hinda Frajman		Alie	Child			Gombin	G
Frajman	Nachman Frajman		Alie	Child			Gombin	G
Frajman	Sura Frajman						Gombin	G
Frajman	(GNU) Frajman		Sura	Child of Sura			Gombin	G
Frajman	(GNU) Frajman		Sura	Child of Sura			Gombin	G
Frankel	Aaron Frankel			Married to Cyvia		Gombin		B
Frankel	Cyvia Frankel			Married to Aaron		Gombin		B
Frankel	Hershel Frankel			Married to Frieda		Gombin		B
Frankel	Frieda Frankel			Married to Hershel		Gombin		B
Frankel	Sholim Frankel			Married to Feiga		Gombin		B
Frankel	Feiga Frankel			Married to Sholim		Gombin		B
Frankel	Isaac Frankel			Married to Feige		Gombin		B
Frankel	Feige Frankel			Married to Isaac		Gombin		B
Fraytik	Israel Fraytik					Gombin		W

10

Family	Person's complete name	Year born	Parents	Other details	Place of birth	Before the war lived in	During the war was in	Source
Fraytik	Chana Fraytik				Gombin	Gombin		W
Frenkel	Itzhok Frenkel			Cap maker, married to Sache	Gombin	Gombin	Gombin	G B M
Frenkel	Sache Frenkel			Married to Itzhok	Gombin	Gombin	Gombin	G B M
Frenkel	Benek Frenkel		tzhok & Sache		Gombin	Gombin	Gombin	B
Frenkel	Hersz Frenkel		tzhok & Sache	Child	Gombin	Gombin	Gombin	G B
Frenkel	Mojshe Frenkel		tzhok & Sache	Child	Gombin	Gombin	Gombin	G B
Frenkel	Aaron Frenkel					Gombin		W
Frenkel	Tzviah Frenkel					Gombin		W
Frenkel	Meir Fishel Frenkel					Gombin		W G
Frenkel	Dyna Frenkel		Majer	Child			Gombin	G
Frenkel	Binem Frenkel					Gombin		W G
Frenkel	Mordechai Frenkel					Gombin		W
Frenkel	Gedaliahu Frenkel					Gombin		W
Frenkel	Ita Frenkel					Gombin		W
Frenkel	Efraim Frenkel					Gombin		W
Frenkel	Shifra Lea Frenkel					Gombin		W
Frenkel	Abram Frenkel	1916		Killed June 28, 1942, buried Ko	Gombin		Konin camp	Y K
Frenkel	Rachel Frajda Frenkel nee Zikhlins	1880	Dov & Liba	Owned house, widow	Gombin	Wloclawek	Gombin	Y
Frenkel	Riwka Frenkel nee Szlang	1904	Gidale & Tzipora	Milliner, married to Meir	Gombin	Sanniki	Sanniki	Y
Frenkel	Szlomo Frenkel	1878	Aharon & Tzvia	Hat maker, married to Feiga	Gombin	Gombin	Gombin	Y G
Frenkel	Fajge Frenkel	1880		Married to Shlomo	Gombin	Gombin	Gombin	Y
Frenkel	Chaja Frenkel	1914	Szlomo & Feiga	Married	Gombin	Gombin	Gombin	Y
Frenkel	Mindl Frenkel nee Bul	1910	Avraham & Ester	Married to Shimon	Gombin	Gombin	Gombin	Y
Frenkel	Efraim Frenkel		Shimon & Mindl nee Bul	Child		Gombin	Gombin	Y
Frenkel	Cesia Frenkel	1921		Pupil, single	Gombin	Gombin	Lodz	Y
Frenkel	Dobra Frenkel	1895	Aharon & Tzvia	Married	Gombin	Gombin	Lodz	Y
Frenkel	Ajzyk Frenkel	1881	Aharon & Tzvia	Hat maker	Gombin	Lodz		Y G
Frenkel	Cywia Frenkel		Ajzyk	Child		Gombin	Gombin	G
Frenkel	Aron Frenkel		Ajzyk	Child			Gombin	G
Frenkel	Pesa Frenkel	1867	Yosef & Khana	Married to Avraham, Lodz hosp	Gombin	Lodz	Lodz	Y L M
Frenkel	Zylbersztej Frenkel	1883		Deported from Malines 15/09/	Gombin	Belgium	Auschwitz camp	Y M
Frenkel	Abram Icek Frenkel	1861		Deported from Malines 26/09/	Gombin	Belgium	Auschwitz camp	Y
Frenkel	Israel Frenkel			Teacher, married to Chaya	Poland	Gombin	Gombin	Y
Frenkel	Chaya Frenkel nee Puro			Married to Israel	Poland	Gombin	Gombin	Y
Frenkel	Abraham Frenkel	1910	Israel & Khaia nee Puro		Poland	Gombin	Gombin	Y
Frenkel	Yetta Yeta Frenkel	1918	Israel & Khaia nee Puro		Poland	Gombin	Gombin	Y
Frenkel	Hersz Frenkel	1914	Israel & Khaia nee Puro		Poland	Gombin	Soviet Union	Y
Frenkel	Chava Frenkel	1927	Israel & Khaia nee Puro	Pupil	Gombin	Gombin	Gombin	Y
Frenkel	Jankiel Frenkel	1872	Dina	Married to Chana	Gombin	Gombin	Gombin	Y
Frenkel	Hershel Leib Frenkel	1912	Yankel & Chana Laja	Married to Dinan	Gombin	Gombin		Y W
Frenkel	Dina Frenkel	1908	Mortchele	Married to Hershel Leib	Gombin	Gombin	Gombin	Y W

11

Family	Person's complete name	Year born	Parents	Other details	Place of birth	Before the war lived in	During the war was in	Source
Frenkel	Jakob Frenkel			Made shoe uppers	Poland	Gombin	Poland	Y W
Frenkel	(GNU) Frenkel		Shlomo	Child of Shlomo			Gombin	G
Frenkel	(GNU) Frenkel		Shlomo	Child of Shlomo			Gombin	G
Frenkel	Cesia Frenkel						Gombin	G
Frenkel	Mindzia Frenkel						Gombin	G
Frenkel	Chana Laja Frenkel						Gombin	G
Frenkel	Chaim Pinkus Frenkel						Gombin	G
Frenkel	Fajwysz Frenkel						Gombin	G
Frenkel	Icchak Frenkel	1922		Single, "sick" deported 19.5.42		Gombin	Konin camp	K
Frenkel	Shloime Frenkel					Gombin		B
Frenkel	Mendel Frenkel					Gombin		B
Frenkel	Cirel Frenkel					Gombin		B
Frenkel	Laitsche Frenkel					Gombin		B
Frenkel	Rywen Hersz Frenkel	1871		Died in Lodz Ghetto	Gombin	Gombin	Lodz	L M
Frenkel	Rywka Frenkel	1883		Kazerne Dossin, deported 12/9	Gombin	Belgium	Auschwitz camp	F M
Fridland	Szmul Grojnem Fridland	1863		Died in Lodz Ghetto	Gombin	Gombin	Lodz	L M
Fridland	Yitzkhak Fridland					Gombin		Y
Fridland	Szlomo Chaim Fridland		Gdaliyahu & Gela	Merchant, married to Ester nee	Gombin	Gombin	Gombin	Y
Fridland	Ester Fridland nee Kulsk	1890	David & Mendel	Married to Shlomo	Kutno	Gombin	Gombin	Y
Fridman	Moshe Fridman	1879		Merchant, married to Tzirel nee	Sochaczew	Gombin	Warsaw	Y R
Fridman	Tzirel Fridman nee Zamosc	1879	Chaim Yehuda & Deborah	Married to Moshe	Gombin	Gombin	Warsaw	Y R
Fridman	Zeev Nakhum Fridman	1886		Merchant, married to Tzipa nee		Gombin	Konin camp	Y W K
Fridman	Tzipa Fridman					Gombin		W
Fridman	Ahuva Fridman	1926	Zeev & Tzipa	Single	Gombin	Gombin	Gombin	Y W
Fried	Abraham Fried					Gombin	Gombin	G
Frizler	Moshe Frizler			Merchant, married to Khana ne	Gombin	Gombin	Gombin	Y W
Frizler	Chana Frizler nee Bornshtein			Married to Moshe	Gombin	Gombin	Gombin	Y W
Frydel	Frenia Frydel		Hersz & Rywka nee Frenkel	Married	Gombin	Lodz	Pinczow	Y
Frydel	Ester Frydel		Hersz & Rywka nee Frenkel	Single	Gombin	Lodz	Lodz	Y
Frydel	Yechiel Frydel		Hersz & Rywka nee Frenkel	Teenager	Gombin	Lodz	Lodz	Y
Frydland	Welwek Frydland	1916		Married to Blumka	Gombin	Gombin	Bialystok	Y H
Frydland	Blumka Frydland			Married to Welwek		Gombin	Bialystok	H
Fuchs	Szmul Uscher Fuchs	1884		Married, buried Konin Catholic	Gombin		Konin camp	Y W G
Fuchs	(GNU) Fucks			Wife of Szmul			Gombin	G
Fuchs	(GNU) Fucks		Szmul	Son of Szmul			Gombin	G
Fuchs	(GNU) Fucks		Szmul	Daughter of Szmul			Gombin	G
Fuchs	(GNU) Fucks		Szmul	Daughter of Szmul			Gombin	G
Fuchs	(GNU) Fucks		Szmul	Daughter of Szmul			Gombin	G
Fuchs	(GNU) Fucks		Szmul	Daughter of Szmul			Gombin	G
Fuks	Laja Fuks nee Konafko		Sucher & Sura	Married to Monek	Gombin	Lodz	Piotrkow Trybunals	Y
Fuks	Szlomo Fuks	1914		Single, "sick" deported 8.7.42		Gombin	Konin camp	K

12

Family	Person's complete name	Year born	Parents	Other details	Place of birth	Before the war lived in	During the war was in	Source
Fuksa	Max Fuksa	1900	Married to Etta	Deported from Drancy 06/03/1...	Gombin	Paris, France	Majdanek camp	Y F M*
Fuksa	Etta Fuksa nee Goldberg	1899	Married to Max	Deported from Drancy 06/03/1...	Gombin	Paris, France	Majdanek camp	F M
Funkenshtein	Shmuel Funkenshtein			Merchant, married to Rakhel n...	Gombin	Wloclawek	Lodz	Y
Funtovitsh	Rachel Funtovitsh nee Holtzman	1895	Yekhezkel & Lea	Merchant, married to Yisrael	Gombin	Lvow		Y
Futerman	Abraham Futerman	1893	Yehoshua	Merchant, married to Khana	Warsaw	Gombin	Warsaw	Y G
Futerman	Hersz Futerman		Abram	Child			Gombin	G
Futerman	Szymon Futerman		Abram	Child			Gombin	G
Futerman	Chana Futerman		Abram	Child			Gombin	G
Futerman	Szmul Futerman		Abram	Child			Gombin	G
Futerman	Zalme Futerman		Abram	Child			Gombin	G
Futerman	(GNU) Futerman		Abram	Son of Abram			Gombin	G
Gajst	Sara Gajst nee Pytel	1863	...osek & Fajga nee Warszaw...	Married to Mojsie	Gombin			Y
Gajst	Gitel Fajga Gajst		Mordka	Child			Gombin	G
Gajst	Hersz Gajst		Mordka	Child			Gombin	G
Gajst	Mojsze Gajst						Gombin	G
Gajst	(GNU) Gajst			Wife of Mojsze			Gombin	G
Gajst	(GNU) Gajst		Mojsze	Son of Mojsze			Gombin	G
Gajst	(GNU) Gajst		Mojsze	Daughter of Mojsze			Gombin	G
Gelbert	Zainvil Gelbert			Married to Malka		Gombin		W
Gelbert	Malka Gelbert nee Kilbert	1887	Yaakov & Feiga	Married to Zainvil	Zychlin	Gombin	Gombin	Y W B
Gelbert	Moshe Gelbert	1914	Zainvil & Malka	Metalworker	Gombin	Gombin	Gombin	Y W B
Gelbert	Yehuda Ber Gelbert	1890	Moshe & Malka	Tailor, married to Khana nee Zo...	Gombin	Gombin	Gombin	Y
Gelbert	Chana Breyne Gelbert	1890	Yitzkhak & Sheina	Married to Ber	Wloclawek	Gombin	Gombin	Y
Gelbert	Mottel Gelbert	1916	Ber & Breina	Tailor, single	Gombin	Gombin		Y
Gelbert	David Gelbert	1919	Ber & Breina	Uppers cutter/tailor, single	Poland	Gombin	Gombin	Y
Gelbert	Yosef Gelbert	1923	Ber & Breina	Tailor, single	Gombin	Gombin	Gombin	Y
Gelbert	Adam Gelbert	1900	Yaakov & Ita	Baker, married to Sara nee Vint...	Gombin	Gombin	Gombin	Y
Gelbert	Rywka Sara Gelbert	1904	Moshe	Married to Adam	Gombin	Gombin	Gombin	Y
Gelbert	Chaja Gelbert	1922	Adam & Rivka	Single	Gombin	Gombin	Gombin	Y
Gelbert	Jakow Gelbert	1924	Adam & Rivka	Single	Gombin	Gombin	Gombin	Y
Gelbert	Nahum Gelbert	1905		Married, buried Konin Catholic...	Gombin		Konin camp	K
Gelbert	Anna Rachel Gelbert		Nuchym	Child		Gombin	Gombin	G
Gelbert	Szmul Gelbert		Nuchym	Child		Gombin	Gombin	G
Gelbert	Bajla Gelbert					Gombin	Gombin	G
Gelbert	Lajzer Gelbert					Gombin	Gombin	G
Gelbert	Mendel Gelbert			Single, deported Konin camp to...		Gombin	Konin camp	K
German	Chaim German			Yeshiva student, single	Gombin	Gombin	Lublin	Y
German	Hinda German					Gombin	Gombin	G
Gersht	Glika Gersht nee Fridel	1900	Yekhezkel & Lea	Married to Yedidia	Gombin	Lodz	Lodz	Y
Gips	Lajb Gips	1909		Merchant, died in Stutthof cam...	Gombin	Gdynia	Stutthof camp	Y W
Gips	Anza Ana Gips	1915	Leib	Single	Gombin	Gombin	Gombin	Y

13

Family	Person's complete name	Year born	Parents	Other details	Place of birth	Before the war lived in	During the war was in	Source
Gips	Lusia Lea Gips	1922	Leib	Pupil, single	Gombin	Gombin	Gombin	Y
Gips	Rozia Gips	1916	Leib	Single	Gombin	Gombin	Gombin	Y
Gips	Ahron Gips	1917	Leib	Pupil, single	Gombin	Gombin	Gombin	Y
Gips	Yosef Glas				Gombin	Gombin		W
Glas	Jcek Majer Glas	1869		Stone cutter, married to Lea ne	Warsaw	Gombin	Gombin	Y W
Glas	Lea Glas nee Szapiro			Married to Icek	Gombin	Gombin	Gombin	Y W
Glas	Szal Glas	1900	Icek & Lea nee Szapiro	Bookkeeper, married to Roza	Gombin	Gombin	Gombin	Y
Glas	Roza Glas	1905		Married to Szaul	Rypin	Gombin	Gombin	Y
Glas	Natan Glas	1930	Shaul & Ruza	Pupil	Gombin	Gombin	Gombin	Y
Glas	Lejb Glas	1904	Icek & Lea nee Szapiro	Pharmacist, married to Hanka r	Gombin	Wieruszow	Auschwitz camp	Y G M
Glas	Hanka Glas nee Kaplan	1910		Married to Leon	Kutno	Wieruszow	Gombin	Y
Glas	Regina Glas	1933	Leon & Hanka nee Kaplan	Pupil	Wieruszow	Wieruszow	Gombin	Y
Glas	Menasze Glas	1906	Icek & Lea nee Szapiro	Pharmacist, married to Meta	Gombin	Konin	Gombin	Y
Glas	Meta Glas	1906		Married to Menasze	Germany	Konin	Gombin	Y
Glas	Ewa Glas	1937	Menasze & Meta	Child	Konin	Konin	Gombin	Y
Glas	Anzia Glas					Gombin		W
Glas	Saul Glas					Gombin		W
Glas	Leon Maitek Glas					Gombin		W
Glikzeliger	Moszek Glikzeliger	1881	Pesakh & Pesia	Merchant, married to Rivka	Poland	Gombin	Warsaw	Y W
Glikzeliger	Rebeka Glikzeliger	1884	Simkha & Lea	Married to Moshe	Gombin	Gombin	Warsaw	Y W
Glikzeliger	Ycek Glikzeliger	1917	Moshe & Rivka	Metalworker, single	Gombin	Gombin	Gombin	Y W
Godlewski	Kazimierz Godlewski	1908			Gombin		Stutthof camp	M
Goldberg	Jurek-Josek Goldberg	1913			Gombin		Czestochowa camp	M
Goldberg	Liba Goldberg nee Charnochapke	1887	Reuven & Khaia	Married to Khanokh	Gombin	Rypin	Rypin	Y
Goldberg	Zalme Jcek Goldberg		Jzrael Mordka	Child			Gombin	G
Goldberg	Rachmiel Goldberg		Jzrael Mordka	Child			Gombin	G
Goldberg	Salomon Goldberg						Gombin	G
Goldberg	Lajb Goldberg	1906		Married, "sick" deported 11.5.4		Gombin	Konin camp	G K
Goldberg	(GNU) Goldberg			Wife of Lajb			Gombin	G
Goldberg	Chana Goldberg		Lajb	Child			Gombin	G
Goldberg	Chawa Goldberg		Lajb	Child			Gombin	G
Goldberg	Szyia Bina Goldberg		Lajb	Child			Gombin	G
Goldberg	(GNU) Goldberg		Lajb	Son of Lajb			Gombin	G
Goldman	Chaja Goldman nee Hodes	1870	Icek & Ruchla nee Bromberg	Married to Uszer	Gombin	Kutno, Poland	Gombin	Y
Goldman	Meir Goldman		Yitzkhak & Khana	Married to Sala nee Zwirek	Gombin	Plock	Plock	Y
Goldman	Abraham Goldman		Yitzkhak & Khana	Merchant, single	Gombin	Gombin	Gombin	Y
Goldman	Gedalja Goldman	1893	Yitzkhak & Khana	Tinsmith, married to Gita nee M	Gombin	Gombin	Konin camp	Y G K
Goldman	Gita Goldman nee Markovitz			Wife of Gedalia			Gombin	G
Goldman	Szajna Goldman		Gedalia	Child			Gombin	G
Goldman	(GNU) Goldman		Gedalia	Daughter of Gedalia			Gombin	G
Goldman	(GNU) Goldman		Gedalia	Daughter of Gedalia			Gombin	G

Family	Person's complete name	Year born	Parents	Other details	Place of birth	Before the war lived in	During the war was in	Source
Goldman	Hersz Goldman		Yitzkhak & Khana	Tinsmith, married	Gombin	Gombin	Gombin	Y
Goldman	Efraim Goldman		Hersz	Child	Gombin	Gombin	Gombin	Y
Goldman	(GNU) Goldman		Hersz	Child	Gombin	Gombin	Gombin	Y
Goldman	Gershon Goldman	1890	Israel & Reizl	Merchant, married to Roza, de	Gombin	Gombin	Konin camp	Y G K
Goldman	Roza Goldman			Seamstress, married to Gersho	Zychlin.	Gombin	Gombin	Y
Goldman	Israel Goldman	1923	Gershon & Roza	Single, "sick" deported 8.7.42		Gombin	Konin camp	Y K
Goldman	Hersh Goldman		Gerszon & Roza	Child		Gombin	Gombin	Y
Goldman	Rakhel Goldman nee Bornshtein		Faivel & Tzvia	Married to Ber	Poland	Gombin	Gombin	Y
Goldman	Bela Goldman	1905			Gombin	Gombin	Warsaw	Y
Goldman	Chana Goldman nee Iakovitz			Married to Yitzkhak		Gombin	Gombin	Y
Goldman	Benjamin Goldman		Yitzkhak & Khana	Tinsmith, married to Lea nee V	Gombin	Gombin	Gombin	Y G
Goldman	Lea Goldman nee Vinter		Tzipora	Married to Beniamin		Gombin	Gombin	Y G
Goldman	Yitzkhak Goldman		Benjamin & Lea nee Vinter	Child		Gombin	Gombin	Y G
Goldman	Berish Goldman		Benjamin & Lea nee Vinter	Child		Gombin	Gombin	Y
Goldman	Wolf Goldman			Merchant, married to Rakhel n	Gombin	Gombin	Gombin	Y
Goldman	Raizel Goldman	1923			Gombin	Gombin	Gombin	Y
Goldman	Khaim Goldman		Wolf & Rakhel nee Bornshte	Child		Gombin	Gombin	Y
Goldman	Avraham Goldman		Wolf & Rakhel nee Bornshte	Child		Gombin	Gombin	Y
Goldman	Chaim Tuvia Goldman	1895		Merchant, married to Khaia ne	Gombin	Gombin	Gombin	Y
Goldman	Chava Goldman	1896	Leib & Frida	Married to Khaim	Gombin	Gombin	Gombin	Y
Goldman	Malka Goldman		Khaim & Khava	Child		Gombin	Gombin	Y
Goldman	Shmuel Goldman		Khaim & Khava	Child		Gombin	Gombin	Y
Goldman	Chana Goldman					Gombin	Gombin	W G
Goldman	Bencjon Goldman					Gombin	Gombin	G
Goldman	Mania Goldman					Gombin	Gombin	G
Goldshmit	Abraham Benjamin Goldshmit	1890	Yerakhmiel & Sara	Merchant, married to Feiga ne	Gombin	Lipno		Y
Goldshtein	(GNU) Goldshtein			Mother of Brana			Gombin	G
Goldshtein	Brana Goldshtein						Gombin	G
Goldshtein	Fradel Goldshtein		Brana	Child			Gombin	G
Goldshtein	Szaja Goldshtein		Brana	Child			Gombin	G
Goldshtein	Shmuel Goldshtein	1881	Moshe	Watchmaker / silversmith, mar	Sochaczew	Gombin	Gombin	Y
Goldshtein	(GNU) Goldshtein		Shmuel	Child		Gombin	Gombin	Y
Goldshtein	Baruch Goldshtein			Single, deported Konin camp to		Gombin	Konin camp	K
Goldshtein	Lajbus Goldshtein			Single, deported Konin camp to		Gombin	Konin camp	K
Goldszlak	Szymon Goldszlak	1907			Gombin		Buchenwald camp	Y M
Goldszlak	Brana Goldszlak		Szymon	Child			Gombin	G
Goldszlak	Sura Goldszlak						Gombin	G
Goldszlak	Brucha Goldszlak						Gombin	G
Goldszlak	Aron Goldszlak						Gombin	G
Goldszlak	Lajzer Icek Goldszlak		Yozef Lajb	Child			Gombin	G
Goldszlak	Chawa Goldszlak						Gombin	G

Family	Person's complete name	Year born	Parents	Other details	Place of birth	Before the war lived in	During the war was in	Source
Goldszlak	Szaje Goldszlak						Gombin	G
Goldszlak	Blima Goldszlak		Wolf	Child			Gombin	G
Goldszlak	Chana Goldszlak		Josek	Child			Gombin	G
Goldszlak	Estera Goldszlak						Gombin	G
Goldszmid	Golda Goldszmid nee Kerber	1873	Barukh	Married to Volf	Gombin	Plock	Plock	Y
Goldszmidt	Jacob Goldszmidt	1885		Tailor, deported from Malines	Gombin	Lens, France	Auschwitz camp	Y F
Gombiner	Jacob Gombiner	1888	Isaac & Chava nee Zayontz	Violinist, married to Etka	Gombin	Wloclawek	Wloclawek	Y
Gombiner	Etka Gombiner	1892		Married to Jacob	Gombin	Wloclawek	Wloclawek	Y
Gordon	Mose Gordon	1885		Merchant, married to Khaia	Gombin	Gombin	Gombin	Y
Gordon	Chaya Gordon	1890		Married to Moshe	Poland	Gombin	Gombin	Y
Gordon	Baruch Gordon	1920	Moshe & Khaia	Single	Gombin	Gombin	Gombin	Y
Gordon	Shlomo Gordon	1918	Moshe & Khaia	Single	Gombin	Gombin	Gombin	Y
Gordon	Eliezer Gordon	1915	Moshe & Khaia	Single	Gombin	Gombin	Gombin	Y
Gordon	Gina Gordon	1908			Gombin		Teheran, Iran	Y
Gordon	Moshe Gordon			Son of Moshe	Gombin	Gombin	Gombin	H
Gordon	Shlomo Gordon				Gombin	Gombin	Gombin	H
Gorker	Godel Gorker	1910		Agent, married to Khana nee Le	Gombin	Gombin	Gombin	Y
Gorker	Chana Gorker nee Levkovitz	1911	Godel & Khana	Married to Godel	Juliszew	Juliszew	Gombin	Y
Gorker	Aharon Gorker			Child		Lvow	Gombin	B
Gostinsky	David Gostinsky			Married to Rivka		Gombin		B
Gostinsky	Rivka Gostinsky			Married to David		Gombin		B
Gostinsky	Rude Gostinsky				Gombin	Gombin	Gombin	B
Gostynska	Etel Gostynska	1872	Zalman & Rakhel		Gombin	Gombin	Gombin	Y
Gostynska	Laja Gostynska						Gombin	G
Gostynski	Estera Gostynska		Laja	Child			Gombin	G
Gostynski	Jta Gostynska		Laja	Child			Gombin	G
Gostynski	Hinda Gostynska		Laja	Child			Gombin	G
Gostynski	Beniamin Gostynski		Laja	Child			Gombin	G
Gostynski	Jakub Gostynski		Laja	Child			Gombin	G
Gostynski	Hersh Pinkhas Gostynski	1911	Yaakov & Yokheved	Butcher, married to Khana nee	Gombin	Gombin	Auschwitz camp	Y W H
Gostynski	Chana Gostynski nee Laski		Zeev & Fradil	Married to Pinchas		Gombin	Gombin	Y H B
Gostinski	Rose Shoshana Gostinski nee Hers		Shmuel & Rivka nee Borenst	Married to Achil	Gombin	Paris, France	Paris, France.	Y
Gostynski	Yakow Gostynski	1883	Moshe & Khaia	Married to Yokheved nee Honi	Gombin	Gombin	Gombin	Y W H
Gostynski	Jochewed Gostynski nee Honigsh	1890	Leibel & Rakhel	Married to Yaakov	Gombin	Gombin	Gombin	Y W H
Gostynski	Moszek Gostynski	1867		Butcher, married to Khaia nee	Poland	Gombin	Poland	Y
Gostynski	Yaakov Gostynski		Mosze & Khaia nee Shtoltzn	Child		Gombin		Y
Gostynski	Dina Gostynski		Mosze & Khaia nee Shtoltzn	Child		Gombin		Y
Gostynski	Jojne Gostynski			Wife of Jojne			Gombin	G
Gostynski	(GNU) Gostynski						Gombin	G
Gostynski	Benjamin Gostynski						Gombin	G
Gottesgnade	Icchak Gottesgnade	1883	Khaim & Rivka	Merchant, married to Dwora	Poland	Poland	Gombin	Y

16

Family	Person's complete name	Year born	Parents	Other details	Place of birth	Before the war lived in	During the war was in	Source
Gottesgnade	Dwora Gottesgnade nee Khaium		Eliezer	Married to Icchak		Poland	Gombin	Y
Gottesgnade	Khaim Reuven Gottesgnade		Icchak	Child		Poland	Gombin	Y
Gottesgnade	Sara Rivka Gottesgnade		Icchak	Child		Poland	Gombin	Y
Gottesgnade	Moszek Gottesgnade						Gombin	G
Gottesgnade	Estera Gottesgnade		Icek	Child			Gombin	G
Gottesgnade	Majer Gottesgnade		Jcek	Child			Gombin	G
Gottesgnade	Chaim Gottesgnade		Jcek	Child			Gombin	G
Gottesgnade	Chaja Gottesgnade		Jcek	Child			Gombin	G
Gottesgnade	Izrael Uszer Gottesgnade	1918			Gombin		Lodz	L M
Grabman	Sura Bina Grabman		Rubin	Child			Gombin	G
Grabman	Lajzer Grabman		Rubin	Child			Gombin	G
Grabman	Chaim Grabman		Rubin	Child			Gombin	G
Greber	Michael Greber					Gombin		W
Greenbaum	Jacob Leib Greenbaum	1883	Abraham & Hinda nee Rosel	Businessman, married to Hena	Gombin	Gombin	Libenau camp	Y W B R
Greenbaum	Hena Greenbaum nee Ryster	1884	Jojne Ryster	Married to Jacob	Gombin	Gombin	Gombin	Y W B R
Greenbaum	Shlomo (Stash) Greenbaum	1910	Jakob & Hena	Married to Helena	Gombin	Gombin	Gombin	W B R
Greenbaum	Helena Greenbaum nee Zayontz	1917	Stash & Helena	Married to Stash	Gombin	Gombin	Gombin	W B R
Greenbaum	Izzidor (Izho) Greenbaum	1941	Stash & Helena	Child	Gombin	Gombin	Gombin	W R B
Greenbaum	Jehoszua Greenbaum	1896	Abraham & Hinda nee Rosel	Married to Sarah, "sick" deport	Gombin	Gombin	Konin camp	K B R
Greenbaum	Sarah Grinbaum		Jehoszua & Sarah	Married to Jehoszua	Gombin	Gombin	Gombin	B R
Greenbaum	Reiselle Grinbaum	1933	Jehoszua & Sarah	Child	Gombin	Gombin	Gombin	B R
Grinberg	Ester Grinberg nee Shlang	1902	Gidale & Tzipora	Seamstress, married	Gombin	Gombin	Gombin	Y
Grinberg	Jakub Haim Grinberg	1886				Gombin	Lodz	Y L
Grinberg	Chana Sura Grinberg	1929				Gombin	Lodz	Y L
Grinberg	Rywka Grinberg	1925				Gombin	Lodz	Y L
Grinberg	Yona Grinberg					Gombin		W
Grinblat	Chaya Grinblat	1918	Yehuda & Bluma	Single	Gombin	Gombin	Gombin	Y
Grinblat	Jehuda Lejb Grinblat	1883	Yosef & Alte	Merchant, married to Blima ne	Radom	Gombin	Gombin	Y W
Grinblat	Blima Rachel Grinblat	1893	Shamai & Charna	Married to Yehuda	Zwolen	Gombin	Gombin	Y W
Grinblat	Israel Grinblat	1916	Jehuda & Rakhel nee Veintr	Shop assistant, single	Gombin	Gombin	Gombin	Y W
Grinblat	Ester Alte Grinblat		Jehuda & Rakhel nee Veintr	Child		Gombin	Gombin	Y W
Grinblat	Yosef Shamai Grinblat		Jehuda & Rakhel nee Veintr	Child		Gombin	Gombin	Y W
Grinblat	Mordekhai Grinblat		Jehuda & Rakhel nee Veintr	Child		Gombin	Gombin	Y W
Grinblat	Jdel Grinblat		Jdel				Gombin	G
Grinblat	Mordka Grinblat		Jdel	Child			Gombin	G
Grinboim	Kuba Grinboim	1900	Eliahu & Ita		Plock	Gombin	Gombin	Y
Grinboim	Iurek Grinboim		Kuba	Child		Gombin	Gombin	Y
Grinboim	(GNU) Grinboim		Kuba	Child		Gombin	Gombin	Y
Gronszki	Szyia Gronszki						Gombin	G
Gronszki	(GNU) Gronszki		Szyia	Child of Szyia			Gombin	G
Gronszki	(GNU) Gronszki		Szyia	Child of Szyia			Gombin	G

17

Family	Person's complete name	Year born	Parents	Other details	Place of birth	Before the war lived in	During the war was in	Source
Gronszki	(GNU) Gronszki		Szyia	Child of Szyia			Gombin	G
Gronszki	(GNU) Gronszki		Szyia	Child of Szyia			Gombin	G
Gross	Witel Gross					Gombin		W
Gross	Sara Gross					Gombin		W
Groybard	Lajwel Groybard			Married, deported Konin camp		Gombin	Konin camp	K
Grynbaum	Jakob Grynbaum	1900	Josef	Dentist, married to Khana nee		Gombin	Lwow	Y
Grynbaum	Anna Grynbaum nee Warchiwkier	1902				Gombin		Y
Grynbaum	Yozef Grynbaum		Yaakov & Khana nee Verkhiv	Child		Gombin	Gombin	Y
Grynbaum	Mira Grynbaum		Yaakov & Khana nee Verkhiv	Child		Gombin	Gombin	Y
Grynberg	Ber Grynberg			Single, deported Konin camp to		Gombin	Konin camp	K
Grynhaus	Max Grynhaus					Gombin		W
Grynspan	Shalom David Grynspan		Jacob			Berlin, Germany	Gombin	Y
Grynspan	Sara Grynspan nee Tyber	1886	Moshe & Golda		Gombin	Berlin, Germany	Gombin	Y B
Grzywacz	Boruch Grzywacz	1907			Gombin		Lodz	L M
Gurker	Israel Gurker			Married to Frieda		Gombin		W B
Gurker	Frieda Gurker nee Boiman	1882	Yaakov	Married to Israel	Gombin	Gombin	Gombin	Y W B
Gurker	Channa Gurker		Israel & Frieda			Gombin	Plock	W B
Gurker	Gad Gurker	1907	Avraham & Frida	Worker, married to Khana	Gombin	Gombin	Gombin	Y
Gurker	Khana Gurker	1910		Married to Gad	Gombin	Gombin	Gombin	Y
Gurker	Avraham Gurker		Gad & Khana	Child		Gombin	Gombin	Y
Gurni	Guta Gurni nee Venetzki			Merchant	Gombin	Warsaw	Gombin	Y
Gutman	Nuchym Gutman						Gombin	G
Gutman	(GNU) Gutman			Wife of Nuchym			Gombin	G
Gutman	Chana Gutman		Nuchym	Child			Gombin	G
Gutman	Aron Josef Gutman		Nuchym	Child			Gombin	G
Gutman	(GNU) Gutman		Nuchym	Child of Nuchym			Gombin	G
Guyer	Yacov Guyer					Gombin		W
Guyer	Neta Guyer					Gombin		W
Guyer	Zelda Guyer					Gombin	Gombin	W
Gvirtzman	Mania Gvirtzman nee Friedel		Hersz & Rywka nee Frenkel	Married	Gombin	Lodz	Lodz	Y
Gzhivatch	Volf Gzhivatch					Gombin	Gombin	B
Hadas	Cheskiel Hadas	1900		Baker, married	Gombin	Zakroczyn	Plock	Y
Haik	Zelda Haik nee Vispa		Avrom & Rakhel	Married to David	Gombin	Tzagnik		Y
Haltrecht	Josef Mieczyslaw Haltrecht	1894		Physician, married	Gombin	Oksa	Oksa	Y
Hamburger	Reuwen Hamburger			Deported Konin camp to Andrz		Gombin	Konin camp	K
Hamer	Abram Hamer						Gombin	G
Hamer	(GNU) Hamer			Wife of Abram			Gombin	G
Hamer	Jzrael Hamer		Abram Chaim	Child			Gombin	G
Hamer	(GNU) Hamer		Abram	Son of Abram			Gombin	G
Hamer	(GNU) Hamer		Abram	Son of Abram			Gombin	G
Hardy	Aaron Hardy		Shimon		Gombin	Gombin	Gombin	Y

18

Family	Person's complete name	Year born	Parents	Other details	Place of birth	Before the war lived in	During the war was in	Source
Hardy	Yaacov Hardy		Avram & Dvora		Gombin	Gombin	Gombin	Y
Hardy	Shimon Hardy		Avram & Dvora			Gombin	Gombin	Y
Hecht	Chana Malka Hecht	1857		Died in Lodz Ghetto	Gombin		Lodz	L M
Helerman	Moshe Hirsz Helerman					Gombin		W
Helerman	Rachel Helerman					Gombin		W
Henzinski	Hinda Henzinski nee Finkelstein	1897		Deported from Drancy 16-09-1	Gombin	Sprendlingen, Gerr	Auschwitz camp	Y F
Herschberg	Sara Rivka Herschberg nee Borens		Joseph & Pesia	Merchant, married to Shmuel	Gombin	Gombin	Poland	Y
Herschberg	Avraham Herschberg		Shmuel & Rivka nee Borenst		Gombin	Gombin	Gombin	Y
Herschberg	Moshe Herschberg		Shmuel & Rivka nee Borenst		Gombin	Gombin	Gombin	Y
Herschberg	Yehushua Herschberg	1905	Shmuel & Rivka nee Bornsh	Married	Gombin	Poland	Poland	Y
Himel	Yaakov Himel	1884			Gombin	Zgierz	Warsaw	Y
Hirschberg	Shmuel Hirschberg			Married to (GNU)		Gombin		B
Hirschberg	(GNU) Hirschberg			Married to Shmuel		Gombin		B
Hirschberg	Abraham Moshe Hirschberg		Shmuel & (GNU) Hirschberg			Gombin		B
Hirschberg	Szyja Hirschberg		Shmuel & (GNU) Hirschberg			Gombin		B
Hirschberg	Rose Hirschberg		Shmuel & (GNU) Hirschberg			Gombin		B
Hochszpigiel	Lajb Hochszpigiel						Gombin	G
Hochszpigiel	Z. Majer Hochszpigiel						Gombin	G
Hodes	Yechezkel Hodes				Gombin	Gombin	Gombin	B
Hodes	Melech Hodes	1905	David & Shosha	Merchant, married to Khana	Gombin	Lodz	Lodz	Y
Hodes	Mosze Hodes	1900	David & Shosha	Merchant, married to Regina	Gombin	Lodz	Lodz	Y
Hodes	Abram Hodes	1872	Pinkhas & Lea	Merchant, married to Peril	Gombin	Lodz	Lodz	Y
Hodes	Simcha Hodes	1876	Pinkhas & Lea	Merchant, married to Gitel nee	Gombin	Lodz	Lodz	Y
Hodis	Ysrael Hodis	1900		Accountant, married to Poza ne	Gombin	Sierpc	Warsaw	Y
Hodys	Icchak Hodys	1886		Married, buried Konin Catholic	Gombin	Gombin	Konin camp	Y K
Hodys	Lazer Ber Hodys					Gombin		W
Hodys	Masza Hodys					Gombin		W
Hodys	Shimon Hodys					Gombin		W
Hodys	Aaron Hodys					Gombin		W
Hodys	Channa Gitel Hodys					Gombin		W
Hodys	Rosa Hodys					Gombin		W
Hodys	Shmil Yakir Hodys					Gombin		W
Hodys	Yehuda Hodys					Gombin		W
Hodys	Hersz Hodys					Gombin		W
Hodys	Avraham Moshe Hodys					Gombin		W
Hodys	Lajb Hodys	1886		Married, "sick" deported 9.4.4		Gombin	Konin camp	G K
Hodys	Josek Hodys		Lajb	Child			Gombin	G
Hodys	Dona Hodys		Lajb	Child			Gombin	G
Hodys	Dan Hodys						Gombin	G
Hodys	Mosze Hodys						Gombin	G
Hodys	Brana Hodys		Nusyn	Child			Gombin	G

19

Family	Person's complete name	Year born	Parents	Other details	Place of birth	Before the war lived in	During the war was in	Source
Hodys	Lajb Hodys			Deported Konin camp to Andrz		Gombin	Konin camp	K
Hodys	Szmuel Hodys			Deported Konin camp to Andrz		Gombin	Konin camp	K
Hodys	Juda Hodys			Deported Konin camp to Andrz		Gombin	Konin camp	K
Hirszberg	Mojsze Hirszberg	1903	Rivka	Merchant, married to Feiga nee	Gombin	Lodz	Lodz	Y
Holzman	Eliahu Holzman					Gombin		W
Holzman	Rasza Holzman					Gombin		W
Holzman	Benjamin Holzman	1881		Died Lodz hospital 09-Apr-1942	Gombin		Lodz	L M
Holzman	Simcha Holzman	1892	Yekhezkel & Lea	Merchant, married to Dina nee	Gombin	Gombin	Gombin	Y
Holzman	Dyjina Dina Holzman nee Halperin		Gedalia & Yehudit	Married to Simkha	Gombin	Gombin		Y
Holzman	Aharon Holzman				Gombin	Gombin		Y
Holzman	Moshe Itzek Holzman	1875	Aron & Reizl	Industrialist	Gombin	Lodz	Warsaw	Y
Holzman	Hersz Eliezer Holzman	1905	Eliahu & Rasha	Merchant, married to Rakhel n	Gombin	Gombin		Y
Holzman	Haja Sara Holzman nee Korn	1905	Tzvi & Frida	Married to Hersz Eliezer	Zychlin	Gombin		Y
Holzman	Khana Holzman		Lejzer & Sara nee Korn	Child		Gombin	Gombin	Y
Holzman	Josef Leib Holzman	1900	Eliahu & Rasha	Merchant, married to Lea nee 2	Gombin	Gombin	Gombin	Y G
Holzman	Lea Holzman nee Zolna			Married to Josef		Gombin	Gombin	Y
Holzman	Andzia Holzman		Yosef & Lea	Child		Gombin	Gombin	Y
Holzman	Sheina Holzman		Yosef & Lea	Child		Gombin	Gombin	Y
Holzman	Ytzkhak Avraham Holzman	1900	Eliahu & Rasha	Egg trader, married to Lea nee	Gombin	Lodz	Gombin	Y
Holzman	Lea Holzman nee Luidor			Teacher, married to Abram	Lodz	Gombin	Gombin	Y
Holzman	Eliahu Holzman		Avraham & Lea nee Luidor	Child	Gombin	Gombin	Gombin	Y
Holzman	Yisrael Holzman				Gombin	Gombin		Y
Holzman	Ester Holzman nee Mantzik			Married to Israel	Gombin	Gombin	Gombin	Y
Holzman	Eliahu Holzman		Israel & Ester	Child	Gombin	Gombin	Gombin	Y
Holzman	Mirl Holzman			Married to Moshe	Wyszogrod.	Gombin	Gombin	Y
Holzman	Khana Holzman		Mosze & Mirl	Child		Gombin		Y
Holzman	Perel Holzman		Mosze & Mirl	Child		Gombin		Y
Holzman	Estera Bajla Holzman	1848		Died in Lodz Ghetto	Gombin		Lodz	L M
Holzman	Mordka Josek Holzman	1869			Gombin		Lodz	L M
Holzman	Jakob Holzman	1866		Died in Lodz Ghetto	Gombin		Lodz	L M
Holzmann	Benjamin Holzmann	1887		Deported from Drancy 07/10/1	Gombin	Nice, France	Auschwitz camp	Y F M
Horowitz	Eva Horowitz nee Szklower	1898	Mendel & Frimel nee Golds	Married to David, deported fro	Gombin	Borgo San Dalmazz	Auschwitz camp	Y F
Hymel	Shlomo Hymel			Deported Konin camp to Andrz		Gombin	Konin camp	K
Iampolski	Sura Estera Iampolski nee Kowalsk	1905			Gombin	France	Auschwitz camp	Y
Jacentowski	Shmuel Jacentowski	1874	Rafael & Lea	Merchant, married to Sara nee	Zdunska Wola	Gombin		Y
Jacentowski	Sara Jacentowski nee Knobel	1876		Married	Gombin	Gombin		Y
Jacentowski	Gershon Jacentowski	1916	Shmuel & Sara	Shoemaker, single	Gombin	Raczonsz		Y
Jacentowski	Motke Jacentowski	1914	Shmuel & Sara	Driver, single	Gombin	Gombin		Y
Jacentowski	Yitzkhak Jacentowski	1908	Shmuel & Sara	Shoemaker, married	Gombin	Plock		Y
Jacentowski	Fishel Jacentowski	1910	Shmuel & Sara	Driver, married	Gombin	Gombin		Y G
Jacentowski	(GNU) Jacentowski			Wife of Fishel	Gombin	Gombin	Gombin	G

20

Family	Person's complete name	Year born	Parents	Other details	Place of birth	Before the war lived in	During the war was in	Source
Jackowski	Lucian Jackowski					Gombin		W
Jacobowicz	Eliah Meir Jacobowicz					Gombin		W
Jacobowicz	Ester Jacobowicz					Gombin		W
Jacobowicz	Hercka Jacobowicz		Szajna Ruchla	Child			Gombin	G
Jacobowicz	Majer Jacobowicz		Szajna Ruchla	Child			Gombin	G
Jankowski	Stephan Jankowski	1900			Gombin			M
Jarlicht	Mordechai Jarlicht					Gombin		W
Jarlicht	Miriam Jarlicht					Gombin		W
Jarlicht	Jakob Josef Jarlicht	1892		Married, "sick" deported 26.9.4		Gombin	Konin camp	K
Jarlicht	Hersz Jarlicht			Single, deported Konin camp to		Gombin	Konin camp	K
Jaskolka	Symcha Jaskolka	1900	Avigdor & Tzipora	Merchant, married to Lea nee A	Gombin	Gombin	Gombin	Y
Jaskolka	Lea Jaskolka nee Ash	1902	Yisrael & Rivka	Married to Simkha	Kutno		Gombin	Y
Jaskolka	Slomo Jaskolka	1923	Simkha & Lea	Pupil, single	Gombin		Gombin	Y
Jaskolka	Zelig Jaskolka		Simkha & Lea	Child			Gombin	Y
Jaskolka	Sara Jaskolka	1920	Simkha & Lea	Single	Gombin	Plock	Plock	Y
Jaswinski	Abram Jaswinski						Gombin	G
Jaswinski	Doba Jaswinski						Gombin	G
Jaswinski	Machel Jaswinski		Abram	Child			Gombin	G
Jaswinski	Icek Jaswinski		Abram	Child			Gombin	G
Jaswinski	Dyna Jaswinski		Abram	Child			Gombin	G
Jaswinski	Sura Jaswinski		Abram	Child			Gombin	G
Joab	Ryfka Joab	1894			Gombin		Lodz	L M
Joab	Brana Itla Joab	1871		Died in Lodz Ghetto	Gombin		Lodz	L M
Jospe	Rosa Jospe nee Cerini	1883	Selmar & Regina	Married to Joseph	Gombin	Oppeln, Germany	Berlin, Germany	Y
Kaczka	Jocheta Kaczka	1866		Died in Lodz Ghetto	Gombin		Lodz	L M
Kaczor	Zipora Kaczor	1898	Dov Ber Kaczor & Shayna Ko	Married	Rypin	Gombin	Gombin	Y
Kaczor	Bina Kaczor						Gombin	G
Kal	Abraham Meir Kal	1876		Married, "sick" deported 11.5.4		Gombin	Konin camp	K
Kalinski	Hersz Kalinski	1900	Shimon & Ester	Merchant, married to Reizil nee	Gombin	Gombin	Gombin	Y
Kalinski	Rajzla Kalinski nee Farba	1902	Shmuel & Khaia	Married to Hersh	Plock	Gombin	Gombin	Y
Kalinski	Shmuel Kalinski		Hersh & Reizil			Gombin		Y
Kalinski	Shimon Kalinski		Hersh & Reizil	Child		Gombin	Gombin	Y
Kalinski	Hinda Kalinski		Hersh & Reizil	Child		Gombin	Gombin	Y
Kalinski	Chana Kalinski		Sura	Child			Gombin	G
Kalinski	Zalme Josek Kalinski		Sura	Child			Gombin	G
Kalinski	Szymon Kalinski		Sura	Child			Gombin	G
Kalmus	Jakob Kalmus	1900	Abraham	Bookkeeper, married to Sara ne	Gombin	Lodz	Lodz	Y
Kalmus	Szlomo Kalmus	1872	Natan & Rakhel	Miller, married to Iaska nee Ko	Gombin	Lodz	Lodz	Y
Kalmus	Dawid Kalmus	1904		Died Lodz hospital 02-May-194	Gombin		Lodz	L M
Kamlazh	Feiwisz Kamlazh			Buried Konin Catholic cemeter	Gombin		Konin camp	K B R
Kampinski	Natan Kampinski	1885		Married, "sick" deported 8.7.42		Gombin	Konin camp	K

Family	Person's complete name	Year born	Parents	Other details	Place of birth	Before the war lived in	During the war was in	Source
Kamski	Gersh Kamski	1912		Driver, married	Gombin	Nesvizh, Belarus	Slutsk, Belarus	Y
Kaploun	Liba Kaploun nee Opatowska			Deported from Malines 24/10/	Gombin	Boitsfort, Belgium	Auschwitz camp	Y
Kapuza	Ester Kapuza nee Tadelis	1904	Shlomo & Rivka	Married to Yosef	Gombin	Warsaw	Warsaw	Y
Karaszovicz	Leib Karaszovicz	1880	Nakhman	Merchant, married to Frida nee	Gombin	Gombin	Gombin	Y
Karaszovicz	Freida Karaszovicz	1870	Shmuel & Khaia	Married to Leib	Gombin	Gombin	Gombin	Y
Karaszovicz	Jenta Karaszovicz	1894	Leib & Frida	School owner, married to Jita	Gombin	Gombin	Gombin	Y
Karmel	Fajga Karmel		Elie Sieradzki	Child			Gombin	G
Karo	Avraham Karo			Married to Tova	Poland	Gombin	Gombin	Y G
Karo	Tova Karo nee Pozner	1903	Khanokh & Shura	Married to Avraham	Gombin	Gombin	Gombin	Y
Karo	Gitel Karo	1931	Avraham & Tova	Pupil	Gombin	Gombin	Gombin	Y
Karo	Gucia Karo		Avraham & Tova		Gombin	Gombin	Gombin	G
Karo	Barukh Karo	1894	Mikhael & Reizl Vispa		Gombin			Y
Karo	Simkha Karo	1898	Mikhael & Reizl Vispa	Married	Gombin			Y
Karo	Feiga Karo	1885	Mikhael & Reizl Vispa		Gombin			Y
Karo	Rakhel Karo	1907	Mikhael & Reizl Vispa	Married	Gombin	Gombin	Gombin	Y
Kaszer	Chaim Kaszer						Gombin	G
Kaszer	Bina Kaszer		Chaim	Child			Gombin	G
Kening	Chaim Pinkus Kening						Gombin	G
Kening	Bajla Kening						Gombin	G
Keler	Shlomo Keler			Merchant, married to Lea	Gombin	Lowicz	Lowicz	Y
Kempinski	Wolf Kempinski	1927			Gombin			Y
Kerber	Majer Kerber	1904			Gombin			Y
Kerber	Abraham Mose Kerber	1870	Barukh	Merchant, married to Lea nee F	Gombin	Plock	Plock	Y
Kerber	Meir Kerber	1904		Married, buried Konin Catholic	Gombin		Konin camp	K
Kerber	Zalman Kerber	1878	Barukh	Merchant, married to Brakha	Gombin	Gombin	Gombin	Y
Kerber	Bracha Yehudit Kerber	1880		Married to Zalman	Gombin	Gombin	Gombin	Y
Kerber	Breina Kerber		Zalman & Yehudit nee Fuks	Child	Gombin	Gombin	Gombin	Y
Kerber	Zalman Kerber	1886	Barukh & Sara	Merchant, married to Rivka nee	Gombin	Gombin	Gombin	Y W
Kerber	Rivka Kerber nee Fuks	1885		Married to Zalman	Gombin	Gombin	Gombin	Y W
Kerber	Brontza Kerber		Zalman & Rivka		Gombin	Gombin	Gombin	Y W
Kerber	Yehudit Kerber					Gombin	Gombin	W
Kerber	Rafael Kerber	1885	Barukh	Tailor, married to Feiga	Gombin	Gombin	Gombin	Y
Kerber	Fajga Kerber	1887		Married to Rafael	Gombin	Gombin	Gombin	Y
Kerber	Baruch Kerber	1922	Rafael & Feiga	Pupil, married	Gombin	Gombin	Gombin	Y
Kerber	Sara Kerber	1921	Rafael & Feiga	Married	Gombin	Gombin	Gombin	Y
Kerber	Hershel Kerber	1874	Ezriel	Married	Gombin	Gombin	Gombin	Y
Kerber	Fajwisz Kerber		Hersz	Married to Lea nee Karo	Gombin	Gombin		Y
Kerber	(GNU) Kerber				Gombin	Gombin		Y
Kerber	Lea Kerber nee Karo	1905	Mikhael & Reizl nee Vispa	Married	Gombin	Gombin		Y
Kerber	Batsheva Kerber		Lea	Child	Gombin	Gombin		Y
Kerber	Roza Kerber		Lea	Child	Gombin	Gombin		Y

22

Family	Person's complete name	Year born	Parents	Other details	Place of birth	Before the war lived in	During the war was in	Source
Kerber	Saral Kerber		Lea	Child	Gombin	Gombin		Y
Kerber	Hersz Kerber			Killed during deportation to car		Gombin	Gombin	W B
Kerber	Marla Kerber					Gombin		W
Kerber	Gerszon Kerber						Gombin	G
Kerber	Frymet Kerber		Gerszon	Child			Gombin	G
Kerber	Josef Kerber						Gombin	G
Kerber	(GNU) Kerber		Josef	Son of Josef			Gombin	G
Kerber	(GNU) Kerber		Josef	Son of Josef			Gombin	G
Kerber	Nacha Kerber						Gombin	G
Kerber	Boruch Kerber						Gombin	G
Kesselman	Yosef Kesselman					Gombin		W
Kessler	Masza Kessler		Majer	Child			Gombin	G
Kessler	Sala Kessler		Majer	Child			Gombin	G
Khmiel	Reizl Khmiel nee Burshtein				Gombin	Gombin		Y
Kilbert	Meir Kilbert	1880		Married to Yeta nee Bzora	Gombin	Gombin	Gombin	Y W
Kilbert	Yita Kilbert	1880	Shmuel & Khaia	Married to Meir	Gombin	Gombin	Gombin	Y W
Kilbert	Chil Kilbert	1888	Yitzkhak	Agriculturist, married	Gombin	Gombin	Gombin	Y
Klinger	Jakob Klinger	1884		Pupil, married to Lea nee Bzora	Zychlin	Gombin	Gombin	Y W
Klinger	Lea Klinger	1886	Shmuel & Khava	Married to Yaakov	Gombin	Gombin	Gombin	Y W
Klinger	Sara Klinger					Gombin		W
Klinger	Slata Klinger					Gombin		W
Klinger	Baila Klinger						Gombin	G
Klinger	Frajda Klinger						Gombin	G
Klinkaowstein	Zyskind Klinkaowstein			Deported Konin camp to Andrz		Gombin	Konin camp	K
Klinski	Hersz Klinski					Gombin		W
Klinski	Arie Klinski					Gombin		W
Knobel	Golda Knobel						Gombin	G
Knobel	Kasryl Knobel		Golda	Child			Gombin	G
Knobel	Chaja Knobel		Golda	Child			Gombin	G
Knopmacher	Jankiel Jakob Knopmacher	1914		Married, "sick" deported 8.7.42	Gombin	Gombin	Konin camp	G K
Knopmacher	Abram Knopmacher		Jakub	Child			Gombin	G
Kocinski	Leja Kocinski	1885		Widow	Gombin	Gombin	Gombin	Y
Kocinski	Eliejzer Kocinski	1915	Lea	Tailor, single	Gombin	Gombin	Gombin	Y
Kocinski	Chaim Kocinski	1914		Tailor, single	Gombin	Gombin	Gombin	Y
Kocinski	Ester Koczynski	1921		Pupil, single	Gombin	Gombin	Gombin	Y
Kohen	Nute Kohen	1859	Moshe & Yokheved	Merchant, married to Rivka	Gombin	Gombin	Gombin	Y
Kohen	Avraham Kohen		Nute	Fruit trader, married to Shosha	Gombin	Gombin	Gombin	Y
Kohn	Cypora Kohn nee Vigdorovitz	1877	Yosef & Khana	Grocer, widow	Gombin	Gombin	Gombin	Y
Kolski	David Kolski	1861		Married to Mindl	Kutno	Kutno, Poland	Gombin	Y
Kolski	Mindl Kolski			Married to David	Kutno	Kutno, Poland	Gombin	Y
Kolski	Ber Kolski	1900	David & Mindl	Mechanic, single	Kutno	Kutno, Poland	Gombin	Y

23

Family	Person's complete name	Year born	Parents	Other details	Place of birth	Before the war lived in	During the war was in	Source
Kolski	Rivka Regina Kolski			Married to Mendel	Gombin	Wloclawek	Wloclawek	Y
Koltanowski	Marie Koltanowski nee Lassmann	1870		Widow, deported from Malines	Gombin	Belgium	Auschwitz camp	Y
Kon	Moshe Kon			Tailor, married to Reyza	Gombin	Gombin	Gombin	Y
Kon	Braina Kon nee Beibuk	1899	Hersh & Khaia	Married to Yitzkhak	Gombin	Gombin	Wyszogrod	Y
Kon	Josek Kon	1889		Died Lodz hospital 19-Jul-1942	Gombin		Lodz	L M
Kon	Arie Kon						Gombin	G
Kon	(GNU) Kon			Wife of Arie			Gombin	G
Kon	Chaim Wolf Kon						Gombin	G
Kon	(GNU) Kon		Chaim Wolf	Son of Chaim Wolf			Gombin	G
Kon	(GNU) Kon		Chaim Wolf	Son of Chaim Wolf			Gombin	G
Kon	Awrum Kon						Gombin	G
Kon	(GNU) Kon			Wife of Awrum			Gombin	G
Kon	Majer Elia Kon						Gombin	G
Kon	Josek Kon		Majer Elia	Child			Gombin	G
Kon	Boruch Kon		Majer Elia	Child			Gombin	G
Kon	(GNU) Kon		Majer Elia	Child of Majer			Gombin	G
Kon	Lajzer Kon						Gombin	G
Kon	Nuta Kon						Gombin	G
Kon	Rajza Kon						Gombin	G
Kon	Estera Kon						Gombin	G
Kon	Josek Kon	1909		Died in Lodz Ghetto	Gombin		Lodz	L M
Kopito	Minka Kopito	1885		Married to David	Gombin	Plock	Plock	Y
Kopito	Rachel Kopito	1878		Married to David	Gombin	Plock	Plock	Y
Kopito	Hinda Kopito	1890	Shimon & Sara	Married to Yosef	Gombin	Plock	Plock	Y
Kot	Razlen Kot nee Menkhe		Josef & Rose nee Bornshteir	Businessman, married to Lejzer	Gombin	Gombin	Gombin	Y
Kot	Sali Kot	1916	Lejzer & Razlen nee Menkhe	Bookkeeper, single	Gombin	Plock	Sierpc	Y
Kot	Mosche Israel Kot	1920		Single, buried Konin Catholic ce	Gombin		Konin camp	Y K
Kotliar	Abraham Kotliar			Married to Manya	Gombin		Warsaw	Y B
Kotliar	Manya Kotliar			Married to Abraham	Gombin		Warsaw	Y B
Kowalski	Khoni David Kowalski	1880		Merchant, married to Mindl	Kutno	Gombin	Gombin	Y
Kowalski	Mindl Feiga Kowalski nee Goldma	1882	Israel & Reizel	Married to Khoni	Gombin	Gombin	Gombin	Y
Kowalski	Hershl Kowalski	1911	Khoni & Mindel nee Goldma		Gombin	Gombin		Y
Kowalski	Sara Kowalsky	1913	Khoni & Mindel nee Goldma	Seamstress, single	Gombin	Paris, France	Paris, France.	Y
Kowalski	Moshe Kowalski	1916	Khoni & Mindel nee Goldma		Gombin	Gombin		Y
Kowalski	Khana Kowalski	1910	Khoni & Mindel nee Goldma		Gombin	Gombin	Gombin	Y
Kowalski	Mendel Kowalski	1923	Khoni & Mindel nee Goldma	Single, "sick" deported 8.7.42	Gombin	Gombin	Konin camp	Y
Kowalski	Rivka Kowalski	1919	Khoni & Mindel nee Goldma		Gombin	Gombin		Y
Kranc	Wigdor Kranc						Gombin	G
Kranc	Gucia Kranc						Gombin	G
Kraszewicz	Sura Kraszewicz						Gombin	G
Kraszewicz	(GNU) Kraszewicz		Sura	Child of Sura			Gombin	G

24

Family	Person's complete name	Year born	Parents	Other details	Place of birth	Before the war lived in	During the war was in	Source
Kraszewicz	Feiga Krasewitz nee Zhelonka	1885	Itzig & Rachel	Deported from Drancy 30/06/1	Gombin	Paris, France	Auschwitz camp	Y F
Kraszewicz	Laib Kraszewicz					Gombin		W
Kraszewicz	Frida Kraszewicz					Gombin		W
Kraszewicz	Lipe Kraszewicz	1898	Lev & Frida	Clothing store, married to Sara	Gombin	Gombin	Gombin	Y
Kraszewicz	Sara Kraszewicz	1899	Israel	Married to Lipman	Gombin	Gombin	Gombin	Y
Kraszewicz	Brakha Kraszewicz		Lipman & Sara	Child		Gombin	Gombin	Y
Kraszewicz	Shmuel Kraszewicz		Lipman & Sara	Child		Gombin	Gombin	Y
Krasiewicz	Selig Meir Krasiewicz	1900	Lev & Frida	Married to Zelda nee Altman	Gombin	Gombin	Gombin	Y
Krasiewicz	Zelda Krasiewicz nee Altman	1902	Ela	Married to Meir	Gombin	Gombin	Gombin	Y
Krasiewicz	Ela Krasiewicz		Selig & Zelda nee Altman	Child		Gombin	Gombin	Y
Kraut	Rakhel Kraut nee Tiber	1887		Married to Meir	Gombin	Lipno	Lipno	Y
Kraut	Shimon Kraut					Gombin		W
Kraut	Hersz Kraut						Gombin	G
Kraut	Lajzer Kraut		Hersz	Child			Gombin	G
Kraut	Alie Kraut		Hersz	Child			Gombin	G
Kroj	Brana Kroj			Died in Lodz Ghetto	Gombin		Lodz	L M
Kroj	Moszek Aron Kroj	1879		Died in Lodz Ghetto	Gombin		Lodz	L M
Kroj	Jakób Berek Kroj	1877		Died in Lodz Ghetto	Gombin		Lodz	L M
Kronzylber	Sura Kronzylber nee Rosenblum	1883		Married to Josef	Gombin		Kutno	Y
Krowiczki	Wigdor Krowiczki						Gombin	G
Kruch	Czarna Kruch	1882	Jakow & Brana	Married to Yitzkhak, ied Lodz h	Gombin	Lodz	Lodz	Y L M
Kruk	Gitek Kruk		Yaakov & Rakhel	House painter, married	Plock	Plock	Gombin	Y
Krul	Ester Krul nee Plonski	1915	Moses & Lea	Married to Leon	Gombin	Lodz	Stutthof camp	Y
Kuchinski	Leyzer Kuchinski	1907		Tailor, married	Gombin	Nesvizh, Belarus	Slutsk, Belarus	Y
Kuchinsky	Moishe Kuchinsky			Tailor, married to Rivka nee Wy	Gombin	Gombin	Gombin	Y W
Kuchinsky	Rivka Kuchinsky					Gombin		W
Kuchinsky	Laibush Kuchinsky		Moishe & Rivka nee Wyspa	Teacher	Gombin	Poland	Poland	Y
Kuchinsky	Shemuel Kuchinsky		Moishe & Rivka nee Wyspa		Gombin	Lodz	Lodz	Y
Kuchinsky	Sura Kuchinsky		Moishe & Rivka nee Wyspa	Married to Avrum	Gombin	Poland	Poland	Y
Kuczinsky	Guershon Kuczinsky	1890	Shalom & Brakha	Tailor, married to Mania	Gombin	Rypin	Gombin	Y
Kuczynski	Szyja Gersen Kuczynski			Married to Ruchla		Gombin	Gombin	Y
Kuczynski	Ruchla Kuczynski			Married to Szyja			Gombin	Y
Kuczynski	Rajza Kuczynski						Gombin	G
Kuczynski	Mariem Kuczynski						Gombin	G
Kukuridza	Arie Kukuridza	1899			Gombin	Gombin		Y
Kukuridza	Dina Kukuridza nee Zilberberg	1898	Eliezer	Married to Arie	Kutno	Gombin	Gombin	Y G
Kukuridza	Malka Kukuridza	1918	Arie & Dina	Single	Gombin	Gombin	Gombin	Y
Kukuridza	Cipora Kukuridza	1920	Arie & Dina	Single	Gombin	Gombin	Gombin	Y
Kukuridsa	Meir Kukuridsa	1924	Arie & Dina	Child	Gombin	Gombin	Gombin	Y
Kukuridza	Baruk Kukuridza	1874	Meir & Tzipora	Tailor, married to Khana nee Se	Kiev, Ukraine	Gombin	Gombin	Y W
Kukuridza	Hana Kukuridza nee Salup	1876	Sender & Rivka	Married to Barukh	Gombin	Gombin	Gombin	Y W

25

Family	Person's complete name	Year born	Parents	Other details	Place of birth	Before the war lived in	During the war was in	Source
Kukuridza	Leib Kukuridza					Gombin		W
Kukuridza	Miriam Kukuridza					Gombin		W
Kukurydza	Wolek Berk Kukurydza	1886		Died Lobau camp, 1942	Gombin		Lobau camp	Y
Kukurydza	Abram Kukurydza			Single, deported Konin camp to		Gombin	Konin camp	K
Kuplewski	Jenta Kuplewski		Nachman	Child			Gombin	G
Kuplewski	Luba Kuplewski		Nachman	Child			Gombin	G
Kutchinski	Raphael Kutchinski					Gombin		B
Kutchinski	(GNU) Kutchinski			Wife or Raphael		Gombin		B
Kutchinski	(GNU) Kutchinski			Son of Raphael		Gombin		B
Kutchinski	(GNU) Kutchinski			Son of Raphael		Gombin		B
Kutnowski	Israel Kutnowski					Gombin		W
Kutshinsky	Moishe Kutshinsky			Married to Chana		Gombin		B
Kutshinsky	Chana Kutshinsky nee Frankel			Married to Moishe		Gombin		B
Lacka	Ester Gitel Lacka		Ester Gitel	Daughter of Ester Gitel			Gombin	G
Lacka	(GNU) Lacka		Ester Gitel				Gombin	G
Lacki	Khana Lacki		Yaakov & Gitel	Married	Gombin	Gombin		Y
Lacki	Lajzer Josek Lacki	1882		Died Lobau camp, 1942	Gombin		Lobau camp	Y
Lacki	Fajwel Lacki		Josek	Child			Gombin	G
Laks	Benjamin Laks	1890		Merchant, married to Feiga	Gombin	Gombin	Gombin	Y G
Laks	Feiga Laks nee Pozner	1892		Married to Beniamin	Gombin	Gombin	Gombin	Y
Laks	Shamai Laks	1923	Benjamin & Feiga nee Pozne	Single, "sick" deported 11.5.42	Gombin	Gombin	Konin camp	Y K
Laks	Gitel Laks	1930	Beniamin & Feiga nee Pozne	Child	Gombin	Gombin	Gombin	Y
Laks	Golda Laks	1927	Beniamin & Feiga nee Pozne		Gombin	Gombin	Gombin	Y
Laks	Yokheved Laks	1918	Beniamin & Feiga		Gombin	Gombin	Gombin	Y
Landau	Itshe Landau			Married to Chajele		Gombin	Warsaw	B
Landau	Chajele Landau			Married to Itshe		Gombin	Warsaw	B
Landschneider	Chil Mayer Landschneider	1892		Deported from Malines 31/07/	Gombin	Belgium	Auschwitz camp	Y
Landsman	Azriel Landsman	1896	Szloma & Laja nee Popiol	Married to Anna, deported from	Gombin	Saint-Sauvant, Fran	Auschwitz camp	Y F M
Laski	Mosze Laski			From Wloclawek		Wloclawek	Gombin	G
Laski	Sura Laski						Gombin	G
Laski	Josef Laski	1904	Moshe	Tailor, married to Ilka nee Roze	Poland	Gombin	Gombin	Y G
Laski	Ela Laski nee Rozenfeld	1898	Kalman & Rivkah		Plock	Gombin		Y
Laski	Moshe Laski	1933	Yosef & Elka nee Rozenfeld			Gombin		Y G
Laski	Rivka Laski	1937	Yosef & Elka nee Rozenfeld	Child		Gombin	Warsaw	Y
Laski	Kalman Laski		Yosef & Elka nee Rozenfeld	Child		Gombin	Warsaw	Y
Laski	Wolf Zeev Laski		Szmul & Zindl	Tinsmith, married to Freida	Gombin	Gombin	Gombin	Y W B
Laski	Freida Laski nee Kilbert		Yaakov & Tzipora	Married to Wolf	Zychlin	Gombin	Gombin	Y W B
Laski	Sara Laski		Wold &Freida	Pupil, single	Gombin	Gombin	Gombin	Y B
Laski	Khana Laski		Wold &Freida	Single	Gombin	Gombin	Gombin	Y B
Laski	Tuwia Laski	1889		Merchant, married to Malka	Gombin	Gombin	Gombin	Y
Laski	Malka Laski			Married to Tuvia	Gombin	Gombin	Gombin	Y

26

Family	Person's complete name	Year born	Parents	Other details	Place of birth	Before the war lived in	During the war was in	Source
Laski	Fryda Laski	1916	Tuvia	Student, single	Gombin	Gombin	Gombin	Y
Laski	Szoszana Laski	1913	Tuvia	Student, single	Gombin	Gombin	Gombin	Y
Laski	Chana Laski	1916	Tuvia & Malka	Student, single	Gombin	Gombin	Gombin	Y
Laski	Tuwja Laski	1905		Merchant, married to Khana	Gombin	Gombin	Gombin	Y W
Laski	Chana Laski	1908	Bluma	Married to Tuvia	Plock	Gombin	Gombin	Y W
Laski	Fradil Laski			Married to Julek	Poland	Gombin	Gombin	Y
Laski	Roiza Laski		Baia & Malka	Teacher, single	Gombin	Gombin	Gombin	Y
Laski	Wolf Laski			Child		Gombin		W G
Laski	Herszel Laski					Gombin		W
Laski	Meir Yosef Laski					Gombin		W G
Laski	Laibisz Laski					Gombin		W
Laski	Mendel Laski	1919	Majer & Dwejra			Gombin		Y G
Laski	Moshe Laski	1891		Married, buried Konin Catholic	Gombin		Konin camp	K
Laskowski	Moshe Laskowski			Deported Konin camp to Andrz		Gombin	Konin camp	K
Lasman	Yehuda Lajb Lasman	1895		Married, "sick" deported 9.4.42		Gombin	Konin camp	G K
Lasman	Sura Lasman			Wife of Jde Lajb			Gombin	G
Lasman	Elie Lajzer Lasman		Yehuda Lajb	Child			Gombin	G
Lasman	Nysyn Lasman		Yehuda Lajb	Child			Gombin	G
Lassmann	Maria Lassmann	1870		Kazerne Dossin, deported tran	Gombin	Belgium	Auschwitz camp	F M
Lederman	Brana Lederman nee Gips				Bodzanow	Bodzanow	Gombin	Y
Lefkowicz	Chaya Lefkowicz nee Luxemburg	1895	Yossel	Married	Gombin	Poland		Y
Leizershtein	Avraham David Leizershtein	1902	Moshe & Lea	Married to Rakhel nee Poddęb	Gombin	Kutno, Poland	Kutno	Y
Lejek	Noech Lejek	1919			Gombin		Auschwitz camp	Y
Lejman	Reizl Lejman	1885	Avraham & Yenta	Married	Gombin	Lodz	Lodz	Y
Lemberg	Zew Lemberg	1891	Avraham & Helena	Uppers cutter/tailor, single	Gombin	Zychlin	Zychlin	Y
Lesinska	Sala Lesinska nee Wolfowicz	1895	Zelig & Ita nee Gips	Clerk, married to Marian	Gombin	Wloclawek	Warsaw	Y
Levin	Mihael Levin			Merchant, single	Gombin	Gombin		Y
Lewinska	Bajla Lewinska	1880		Died in Lodz Ghetto	Gombin		Lodz	L M
Lewkowicz	Sura Lewkowicz	1864		Died in Lodz Ghetto	Gombin		Lodz	L M
Lewkowicz	Dawid Lewkowicz	1878		Died Lodz hospital 21-Jan-1942	Gombin		Lodz	L M
Lewkowicz	Haja Lewkowicz nee Luksemburg		Yoseph	Married to Mikhael	Gombin	Lowicz	Warsaw	Y
Lewkowicz	Roza Rivka Lewkowicz	1911	Menashe & Hinda	Married	Plock	Plock	Gombin	Y
Lewkowicz	Fela Lewkowicz		Rozka	Child		Plock	Gombin	Y
Liberman	Pinchas Shalom Liberman						Gombin	G
Libfrojnd	Abram Hersl Libfrojnd	1900	Leizer & Moshe	Merchant, married to Brakha n	Sanniki	Sanniki	Gombin	Y
Libfrojnd	Bracha Libfrojnd nee Bzhezinski	1907	Tzvi & Sara	Married to Avraham	Sochaczew	Sanniki	Gombin	Y
Libfrojnd	Lajb Libfrojnd	1911		Single, "sick" deported 19.5.42		Gombin	Konin camp	K
Lichtensztein	Hanich Lichtensztein	1877		Married, "sick" deported 8.7.42		Gombin	Konin camp	K
Lifsin	Moszie Lifsin	1892					Gombin	G
Lipszyc	Slomo Lipszyc	1892		Married to Feiga, buried Konin	Gombin	Gombin	Konin camp	Y K
Lipszyc	Feiga Lipszyc nee Temerson	1894				Gombin	Gombin	Y

27

Family	Person's complete name	Year born	Parents	Other details	Place of birth	Before the war lived in	During the war was in	Source
Lipszyc	Sara Lipszyc	1915	Shlomo & Feiga	Single	Gombin	Gombin		Y
Lipszyc	Abram Lipszyc	1911	Shlomo & Feiga	Merchant, single	Gombin	Gombin		Y
Lipszyc	Natan Lipszyc	1913	Shlomo & Feiga	Merchant, single	Gombin	Gombin	Gombin	Y
Liserstain	Lea Liserstain					Gombin	Gombin	Y
Litvin	Mojshe Litvin		Yitzkhak & Perel	Businessman, married to Chava	Opoczno	Gombin	Gombin	Y
Litvin	Khava Litvin nee Spiewak				Wyszogrod	Gombin	Gombin	Y
Litvin	Rivka Litvin		Mojshe & Khava nee Shpiva	Student	Gombin	Gombin	Gombin	Y
Litvin	Mordechaj Litvin		Mojshe & Khava nee Shpiva	Student	Gombin	Gombin	Gombin	Y
Litvin	Yitzkhak Litvin		Mojshe & Khava nee Shpiva	Student	Gombin	Gombin	Gombin	Y
Litvin	Majer Litvin		Mojshe & Khava nee Shpiva	Student	Gombin	Gombin	Gombin	Y
Litvin	Mordhai Litvin		Mojshe & Khava nee Shpiva	Single	Gombin	Gombin	Gombin	Y
Litvin	Ester Litvin		Mojshe & Khava nee Shpiva	Child	Gombin	Gombin	Gombin	Y G
Lopata	Israel Lopata	1890		Butcher, married to Sara	Poland	Gombin	Gombin	Y
Lubet	Jachla Lubet			Married to Avraham	Gombin	Lodz	Lodz	Y
Lubet	Jite Lubet	1922	Avraham & Rakhel	Single	Gombin	Lodz	Lodz	Y
Lubet	Cwi Lubet	1916	Avraham & Yokheved	Merchant, married	Gombin	Lodz	Lodz	Y
Lubinski	Rabbi Menahem Lubinski		Binem & Miriam	Rabbi	Gombin	Gombin	Gombin	Y B
Lubinski	Chil Meir Lubinski		Binem & Miriam		Gombin		Lodz	Y B
Lubinski	Devorah Lubinski		Binem & Miriam		Gombin		Auschwitz camp	Y B
Lubranecki	Helena Lubranecki nee Likhtensht	1895		Merchant, married to Shmuel	Warsaw	Gombin	Gombin	Y
Luksenburg	Yossel Luksenburg	1870		Married	Gombin			Y
Luksenburg	Moshe Luksenburg		Yossel		Gombin			Y
Luksenburg	Rosa Luksenburg	1905	Yossel	Single	Gombin			Y
Luksenburg	Eliahu Luksenburg				Gombin	Lodz	Lodz	Y
Luksenburg	Jchezkel Luksenburg	1895	Yosef	Butcher, married to Feiga nee +	Gombin	Lodz	Lodz	Y
Luksenburg	Faiga Luksenburg nee Holtzman	1898	Eliahu & Rasha nee Zlotnik	Married to Yehezkel	Gombin	Lodz	Lodz	Y
Luksenburg	Baltche Luksenburg		Yekhezkel & Feiga	Child	Gombin	Lodz	Lodz	Y
Luksenburg	Rakhel Luksenburg		Yekhezkel & Feiga	Child	Gombin	Lodz	Lodz	Y
Luksenburg	Ruda Laja Luksenburg	1923			Gombin		Lodz	L M
Lupato	Malka Lupato			Married	Poland	Gombin	Gombin	Y
Luria	Chaim Luria	1893	Mordekhai	Married to Ruchla	Gombin	Gombin	Gombin	Y W R
Luria	Ruchla Luria nee Stupaj	1895	Mosche & Necha	Married to Chaim	Gombin	Gombin	Gombin	Y W R
Luria	Rachel Luria	1922	Chaim & Ruchla	Single	Gombin	Gombin	Gombin	Y W R
Luria	Mordchai Luria	1925	Chaim & Ruchla	Single	Gombin	Gombin	Gombin	Y W R
Luria	Mosze Luria	1895		Tinsmith, married to Miriam	Gombin	Gombin		Y
Luria	Mirjam Luria nee Goldman	1897		Married to Moshe	Gombin	Gombin		Y
Luria	Michla Luria	1917	Moshe & Miriam	Pupil, single	Gombin	Gombin	Warsaw	Y
Luria	Mordcha Luria	1920	Moshe & Miriam	Tinsmith	Gombin	Gombin	Warsaw	Y
Luria	Jojna Luria		Szymon	Child		Gombin	Gombin	G
Luria	Estera Luria					Gombin	Gombin	G
Luria	Lajb Luria			Executed June 11, 1942 in Koni	Gombin	Gombin	Konin camp	K

28

Family	Person's complete name	Year born	Parents	Other details	Place of birth	Before the war lived in	During the war was in	Source
Luszynski	Sender Luszynski	1877		Merchant, single	Gombin	Gombin	Gombin	Y W
Luszynski	Lea Luszynski					Gombin	Gombin	W
Luszynski	Natan Luszynski	1899	Sender & Lea	Married, "sick" deported 8.7.42	Gombin	Gombin	Konin camp	Y K
Luszynski	Awraham Luszynski	1900	Sender & Lea	Clerk, married to Mania nee Te	Gombin	Gombin	Gombin	Y
Luszynski	Mania Lusinski nee Temerson	1903		Married to Avraham	Gombin	Gombin	Gombin	Y
Lusinski	Shlomo Lusinski		Abraham & Mania nee Tem	Child		Gombin	Gombin	Y
Luszynski	Hersz Luszynski	1899	Sender & Lea	Merchant, married to Shulamit	Gombin	Gombin	Gombin	Y
Luszynski	Shulamit Luszynski	1901		Married to Hersh	Gombin	Gombin	Gombin	Y
Luszynski	Hela Luszynski	1924	Hersh & Shulamit	Single	Gombin	Gombin	Gombin	Y
Luszynski	Nissan Luszynski					Gombin		W
Luszynski	Miriam Luszynski					Gombin		W
Luszynski	Izhak Luszynski					Gombin		W
Luszynski	Frymet Luszynski					Gombin		W
Luszynski	Ester Luszynski					Gombin		W
Luszynski	Toba Luszynski					Gombin	Gombin	G
Luszynski	Wolf Zeev Luszynski	1885		Married, "sick" deported 11.5.4		Gombin	Konin camp	G K
Luszynski	Hersz Luszynski					Gombin	Gombin	G
Luszynski	Jakob Luszynski			Married, deported Konin camp		Gombin	Konin camp	K
Macher	Richard Macher	1885			Gombin			M
Maidad	Chana Maidad	1882	Shmuel & Khava	Married to Flank	Gombin	Gombin	Gombin	Y
Mainczyk	Laibisz Mainczyk					Gombin	Gombin	W G
Mainczyk	Szlama Mainczyk			Married, deported Konin camp		Gombin	Konin camp	G K
Mainczyk	(GNU) Mainczyk			Wife of Szlama			Gombin	G
Mainczyk	Chaja Mainczyk		Szlama	Child			Gombin	G
Mainczyk	Pinkus Mainczyk		Szlama	Child			Gombin	G
Mainczyk	(GNU) Mainczyk		Szlama	Child of Szlama			Gombin	G
Mainczyk	(GNU) Mainczyk		Szlama	Child of Szlama			Gombin	G
Mainczyk	Szmaja Mainczyk	1917		Single, "sick" deported 26.9.42		Gombin	Konin camp	K
Majdat	Hersz Majdat	1894		Died in Lodz Ghetto	Gombin		Lodz	L M
Makarowsky	Nuchym Makarowsky	1897		Deported from Drancy 16/09/1	Gombin	Paris, France	Auschwitz camp	Y F M
Makower	Rywka Makower			Single		Gombin		H
Makowski	Rachel Makowski nee Karo	1907		Deported from Drancy 14/08/1	Gombin	Paris, France	Auschwitz camp	Y F M
Malamut	Gershon Khanokh Malamut	1893		Merchant, married to Ester		Lodz	Lodz	Y
Mantchik	Esther Mantchik nee Skurka	1917	Hersh & Hodes		Gombin	Gombin	Gombin	B
Marcus	Moritz Marcus			Merchant, married to Bezya ne	Gombin	Plock		Y
Markiewicz	Jakob Markiewicz	1918			Gombin		Buchenwald camp	Y M
Markiewicz	Udem Markiewicz						Gombin	G
Markiewicz	(GNU) Markiewicz			Wife of Udem			Gombin	G
Markiewicz	Ajzyk Markiewicz		Szmul	Child			Gombin	G
Markiewicz	Luzer Markiewicz		Szmul	Child			Gombin	G
Markiewicz	Jta Markiewicz						Gombin	G

29

Family	Person's complete name	Year born	Parents	Other details	Place of birth	Before the war lived in	During the war was in	Source
Markiewicz	Zalman Markiewicz		Hersz	Child			Gombin	G
Markiewicz	Chana Markiewicz		Hersz	Child			Gombin	G
Markiewicz	Izrael Markiewicz						Gombin	G
Markiewicz	(GNU) Markiewicz		Izrael	Wife of Izrael			Gombin	G
Markiewicz	(GNU) Markiewicz		Izrael	Daughter of Izrael			Gombin	G
Markiewicz	(GNU) Markiewicz		Izrael	Boy of Izrael			Gombin	G
Markiewicz	(GNU) Markiewicz		Izrael	Boy of Izrael			Gombin	G
Markowicz	Szmuel Markowicz	1912		Married, "sick" deported 8.7.42		Gombin	Konin camp	K
Masfaum	Moniek Masfaum	1921		Single	Gombin	Gombin	Gombin	Y
Mastbaum	Leibl Mastbaum			Baker, Married to Leie	Poland	Gombin	Gombin	Y G B
Mastbaum	Malke Leie Mastbaum nee Seidelm			Married to Leibl	Poland	Gombin	Gombin	Y G B
Mastbaum	Mordechai Mastbaum		Leibl & Leie nee Seidelman	Hairdresser, single	Gombin	Gombin	Poland	Y
Mastbaum	(GNU) Mastbaum		Leibl & Leie nee Seidelman	Child of Leibl & Leie			Gombin	G
Maydat	Aron Maydat	1920		Driver, single	Gombin	Nesvizh, Belarus	Slutsk, Belarus	Y
Maydat	Herszel Maydat			Married, deported Konin camp		Gombin	Konin camp	W K
Melamed	Genendla Melamed	1867		Died Lodz hospital 02-Jul-1942	Gombin		Lodz	L M
Menche	Chaim Menche	1892	Josef & Rose nee Bornshteir	Businessman, married to Sara	Gombin	Plock	Gombin	Y
Menche	Sara Menche nee Gutman	1890		Married to Chaim	Plock	Plock	Gombin	Y
Menche	Szlama Menche	1892		Died in Lodz Ghetto	Gombin		Lodz	L M
Menche	Abram Lajzer Menche	1914			Gombin		Lodz	L M
Migdal	Rivka Mia Migdal		Meine		Gombin	Lodz	Lodz	Y
Milewski	Mordechai Milewski					Gombin		W
Milewski	Channa Milewski					Gombin		W
Milewski	Wladyslaw Milewski	1897			Gombin		Bergen-Belsen Cam	M
Milgrom	Rafael Milgrom		Mordekhai & Breina	Manager		Gombin	Gombin	Y
Milgrom	Rakhel Milgrom			Vacation home, married to Raf		Lowicz	Gombin	Y
Milgrom	Aharon Milgrom	1916	Rafael & Rakhel	Worker, single		Lowicz	Gombin	Y
Minc	M. Minc				Gombin		Gombin	G
Minski	Abram Minski	1918			Gombin		Brieskow camp	M
Miotla	Bluma Miotla	1875	Yosef & Khana	Married	Gombin	Plock	Plock	Y
Miotla	Szmul Wolf Miotla				Gombin		Auschwitz camp	G M
Miotla	(GNU) Miotla			Wife of Szmul			Gombin	G
Miotla	Dawid Zelig Miotla		Szmul Wolf	Child			Gombin	G
Miotla	Tojwie Miotla		Szmul Wolf	Child			Gombin	G
Miotla	(GNU) Miotla		Szmul Wolf	Child of Szmul			Gombin	G
Mitelpunkt	Aron Mitelpunkt		Anszel	Child			Gombin	G
Mitelpunkt	Frajda Mitelpunkt		Anszel	Child			Gombin	G
Mitelpunkt	Lajb Mitelpunkt						Gombin	G
Mitelpunkt	(GNU) Mitelpunkt			Wife of Lajb			Gombin	G
Mitelpunkt	(GNU) Mitelpunkt		Lajb	Child of Lajb			Gombin	G
Mitelpunkt	(GNU) Mitelpunkt		Lajb	Son of Lajb			Gombin	G

Family	Person's complete name	Year born	Parents	Other details	Place of birth	Before the war lived in	During the war was in	Source
Mitelpunkt	Mordechai Mitelpunkt			Single, deported Konin camp to		Gombin	Konin camp	K
Mojne	Jechiel Mojne	1888		Widower, "sick" deported 9.4.		Gombin	Konin camp	K
Mokotov	Yidl Mokotov			Married to Rokhl		Gombin		B
Mokotov	Rokhl Mokotov			Married to Yidl		Gombin		B
Mokotov	Moishe Mokotov		Yidl & Rokhl			Gombin		B
Monszajn	Chana Monszajn	1877		Died Lodz hospital 03-Nov-194	Gombin		Lodz	L M
Mose	Lajb Mose						Gombin	G
Mose	Hersz Mose						Gombin	G
Mose	Dawid Mose						Gombin	G
Moskewicz	Jakew Moskewicz						Gombin	G
Moskewicz	(GNU) Moskewicz			Wife of Jakew			Gombin	G
Mossman	Manus Kalman Mossman		Sidney & Gittel nee Rhyzmir	Married to Chaya	Poland	Gombin	Poland	Y
Mossman	Chaya Mossman			Married to Manus		Gombin	Poland	Y
Moszkiewicz	Hersz Moszkiewicz						Gombin	G
Moszkiewicz	(GNU) Moszkiewicz			Wife of Hersz			Gombin	G
Moszkiewicz	(GNU) Moszkiewicz		Hersz	Daughter of Hersz			Gombin	G
Moszkiewicz	(GNU) Moszkiewicz		Hersz	Daughter of Hersz			Gombin	G
Moszkiewicz	(GNU) Moszkiewicz		Hersz	Daughter of Hersz			Gombin	G
Moszkiewicz	(GNU) Moszkiewicz		Hersz	Daughter of Hersz			Gombin	G
Moszkiewicz	(GNU) Moszkiewicz		Hersz	Son of Hersz			Gombin	G
Motilinski	Machla Izhak Motilinski					Gombin		W
Motilinski	Sala Motilinski					Gombin		W
Motilinski	Chaim Motilinski					Gombin		W
Motilinski	Golda Mirel Motilinski					Gombin		W
Motyl	Jakob Lajb Motyl	1893		Died Konin camp 31-01-1943	Gombin			Y
Mozelman	Yoel Mozelman			Married to Khaia	Poland	Gombin	Warsaw	Y
Mozelman	Haia Mozelman		Yitzkhak & Sara	Married to Yoel	Poland	Gombin	Warsaw	Y
Mrzywarc	Szaja Mrzywarc						Gombin	G
Mrzywarc	Fradil Mrzywarc						Gombin	G
Munczek	Lajb Munczek	1899		Married, buried Konin Catholic	Gombin		Konin camp	K
Mucni	Aharon Mucni	1875		Married, "sick" deported 11.5.4		Gombin	Konin camp	K
Nachbin	Rozalia Nachbin nee Tzuk	1890	David & Miriam	Merchant, married to Shmuel	Gombin	Lipno	Warsaw	Y
Najdorf	Abraham Israel Najdorf	1882		Died Konin camp	Gombin	Gombin	Konin camp	Y K B
Najman	Trana Najman nee Pankier	1880	Abram & Malka nee Budnik	Married to Mordka	Kutno	Gombin	Kutno	Y
Najman	Szmul Najman						Gombin	G
Najman	(GNU) Najman		Szmul	Wife of Szmul			Gombin	G
Najman	Chil Najman		Szmul	Child			Gombin	G
Najman	Szyja Najman		Szmul	Child			Gombin	G
Najman	Jankiel Najman		Szmul	Child			Gombin	G
Najman	(GNU) Najman		Szmul	Child of Szmul			Gombin	G
Najman	(GNU) Najman		Szmul	Child of Szmul			Gombin	G

Family	Person's complete name	Year born	Parents	Other details	Place of birth	Before the war lived in	During the war was in	Source
Najman	Marien Najman				Gombin		Lodz	L
Natanovitz	Meir Natanovitz			Merchant, married to Dvora nee	Gombin	Klodawa		Y
Natanovitz	Aharon Fabian Natanovitz	1885	Natan & Gerda	Bookkeeper, married to Mindla	Gombin	Warsaw	Warsaw	Y
Nejmann	Rejzel Nejmann nee Arbeitsman		Josef & Roda	Married to David	Gombin	Gostynin	Gostynin	Y
Nowak	Szulim Nowak						Gombin	G
Nowak	(GNU) Nowak			Wife of Szulim			Gombin	G
Nowak	Zelig Nowak		Szulim	Child			Gombin	G
Nowak	Mariem Nowak		Szulim	Child			Gombin	G
Nowak	Szmul Nowak		Szulim	Child			Gombin	G
Nowak	Chil Nowak						Gombin	G
Nowak	(GNU) Nowak			Wife of Chil			Gombin	G
Nowak	Rojza Nowak		Chil	Child			Gombin	G
Nowak	Abram Nowak			Married, deported Konin camp		Gombin	Konin camp	K
Nowak	Szmul Nowak		Abram	Child			Gombin	G
Nowak	Jcek Nowak		Abram	Child			Gombin	G
Nowak	Szulim Nowak		Abram	Child			Gombin	G
Nutkowicz	Natan Nutkowicz	1888		Rabbi of Gombin, married to Ra	Rypin	Gombin	Warsaw	Y G
Nutkowicz	Raca Nutkowitz	1894	Tzvi	Married to Natan	Gombin	Rypin	Gombin	Y G
Nysenjolc	(GNU) Nysenjolc			Child			Gombin	G
Odera	Shimshon Odera					Gombin		W
Odera	Lazer Odera					Gombin		W
Odera	Shmuel Odera					Gombin		W
Odera	Gnendel Ita Odera					Gombin		W
Odera	Hilel Odera			Wife of Hilel			Gombin	G
Odera	(GNU) Odera		Hilel	Child			Gombin	G
Odera	Chaim Odera		Hilel	Child			Gombin	G
Odera	Wolf Ber Odera		Hilel	Daughter of Hilel			Gombin	G
Odera	(GNU) Odera		Hilel	Died Lodz hospital 03-Nov-1943	Gombin		Lodz	L M
Offenbach	Sura Offenbach	1874					Gombin	G
Ogrodnik	Elie Majer Ogrodnik			Deported from Drancy 11-09-1	Gombin	Millau, France	Auschwitz camp	F
Olszer	Jacques Olszer	1903		Merchant, married	Gombin	Gombin	Gombin	Y
Opatowski	Nachman Opatowski	1892		Single	Gombin	Gombin	Gombin	Y
Opatovski	Awraham Opatovski	1922	Nachman	Pupil, single	Gombin	Gombin	Gombin	Y
Opatovski	Gitl Opatowski	1924	Nachman	Clerk, single	Gombin	Gombin	Gombin	Y
Opatovski	Mordechaj Opatowski	1920	Nachman		Gombin	Gombin	Gombin	Y
Opatowski	Yacov Opatowski					Gombin		W
Opatowski	Moshe Opatowski					Gombin		W
Opatowski	Zasza Opatowski					Gombin		W
Opatowski	Rivka Opatowski			Furrier, married to Golda, "sick	Gombin	Gombin		W
Opatowski	Israel Opatowski	1892	Zisja	Marrited to Israel	Gombin	Gombin	Gombin	Y
Opatowski	Golda Opatowski nee Rozemberg					Gombin	Gombin	Y

32

Family	Person's complete name	Year born	Parents	Other details	Place of birth	Before the war lived in	During the war was in	Source
Opatowski	Estera Opatowski nee Guterman	1900		Deported from Drancy 24-08-1	Gombin	Paris, France	Auschwitz camp	Y F
Opatowski	Zisja Opatowski			Married to Chawa	Gombin	Gombin	Gombin	Y
Opatowski	Chawa Opatowski			Married to Zisja			Gombin	G
Opatowski	(GNU) Opatowski		Zisja & Chawa	Child			Gombin	G
Opatowski	(GNU) Opatowski		Zisja & Chawa	Child			Gombin	G
Opatowski	(GNU) Opatowski		Zisja & Chawa	Child			Gombin	G
Opatowski	Yosef Opatowski			Married to Miriam		Gombin		B
Opatowski	Miriam Opatowski			Married to Yosef		Gombin		B
Opatowski	Libe Opatowski		Yosef & Miriam			Gombin		B
Opatowski	Moishe Opatowski		Yosef & Miriam			Gombin		B
Opatowski	Zishe Opatowski		Yosef & Miriam			Gombin		B
Opatowski	Yankl Opatowski		Yosef & Miriam			Gombin		B
Opatowski	Sorele Opatowski		Yosef & Miriam	Married to Lipe		Gombin		B
Opatowski	Lipe (SU)			Married to Sorele		Gombin		B
Opatowski	Rafel Opatowski			Married to (GNU) nee Kutchins		Gombin		B
Opatowski	(GNU) nee Kutchinsky			Married to Rafel		Gombin		B
Opatowski	(GNU) Opatowski		Rafel & (GNU) nee Kutchinsl	Child		Gombin		B
Opatowski	(GNU) Opatowski		Rafel & (GNU) nee Kutchinsl	Child		Gombin		B
Orbach	Moshe Lajb Orbach	1896		Married, "sick" deported 9.4.42		Gombin	Konin camp	K B
Orenstein	Yankel Orenstein			Married to Hannah	Gombin		Warsaw	Y B
Orenstein	Hannah Orenstein			Married to Yankel	Gombin		Warsaw	Y B
Orenstein	Harry Orenstein			Married to Braindel	Gombin		Warsaw	Y B
Orenstein	Braindel Orenstein			Married to Harry	Gombin		Warsaw	Y B
Orenstein	Philip Orenstein			Married to Golda	Gombin		Warsaw	Y B
Orenstein	Golda Orenstein			Married to Philip	Gombin		Warsaw	Y B
Ostrowitch	Brana Ostrowitch nee Gerszt	1899		Deported from Drancy 4-11-19	Gombin	Montreuil, France	Auschwitz camp	F
Ostrowski	Jadwiga Ostrowski	1913		Died in Auschwitz	Gombin		Auschwitz camp	M
Palka	Miriam Palka	1921	Aharon & Rivka nee Pozner	Pupil	Gombin	Gombin	Gombin	Y
Palka	Gitel Palka	1923	Aharon & Rivka nee Pozner		Gombin	Gombin		Y
Palka	Shame Palka		Aharon & Rivka nee Pozner		Gombin	Gombin		Y
Palka	Khaia Palka	1930	Aharon & Rivka nee Pozner	Pupil	Gombin	Gombin	Gombin	Y
Pelka	Gucia Pelka	1923			Gombin		Kutno	U
Pelka	Henoch Pelka	1901			Gombin		Kutno	U
Pelka	Sura Pelka	1897			Gombin		Kutno	U
Pelka	Abram Hersch Pelka	1938			Gombin		Kutno	U
Pelka	Hena Pelka	1929			Gombin		Kutno	U
Pelka	Chaja Laja Pelka						Gombin	G
Pelka	Srulek Pelka		Jcchok	Child			Gombin	G
Pelka	Felcia Pelka		Jcchok	Child			Gombin	G
Pelka	Jzrael Pelka		Jcchok	Child			Gombin	G
Pelka	Jakob Pelka	1895		Married, "sick" deported 8.7.42		Gombin	Konin camp	K

33

Family	Person's complete name	Year born	Parents	Other details	Place of birth	Before the war lived in	During the war was in	Source
Pelka	Moshe Pelka	1891		Married, "sick" deported 8.7.42	Gombin	Gombin	Konin camp	K
Papierczyk	Ester Papierczyk	1892		Married to Kopel	Gombin	Plock	Plock	Y
Papierczyk	Kopl Papierczyk	1888	Etel	Merchant, married to Ester	Gombin	Plock	Plock	Y
Perczak	Tova Perczak	1892	Mosche	Single	Gombin	Gombin		Y
Perczak	Avraham Laib Perczak					Gombin		W
Perczak	Toybe Perczak					Gombin		W
Perczak	Fiszel Perczak					Gombin		W
Perczak	Moshe Perczak					Gombin		W
Perczak	Dvora Perczak					Gombin		W
Perczak	Ruda Perczak		Ruda	Child			Gombin	G
Perczak	Estera Rywka Perczak						Gombin	G
Philips	Elhanan Yacov Philips					Gombin		W
Philips	Channa Shaina Philips					Gombin		W
Piasechni	Shmuel Piasechni	1904		Tailor, married to Khana nee Pi	Gombin	Lowicz	Lowicz	Y
Piasecko	Smuel Piasecko	1900		Glassmaker, married to Batia n	Gombin	Gombin	Wilno	Y
Piaseczner	Berta Piaseczner	1908		Married to Szmul	Gombin	Gombin	Wilno	Y
Pietrkowsky	Mirjam Pietrkowsky	1910	Khaim & Breina	Merchant, married, ied Lodz ho	Gombin	Lodz	Lodz	Y L
Pinchowski	Joseph Pinchowski			Married to Deborah		Gombin		B
Pinchowski	Deborah Pinchowski nee Frankel			Married to Joseph		Gombin		B
Pindek	Mordka Pindek			Merchant, married to Rivka nee	Gombin	Gombin	Gombin	Y
Pindek	Rivka Pindek nee Bornshtein		Faivel & Tzvia	Married to Mordekhai	Gombin	Gombin	Poland	Y
Pindek	Pola Pindek		Mordekhai & Rivka	Single	Gombin	Gombin	Gombin	Y
Pindek	Icchak Pindek	1891		Married, "sick" deported 8.7.42	Gombin	Gombin	Konin camp	K
Piotrkowski	Mariem Piotrkowski	1893		Died in Lodz Ghetto Hospital	Gombin		Lodz	L M
Pitterman	Abram Pitterman			Deported Konin camp to Andrz		Gombin	Konin camp	K
Pitterman	Zalman Pitterman			Deported Konin camp to Andrz		Gombin	Konin camp	K
Pioro	Izzidor Pioro					Gombin		W
Piuro	Abe Piuro	1900		Butcher, married to Adela	Tuszyn	Gombin	Gombin	Y
Piuro	Adela Piuro nee Ianovski	1902	Yokhanan & Tova	Married to Aba	Zdunska Wola	Gombin	Gombin	Y
Piuro	Chaja Piuro	1925	Abe & Adela		Gombin	Gombin		Y
Piuro	Haya Piuro	1925	Abe & Adela	Pupil	Gombin	Gombin	Gombin	Y
Piuro	Fishel Piuro	1927	Abe & Adela		Gombin	Gombin		Y
Plazewski	Leo Plazewski	1882		Died Dachau camp 10-02-1941	Gombin	Gombin	Dachau camp	M
Plewa	Anka Khana Plewa	1914		Married to Eliezer	Gombin	Zakroczyn	Warsaw	Y
Plonski	Shlomo Plonski	1868		Widower	Gombin	Gombin		Y
Plonski	Sara Rivka Plonski					Gombin		W
Plonski	Rakhel Plonski	1911	Shlomo & Rivka	Single	Gombin	Gombin		Y W
Plonski	David Plonski	1902	Shlomo & Rivka	Photographer, married	Gombin	Gombin		Y W
Plonski	Moshe Plonski	1904	Shlomo & Rivka		Gombin	Gombin		Y W
Plonski	Gedalia Plonski	1907	Shlomo & Rivka		Gombin	Gombin		Y W M
Plonski	Leibush Plonski	1899	Shlomo & Rivka	Married	Gombin	Gombin	Gombin	Y W

34

Family	Person's complete name	Year born	Parents	Other details	Place of birth	Before the war lived in	During the war was in	Source
Plonski	Mosze Plonski	1904		Tailor, married to Charna nee	Gombin	Lodz	Bialystok	Y
Plonski	Bernard Plonski	1907	Moses & Lea nee Zonenberg		Gombin		Auschwitz camp	Y M
Plonski	Mendel Plonski	1926	Moses & Lea nee Zonenberg		Gombin	Lodz	Lodz	Y
Plonski	Roza Plonski	1919	Moses & Lea nee Zonenberg	Single	Gombin	Lodz	Ukraine	Y
Plonski	Szyja Plonski	1876		Died Lobau camp 31-01-1942	Gombin		Lobau camp	Y G
Plonski	(GNU) Plonski			Wife of Szyia			Gombin	G
Plonski	Gucia Plonski		Szyia	Child			Gombin	G
Plonski	Mindla Plonski		Szyia	Child			Gombin	G
Plonski	Abram Chaim Plonski		Szyia	Child			Gombin	G
Plonski	Jerychum Plonski		Szyia	Child			Gombin	G
Plutzer	Faigue Plutzer nee Vispa		Avrom & Rakhel	Married to Hamoucher	Gombin	Tzagnik	Tzagnik	Y
Pocmanter	Jecel Pocmanter	1924		Died Lodz hospital 15-Jan-1942	Gombin		Lodz	L M
Pocmanter	Lajbus Pocmanter		Szymon	Child			Gombin	G
Pocmanter	Ajzyk Pocmanter		Szymon	Child			Gombin	G
Polasinski	Malka Polasinski	1906		Died Lodz hospital 28-Apr-1943	Gombin		Lodz	L M
Portugal	Fiszel Portugal	1911		Died Poznan camp 18-01-1943	Gombin		Poznan camp	Y
Portugal	Abram Portugal		Abram	Child			Gombin	G
Portugal	Chaja Portugal						Gombin	G
Portugal	Hersz Portugal						Gombin	G
Posner	Moszek Posner	1914			Gombin		Buchenwald camp	Y M
Potchekho	Ruven Yekhezkl Potchekho			Married to Pese	Gombin	Gombin	Gombin	B
Potchekho	Pese Dvoyre Potchekho			Married to Ruven	Gombin	Gombin	Gombin	B
Potchekho	Khone Yakov Potchekho		Ruven & Pese		Gombin	Gombin	Gombin	B
Poznanski	Shmuel Aba Poznanski	1890	Feiga	Merchant, married to Zelda ne	Gombin	Gombin	Gombin	Y G
Poznanski	Zelda Poznanski nee Piasechni	1893	Yitzkhak	Married to Shmuel	Gombin	Gombin	Gombin	Y G
Poznanski	Chim Poznanski	1923	Shmuel & Zelda	Pupil, single	Gombin	Gombin	Gombin	Y G
Poznanski	Chaim Israel Poznanski	1907		Single, buried Konin Catholic ce	Gombin	Gombin	Konin camp	Y K
Pozner	Shimshon Pozner		Heniek & Shura	Shoemaker	Gombin	Gombin	Gombin	Y
Prawda	Faivish Prawda					Gombin		W
Prawda	Feiga Malka Prawda					Gombin		W
Prawda	Avraham Prawda					Gombin		W
Prawda	(GNU) Prawda		Faivel & Tzvi	Married to Avraham		Gombin		W
Preizler	Khana Preizler nee Bornshtein	1890	Feiga	Married	Gombin		Poland	Y
Props	Tzvi Hersz Props			Married to Bronia nee Zamosc	Kutno	Gombin	Gombin	Y R
Props	Bronia Props nee Zamosc		Chaim Yehuda & Dvora	Married to Tzvi Hersz	Gombin	Gombin	Gombin	R
Props	David Props		Tzvi Hersz & Bronia	Child	Gombin	Gombin	Gombin	Y R
Props	Dvora Props		Tzvi Hersz & Bronia	Child	Gombin	Gombin	Gombin	Y R
Pyascki	Zelik Pyascki				Gombin	Gombin		W
Pytel	Josef Pytel			Perished in Konin camp		Gombin	Konin camp	K
Pytel	Wolf Pytel	1902			Gombin		Auschwitz camp	Y M
Pytel	Harry Pytel					Gombin		W

35

Family	Person's complete name	Year born	Parents	Other details	Place of birth	Before the war lived in	During the war was in	Source
Pytel	Lajzer Pytel			Child			Gombin	G
Pytel	Ela Pytel		Jcze	Child			Gombin	G
Pytel	Jta Pytel		Jcek	Child			Gombin	G
Pytel	Tauba Pytel nee Danielewicz			Widow of Icek Pytel	Kowal	Gombin		R
Pytel	Bajla Dyna Pytel		Icek & Tauba		Gombin	Gombin		R
Pytel	Dwojra Pytel		Icek & Tauba		Gombin	Gombin		R
Pytel	Kejla Danielewicz nee Pytel		Icek & Tauba	Married	Gombin	Gombin		R
Pytel	Chana Gowshorowski nee Pytel		Icek & Tauba	Married	Gombin	Gombin		R
Pytel	Zelman Pytel		Icek & Tauba	Perished with wife Dwojra and	Gombin	Gombin		R
Rabinowicz	Benjamin Rabinowicz	1910	Eliahu & Sara	Watchmaker, married to Charr	Gombin	Gombin	Gombin	Y
Rabinowicz	Czarny Rabinowicz nee Zilber	1910	Mendel	Married to Benjamin		Gombin	Gombin	Y
Rafel	Chaim Rafel	1886		Deported from Drancy 13-Feb-	Gombin	Paris, France	Auschwitz camp	Y F
Rafel	Bina Rafel						Gombin	G
Rafel	Hersz Rafel						Gombin	G
Rafel	(GNU) Rafel			Wife of Hersz			Gombin	G
Rafel	(GNU) Rafel		Hersz	Child of Hersz			Gombin	G
Rafel	(GNU) Rafel		Hersz	Child of Hersz			Gombin	G
Raichert	Abram Reichert	1901		Furrier, deported from Malines	Gombin	Berlin, Germany	Auschwitz camp	Y
Rayk	Natan Rayk					Gombin		W
Rayk	Helena Rayk					Gombin		W
Rayk	Henach Rayk			Married, deported Konin camp		Gombin	Konin camp	K
Rambam	Moses Rambam	1896		Bookkeeper, married to Ester n	Gombin	Bochum, Germany	Auschwitz camp	Y
Rembaum	Icek Rembaum	1902	Mendel & Tirtza	School director, married to Git	Plock	Gombin	Gombin	Y G
Rembaum	Gita Rembaum nee Rusak	1906	Khaim & Ester	Married	Sierpc	Gombin	Gombin	Y
Rembaum	Ester Toshia Rembaum		Icek & Gita nee Rusak	Child			Gombin	Y
Rembaum	Elje Rembaum						Gombin	G
Rewzin	Eliezer Rewzin		Jcek & Lea	Pharmacist, married to Chana	Warsaw	Gombin	Warsaw	Y
Rewzin	Chana Rewzin nee Glas		Eliezer & Chana	Pharmacist, married to Eliezer	Gombin	Gombin	Warsaw	Y
Rewzin	Josef Rewzin		Eliezer & Chana	Pupil, single	Gombin	Gombin	Warsaw	Y
Rewzin	Bella Rewzin			Pupil, single		Gombin	Warsaw	Y
Rissmann	Manele Rissmann	1870	Pinchus & Nacha nee Laski	Manager, married to Sara	Gombin	Gombin	Gombin	Y W B
Rissmann	Sara Rissmann	1876		Married to Manele (3rd wife)	Gombin	Gombin	Gombin	Y B
Rissmann	Zelda Rissman	1920	Manele & Sara	Married	Gombin	Gombin	Gombin	Y W B
Rissmann	Shaja Rissman		Manele & Sara		Gombin	Gombin	Gombin	W B
Rissmann	Chava Rissman				Gombin	Gombin	Gombin	W
Rogojinsky	Leibl Rogojinsky	1905	Khil	Merchant, single	Gombin	Gombin	Gombin	Y
Rogojinsky	Icil Yekhiel Rogojinsky	1892	Leibel & Pesa	Merchant, married	Szeyacz	Gombin	Gombin	Y
Rogozinski	Wolf Rogozinski			Buried Konin Catholic cemetery	Gombin		Konin camp	K
Rogozinski	Abram Rogozinski	1925		Buried Konin Catholic cemetery	Gombin		Konin camp	Y K
Rogozinski	Czeslaw Rogozinski	1913			Gombin		Czestochowa camp	M
Rosen	Bracha Rosen nee Luxemburg	1880	Moshe & Miriam	Married	Lodz	Lodz	Lodz	Y

36

Family	Person's complete name	Year born	Parents	Other details	Place of birth	Before the war lived in	During the war was in	Source
Rosen	Avraham Moshe Rosen	1900	Michael & Brucha	Married	Gombin	Poland	Poland	Y
Rosenbaum	Alter Rosenbaum	1870		Deported from Malines 12/09/	Gombin	Wuerzburg, Germa	Auschwitz camp	Y M
Rosenberg	Abraham Rosenberg			Executed June 11, 1942 in Koni	Gombin	Gombin	Konin camp	K
Rosenberg	Pinhas Rosenberg	1870	Avraham & Yenta	Married to Perel	Gombin	Warsaw	Kalisz	Y
Rosenberg	Bajla Rosenberg nee Finkenstein						Gombin	G B
Rosenberg	(GNU) Rosenberg		Bajla	Daughter of Bajla			Gombin	G B
Rosenberg	(GNU) Rosenberg		Bajla	Son of Bajla			Gombin	G B
Rosenberg	(GNU) Rosenberg		Bajla	Son of Bajla			Gombin	G B
Rosenblum	Nekhama Rosenblum nee Luksenb	1875	Moshe & Miriam	Married to Henoch	Gombin	Lodz	Lodz	Y
Rosental	David Rosental	1856	Aharon	Merchant, married to Sara nee	Gombin	Warsaw	Warsaw	Y
Rotblat	Rachel Rotblat		Yitzkhak & Sara	Married	Poland	Gombin		Y
Rotblat	Tova Rotblat		Rakhel	Single	Poland	Gombin		Y
Rotblat	Adina Rotblat		Rakhel	Child		Gombin		Y
Rotblat	Gitl Rotblat		Rakhel			Gombin		W
Rotblat	Lea Rotblat		Rakhel			Gombin		W
Rothstein	Chayele Rothstein nee Brzezinski		Abraham & Chana	Married to (GNU) Rothstein	Gombin	Gombin	Gombin	Y B
Rothstein	(GNU) Rothstein			Married to Chayele		Gombin	Gombin	B
Rozanski	Hinda Rozanski nee Hodys	1902		Deported from Beaune la Rolar	Gombin	Paris, France	Theresienstadt can	Y F
Rozen	Bracha Rozen	1880	Khaim & Rada	Widow	Gombin	Gombin	Otwock	Y
Rozenberg	Menashe Rozenberg	1882	Moshe & Khaia	Tailor, married to Perel nee Tz	Gombin	Gombin	Gombin	Y W
Rozenberg	Khaia Pearl Rozenberg				Gombin	Gombin	Gombin	W
Rozenberg	Mania Rozenberg	1922	Menashe & Khaia	Single	Gombin	Gombin	Gombin	Y W
Rozenberg	Yaakov Rozenberg	1917	Menashe & Khaia	Single	Gombin	Gombin	Gombin	Y W
Rozenberg	Chana Rozenberg		Estera	Child	Gombin	Gombin	Gombin	G
Rosenblum	Chaja Rozenblum nee Wispa	1911		Deported from Pithiviers 07/08	Gombin	Montreuil, France	Auschwitz camp	Y F M
Rozenblum	Towa Rozenblum nee Temerson	1897	Mendel & Sara	Married to Hirsh	Gombin	Kutno, Poland	Kutno	Y
Rozenblum	Dawid Rozenblum	1891		Married, "sick" deported 11.5.		Gombin	Konin camp	K
Rozenfeld	Aharon Rozenfeld	1909		Baker, married, deported Koni	Gombin	Gombin	Konin camp	Y K
Rozenfeld	Khaia Rozenfeld nee Gurker	1909	Avraham & Frida	Married to Aharon	Gombin	Gombin	Gombin	Y
Rozenfeld	Shlomo Rozenfeld		Aharon	Child		Gombin	Gombin	Y
Rozenfeld	Avraham Rozenfeld		Aharon	Child		Gombin	Gombin	Y
Rozenman	Icze Rozenman					Gombin	Gombin	G
Rozental	Hersz Rozental	1886		Died Lodz hospital 23-Aug-194	Gombin		Lodz	L M
Rudnik	Zelig Rudnik	1888	Avraham & Lea	Photographer, married to Hind	Lodz	Gombin		Y W G
Rudnik	Mona Rudnik		Zelig & Hinda nee Shvartz	Child		Gombin		Y W
Rudnik	(GNU) Rudnik		Zelig & Hinda nee Shvartz	Child		Gombin		Y W
Rutkowski	Edmund Rutkowski	1913			Gombin			M
Rusak	Borukh Ozer Rusak			Married to Khaya Iteh		Gombin		B
Rusak	Khaya Iteh Rusak			Married to Borukh Ozer		Gombin		Y B
Rusak	Nekhe Rusak	1903	Borukh & Khaya	Single	Gombin	Gombin	Gombin	Y B
Rusak	Menachem Mendel Rusak	1914	Borukh & Khaya	Single	Gombin	Gombin	Gombin	Y B

37

Family	Person's complete name	Year born	Parents	Other details	Place of birth	Before the war lived in	During the war was in	Source
Rusak	Yankl Jacow Rusak	1897	Borukh & Khaya	Merchant, married to Iteh Mir	Gombin	Lowicz	Warsaw	Y B
Rusak	Iteh Miriam Rusak			Married to Yankl		Gombin		Y B
Rusak	Khanele Rusak		Yankl & Iteh	Child		Gombin		Y B
Rusak	Eliezer Rusak		Yankl & Iteh	Child		Gombin		Y B
Rusak	Aron Dovid Rusak		Yankl & Iteh	Child		Gombin		Y B
Rusak	Yehuda Tzvi Rusak	1904	Borukh & Khaya	Merchant, married to Khaia, "s	Gombin	Gombin	Konin camp	Y B
Rusak	Khaia Rusak	1910		Married to Yehuda Tzvi		Gombin	Gombin	Y B
Rusak	(GNU) Rusak		Yehuda & Khaia	Child	Gombin	Gombin	Gombin	Y B
Rusak	(GNU) Rusak		Yehuda & Khaia	Child	Gombin	Gombin	Gombin	Y B
Rusak	Shmuel Rusak	1910	Borukh & Khaya	Married to Nekheh	Gombin	Warsaw	Mauthausen camp	Y B M
Rusak	Nekheh Genendel Rusak	1912		Married to Shmuel		Warsaw		Y B
Rusak	(GNU) Rusak		Shmuel & Nekheh	Child		Warsaw		Y B
Rusak	Chajim Dov Rusak	1870		Married	Poland	Gombin	Gombin	Y
Rusak	Chune Rusak	1912	Chaim & Bronia nee Bauma	Married to Edzia	Gombin	Warsaw	Auschwitz camp	Y M
Rusak	Beila Rusak nee Gordon	1914	Moshe & Khaia	Married to Khaim	Poland	Gombin	Gombin	Y
Rusak	Arie Rusak		Khaim & Bila nee Gordon	Child		Gombin	Gombin	Y
Rusak	Rizel Figel Rusak nee Berliner	1885			Gombin	Lodz	Lodz	Y
Ruzga	Yacov Ruzga			Married to Rachel		Gombin		W B
Ruzga	Rachel Laja Ruzga			Narried to Yacov		Gombin		W B
Ruzga	Zysha Ruzga		Yacov & Rachel			Gombin		B
Ruzga	Shmuel Ruzga		Yacov & Rachel			Gombin		B
Ruzga	Moishe Ruzga		Yacov & Rachel			Gombin		B
Ruzga	Avrumele Ruzga		Yacov & Rachel			Gombin		B
Ruzga	Esther Ruzga		Yacov & Rachel			Gombin		B
Rybak	Chana Rybak		Lajb	Child			Gombin	G
Rybak	Jankiel Rybak		Lajb	Child			Gombin	G
Rybak	Mosze Rybak		Chaim	Child			Gombin	G
Ryczke	Ester Ryczke nee Prost	1869			Gombin	Konin		Y
Ryster	Mordko Ryster	1896		Deported Konin camp to Andrz	Gombin	Castrop Rauxel, Ge	Sachsenhausen cam	Y
Ryster	Wolf Ryster			Died in Lodz Ghetto		Gombin	Konin camp	G K
Ryster	Hersz Dawid Ryster	1921			Gombin		Lodz	L M
Ryster	Towie Ryster	1888			Gombin		Lodz	L M
Ryster	Chaim Jojne Ryster	1913			Gombin			M
Sadowski	Pinkus Sadowski					Gombin	Gombin	G
Samulewicz	Bronia Samulewicz nee Borenstein					Gombin		Y
Samulewicz	Moshe Samulewicz		Efraim	Dentist		Gombin	Gombin	Y
Sannicki	Hersz Sannicki	1905	Nakhum & Lea	Metalworker, married to Dore	Gombin	Gombin		Y
Sannicki	Cirla Sannicki	1908	Nakhum & Lea		Gombin	Gombin		Y
Sannicki	Ester Sannicki				Gombin	Gombin		W
Sannicki	Channa Sannicki				Gombin	Gombin		W
Sannicki	Rivka Lea Sanicki nee Gostynska				Gombin	Gombin		Y W

38

Family	Person's complete name	Year born	Parents	Other details	Place of birth	Before the war lived in	During the war was in	Source
Sannicki	Rojza Sannicki		Jojne	Child			Gombin	G
Sannicki	Chana Sannicki		Jojne	Child			Gombin	G
Sannicki	Wolf Sannicki		Jojne	Child			Gombin	G
Sannicki	Szmul Sannicki						Gombin	G
Sannicki	(GNU) Sannicki			Wife of Szmul			Gombin	G
Sannicki	(GNU) Sannicki		Szmul	Daughter of Szmul			Gombin	G
Sannicki	Moshe Sannicki	1906		Married, "sick" deported 11.5.4		Gombin	Konin camp	K
Sapirsztein	Szosza Sapirsztein nee Blumenfeld	1854	Arie & Sara	Married to Yekutiel	Gombin	Bialystok	Bialystok	Y
Schapiro	Guerchon Azriel Schapiro	1915	Yehuda & Dina	Musician, married	Gombin	Przasnysz	Bialystok	Y
Schwartz	Abraham Schwartz			Married to Ruchele		Gombin		B
Schwartz	Ruchele Schwartz nee Gurker		Israel & Zelda	Married to Abraham		Gombin		B W
Schenwald	Dwojra Schenwald	1890			Gombin		Lodz	L
Seideman	Chaim David Seideman			Wholesaler, married to Chana	Gombin	Gombin	Gombin	Y
Seideman	Chana Seideman nee Wyspa		Yitzchak & Dvorah nee Ettin	Married to Chaim	Gombin	Gombin	Gombin	Y
Seideman	Rivka Seideman	1927	Chaim & Chana nee Wyspa	Single	Gombin	Gombin	Gombin	Y
Seideman	Avrum Seideman	1929	Chaim & Chana nee Wyspa	Single	Gombin	Gombin	Gombin	Y
Seideman	Sura Seideman		Chaim & Chana nee Wyspa	Single	Gombin	Gombin	Gombin	Y
Seideman	Hersch Seideman	1914		Died Lobau camp 6-03-1942	Gombin	Gombin	Lobau camp	Y
Seidman	Daniel Seidman			Married to Ester	Poland	Gombin	Gombin	Y
Sender	Icek Sender	1916		Deported from Pithiviers 17-07	Gombin	Paris, France	Auschwitz camp	F M
Senderovicz	Hersz Chaim Senderovic	1885	Feibel & Lea	Merchant, widower	Gombin	Gombin	Gombin	Y
Senderovicz	Icze Senderovicz	1900		Hardware store, married to Kh	Gombin	Zychlin	Zychlin	Y
Senderowicz	Rywka Senderowicz	1918			Gombin	Lodz	Lodz	Y
Senderowicz	Moniek Senderowicz	1924			Gombin	Lodz	Lodz	Y
Senderowicz	Duvidl Senderowicz	1927			Gombin	Lodz	Lodz	Y
Senderowicz	Nachszon Senderowicz						Gombin	G
Senderowicz	Hersz Senderowicz			Wife of Hersz			Gombin	G
Senderowicz	(GNU) Senderowicz			Wife of Hersz			Gombin	G
Senderowicz	(GNU) Senderowicz		Hersz	Son of Hersz			Gombin	G
Senderowicz	(GNU) Senderowicz		Hersz	Son of Hersz			Gombin	G
Shachar	Avraham Pinchas Shachar			Married to Chava		Gombin		W B
Shachar	Chava Shachar			Married to Avraham Pinchas		Gombin	Gombin	W B
Shacher	Krause Shacher			Married to Hyman		Gombin	Gombin	B
Shacher	Chaskel Shacher		Hyman & Krause			Gombin	Gombin	B
Shacher	Lajele Shacher		Hyman & Krause			Gombin	Gombin	B
Shacher	Shmulik Shacher		Hyman & Krause			Gombin	Gombin	B
Shacher	(GNU) Shacher			Married to Shmulik		Gombin	Gombin	B
Shacher	Rafel Shacher			Married to Zelda		Gombin		B
Shacher	Zelda Shacher			Married to Rafel		Gombin		B
Shacher	David Shacher		Rafel & Zelda			Gombin		B
Shacher	Bunim Shacher		Rafel & Zelda	Married to Sylvia		Gombin		B

39

Family	Person's complete name	Year born	Parents	Other details	Place of birth	Before the war lived in	During the war was in	Source
Shacher	Sylvia Shacher			Married to Bunim		Gombin		B
Shacher	Alexander Shacher		Rafel & Zelda	Married to Gussie		Gombin		B
Shacher	Gussie Shacher			Married to Alexander		Gombin		B
Shacher	Isaac Shacher		Rafel & Zelda	Married to Beckie		Gombin		B
Shacher	Beckie Shacher			Married to Isaac		Gombin		B
Shapiro	Moishe Shapiro	1903			Gombin	Gombin	Gombin	Y
Shapiro	Zisl Shapiro nee Beibuk	1907			Gombin	Gombin	Gombin	Y
Shapiro	Abram Shapiro	1934	Moishe & Zysl nee Beibuk	Child	Gombin	Gombin	Gombin	Y G
Shapiro	Szlama Shapiro	1902		Married, "sick" deported 9.4.42		Gombin	Konin camp	K
Shapiro	Mendl Shapiro			Married to Tobe		Gombin		B
Shapiro	Tobe Shapiro nee Volman		Yosef	Married to Mendl		Gombin		B
Shchigel	Avrom Moishe Shchigel			Married to Royze		Gombin		B
Shchigel	Royze Shchigel			Married to Avrom		Gombin		B
Shchigel	Leybl Shchigel		Avrom & Royze			Gombin		B
Shchigel	Khaya Sore Shchigel		Avrom & Royze			Gombin		B
Shilski	Bilha Shilski nee Rafael	1888	Avraham & Rakhel	Married to Shlomo	Gombin	Lodz	Lodz	Y
Shlekhter	Eliahu Shlekhter	1895	Hirsh & Sara	Worker, married to Rela	Plock	Plock	Gombin	Y
Shpigel	Etl Shpigel	1880	Yosef & Adela	Married to Yaakov	Gombin	Gombin	Gombin	Y
Shtolzman	Mayla Shtolzman	1904	Khanokh & Hendlia	Married	Bodzanow	Poland	Gombin	Y
Shvartz	Hinda Shvartz nee Zaiontz	1900	Leib & Sara	Married to Nisan	Gombin	Gombin	Gombin	Y
Shvartz	Khaia Shvartz	1932	Nisan & Hinda	Child	Gombin	Gombin	Gombin	Y
Shvartz	Aron Shvartz			Married to Bila	Gombin	Gombin	Gombin	Y W
Shvartz	Bila Shvartz			Married to Aron	Gombin	Gombin	Gombin	Y W
Shvartz	Sara Shvartz		Aron & Bila		Gombin	Gombin		Y W
Shvartz	Rivka Shvartz		Aron & Bila		Gombin	Gombin		Y W
Shvartz	Hersh Ber Shvartz					Gombin		W
Shvartz	Izhak Shvartz					Gombin		W
Shvartzberg	Mordechai Shvartzberg					Gombin		W B
Shvartzberg	Yehudit Shvartzberg					Gombin		W B
Sidlo	Malka Sidlo nee Tadelis	1912	Shlomo & Rivka	Married to Yitzkhak	Gombin	Warsaw	Warsaw	Y
Sieradzcki	Eliasz Sieradzcki						Gombin	G
Sieradzcki	Rywcia Sieradzcki		Eliasz	Child			Gombin	G
Sieradzcki	Luzer Sieradzcki		Eliasz	Child			Gombin	G
Sikirka	Ithak Sikirka			Community leader, married to	Poland	Gombin		Y W B
Sikirka	Sara Sikirka		Elkhanan & Adina	Married to Yitzkhak	Poland	Gombin		Y W
Sikirka	Simha Sikirka		Yitzkhak & Sara	Married to Riza	Poland	Gombin	Gombin	Y W
Sikirka	Yehoszua Sikirka		Yitzkhak & Sara	Single	Poland	Gombin		Y W
Sikirka	Hirsh Leib Sikirka		Yitzkhak & Sara	Deputy mayor, married to Gita	Poland	Gombin	Warsaw	Y W
Sikirka	Ghita Sikirka			Married to Hirsh	Poland	Gombin	Warsaw	Y W
Sikirka	Hinda Sikirka		Hirsh & Gita	Single	Poland	Gombin	Warsaw	Y W
Silberman	Lee Silberman			Married to Helen		Gombin	Warsaw	Y B

Family	Person's complete name	Year born	Parents	Other details	Place of birth	Before the war lived in	During the war was in	Source
Silberman	Helen Silberman			Married to Lee	Gombin	Gombin	Warsaw	Y B
Skorkowski	Chawa Skorkowski	1914		Married to Sender	Gombin	Lodz	Lodz	Y
Skorkowski	Sara Skorkowski nee Hodes	1878	Pinkhas & Lea	Married to Mendel	Gombin	Lodz	Lodz	Y
Slan	Saul Slan					Gombin		W
Sloma	Abram Hersz Sloma						Gombin	G
Sloma	Szajndla Sloma						Gombin	G
Sloma	(GNU) Sloma		Abram Hersz	Child of Abram			Gombin	G
Sloma	(GNU) Sloma		Abram Hersz	Child of Abram			Gombin	G
Sloma	(GNU) Sloma		Abram Hersz	Child of Abram			Gombin	G
Sochaczewski	Moshe Aharon Sochaczewski					Gombin		W
Sochaczewski	Channa Gitel Sochaczewski					Gombin		W
Sochaczewski	Abraham Eli Sochaczewski			Married to Miriam nee Kozinsk	Poland	Gombin	Gombin	Y W B
Sochaczewski	Mirjam Sochaczewski nee Kuchins			Married to Avraham	Poland	Gombin	Gombin	Y W B
Sochaczewski	Tova Sochaczewski		Avraham & Miriam	Married	Gombin	Gombin	Gombin	Y W B
Sochaczewski	Pesach Sochaczewski	1907	Avraham & Miriam	Carpenter	Gombin	Gombin		Y W H B
Sochaczewski	Mosze Sochaczewski		Avraham & Miriam	Married	Gombin	Gombin	Gombin	Y W B
Sochaczewski	Szlomo Sochaczewski		Avraham & Miriam	Married	Gombin	Gombin	Gombin	Y W B
Sochaczewski	Rubin Sochaczewski		Avraham & Miriam	Married	Gombin	Gombin	Gombin	Y W B
Sochaczewski	Jonatan Sochaczewski		Avraham & Miriam	Married	Gombin	Gombin	Gombin	Y W G B
Sochaczewski	Jakov Sochaczewski	1900	Avraham & Miriam	Married	Gombin	Gombin	Gombin	Y W B
Sochacki	Moishe Aaron Sochacki			Married to Chana Gitel		Gombin		B
Sochacki	Chana Gitel Sochacki			Married to Moishe Aaron		Gombin		B
Sochacki	Nathan Sochacki		Moishe & Chana			Gombin		B
Sochacki	David Sochacki		Moishe & Chana			Gombin		B
Sochacki	Symcha Sochacki		Moishe & Chana			Gombin		B
Sochacki	Nusyn Sochacki						Gombin	G
Sochacki	(GNU) Sochacki			Wife of Nusyn			Gombin	G
Sochacki	Szmul Sochacki		Nussyn	Child			Gombin	G
Sochacki	Jcek Sochacki		Nussyn	Child			Gombin	G
Sochacki	Majer Sochacki						Gombin	G
Sochacki	(GNU) Sochacki			Wife of Majer			Gombin	G
Sochacki	Abram Sochacki			Child			Gombin	G
Sochacki	Chaim Sochacki						Gombin	G
Sohacky	Simon Sohacky	1901	Tuvia & Tzipora	Tailor, married to Miriam nee K	Gombin	Gombin	Gombin	Y
Sohacky	Miriam Sohacky nee Kukuridza	1903	Barukh & Khana	Seamstress, married to Shimon	Gombin	Gombin	Gombin	Y
Sohacky	Khaim Sohacky	1923	Simon & Miriam nee Kukuri	Child		Gombin	Gombin	Y
Sohacky	Tuvia Sohacky	1931	Simon & Miriam nee Kukuri	Child		Gombin	Gombin	Y
Solomon	Yacov Solomon					Gombin		W
Solomon	Tzvi Solomon					Gombin		W
Solomon	Yosef Solomon					Gombin		W
Speishendler	Yechiel Machl Speishendler			Married to Bela		Gombin	Lowitz	B

41

Family	Person's complete name	Year born	Parents	Other details	Place of birth	Before the war lived in	During the war was in	Source
Speishendler	Bela Speishendler nee Tyber		Lajzer & Mindel	Married to Yechiel Machl		Gombin	Lowitz	B
Speishendler	Edzia Speishendler		Yechiel Machl & Bela			Gombin	Lowitz	B
Speishendler	Lajser Speishendler		Yechiel Machl & Bela			Gombin	Lowitz	B
Speishendler	Schlojme Leib Speishendler			Married to Cypra		Gombin		B
Speishendler	Cypra Speishendler			Married to Schlojme Leib		Gombin		B
Speishendler	Abraham Speishendler		Schlojme Leib & Cypra			Gombin		B
Speishendler	Michael Speishendler		Schlojme Leib & Cypra			Gombin		B
Speishendler	Sarah Speishendler		Schlojme Leib & Cypra			Gombin		B
Spiel	Meir Spiel	1882		Married, "sick" deported 11.5.4		Gombin`	Konin camp	K
Spiewak	Naftali Spiewak	1892	Jidel & Rivka	Watchmaker, married to Ruche	Wyszogrod	Gombin	Gombin	Y
Spiewak	Ruchel Spiewak nee Bzhezhina	1898	Yechezkiel & Sara	Married to Naftali	Kutno	Gombin	Gombin	Y
Spiewak	Yechezkiel Spiewak	1920	Naftali & Rakhel nee Bzhezh	Student	Gombin	Gombin	Gombin	Y
Spiewak	Leah Spiewak	1926	Naftali & Rakhel nee Bzhezh	Student	Gombin	Gombin	Gombin	Y
Spiewak	Chava Spiewak	1927	Naftali & Rakhel nee Bzhezh	Student	Gombin	Gombin	Gombin	Y
Spodek	Mosze Spodek	1890		Merchant, married to Feiga ne	Lowicz	Lowicz	Gombin	Y
Spodek	Fajge Ita Spodek nee Senderovitz	1890	Feibel & Lea	Married to Moshe	Gombin	Lowicz	Gombin	Y
Spodek	Ahron Spodek	1918	Moshe & Ita	Merchant, single	Lowicz	Lowicz	Gombin	Y
Stan	Itcze Stan					Gombin		W
Stempa	Fajga Stempa	1896			Gombin			M
Stern	Shaul Stern	1870		Married to Mindl	Gombin	Gombin	Gombin	Y W
Stern	Mindl Stern nee Holtzman			Married to Shaul	Gombin	Dobrzykow	Gombin	Y W
Stern	Dina Stern	1903	Shaul & Mindl		Dobrzykow	Dobrzykow	Gombin	Y
Stern	Izchak Stern	1908	Shaul & Mindl	Married to Leahnee Pokorski	Dobrzykow	Dobrzykow	Gombin	Y W
Stern	Leah Stern nee Pokorski	1911		Married to Izchak	Plock	Gombin	Gombin	Y W
Stern	Sarah Stern	1940	Izchak & Lea nee Pokorski	Child	Gombin	Gombin	Gombin	Y W
Stern	Fraidel Stern		Jzrael	Child			Gombin	G
Stolcman	Tacov Stolcman					Gombin		W
Stolcman	Rasza Stolcman					Gombin		W
Stolcman	Blima Stolcman						Gombin	G
Stolcman	Zygmunt Stolcman						Gombin	G
Stolcman	Hersz Stolcman						Gombin	G
Stupaj	Lajzer Stupaj					Gombin		W
Stupaj	Razel Stupaj					Gombin		W
Stupaj	Mosche Stupaj	1862	Josek & Ruchla	Married to Necha	Plock	Gombin	Gombin	Y W R
Stupaj	Necha Stupaj nee Stupaj	1867	Avram & Michle	Married to Mosche	Gombin	Gombin	Gombin	Y W R
Stupaj	Iosif Arie Stupaj	1897		Waggoner, married to Gitele	Gombin	Gombin	Gombin	Y G
Stupaj	Gitele Stupaj nee Beibuk	1902		Married to Yosif	Gombin	Gombin	Gombin	Y G
Stupaj	Hinda Stupaj	1927	Iosif & Gitel nee Beibuk	Pupil	Gombin	Gombin	Gombin	Y G
Stupaj	Ester Stupaj	1930	Iosif & Gitel nee Beibuk	Pupil	Gombin	Gombin	Gombin	Y G
Stykowczki	Chaja Stykowczki		Jakub	Child			Gombin	G
Stykowczki	Abram Stykowczki		Jakub	Child			Gombin	G

42

Family	Person's complete name	Year born	Parents	Other details	Place of birth	Before the war lived in	During the war was in	Source
Sukhetzki	Bela Sukhetzki	1907	Barukh	Uppers cutter/tailor, married	Gombin		Gombin	Y
Szacher	Rajza Szacher						Gombin	G
Szacher	(GNU) Szacher		Rajza	Daughter of Rajza			Gombin	G
Szacher	(GNU) Szacher		Rajza	Daughter of Rajza			Gombin	G
Szacher	(GNU) Szacher		Rajza	Son of Rajza			Gombin	G
Szacher	(GNU) Szacher		Rajza	Son of Rajza			Gombin	G
Szafir	Szlomo Szafir	1895		Merchant, married to Khava ne	Gombin	Warsaw	Warsaw	Y
Szczygiel	Simcha Szczygiel	1899	Faivel & Hinda Ester	Married to Chana	Sanniki	Gombin	Warsaw	Y R
Szczygiel	Chaia Brakha Szczygiel		Smkha & Khina	Married		Gombin	Gombin	Y
Szczawinski	Majlech Szczawinski	1899		Married, buried Konin Catholic	Gombin	Gombin	Konin camp	Y K G
Szemiontek	Ester Szemiontek	1870				Piotrkovitz	Gombin	Y
Szemiontek	Jochewet Szemiontek	1904	Leib & Ester	Married	Slubice	Gombin	Gombin	Y
Szerawinski	Gerszon Szerawinski		Majloch	Child			Gombin	G
Szklarek	Abram Szklarek			Single, deported Konin camp to		Gombin	Konin camp	K
Szklower	Yosef Szklower	1905		Merchant, married to Frida nee	Gombin	Wloclawek	Wloclawek	Y
Szklower	Schmul Moschek Szklower	1898	Mendel & Frimet nee Goldse		Gombin	Berlin, Germany	Auschwitz camp	Y M
Szlanchtus	Laibisz Szlanchtus					Gombin		W
Szlang	Gdaliyahu Noakh Szlang	1878	Ahaaron & Rikel	Rabbi, merchant, married to Fa	Zakroczym	Gombin	Gombin	Y G
Szlang	Fajge Szlang			Married to Gdaliyahu	Poland	Gombin	Gombin	Y
Szlang	Moses Israel Szlang	1911	Gdaliyahu & Fajge	Married, buried Konin Catholic	Gombin	Gombin	Konin camp	Y K
Szlang	Mendel Szlang	1913	Gdaliyahu & Fajge	Married	Gombin	Warsaw	Warsaw	Y
Szlang	Ester Szlang	1901	Gdaliyahu & Fajge		Gombin	Gombin	Gombin	Y
Szlang	Rywka Szlang	1907	Gdaliyahu & Fajge	Seamstress, married to Meir	Gombin	Sanniki	Gostynin	Y
Szlang	Lea Szlang	1906	Gdaliyahu & Fajge	Kindergarten teacher, single	Gombin	Gombin	Gombin	Y
Szlang	Myriam Szlang	1910	Gdaliyahu & Fajge	Merchant, married to Hershel	Gombin	Warsaw	Warsaw	Y
Szleifer	Temtja Szleifer nee Temerson	1900			Gombin	Kutno, Poland	Kutno	Y
Szlejfer	Kalman Szlejfer	1888		Married to Khaia nee Binenfeld	Gombin	Warsaw	Warsaw	Y
Szmigel	Wolf Beer Szmigel	1875	Yitzkhak & Luba	Bookkeeper	Gombin	Lodz	Lodz	Y
Szochaczewski	Yona Szochaczewski					Gombin		W
Szochaczewski	Lea Szochaczewski					Gombin		W
Szperling	Aron Szperling						Gombin	G
Szperling	(GNU) Szperling			Wife of Aron			Gombin	G
Szperling	Sura Szperling		Aron	Child			Gombin	G
Szpilfogiel	Moszek Szpilfogiel						Gombin	G
Szpilfogiel	(GNU) Szpilfogiel		Moszek	Daughter of Moszek			Gombin	G
Szpilfogiel	(GNU) Szpilfogiel		Moszek	Daughter of Moszek			Gombin	G
Szpilfogiel	(GNU) Szpilfogiel		Moszek	Daughter of Moszek			Gombin	G
Szpilfogiel	(GNU) Szpilfogiel		Moszek	Son of Moszek			Gombin	G
Szpilfogiel	Sala (Sara) Szpilfogiel		Izrael Mordka	Child			Gombin	G
Szpilfogiel	Pesa Szpilfogiel		Izrael Mordka	Child			Gombin	G
Sztajnfeld	Gitla Machla Sztajnfeld	1880		Died in Lodz Ghetto	Gombin		Lodz	L M

43

Family	Person's complete name	Year born	Parents	Other details	Place of birth	Before the war lived in	During the war was in	Source
Sztajnke	Sura Sztajnke nee Zychlinska	1908		Married to Pinkus	Gombin	Kutno, Poland	Kutno	Y
Sztern	Izaak Sztern	1908	Shaul & Mindl	Hairdresser, married to Lea	Gombin	Gombin	Gombin	Y
Sztern	Lea Sztern	1916		Married to Yitzkhak	Plock	Gombin	Gombin	Y
Sztern	Mordekhai Sztern		Izaak & Lea	Child	Gombin	Gombin		Y
Sztern	Sara Sztern		Izaak & Lea	Child	Gombin	Gombin	Gombin	Y
Sztern	Szaul Sztern	1878	Yitzkhak & Sara	Merchant, married to Mindl ne	Gombin	Gombin	Gombin	Y
Sztern	Mindl Sztern nee Holtzman	1886	Zalman & Lea	Married to Shaul	Gombin	Gombin	Gombin	Y
Sztern	Dyna Sztern	1905	Shaul & Mindl	Single	Gombin	Gombin	Gombin	Y
Sztern	Bluma Sztern	1870		Died Lodz hospital 08-Jul-1942	Gombin		Lodz	L M
Sztern	Motyl Sztern						Gombin	G
Sztern	Sura Sztern						Gombin	G
Sztiglic	Icchak Sztiglic			Deported Konin camp to Andrz		Gombin	Konin camp	K
Sztolcman	Rosalja Sztolcman		Rosalya			Gombin		B
Sztolcman	Helena Sztolcman		Rosalya			Gombin		B
Sztolcman	Moniek Sztolcman		Rosalya			Gombin		B
Sztolcman	Alfred Sztolcman		Rosalya			Gombin		B
Sztolcman	Chana Sztolcman			Married to Menashe		Gombin		B
Sztolcman	Chanele Sztolcman			Married to Lejbel		Gombin		B
Szulc	Majer Szulc	1870	Yosef & Mindl	Married to Ester nee Bleikh	Gombin	Kolo		Y
Szulman	Towia Szulman	1876	Shmuel & Lea nee Zilberstei	Married to Frajda nee Karo	Gombin	Lodz	Lodz	Y L M
Szwarc	Chaia Szwarc	1922	Natan & Hinda	Single	Gombin	Gombin	Gombin	Y
Szwarc	Icchak Szwarc	1896		Married, "sick" deported 8.7.42		Gombin	Konin camp	K
Szwarc	Hynda Szwarc nee Zaiontz	1900	Leib & Sara	Seamstress, married to Natan	Gombin	Gombin	Gombin	Y
Szwarc	Abraham Szwarc		Sala			Gombin	Gombin	G
Szyber	Marysia Szyber		Sala	Student, killed during bombarn	Plock	Plock	Gombin	Y
Szykorski	Gitel Szykorski		Gitel	Daughter of Gitel			Gombin	G
Szykorski	(GNU) Szykorski		Gitel	Son of Gitel			Gombin	G
Szykorski	(GNU) Szykorski						Gombin	G
Szymbaum	Abraham Szymbaum	1893		Married, buried Konin Catholic	Gombin		Konin camp	K
Tadelis	Elimelech Tadelis					Gombin		W
Tadelis	Awram Tadelis	1896	Mosche & Khava nee Blusht	Tailor, married to Sheindl	Gombin	Leipzig, Germany	Leipzig, Germany	Y W M
Tadelis	Chaja Ester Tadelis	1908	Mosche & Khava nee Blusht		Gombin	Kalisz	Lublin	Y W
Tadelis	Izchak Tadelis	1903	Mosche & Khava nee Blusht	Weaver, married to Regina	Gombin	Poznan		Y W
Tadelis	Jacob Tadelis	1910	Mosche & Khava nee Blusht	Tailor, single	Gombin	Kalisz	Kalisz	Y W
Tadelis	Shlomo Tadelis	1882	Avraham & Rakhel	Merchant, married to Rivka nee	Gombin	Warsaw	Warsaw	Y W
Tadelis	Rivka Tadelis				Gombin	Warsaw	Warsaw	Y W
Tadelis	Khaim Tadelis	1915	Shlomo & Rivka	Clerk, married	Gombin	Warsaw	Warsaw	Y W
Tadelis	Josef Tadelis	1919	Shlomo & Rivka	Physician, single	Gombin	Warsaw	Warsaw	Y W
Tadelis	Sara Tadelis	1907	Shlomo & Rivka	Seamstress, married	Gombin	Warsaw	Warsaw	Y W
Tadelis	Shoshana Tadelis nee Volman	1880	Tzali	Merchant, married to Melekh	Gombin	Gombin	Gombin	Y
Tadelis	Miriam Tadelis		Melekh & Shoshana nee Vol	Child		Gombin	Gombin	Y

44

Family	Person's complete name	Year born	Parents	Other details	Place of birth	Before the war lived in	During the war was in	Source
Tadelis	Mosche Aron Tadelis		Ytzkhak & Pesa	Teacher, married to Chawa	Gombin	Kalisz	Lublin	Y
Tadelis	Chawa Tadelis nee Blushtein		Shmuel & Sara	Married to Aron	Gombin	Kalisz	Lublin	Y
Tadelis	Tzirel Cesia Tadelis	1882		Married to Moshe	Gombin	Gombin	Gombin	Y
Tadelis	Jidel Izak Tadelis	1907	Moshe & Tzirel	Hospital clerk, single	Gombin	Gombin	Gombin	Y
Tadelis	Gerszon Tadelis	1905	Moshe & Tzirel	Merchant, married	Gombin	Gombin	Gombin	Y
Tadelis	Sara Tadelis	1909	Moshe & Tzirel	Married	Gombin	Gombin	Gombin	Y
Tadelis	Jakob Tadelis			Single, deported Konin camp to		Gombin	Konin camp	K
Tajfeld	Noach Tajfeld					Gombin		W
Tajfeld	Ita Miriam Tajfeld					Gombin		W
Tajfeld	Hersz Tajfeld					Gombin		W
Tajfeld	Channa Tajfeld					Gombin		W
Tajfeld	Sara Tajfeld					Gombin		W
Tajfeld	Chuna Tajfeld	1866	Simje & Ryfka nee Kowalska	Baker, married to Mirla nee Fro	Gombin	Mlawa	Mlawa	Y
Tajfeld	Mordka Tajfeld	1923		Died Lodz hospital 07-Feb-1942	Gombin		Lodz	L M
Tajfeld	Perec Tajfeld	1857		Died in Lodz Ghetto	Gombin		Lodz	L M
Tajfeld	Moszek Tajfeld	1921			Gombin		Lodz	L M
Tatarek	Zalma Tatarek	1898		Merchant, married to Nekha	Gombin	Gombin	Gombin	Y
Tatarek	Nacha Tatarek nee Bornshtein	1902	Faivel & Tzivia	Married to Zelma	Gombin	Gombin	Gombin	Y
Tatarek	Uziel Tatarek	1924	Zelma & Nekha nee Bornsht	Child		Gombin	Gombin	Y
Tatarek	Faivel Tatarek	1926	Zelma & Nekha nee Bornsht	Child		Gombin	Gombin	Y
Tatarka	Maier Tatarka	1889	Abram & Golda	Married to Raizele, deported K	Gombin	Gombin	Konin camp	Y W B
Tatarka	Raizel Khaia Tatarka	1890	Matis & Rivka	Married to Maier	Gombin	Gombin	Poland	Y W B
Tatarka	Leib Tatarka	1925	Maier & Khaia	Single, deported Konin camp to	Gombin	Gombin	Konin camp	Y K B
Tatarka	Tobi Tatarka	1923	Maier & Khaia	Single	Gombin	Gombin	Poland	Y B
Tatarka	Riwka Tatarka	1926	Maier & Khaia	Child	Gombin	Gombin	Gombin	Y B
Tatarka	Feiwel Tatarka	1922		Died Poznan camp 25-01-1943	Gombin	Gombin	Poznan camp	Y
Tatarka	Szymszon Tatarka		Josef & Fajga	Baker, married to Laja nee Jast	Gombin	Zychlin	Zychlin	Y
Tatarka	Zalman Tatarka	1921					Mauthausen camp	Y
Tatarka	Chane Tatarka				Gombin	Gombin	Gombin	B
Taub	Feiga Taub nee Birnboim		Sender	Married to Tuvia	Gombin	Jilow	Jilow	Y
Tauber	Abraham Tauber	1901			Gombin		Majdanek camp	Y
Tauber	Tzwi Tauber	1910		Merchant, married to Reiza nee	Poland	Gombin	Gombin	Y
Tauber	Reiza Tauber nee Zolno	1913	Zeev & Rakhel	Married to Tzvi	Gombin	Gombin	Gombin	Y
Tauber	Sender Tauber			Married to Shem		Gombin	Gombin	Y
Tauber	Israel Tauber					Gombin		W
Tcuk	Menachem Tcuk					Gombin		W
Tcuk	Izhak Tcuk					Gombin		W
Tcuk	Moshe Tcuk					Gombin		W
Teefeld	Benjamin Teefeld	1926		Died Flossenbuerg camp	Gombin		Flossenburg camp	Y
Teifeld	Abraham Teifeld					Gombin		B
Teifeld	Ester Teifeld					Gombin		B

45

Family	Person's complete name	Year born	Parents	Other details	Place of birth	Before the war lived in	During the war was in	Source
Teifeld	Sara Teifeld					Gombin		B
Temersohn	Chaya Temersohn nee Vladislavski	1871		Widow of Moise	Plock	Gombin	Gombin	Y B
Temersohn	Roza Temersohn	1908	Moise & Khaia nee Vladislav	Single	Gombin	Gombin	Gombin	Y B
Temersohn	Mania Temersohn	1909	Moise & Khaia nee Vladislav	Single	Gombin	Gombin	Gombin	Y B
Temersohn	Isaac Temersohn	1911	Moise & Khaia nee Vladislav	Single	Gombin	Gombin	Gombin	Y
Temersohn	Mendel Temersohn	1865		Wine merchant, married	Gombin	Gombin	Gombin	Y
Temersohn	Aba Temersohn	1892	Mendel & Sara	Iron dealer, married to Elka nee	Gombin	Kutno, Poland	Kutno	Y
Temersohn	Icchak Temersohn	1915		Merchant, single	Gombin	Gombin	Gombin	Y
Temersohn	Sala Temersohn						Gombin	G
Temersohn	Rywcia Temersohn						Gombin	G
Temersohn	Herszek Temersohn						Gombin	G
Temersohn	Chaja Temersohn						Gombin	G
Temerson	Arie Yehuda Temerson	1909	Aba & Elka nee Shtrom	Rabbi	Kutno	Gombin	Gombin	Y
Temmerzon	Tova Temmerzon nee Bochko			Married to Yehuda		Gombin		Y
Temerson	Sara Temerson		Jehuda & Tova nee Bochko	Child		Gombin	Gombin	Y
Temerson	Ester Temerson		Jehuda & Tova nee Bochko	Child		Gombin	Gombin	Y
Temerzon	Avraham Temerzon			Clerk, married to Mania		Gombin		Y
Temerzon	Iosi Temerzon		Avraham & Mania	Child		Gombin		Y
Terfeld	Hirsh Terfeld			Married to Sara nee Lidzbarski	Poland	Gombin	Poland	Y
Terfeld	Sara Terfeld nee Lidzbarski		Meyir & Lea	Married to Hersh	Tomaszow Mazow	Gombin	Gombin	W
Tiber	Avraham Meir Tiber				Gombin	Gombin	Gombin	W
Tiber	Frida Tiber				Gombin	Gombin	Gombin	W
Tiber	Zipora Tiber	1918	Avraham & Frida	Clerk, single	Gombin	Gombin	Gombin	Y W H
Tiber	Miriam Tiber	1919	Avraham & Frida	Seamstress, single	Gombin	Gombin	Gombin	Y W H
Tiber	Fajga Tiber nee Holtzman	1880	Zalman & Lea	Merchant, widow of Natan	Gombin	Gombin	Gombin	Y
Tiber	Hersz Tiber	1906	Natan & Feiga	Merchant, married to Rada nee	Gombin	Gombin	Gombin	Y
Tiber	Natek Tiber		Hersz & Raca nee Zolna			Gombin		Y
Tiber	Mordchai Tiber			Merchant, married	Gombin	Grodzisk Mazowie	Grodzisk Mazowie	Y
Tiber	Symcha Tiber	1904	Leizer & Mindla nee Lubinsk	Married to Fajga	Gombin	Gombin	Auschwitz camp	Y
Tiger	Lemel Tiger	1901		Married, "sick" deported 8.7.42		Gombin	Konin camp	K
Topial	Mordko Topial	1917			Gombin		Lublin	Y
Topial	Szlama Lajb Topial						Gombin	G
Topial	Gnendla Topial						Gombin	G
Tvorkov	Nekhama Tvorkov nee Bornshtein		Faivel & Tzvia	Married	Gombin	Gombin	Poland	Y
Tyba	Mindl Tyba	1882		Married	Gombin	Gombin	Gombin	Y
Tyba	Yechiel Meir Tyba	1910	Mindl	Merchant, married	Gombin	Gombin	Gombin	Y
Tyber	Gerszon Israel Tyber	1896		Merchant, buried Konin Catholic	Gombin	Gombin	Konin camp	Y K
Tyber	Zelig Tyber	1890	Moshe & Golda	Merchant, married to Gitel	Gombin	Kutno, Poland	Gombin	Y
Tyber	Abraham Tyber		Tzvi & Ita	Clerk, married to Frida nee Eng	Gombin	Gombin	Gombin	Y
Tyber	Jakob Israel Tyber	1886		Married to Roza, buried Konin	Gombin	Gombin	Konin camp	Y W K G
Tyber	Roza Tyber			Married to Jakob	Gombin	Gombin	Gombin	W G

46

Family	Person's complete name	Year born	Parents	Other details	Place of birth	Before the war lived in	During the war was in	Source
Tyber	Juda Tyber		Jakub & Roza	Child			Gombin	G
Tyber	Chana Tyber						Gombin	G
Tyber	Mania Tyber						Gombin	G
Tyber	Mordechai Tyber					Gombin		B
Tyber	Debora Tyber					Gombin		B
Tyber	Bluma Tyber					Gombin		B
Tyber	Simcha Tyber					Gombin	Auschwitz camp	B M
Tyber	(GNU) Tyber		Simcha	Wife of Simcha Tyber		Gombin		B
Tyber	(GNU) Tyber		Simcha	Daughter of Simcha Tyber		Gombin		B
Tyber	(GNU) Tyber		Simcha	Son of Simcha Tyber		Gombin		B
Tyber	Jechiel Meyer Tyber	1889	Lajzer & Mindel	Married, buried Konin Catholic	Gombin	Gombin	Konin camp	Y K B
Tyber	Yehuda Tyber		Lajzer & Mindel		Gombin	Gombin		B
Tyber	Ester Tyber		Yehuda		Gombin	Gombin		B
Tyber	Rachcia Tyber		Yehuda		Gombin	Gombin		B
Tyber	Jankiel Mordka Tyber	1886		Died in Lodz Ghetto	Gombin		Lodz	L M
Tzadek	Merale Tzadek nee Frenkel	1902	Jankiel & Lea	Married to Schmil	Gombin	Lodz	Lodz	Y
Tzelemensky	Moishe Leyb Tzelemensky			Married to Sayne		Gombin		B
Tzelemensky	Shayne Bine Tzelemensky			Married to Moishe		Gombin		B
Tzelemensky	Leah Tzelemensky		Moishe & Shayne			Gombin		B
Tzelemensky	Avrom Tzelemensky		Moishe & Shayne			Gombin		B
Tzelemensky	Bayle Tzelemensky		Moishe & Shayne			Gombin		B
Tzelemensky	Feyge Tzelemensky		Moishe & Shayne			Gombin		B
Tzelemensky	Yosef Tzelemensky		Moishe & Shayne	Married to Khane		Gombin		B
Tzelemensky	Khane Tzelemensky			Married to Yosef		Gombin		B
Tzelemensky	(GNU) Tzelemensky		Yosef & Khane	Child		Gombin		B
Unger	Zalman Unger	1896	Yakow & Ita nee Ribski	Rabbi, married to Sara	Wloclawek	Gombin	Gombin	Y
Unger	Sara Unger			Married to Zalman		Gombin	Gombin	Y
Urbakh	Rakhel Urbakh nee Kilbert	1870	Yaakov	Married to Ytzkhak	Zychlin	Zychlin	Zychlin	Y
Vanger	Rivka Vanger nee Plonski	1913	Moses & Lea nee Zonenberg	Married to Leon	Gombin	Lodz	Lodz	Y
Veitzman	Khana Veitzman nee Kerber	1897	Leibel & Lea	Married to Mendel	Gombin	Gombin	Lodz	Y
Veitzman	Khelcha Veitzman	1927	Mendel & Khana nee Kerber	Pupil, single	Gombin	Gombin	Gombin	Y
Vespa	Avram Moshe Vespa			Married to Jankiel	Gombin	Gombin	Gombin	Y
Volman	Mordekhai Volman			Iron dealer		Gombin		Y
Volman	Gita Volman			Married to Mordekhai	Poland	Gombin	Gombin	Y
Volman	Zisl Volman					Gombin		B
Volman	Khava Volman		Zisl	Married to Lejzer		Gombin		B
Volman	Shlomo Volman		Zisl	Married, deported Konin camp		Gombin	Konin camp	B K
Volman	(GNU) Volman		Shlomo	Wife of Shlomo Wolman		Gombin		B
Volman	(GNU) Volman		Shlomo	Child of Shlomo Wolman		Gombin		B
Volman	Yosef Volman		Yosef			Gombin		B
Volman	Brandl Volman					Gombin		B

47

Family	Person's complete name	Year born	Parents	Other details	Place of birth	Before the war lived in	During the war was in	Source
Volman	Wolf Volman		Yosef			Gombin		B
Volman	Moishe Volman		Yosef	Married to Rokhl		Gombin		B
Volman	Rokhl Volman			Married to Moishe		Gombin		B
Vrubel	Fraidl Vrubel					Gombin		B
Vrubel	(GNU) Vrubel			Daughter of Fraidl		Gombin		B
Vrubel	(GNU) Vrubel			Mother of Fraidl		Gombin		B
Wagner	Pesach Wagner	1902		Merchant, married to Tova	Gombin	Lodz	Lodz	Y
Wahrhaftig	Eliakim Wahrhaftig	1922	Natan & Mirl	Metalworker, single	Gombin	Przemysl	Przemysl	Y
Wajcman	Mendel Menakhem Wajcman	1897	Meir & Simkha nee Magnes	Married to Khana nee Kerber	Plock	Gombin	Gombin	Y
Waldman	Dina Waldman nee Hodes	1882	Pinkhas & Lea	Married to Yisrael	Gombin	Lodz	Lodz	Y
Wandt	Moszek Wandt					Gombin	Gombin	G
Wandt	Mendel Wandt	1906	Icek & Chaja nee Nupenowic	Brother of Mosze From Gostyn	Gombin	Gombin	Auschwitz camp	Y W G M
Wandt	Chaja Wandt					Gombin		W
Warszawer	Elie Warszawer						Gombin	G
Warszawer	(GNU) Warszawer			Wife of Elie			Gombin	G
Warszawer	Chana Warszawer		Elie	Child			Gombin	G
Warszawer	Jta Warszawer		Elie	Child			Gombin	G
Warszawer	Mordka Warszawer		Elie	Child			Gombin	G
Warszawer	Majer Warszawer						Gombin	G
Waserman	Sara Waserman				Gombin	Plock		Y
Wasowicz	Wiktor Wasowicz	1879		Died Lodz hospital 21-Feb-1942	Gombin		Lodz	L M
Weinbaum	Yiechiel Weinbaum					Gombin		W
Weisman	Jechiel Weisman	1901		Married, "sick" deported 19.5.4		Gombin	Konin camp	K
Wiener	Chana Wiener	1897		Deported from Lodz Transport	Gombin		Lodz	Y L
Wiener	Eljasz Nechamja Wiener	1935	Chana	Deported from Lodz Transport	Gombin		Lodz	Y L
Wiener	Golda Wiener	1929	Chana	Deported from Lodz Transport	Gombin		Lodz	Y L
Wiener	Pesa Wiener	1922	Chana	Deported from Lodz Transport	Gombin		Lodz	Y L
Wiener	Rachmil Izrael Icek Wiener	1922	Chana	Deported from Lodz Transport	Gombin		Lodz	Y L
Wiener	Rywka Wiener	1926	Chana	Deported from Lodz Transport	Gombin		Lodz	Y L
Wigdorowich	Hirsh Wigdorowich		Eliezer	Married to Sara	Gombin	Ostrowiec	Ostrowiec	Y
Wigdorowicz	Boruch Wigdorowicz	1900	Yakov & Malkah	Married	Gombin	Gombin		Y
Winawer	Mirjam Winawer nee Charnochap	1880	Reuven & Lea	Married to Eliezer	Gombin	Warsaw	Warsaw	Y
Winiarska	Ruchla Winiarska	1890			Gombin	Wloclawek		Y
Wirobig	Abraham Chaim Wirobig				Gombin	Gombin		W
Wirobig	Fraide Wirobig	1870	Zalman & Rakhel	Married	Gombin	Gombin	Gombin	Y
Wirobig	Haia Sura Wirobig	1860	Zalman & Rakhel	Married to Yosef	Gombin	Gombin	Gombin	Y
Wirobig	Berl Wirobig	1908	Yosef & Sara	Married to Liuba	Gombin	Wilno	Wilno	Y
Wirobig	Janke Yaakov Wirobig	1910	Yosef & Sara		Gombin	Gombin	Gombin	Y
Wirobig	Edel Wirobig	1906	Yosef & Sara	Merchant, married to Angela	Gombin	Gombin	Gombin	Y G
Wirobig	David Wirobig		Idl & Angela	Child	Gombin	Gombin	Gombin	Y
Wirobig	Yosef Wirobig		Idl & Angela	Child	Gombin	Gombin	Gombin	Y G

48

Family	Person's complete name	Year born	Parents	Other details	Place of birth	Before the war lived in	During the war was in	Source
Wirobig	Moshe Wirobig		Icl & Angela	Child	Gombin	Gombin	Gombin	Y G
Witelzon	Israel Witelzon	1882	Moshe & Rivka	Merchant, married to Lea nee V	Gombin	Sosnowice	Sosnowice	Y
Witislawski	Jakob Witislawski	1875		Married, "sick" deported 11.5.4		Gombin	Konin camp	K
Wojdeslawski	Mordechai Wojdeslawski			Married to Nacha nee Rissman		Gombin	Gombin	Y W B
Wojdeslawski	Nacha Wojdeslawski nee Rissman	1901	Manele & Chaya nee Hambu	Married to Mordechai	Gombin	Gombin	Gombin	Y W B
Wojdeslawski	Yosef Wojdeslawski	1909			Gombin	Gombin	Buchenwald camp	Y W M
Wojdeslawski	Ester Wojdeslawski				Gombin	Gombin	Gombin	W
Wojdeslawski	Chaja Wojdeslawski				Gombin	Gombin	Gombin	W
Wojdeslawski	Brana Wojdeslawski						Gombin	G
Wojdeslawski	Liber Wojdeslawski						Gombin	G
Wojdeslawski	Chana Wojdeslawski		Ambram Mosze	Child			Gombin	G
Wojdeslawski	Icchak Wojdeslawski			Deported Konin camp to Andrz		Gombin	Konin camp	K
Wojdeslawski	Hersz Wojdeslawski			Single, deported Konin camp to		Gombin	Konin camp	K
Wojdeslawski	Fiszel Wojdeslawski			Deported Konin camp to Andrz		Gombin	Konin camp	K
Wojdeslawski	Abram Wojdeslawski			Deported Konin camp to Andrz		Gombin	Konin camp	K
Wojdeslawski	Hersh Josel Wojdeslawski			Married to Chaja Tobe		Gombin		B
Wojdeslawski	Chaja Tobe Wojdeslawski			Married to Hersh Josel		Gombin		B
Wojdeslawski	Jankiel Wojdeslawski		Hersh Josel & Chaja Tobe	Child		Gombin		B
Wojdeslawski	Feiga Ruchel Wojdeslawski		Hersh Josel & Chaja Tobe	Child		Gombin		B
Wojdeslawski	Perele Wojdeslawski		Hersh Josel & Chaja Tobe	Child		Gombin		B
Wojdeslawski	Abraham Wojdeslawski			Married to Malka		Gombin		B
Wojdeslawski	Malka Wojdeslawski			Married to Abraham		Gombin		B
Wojdeslawski	Mordecai Wojdeslawski		Abraham & Malka			Gombin		B
Wojdeslawski	Rachel Wojdeslawski		Abraham & Malka			Gombin		B
Wojdeslawski	Laja Wojdeslawski		Abraham & Malka			Gombin		B
Wojdeslawski	Jachet Wojdeslawski	1870		Died in Lodz Ghetto	Gombin		Lodz	L M
Wojdeslawski	Gabrjel Wojdeslawski	1887		Died in Lodz Ghetto	Gombin		Lodz	L M
Wojdeslawski	Lajbel Wojdeslawski	1878		Died in Lodz Ghetto	Gombin		Lodz	L M
Wojdeslawski	Pinkus Wojdeslawski	1886		Died in Lodz Ghetto	Gombin		Lodz	L M
Wojdkowski	Edmund Wojdkowski	1891			Gombin			M
Wolf	Ruchla Wolf nee Gips	1901			Gombin		Lodz	L M
Wolf	Lemel Wolf	1922			Gombin		Lodz	L M
Wolf	Izhak Wolf					Gombin		W
Wolf	David Ber Wolf					Gombin		W
Wolf	Israel Zeev Wolf					Gombin		W
Wolfowicz	Awraham Wolfowicz	1880	Zelig & Yta nee Gips	Merchant, married to Mala	Gombin	Gombin	Lodz	Y
Wolfowicz	Mala Wolfowicz			Married to Awraham	Gombin	Gombin	Gombin	Y
Wolfsztajn	Ester Wolfsztajn nee Volfovitz	1901	Awraham & Mala	Married to Jakob	Gombin	Lodz	Lodz	Y
Wolfovicz	Mieczyslaw Wolfovicz	1918	Jakub & Sala nee Domb	Worker, single	Gombin	Gombin	Lodz	Y
Wolfowicz	Marek Wolfowicz	1890	Zelig & Yta	Merchant, married to Mania	Gombin	Gombin	Warsaw	Y W
Wolfowicz	Mania Wolfowicz nee Glas	1898	Majer & Lea nee Szapiro	Married to Marek	Gombin	Gombin	Warsaw	Y W

49

Family	Person's complete name	Year born	Parents	Other details	Place of birth	Before the war lived in	During the war was in	Source
Wolfowicz	Seweryn Wolfowicz	1913	Izaak & Sala nee Fogel	Physician, married to Mira nee	Gombin	Kiernozia	Kiernozia	Y
Wolfowicz	Icchak Wolfowicz	1895		Married, "sick" deported 11.5.4		Gombin	Konin camp	K
Wolfsztajn	Estera Wolfsztajn	1900		Died in Lodz Ghetto	Gombin		Lodz	L M
Wolman	Toba Wolman						Gombin	G
Wolman	Gucia Wolman						Gombin	G
Wolman	Lajbisz Wolman	1901		Buried Konin Catholic cemetery	Gombin	Gombin	Konin camp	K
Wolman	Elazar Wolman			Mentioned in Aaronson's book		Gombin	Konin camp	K
Wolman	Zipora Wolman					Gombin		W
Wolman	Gitel Wolman					Gombin		W
Wollmann	Lajzer Wollmann	1900		Died Konin camp 20-06-1942	Gombin		Konin camp	Y
Wonsowicz	Victor Wonsowicz	1882	Gedalia & Roda	Teacher, married to Perla	Gombin	Lodz	Lodz	Y
Wruble	Eliahu Wruble	1877		Married, "sick" deported 11.5.4		Gombin	Konin camp	K
Wruble	Zalme Lajb Wruble					Gombin	Gombin	G
Wruble	(GNU) Wruble		Zalme Lajb	Child		Gombin	Gombin	G
Wruble	Bynem Wruble			Single, deported Konin camp to		Gombin	Auschwitz camp	K M
Wruble	Ezra Wruble	1915		Merchant, married to Yafa nee	Poland	Gombin	Gombin	Y W
Wruble	Yenta Wruble	1918	Avraham & Yokheved	Married to Ezra	Gombin	Gombin	Gombin	Y W
Wruble	Omek Wruble					Gombin		W
Wruble	Andzia Wruble					Gombin		W
Wruble	Hersh Yakov Wruble					Gombin		W
Wruble	Hinda Wruble					Gombin		W
Wruble	Shmuel Wruble					Gombin		W
Wrobel	Faibis Wrobel	1904		Tailor, married to Lea nee Liber	Gombin	Gombin	Gombin	Y
Wrobel	Arye Wrobel	1933	Feibish & Lea	Child	Gombin	Gombin	Poland	Y
Wrobel	Malka Wrobel	1931	Feibish & Lea	Child	Gombin	Gombin	Poland	Y
Wrobel	Lea Wrobel nee Liberman	1907		Married	Gombin	Poland	Poland	Y
Wrobel	Jakub Wrobel	1888	Maier & Khana		Gombin	Gombin	Gombin	Y W
Wrobel	Malka Wrobel nee Helmer	1904	Binem	Married to Jakub	Poland	Gombin	Gombin	Y W
Wrobel	Binem Wrobel	1924	Jakub & Malka	Married to Hannah	Gombin	Gombin	Auschwitz camp	Y W
Wrobel	Israel Wrobel	1908	Jakub & Malka		Gombin	Gombin	Auschwitz camp	Y W
Wrobel	Sender Wrobel	1907		Married, buried Konin Catholic	Gombin	Gombin	Konin camp	Y W K
Wygdorowicz	Mojshe Wygdorowicz			Merchant, married to Sarah	Gombin	Gombin	Gombin	Y
Wygdorowicz	Sarah Wygdorowicz nee Shpivak		Jidel & Rivka	Married to Mojshe	Wyszogrod	Gombin	Gombin	Y
Wygdorowicz	Ryvka Wygdorowicz		Mojshe & Sara nee Shpivak	Student	Gombin	Gombin	Gombin	Y
Wyrobek	Jdel Wyrobek						Gombin	G
Wyrobek	Moszek Wyrobek		Jdel	Child			Gombin	G
Wyrobek	Josek Wyrobek		Jdel	Child			Gombin	G
Wyrobek	Miriam Wyrobek			Married to Avraham	Gombin	Gombin	Gombin	Y
Wyrobek	Awraham Wyrobek			Merchant, married to Miriam	Gombin	Gombin	Gombin	Y
Wyrobek	Faivel Wyrobek		Awraham & Miriam	Child		Gombin	Gombin	Y
Wyspa	Sura Wyspa nee Stupaj	1897	Mosche & Necha	Married to Hersch, son of Luze	Gombin	Gombin	Gombin	Y W R

50

Family	Person's complete name	Year born	Parents	Other details	Place of birth	Before the war lived in	During the war was in	Source
Wyspa	Luzer Wyspa	1925	Hersch & Sura		Gombin	Gombin	Gombin	Y W R
Wyspa	Yitzchak Wyspa	1856	Aryeh & Sura	Baker, married to Dvorah nee E	Gombin	Gombin	Gombin	Y
Wyspa	Hersch Wyspa	1900	Elzasz & Ida	Deported from Malines 15/01/	Gombin	Belgium	Auschwitz camp	Y R M
Wyspa	Moshe Aron Wyspa					Gombin		W
Wyspa	Yochevet Wyspa					Gombin		W
Wyspa	Izhak Wyspa					Gombin		W
Wyspa	Razel Wyspa					Gombin		W
Yarlikht	Leah Yarlikht			Widow of Aron David		Gombin		B
Yarlikht	Nekhe Yarlikht		Aron David & Leah			Gombin		B
Yarlikht	Mindl Yarlikht		Aron David & Leah			Gombin		B
Yarlikht	Yitzhak Yarlikht		Aron David & Leah			Gombin		B
Yarlikht	Hershke Yarlikht		Aron David & Leah			Gombin		B
Yarlikht	Moishe Yarlikht		Aron David & Leah			Gombin		B
Yarlikht	Yakov Yosef Yarlikht		Aron David & Leah	Married to Gitele		Gombin		B
Yarlikht	Gitele Yarlikht			Married to Yakov		Gombin		B
Yarlikht	Hershel Yarlikht		Yakov & Gitele	Child		Gombin		B
Yarlikht	Rivtche Yarlikht		Yakov & Gitele	Child		Gombin		B
Yarlikht	Iteh Miriam Yarlikht		Aron David & Leah	Married to Yankl		Gombin		B
Yarlikht	Yankl (SU)			Married to Iteh Miriam		Gombin		B
Yarlikht	Khanele Yarlikht		Iteh Miriam & Yankl	Child		Gombin		B
Yarlikht	Eliezer Yarlikht		Iteh Miriam & Yankl	Child		Gombin		B
Yarlikht	Aron Dovid Yarlikht		Iteh Miriam & Yankl	Child		Gombin		B
Yentes	Ytzkhak Avraham Yentes	1904			Gombin	Nowy Dwor Mazov	Warsaw	Y
Zadok	Shmuel Zadok					Gombin		W
Zadok	Machla Zadok					Gombin		W
Zafran	Chawa Zafran nee Bich	1901	Menakhem & Sara	Married to Yisrael	Zychlin	Zychlin	Gombin	Y
Zaiontz	Idit Etel Zaiontz nee Zhelonka	1913	Yisrael & Khava nee Helman	Married to Khaim	Gombin	Danzig	Warsaw	Y
Zajac	Israel Zajac	1907		Deported from Pithiviers 17/07	Gombin	Paris, France	Auschwitz camp	Y F M
Zajac	Lipman Zajac						Gombin	G
Zajac	Dorcia Zajac		Lipman	Child			Gombin	G
Zajac	(GNU) Zajac		Lipman	Child of Lipman			Gombin	G
Zajac	(GNU) Zajac		Lipman	Child of Lipman			Gombin	G
Zajac	Jehoszua Melech Zajac	1887		Married, "sick" deported 26.9.4		Gombin	Konin camp	K
Zayac	Henry Zayac			Married to Susan Gertrude		Gombin		B
Zayac	Susan Gertrude Zayac			Married to Henry		Gombin		B
Zayac	Ethel Zayac		Henry & Susan			Gombin		B
Zayac	Ruth Zayac		Henry & Susan			Gombin		B
Zayac	Israel Zayac		Ruth	Child of Ruth		Gombin		B
Zayac	Hershel Zayac		Henry & Susan			Gombin		B
Zayac	Shai Zayac		Henry & Susan			Gombin		B
Zayac	Morris Zayac		Henry & Susan			Gombin		B

51

Family	Person's complete name	Year born	Parents	Other details	Place of birth	Before the war lived in	During the war was in	Source
Zeideman	Hersh Nathan Zeideman					Gombin		B
Zeideman	Meyer Zeideman			Married to Rosa		Gombin		B
Zeideman	Rosa Zeideman nee Hodys			Married to Meyer		Gombin		B
Zeideman	Chaskel Zeideman		Meyer & Rosa			Gombin		B
Zeideman	Raizel Zeideman					Gombin		B
Zeideman	Gitel Zeideman					Gombin		B
Zajdman	Shmuel Zajdman		Feibish & Reizl	Pupil, single	Gombin	Gostynin	Gostynin	Y
Zajdman	Golda Zajdman		Feibush & Reizil	Seamstress, single	Gombin	Gostynin	Gombin	Y
Zajdman	Moshe Zajdman		Feibish & Reizl	Uppers cutter/tailor, single	Gombin	Gostynin	Gombin	Y
Zajdman	Zelda Zajdman	1924	Zeev	Student, single	Gombin	Gombin	Gombin	Y
Zajdman	Jechiel Meir Zajdman	1892		Peddler, married to Etka nee Pr	Zychlin	Gombin	Gombin	Y W G
Zajdman	Etka Zajdman nee Pravda	1897	Feibush & Rakhel	Seamstress, married to Yekhie	Gombin	Gombin	Gombin	Y W
Zajdman	Roza Zajdman	1922	Jechiel & Etka nee Pravda	Underwear maker, single	Gombin	Gombin	Gombin	Y W
Zajdman	Ester Zajdman	1926	Jechiel & Etka nee Pravda	Child	Gombin	Gombin	Gombin	Y W G
Zajdman	Favish Zajdman					Gombin		W
Zajdman	Razel Zajdman					Gombin		W
Zajdman	Moshe Zajdman					Gombin		W
Zajdman	Mordechai Zajdman					Gombin		W
Zajonc	Lejb Zajonc	1876	Menashe & Sara	Merchant, married to Sara nee	Gombin	Gombin	Gombin	Y W
Zajonc	Sara Zajonc nee Gelbard	1886	Shalom & Khaia	Married to Leib	Gombin	Gombin	Gombin	Y W
Zajonc	Szejndl Zajonc	1902	Leib & Sara		Gombin	Gombin	Gombin	Y W
Zajonc	Mirl Zajonc	1904	Leib & Sara		Gombin	Gombin	Gombin	Y W
Zajonc	Menasze Zajonc	1907	Leib & Sara	Tailor, married to Rakhel	Gombin	Paris, France	Auschwitz camp	Y W
Zajonc	Jecheskel Zajonc	1917	Leib & Sara	Tailor, single	Gombin	Gombin	Gombin	Y W
Zajonc	Herszl Zajonc	1882	Menashe & Sara	Merchant, married to Fruma ne	Gombin	Gombin	Gombin	Y
Zajonc	Fruma Zajonc	1887	Mordekhai & Freida	Married to Hershel	Gombin	Gombin	Gombin	Y
Zajonc	Ester Zajonc	1913	Hershel & Fruma	Single	Gombin	Gombin	Gombin	Y
Zajonc	Menasze Zajonc	1915	Hershel & Fruma	Single	Gombin	Gombin	Gombin	Y
Zajonc	Sara Zajonc	1914	Hershel & Fruma	Single	Gombin	Gombin	Gombin	Y
Zajonc	Chaim Zajonc	1910	Hershel & Fruma	Merchant, single	Gombin	Gombin	Gombin	Y
Zajonc	Golda Zajonc	1917	Hershel & Fruma	Single	Gombin	Gombin	Gombin	Y
Zajonc	Zisl Zysl Zajonc	1921	Hershel & Fruma	Single	Gombin	Gombin	Gombin	Y
Zajonc	Mojsze Zajonc	1882	Menashe & Sara	Merchant, married to Hinda ne	Gombin	Gombin	Gombin	Y
Zajonc	Hynda Zajonc		Khaim	Married to Moshe	Gombin	Gombin	Gombin	Y B
Zajonc	Chaim Zajonc	1922	Moshe & Hinda	Single	Gombin	Gombin	Gombin	Y
Zalcman	Yakov David Zalcman					Gombin		W G
Zalcman	(GNU) Zalcman		Yakov	Child			Gombin	G
Zalcman	(GNU) Zalcman		Yakov	Child			Gombin	G
Zalesinski	Ichak Jerzyk Zalesinski	1922	Aharon & Ela	Pupil	Wloclawek	Wloclawek	Gombin	Y
Zaleska	Ela Zaleska						Gombin	G
Zaleska	Jerzy Zaleska						Gombin	G

52

Family	Person's complete name	Year born	Parents	Other details	Place of birth	Before the war lived in	During the war was in	Source
Zamosc	Abraham Zamosc	1887	Chaim Yehuda & Dvora	Bank manager, single	Gombin	Gombin	Warsaw	Y R
Zamosc	Leib Zamosc	1899	Chaim Yehuda & Dvora	Uppers cutter/tailor, married to Gombin	Gombin	Gombin	Gombin	Y G R
Zamosc	Chana Zamosc nee Pioro	1901	Michel & Ita nee Zchlova	Married to Leib	Gombin	Gombin	Gombin	Y R
Zamosc	Chaim Zamosc	1935	Leib & Chana	Child	Gombin	Gombin	Gombin	G R
Zalcman	Meir Zalcman			Single, deported Konin camp to		Gombin	Konin camp	K
Zandberg	Josef Zandberg	1890	Moshe & Gitel	Merchant, married to Volf	Gombin	Lodz	Lodz	Y
Zandberg	Khanokh Zandberg	1875	Moshe & Gitel	Merchant, married to Yenta	Gombin	Gombin	Gombin	Y W
Zandberg	Yente Zandberg	1887	Moshe & Malka	Grocer, married to Khanokh	Gombin	Gombin	Gombin	Y W
Zandberg	Mosze Zandberg	1918	Khanokh & Yenta	Single	Gombin	Gombin	Gombin	Y W
Zandberg	Sarah Zandberg	1913	Khanokh & Yenta	Seamstress, single	Gombin	Gombin	Gombin	Y W
Zandberg	Tobia Zandberg	1924	Khanokh & Yenta	Pupil, single	Gombin	Gombin	Gombin	Y W
Zandberg	Chucho Zandberg		Khanokh & Yenta	Child	Gombin	Gombin	Gombin	Y W
Zandberg	Riwka Zandberg	1916	Khanokh & Yenta	Nanny, single	Gombin	Gombin	Gombin	Y W
Zawierucha	Perla Zawierucha nee Gastenski	1890		Deported from Drancy 29/07/1	Gombin	Paris, France	Auschwitz camp	Y F M
Zawierucha	Fajga Zawierucha	1924	Perla	Deported from Drancy 29/07/1	Gombin	Paris, France	Auschwitz camp	Y F M
Zawierucha	Riwka Zawierucha	1919	Perla	Deported from Drancy 29/07/1	Gombin	Paris, France	Auschwitz camp	Y F M
Zeidman	Ester Zeidman	1908		Married to Daniel	Poland	Gombin	Gombin	Y
Zelenka	Azriel Zelenka	1908			Gombin	Gombin		Y
Zelenko	Nevakh Zelenko	1900	Icsel	Metalworker	Gombin	Gombin		Y
Zelenko	Fradlya Zelenko	1905	Mikhel		Warsaw	Gombin		Y
Zelenko	Iosif Ber Zelenko	1929	Nevakh		Gombin	Gombin		Y
Zelonka	Shaja Zelonka		Shaja & Dina	Married to Dina		Gombin		B
Zelonka	Dina Zelonka		Shaja & Dina	Married to Shaja		Gombin		B
Zelonka	Minia Zelonka		Shaja & Dina			Gombin		B
Zelonka	Chaim Zelonka					Gombin		B
Zelonka	David Zelonka				Gombin	Gombin		Y
Zhelonka	Natan Zhelonka	1890	Aizik & Rakhel	Shoemaker, married to Brakha	Gombin	Paris, France	Paris, France.	Y
Zhelonka	Khava Zhelonka nee Helman	1890	Dov & Rivka	Married to Yisrael	Lowicz	Gombin	Gombin	Y
Zhelonka	Leib Zhelonka	1914	Yisrael & Khava nee Helman	Furrier	Gombin	Gombin	Paris, France.	Y
Zhalne	Sore Zhalne nee Shvartz			Married to Yisroel		Gombin		B
Zhalne	Aron Wolf Zhalne		Yisroel & Sore	Child		Gombin		B
Zholne	Volf Zholne			Married to Beyle		Gombin		B
Zholne	Beyle Zholne			Married to Volf		Gombin		B
Zholne	Dvoyre Zholne		Volf & Beyle			Gombin		B
Zholne	Rohel Zholne		Volf & Beyle			Gombin		B
Zholne	Leah Zholne		Volf & Beyle			Gombin		B
Zholne	Sore Zholne		Volf & Beyle			Gombin		B
Zholne	Dena Zholne		Volf & Beyle			Gombin		B
Zichlinski	Jakob Zichlinski			Married to Raizel	Gombin	Gombin	Gombin	Y
Zichlinski	Raizel Zichlinski			Married to Jakob	Lodz	Gombin	Gombin	Y
Zichlinski	Yosef Zichlinski	1904	Yaakov & Reizel	Married	Gombin	Gombin	Gombin	Y

Family	Person's complete name	Year born	Parents	Other details	Place of birth	Before the war lived in	During the war was in	Source
Zichlinski	Chana Zichlinski	1906	Yaakov & Reizel	Married	Gombin	Gombin	Gombin	Y
Zichlinski	Rachel Zichlinski	1906	Tuvia	Married	Gombin	Gombin	Warsaw	Y
Ziegelman	Avraham Ziegelman	1903		Merchant	Gombin	Gombin		Y
Zielonka	Fishel Ber Zielonka	1889		Married to Mata, buried Konin	Gombin	Danzig	Konin camp	Y W K
Zielonka	Mata Zielonka			Married to Fishel	Gombin	Danzig		W
Zielonka	Leon Zielonka	1913	Fishel & Mata	Deported from Drancy 02/03/	Gombin	Bourges, France	Auschwitz camp	Y W F M
Zielonka	Moshe Zielonka					Gombin		W
Zielonka	David Hersz Zielonka					Gombin		W
Zielonka	Chava Zielonka					Gombin		W
Ziezyc	Leib Ziezyc					Gombin		Y
Ziezyc	Israel Ziezyc	1917	Shmuel	Student, single	Gombin	Gombin	Gombin	Y
Ziezyc	Yehudit Ziezyc	1909	Shmuel	Married	Gombin	Gombin	Gombin	Y
Ziezyc	Jakob Ziezyc	1903		Uppers cutter/tailor, married to	Gombin	Gombin	Gombin	Y
Ziezyc	Tzipora Ziezyc nee Bul	1905	Avraham & Malka	Married to Yaakov	Gombin	Gombin	Gombin	Y
Zigelman	Khaia Ester Zigelman nee latzento	1906	Shmuel & Sara	Married	Gombin	Gombin		Y
Zilonka	Faivel Zilonka	1888		Married	Gombin	Paris, France		Y
Zimalinski	Avraham Zimalinski			Married to Gitla		Gombin		W B
Ziselstein	Cypra Ziselstein						Gombin	G
Zolna	Mendel Zolna						Gombin	G
Zolna	Mariem Zolna		Mendel	Child			Gombin	G
Zolna	Szlama Jcze		Mendel	Child			Gombin	G
Zolna	(GNU) Zolna		Mendel	Child of Mendel			Gombin	G
Zolna	Tolcia Zolna						Gombin	G
Zolna	Bajla Zolna						Gombin	G
Zolna	Frania Zolna						Gombin	G
Zolna	Zeev Zolna					Gombin		W
Zolna	Beila Zolna					Gombin		W
Zolna	Hersz Nissim Zolna					Gombin		W
Zolna	Sara Rivka Zolna					Gombin		W
Zolna	Meilach Zolna	1902	Ichok & Liba	Single, "sick" deported 11.5.42	Gombin	Plock	Starachowice	Y
Zolna	Elchanan Zolna	1908				Gombin	Konin camp	K
Zolno	Zeev Zolno	1885		Merchant, married to Ester nee	Polanowice	Gombin	Gombin	Y
Zolno	Ester Zolno nee Rosek	1890	Khaim & Brakha	Married to Zeev	Gombin	Gombin	Gombin	Y
Zolno	Frida Zolno	1919	Zeev & Ester	Single	Gombin	Gombin	Gombin	Y
Zolno	Khana Zolno	1917	Zeev & Ester		Gombin	Gombin		Y
Zolonc	Gitl Zolonc	1923	Moshe & Hinda	Married	Wisnicz	Gombin	Gombin	Y
Zurawski	Ester Yenta Zurawski	1901	Hersh & Khana	Married to Avraham	Gombin	Zychlin		Y
Zurkowska	Chana Zurkowska			Single, sister of Rachel engaged	Gombin	Gombin	Gombin	H
Zurkowska	Rachel Zurkowska			Single, sister of Chana	Gombin	Gombin	Gombin	H
Zwang	David Zwang	1903	Hanyne & Fajga nee Rciola	Married to Bina	Kutno		Gombin	Y M
Zychlinska	Chawa Zychlinska						Gombin	G

54

Family	Person's complete name	Year born	Parents	Other details	Place of birth	Before the war lived in	During the war was in	Source
Zychlinska	Ester Zychlinska	1909	Miriam	Married	Gombin	Gombin	Gombin	Y
Zychlinska	Anka Zychlinska		Abraham & Gertrude		Gombin	Gombin	Warsaw	Y B
Zychlinska	Lajka Zychlinska		Anka	Daughter of Anka	Gombin	Gombin	Warsaw	Y B
Zychlinska	(GNU) Zychlinska		Lajka	Son of Lajka		Gombin	Warsaw	B
Zychlinski	Shlomo Zychlinski			Tanner, married to Hanna nee		Gombin	Gostynin	Y
Zychlinski	Helen Zychlinski	1925	Shlomo & Hanna nee Gomb	Single	Gombin	Gombin	Gostynin	Y
Zychlinski	Fela Zychlinski	1923	Shlomo & Hanna nee Gomb	Factory worker, single	Gombin	Gombin	Gostynin	Y
Zychlinski	Avraham Zychlinski			Married, deported Konin camp		Gombin	Konin camp	W K
Zychlinski	Gitel Zychlinski					Gombin		W
Zyg	Natan Zyg	1881	Khaim & Rakhvula	Hairdresser, married to Sala ne	Plock	Gombin	Gombin	Y
Zyg	Sala Zyg nee Rozahegi	1886		Married to Natan	Plock	Gombin	Gombin	Y
Zyg	Rukhshe Zyg	1907	Natan & Sala	Child	Gombin	Gombin	Gombin	Y
Zyg	Rubin Zyg	1922	Natan & Sala	Dentist, single	Gombin	Gombin	Gombin	Y
Zyg	Ruchcia Zyg	1911		Married to Leibish	Raciaz	Plock	Gombin	Y
Zyger	Rywen Zyger	1897		Married, buried Konin Catholic	Gombin	Gombin	Konin camp	Y K G
Zyger	(GNU) Zyger			Wife of Rywen			Gombin	G
Zyger	Yosef Lajb Zyger		Rywen	Child			Gombin	G
Zyger	Jcek Zyger		Rywen	Child			Gombin	G
Zyger	Frymet Zyger		Rywen	Child			Gombin	G
Zyger	Luna Zyger		Rywen	Child			Gombin	G
Zyger	Jcek Jankew Zyger		Beniamin	Child			Gombin	G
Zyger	Szmul Zyger		Beniamin	Child			Gombin	G
Zyger	Jakub Zyger		Chil Yosek	Child			Gombin	G
Zyger	Chil Zyger	1907			Gombin		Buchenwald camp	Y M
Zylberberg	Szrul Zylberberg	1883		Deported from Drancy 06/03/1	Gombin	Montauban, Franc	Auschwitz camp	Y F M
Zylberman	Abram Zylberman	1922		Died Lodz hospital 04-May-194	Gombin		Lodz	L M
Zylberman	Icek Zylberman	1869		Widower	Gombin	Lodz	Kutno	Y
Zylberman	Moszek Zylberman						Gombin	G
Zylberman	Wolf Ber Zylberman						Gombin	G
Zylbersztein	Rywka Zylbersztein nee Frenkel	1883		Married, deported from Maline	Gombin	Belgium	Auschwitz camp	Y
Zylbersztein	Shlomo Zylbersztein					Gombin		W
Zylbersztein	Miriam Zylbersztein					Gombin		W
Zylbersztein	Yacob Zylbersztein					Gombin		W
Zysier	Beniamin Zysier						Gombin	G
Zysier	(GNU) Zysier			Wife of Beniamin			Gombin	G

55